# CONTROVERSIES IN INNOCENCE CASES IN AMERICA

Controversies in Innocence Cases in America *edited by Sarah Lucy Cooper is an excellent anthology which focuses on all the major problems associated with wrongful conviction. The authors are well qualified in the subject they write about—the book's organization is clear and its findings convincing. We need more books like this in the future in order to bring to light the many mistakes that are made in determining guilt in our criminal justice system.*

Mark Pogrebin, University of Colorado Denver, USA

AF834303

# Controversies in American Constitutional Law

*Series Editors*:

Jon Yorke and Anne Richardson Oakes, Centre for American Legal Studies, School of Law, Birmingham City University, UK

*Controversies in American Constitutional Law* presents and engages with the contemporary developments and policies which mould and challenge US constitutional law and practice. It deals with the full spectrum of constitutional issues, publishing work by scholars from a range of disciplines who tackle current legal issues by reference to their underlying legal and political histories and the philosophical perspectives that they represent. Its cross-disciplinary approach encourages analysis of past, present and future challenges to the idea of US constitutionalism and the power structures upon which it rests. The series provides a forum for scholars to challenge the boundaries of US constitutional law and engages with the continual process of constitutional refinement for the protection of individual rights and liberties, within an evolving framework of legitimate government.

CALS promotes research, scholarship, and educative programs in all areas of US law, and is the home of the *British Journal of American Legal Studies*. Faculty members have extensive experience in submitting *amicus curiae* briefs to the United States Supreme Court and lower federal courts, and advising on criminal justice issues in many states. CALS coordinates the largest British law undergraduate internship program to the United States. Through this program, and members' research, CALS has created relationships with over 100 partners in over 25 states. CALS faculty advise public bodies, provide professional training, and speak at conferences across the USA.

# Controversies in Innocence Cases in America

Edited by

SARAH LUCY COOPER
*Birmingham City University, UK*

Routledge
Taylor & Francis Group
LONDON AND NEW YORK

First published 2014 by Ashgate Publishing

Published 2016 by Routledge
2 Park Square, Milton Park, Abingdon, Oxfordshire OX14 4RN
711 Third Avenue, New York, NY 10017, USA

First issued in paperback 2016

*Routledge is an imprint of the Taylor & Francis Group, an informa business*

Copyright © Sarah Lucy Cooper 2014

Sarah Lucy Cooper has asserted her right under the Copyright, Designs and Patents Act, 1988, to be identified as the editor of this work.

All rights reserved. No part of this book may be reprinted or reproduced or utilised in any form or by any electronic, mechanical, or other means, now known or hereafter invented, including photocopying and recording, or in any information storage or retrieval system, without permission in writing from the publishers.

Notice:
Product or corporate names may be trademarks or registered trademarks, and are used only for identification and explanation without intent to infringe.

**British Library Cataloguing in Publication Data**
A catalogue record for this book is available from the British Library

**Library of Congress Cataloging-in-Publication Data**
Cooper, Sarah Lucy.
Controversies in innocence cases in America / By Sarah Lucy Cooper.
p. cm. -- (Controversies in American constitutional law)
Includes bibliographical references and index.
ISBN 978-1-4094-6354-2 (hardback)
1. Judicial error--United States. 2. False imprisonment--United States. 3. Criminal justice, Administration of--United States. I. Title.
KF9756.C66 2014
345.73'0122--dc23

2013041849

ISBN 13: 978-1-138-24911-0 (pbk)
ISBN 13: 978-1-4094-6354-2 (hbk)

# Contents

# Notes on Contributors

**Francine Banner** is an Associate Professor at Arizona Summit Law School, where she teaches constitutional law, criminal law, and criminal procedure. She received her JD from New York University School of Law and her PhD in Justice Studies from Arizona State University. She has published numerous articles on capital punishment, terrorism, and other issues related to gender, justice, and human rights.

**Sarah Lucy Cooper** is a Senior Lecturer in Law and founding member of the Centre for American Legal Studies at Birmingham City University in the United Kingdom, where her teaching focuses on English and American criminal procedure, practice, and reform. Sarah leads criminal law on the LL.B and carries out her research in the Centre for American Legal Studies. She is a barrister and Lord Denning Scholar of the Bar of England and Wales, and has interned as a research assistant for a federal capital defense team in Arizona and California, and the Community Relations Trust of Jersey. She has been a *pro bono* academic for charities Amicus and Reprieve since 2007. Since 2010, Sarah has been a fellow at the Arizona Justice Project—a non-profit organization that considers claims of "innocence" and "manifest injustice" from Arizona inmates—at Arizona State University. In that time, she has worked on multiple post-conviction relief and clemency petitions, grappling with issues surrounding actual innocence, forensic science, medical science, confessions, and disproportionate sentencing. In 2012, Sarah's work was documented by Barry Siegel in his non-fiction book, MANIFEST INJUSTICE: THE TRUE STORY OF A CONVICTED MURDERER AND THE LAWYERS WHO FOUGHT FOR HIS FREEDOM. Sarah has published and presented her scholarship in Europe and the USA, and was recently shortlisted for Birmingham Law Society's 2012 Pro Bono Lawyer of the Year Award, and the Bar Pro Bono Unit's 2013 Sydney Elland Goldsmith Award.

**Deborah Davis**, PhD, is Professor of Psychology at the University of Nevada, Reno. She has worked on over 100 cases as a jury consultant, and more than 200 cases as an expert witness on issues of witness memory, coerced confessions, and sexual consent; and she lectures at continuing legal education seminars on these topics. Dr. Davis teaches courses relevant to the legal system—including psychology and law, memory on trial, and forensic psychology—and publishes extensively on these topics and others.

**Jules Epstein** is Professor of Law at Widener University School of Law, where he teaches evidence, criminal procedure, and criminal law. He has published extensively regarding the death penalty, eyewitness identification, and evidence. He is faculty for the National Judicial College, where he teaches evidence and capital case courses. Professor Epstein has taught courses on eyewitness evidence nationally, published extensively on the subject, and testified as an expert witness. In the area of forensics, Professor Epstein has worked on two DNA workgroups and in capital case training for the National Institute of Justice, and on an expert working group on latent print issues for the National Institute for Standards and Technology. Professor Epstein has lectured on forensics to judges and attorneys.

**Keith Findley** is an Assistant Professor at the University of Wisconsin Law School. After 21 years on the Law School's clinical faculty and six years as a public defender in Wisconsin, he joined the Law School's tenure-track faculty in 2012. He teaches courses on wrongful convictions, criminal procedure, and evidence. He also serves as co-director of the Wisconsin Innocence Project, a clinical program at the Law School's Frank J. Remington Center which he co-founded in 1998. He also serves as President of the Innocence Network, an affiliation of 65 innocence projects in the United States, Canada, the United Kingdom, the Netherlands, Australia, and New Zealand. Professor Findley's primary areas of expertise are in wrongful convictions, criminal defense, forensic science, evidence, and appellate advocacy. He has published numerous articles on these and related topics. He has litigated hundreds of post-conviction and appellate cases at all levels of state and federal courts, including the United States Supreme Court.

**Lissa Griffin** is a Professor of Law at Pace Law School in White Plains, New York. She is an expert in criminal procedure and comparative criminal procedure, and has written extensively on the causes and correction of wrongful convictions, from both a domestic and comparative perspective. She is the author of two treatises, FEDERAL CRIMINAL APPEALS and MULTI-DEFENDANT CRIMINAL CASES: FEDERAL LAW AND PROCEDURE (with Stacy Caplow), and of many other criminal procedure articles. Before joining Pace, Professor Griffin was involved in criminal and civil appellate litigation. She currently teaches criminal procedure, comparative criminal procedure, evidence, professional responsibility, and lawyering skills. Professor Griffin has served several times as faculty in residence at Pace's semester abroad program at University College, London.

**Richard A. Leo**, PhD, JD, is a Visiting Professor at the University of California, Los Angeles School of Law (2013–14), and a professor and Dean's Circle Research Scholar at the University of San Francisco School of Law. He is nationally and internationally recognized for his pioneering empirical research on police interrogation practices, the impact of Miranda, psychological coercion, false confessions, and wrongful convictions. He has authored more than 80 articles in leading scientific and legal journals as well as several books, including the multiple award-winning *Police Interrogation and American Justice* (Harvard University Press, 2008). He has won numerous individual and career achievement awards for research excellence and distinction, including the William J. Chambliss Lifetime Achievement Award from the Society for the Study of Social Problems; the Saleem Shah Career Achievement Award from the American Psychological Association; the Paul Tappan Award from the Western Society of Criminology; and the Ruth Shonle Cavan Young Scholar Award from the American Society of Criminology. He has also received awards for his scholarship from the Law and Society Association, the Academy of Criminal Justice Sciences, the American Psychology-Law Society, the American Academy of Forensic Psychology, the American Sociological Association, and the Pacific Sociological Association; and he has been the recipient of Soros and Guggenheim fellowships.

**Carrie Leonetti** is an Associate Professor at the University of Oregon School of Law. Her major fields of research and interest are constitutional criminal procedure and adjudication, forensic science and criminal law, and rule-of-law reform. In 2011–12, she was awarded a J.W. Fulbright Foreign Scholar grant to teach at the Faculty of Criminalistics, Criminology, and Security Studies at the University of Sarajevo and to research eyewitness-identification reform in Bosnia and Herzegovina. Her numerous publications include *Independent and Adequate: Maryland's State Exclusionary Rule for Illegally Obtained Evidence*, BALTIMORE LAW REVIEW (2009); *Open Fields in the Inner City: Application of the Curtilage Doctrine to Urban and Suburban Areas*, in THE FOURTH AMENDMENT: SEARCHES AND SEIZURES: ITS CONSTITUTIONAL HISTORY AND THE CONTEMPORARY DEBATE (Cynthia Lee ed., 2011); *When the Emperor Has No Clothes: A Proposal for Defensive Summary Judgment in Criminal Cases*, S. CAL. L. REV. (2011); *When the Emperor Has No Clothes II: A Proposal for a More Serious Look at "the Weight of the Evidence"*, N.Y.U. J.L. & LIBERTY (2013); and *When the Emperor Has No Clothes III: Personnel Policies and Conflicts of Interest in Prosecutors' Offices*, CORNELL J.L. & PUBL. POL'Y (2012). She lives with her husband, son, and Frisbee hound in Eugene, Oregon.

**Jacqueline McMurtrie** is an Associate Professor at the University of Washington School of Law and the director of the Innocence Project Northwest. She joined the faculty in 1989 after a career as a public defender and founded the Innocence Project Northwest in 1997. The Innocence Project Northwest has overturned the convictions of numerous wrongly convicted prisoners. Its recent successes include the exonerations of four clients who served a combined total of 47 years in prison for crimes they did not commit. Professor McMurtrie is a founding member of the Innocence Network, serves on its Board of Directors, and co-chairs its Committee on Amicus Policies. She is also currently the vice-chair of the Washington State Bar Association Council on Public Defense. Professor McMurtrie's research and teaching interests revolve primarily around criminal law and appellate/post-conviction practice, with a particular emphasis on wrongful convictions. She obtained her undergraduate and law degrees from the University of Michigan.

**Nancy Marion** is a Professor of Political Science at the University of Akron, Ohio. She holds a PhD in political science/public policy from the State University of New York at Binghamton. She is the author of several books and numerous scholarly articles on the interplay of politics and criminal justice.

**Lesley C. Risinger** became involved in the plight of the convicted innocent in 1991 when the chance reading of an article in the Jersey Journal led her and her mother, attorney Priscilla Read Chenoweth, to undertake to free Luis Kevin Rojas, a young man from Weehawken who had been convicted of the 1990 shooting murder of another young man on a Greenwich Village street. Over the next seven years they were instrumental in reinvestigating the case, gaining a reversal of the conviction, and finally obtaining an acquittal which led to Mr. Rojas's complete exoneration and compensation by the New York Court of Claims. This experience more or less inevitably led Ms. Risinger toward law school. She graduated *magna cum laude* from Seton Hall Law School in 2003, and thereafter undertook to review the case of Fernando Bermudez at his request when his federal habeas corpus proceeding was in the process of being denied. Over the next four years, Ms. Risinger reinvestigated Mr. Bermudez's case, marshaled the case for innocence, and assembled a team that won Mr. Bermudez complete exoneration by Justice John Cataldo in the New York Supreme Court in Manhattan in November of 2009. She became the founder and director of the Last Resort Exoneration Project at Seton Hall Law School in February of 2011. This project is dedicated to the freeing of the convicted innocent in the prisons of New Jersey. Ms. Risinger has acted as a consultant to the New York Attorney General's Office on the effect of post-conviction rules on the convicted innocent. She teaches a course in exonerations at Seton Hall Law School and has lectured at Yale Law School on the difficulties involved in obtaining exoneration. She is the co-author, with her husband, Professor D. Michael Risinger, of *Innocence is Different: Taking Innocence into Account in Reforming Criminal Procedure*, 56 N.Y.L.S. Law Rev. 935 (2012).

**D. Michael Risinger** is the John J. Gibbons Professor of Law at Seton Hall University School of Law, where he is also the Associate Director of the Last Resort Exoneration Project. He holds a BA from Yale University and a JD from Harvard Law School. He is a past chair of the Association of American Law Schools (AALS) Section on Civil Procedure; the past chair of the AALS Section on Evidence; a life member of the American Law Institute; and was for 25 years a member of the New Jersey Supreme Court Committee on Evidence, which was responsible for the current version of the New Jersey Rules of Evidence. He is the author of two chapters in Faigman et al., Modern Scientific Evidence (2006) (*Handwriting Identification* and *A Functional Taxonomy of Expertise*. He is also the author of articles on a diverse range of subjects, including many articles on expert evidence issues. In recent years he has devoted the bulk of his time to issues concerning the convicted innocent.

**Carrie Sperling** is an Associate Clinical Professor at the University of Wisconsin Law School, where she directs students in the school's Innocence Clinic. Professor Sperling's legal career has centered on public interest law, first as director of the American Civil Liberties Union's (ACLU) North Texas region, then as an advocate in federal courts for inmates on Texas's death row, and as the first Executive Director of the Arizona Justice Project—one of the nation's first innocence projects. Sperling writes in the area where law and science intersect, and she has developed a particular interest in convictions based on shaken baby syndrome. Some of her cases have been featured in The New York Times, The Wall Street Journal, The Guardian, The Dallas Morning News, Slate, The Sacramento Bee, and the Phoenix New Times. Before joining Wisconsin Law School, Professor Sperling was an associate clinical professor at Sandra Day O'Connor College of Law at Arizona State University. She also served as a law clerk to the Hon. Jerry Buchmeyer, US District Judge, and the Hon. Paul D. Stickney, US Magistrate Judge in the Northern District of Texas.

**Michael J. Williams** is a doctoral student in the interdisciplinary social psychology program at the University of Nevada, Reno. He is a National Science Foundation graduate research fellow, funded to conduct research toward enhancing the effectiveness of interrogation techniques in military and federal intelligence-gathering contexts, including research sponsored by the High-Value Detainee Interrogation Group, under the auspices of the FBI.

**Marvin Zalman** is a Professor of Criminal Justice at Wayne State University in Detroit, Michigan. He has researched and written on a variety of policy issues, including physician-assisted suicide, drug asset forfeiture, domestic violence, jail crowding lawsuits, civil liberties, and judicial sentencing. His writings on constitutional criminal procedure include articles on Miranda rights, the Fourth Amendment, and venue, and a text—CRIMINAL PROCEDURE: CONSTITUTION AND SOCIETY (6th ed., 2011). He serves on the editorial advisory boards of the CRIMINAL JUSTICE POLICY REVIEW, CRIMINAL JUSTICE REVIEW, AND THE CRIMINAL LAW BULLETIN. His works on wrongful convictions include studies of the incidence of wrongful convictions, innocence as a reform movement, and theoretical approaches to wrongful conviction, in a number of articles, chapters, encyclopaedia articles, and an annotated bibliography.

# Foreword

We have a confession to make. We were supposed to contribute to this collection. In our proposed chapter—*Life in the Trenches: The Real World of Innocence Work*—we were going to discuss the many and complex challenges we face each day at the Arizona Justice Project, a small non-profit organization dealing with innocence and "manifest injustice" cases in Arizona. We really wanted to tell our story, but it never happened. Why? It didn't happen because, like every inmate we represent (and we bet every author in this collection), we fight time—sometimes for it, sometimes against it. But we do fight it *all* the time.

Since Sarah rallied this collection in the summer of 2011, the Arizona Justice Project has represented 10 people who have been released from prison. Not all of our clients were proven factually innocent, but all of them had suffered a manifest injustice in some way, shape or form. Two of those cases—the Bill Macumber case and the Louis Taylor case—were our largest and oldest cases. The Project investigated both cases for over a decade before reaching a resolution that led to the release of Mr. Macumber in 2012 and the release of Mr. Taylor in 2013. Prior to that, Louis Harper was released in December 2011 after we reached an agreement with the state for a re-sentencing. Louis Harper was convicted of selling $20 worth of crack cocaine to undercover officers, and sentenced to 50 years in prison. We took the case because of the egregious sentence, which the state ultimately agreed was too harsh for the crime. After serving over 21 years in prison, Louis was freed. In 2012, the Project successfully represented Drayton Witt and Armando Castillo—whose convictions were based on a faulty diagnosis of Shaken Baby Syndrome. Drayton was released in May, 2012 and Armando's case was resolved in August, 2012. In both cases, the Justice Project presented new evidence in the form of expert medical opinion with regard to the cause of death. Betty Smithey—America's longest-serving female prisoner—was also released in August, 2012 after the Justice Project successfully represented her in clemency proceedings. Soon after that success, Khalil Rushdan was also released, after a federal judge found his murder conviction was the product of a "vindictive prosecution." In addition to all this casework, a Justice Project volunteer attorney, Professor Bob Bartels, took one of our cases all the way to the United States Supreme Court in 2012, where a majority of the Justices found in favor of our client, Luis Martinez, and recognized the need for effective assistance of counsel with regards to constitutional claims raised in appellate proceedings. In 2013, the Justice Project successfully represented a woman who had been diagnosed with Battered Women's Syndrome in parole proceedings. Justice Project client Donna Bennett, whose first degree murder conviction was vacated several years ago after a Justice Project volunteer attorney proved she did not kill her child, was also freed in 2013. Prior to the summer of 2011, another client was released. Larry Bishop, who was wrongfully convicted of first degree murder, ultimately entered into a plea agreement, and instead of serving life in prison he served 15 years. Larry was released in June 2011. In December 2010, John Watkins' rape conviction was vacated after DNA testing proved his innocence on that charge.

Our relationship doesn't stop when a client is released. Each time a client re-enters society we continue to support them, as often the people at the Justice Project are the only support system they have in the outside world. We have helped clients find homes and jobs, secure welfare benefits, set up bank accounts, and acquire basic clothing and counseling.

We have also had our fair share of disappointments since the summer of 2011. A Justice Project client passed away months before his release on parole. We have lost cases in trial courts, appellate courts, and federal courts, as well as suffered disappointing clemency and parole decisions. And each time this has happened, we have shouldered not only our client's frustration, but that of their families, friends and supporters too.

In addition to case representation, the Justice Project has worked with Pulitzer Prize winning author Barry Siegel, who wanted to tell Bill Macumber's story—a complex story about a third-party confession the jury never heard, an independent witness that corroborated the confession, and compromised forensic evidence. Macumber, in 38 years of incarceration, never wavered from professing his innocence. Barry's book, MANIFEST INJUSTICE: THE TRUE STORY OF A CONVICTED MURDERER AND THE LAWYERS WHO FOUGHT FOR HIS

FREEDOM, was published in January, 2013. Nightline, Dateline, CNN, NPR, and local news, radio, and print have covered this incredible case. Similarly, Louis Taylor's release generated media interest from across the world, most of which our five-man band handled.

Since the summer of 2011, our Project has received over 550 new requests for assistance, and we continue to handle between 40 and 50 active cases at any one time. We have also continued our efforts to apply for grant money, organize fundraising and educational events, engage in policy and political dialogues, train law students, and supervise college and law school externs.

These successes and challenges are not unique to the Arizona Justice Project, but are shared to varying extents by every other similar organization in America. To that end, we hope we provide a fair representation of what life really is like "in the trenches" in this Foreword. We are proud to be a part of the Innocence Movement in America (and beyond) and to work with such hard-working and inspiring people every day.

Our experiences and feeling of privilege are why we want to underscore the importance and excellence of this edited collection. Like many of this collection's contributors, we have a front row seat to the "controversies in innocence cases in America," and can vouch that the themes discussed in this collection are contemporary, exciting, and very worthwhile of discussion. In fact, we can prove it by sharing how our own experiences fit in with each section of the collection.

Part I charts the rise of the Innocence Movement in America, discussing its successes and failures, and the establishment of the Innocence Network. The Arizona Justice Project is one of the Network's oldest members and, like the Network, it continues to evolve. Since 1998, the Project has gone from being run out of the hip pocket of its founder's legal secretary, to having three full-time and two part-time members of staff, an office space, and support from all three Arizona law schools. In that time, we have also witnessed the debate about innocence in America reframed by scores of "powerful narratives" emanating from the rising tally of DNA exonerations, as Professor Findley notes in Chapter 1. We have also had the "transformative effect" on our clients that Professor McMurtrie considers in Chapter 2. Many of our clients consider us to be their "second family."

We have first-hand experience of each of the common causes of wrongful convictions discussed in Part II, namely eyewitness misidentification, false confessions, the suppression of exculpatory evidence, inadequate lawyering, and asymmetrical resources The Arizona Justice Project's first DNA exoneree, John Watkins, served over seven years in prison for a rape he did not commit, before DNA exonerated him. John was 20 years old when police lied to him that his fingerprints were found at the crime scene, his parents had not confirmed his alibi, and he had failed a voice stress test. They also fed him details of the crime, promised leniency in return for a confession, and interrupted his many denials. In less than five hours, John falsely confessed to rape. John was also erroneously identified as the perpetrator by the victim. The victim alleged the rapist wore a white T-shirt. Subsequently, when the victim was shown a photo line-up, only one man was wearing a white T-shirt—John Watkins. Unsurprisingly, she picked him out. As such, John's experiences stress the importance of the research carried out by Professor Leo, Professor Davis, and Michael J. Williams into the frequency of interrogation-induced confessions in Chapter 4, and Professor Epstein's critical overview of eyewitness misidentifications and potential system responses to ameliorate this "American conundrum" in Chapter 3.

Similarly, we can give credence to Professor Griffin's conclusion, in Chapter 5, that the "*Brady* doctrine has not been successful in providing meaningful protection of the innocent." In Louis Taylor's case, a jailhouse snitch testified that Louis had told him he set the fire that killed 29 people at the famous Pioneer Hotel in Tucson, Arizona. The snitch recanted immediately after he gave testimony. After being visited by the State, however, the snitch recanted his recantation. We also found a scientific report that had never been disclosed to the defense. The report discredited the snitch's testimony; and, had it been admitted into evidence at trial, it would have called into question the snitch's truthfulness.

It is important to note these common causes are not alone. As pointed out by Professor Leonetti in Chapter 6, invalidated and/or unreliable forensic science, poor cross-examination, and inappropriate plea bargaining all contribute to the conviction of the innocent. We have experience with most of these issues, too.

Part III largely reflects the challenges and debates we engage in daily. In innocence cases, we certainly are the "innocence lawyer" described by D. Michael Risinger and Lesley C. Risinger in Chapter 7. In innocence cases, after a employing a strict screening procedure, we signal a "well-warranted belief" in the actual innocence of our clients, and expel countless hours and resources on reinvestigation. How this atypical role impacts our typical ethical obligations as criminal defense lawyers is well worth a debate. Similarly, the fictitious story of defendant "Michael," which Professor Sperling tells in Chapter 8 in order to illustrate the "labyrinth" of procedures an inmate must navigate to attain post-conviction conviction relief, is all too familiar. In fact, Michael's story is better described as non-fiction. In Arizona, the threshold for proving post-conviction relief, on the basis of innocence, is "clear and convicting evidence," and, as far as we know, no one in Arizona has succeeded on that claim. This lack of precedent not only demonstrates how difficult it is to achieve post-conviction relief, but also perhaps highlights the difference DNA evidence can make to a case, as considered by Dr. Banner in Chapter 9. Moreover, as well as needing to satisfy a very high standard of proof, we must contend with due diligence requirements that can be significantly hampered by our revolving volunteer base, state push-back, lost files, old files, destroyed evidence, and lack of funding. Bill Macumber's case is a perfect example of us encountering all these issues. Four generations of law students worked on Bill's case over the course of 14 years. The files dated back to 1962, were in an aging condition and difficult to piece together, and the evidence had been destroyed and/or auctioned decades before our investigation began. Every time we made a records request to the police, new material was disclosed. For years we operated on a very small budget and relied on volunteers to carry out research and on experts to work for free or for a reduced fee. As such, Professor Leonetti's point in Chapter 6—that the defense (home and abroad) deserves symmetrical funding and resources to the prosecution—is critical.

Finally, Part IV discusses themes of innocence reform. The Arizona Justice Project has engaged in a number of efforts aimed at making positive changes to the Arizona criminal justice system. We have supported the development of a state compensation statute that would provide individuals who have been wrongfully convicted with compensation upon their release, and supported initiatives aimed at ensuring the recording of police interrogations and improving the reliability of eyewitness identifications. Unfortunately, though, we have not been able make any of these reform ideas "stick," yet. We did, however, persuade the Arizona Board of Executive Clemency in 2011 to fast-track inmates with prior recommendations for release through the state's clemency process. How all these activities fit within the theory of innocence reform frameworks discussed by Professor Zalman and Professor Marion in Chapter 10 is interesting. Needless to say, when engaging in reform efforts, we have encountered some of the issues the editor of the collection, Sarah Lucy Cooper, highlights in Chapter 11 in the context of innocence commissions. For example, we have faced a lack of political will to make changes in favor of inmates amidst a "tough-on-crime" political climate, and lacked resources to devote towards reform efforts and drive them forward. We have also come to understand the importance of carefully framing our contributions so as to make them as attractive as possible to as many of the various stakeholders in our state's criminal justice system as possible. To that end, we are lucky to share productive relationships with law schools, private attorneys, public defenders, and district attorneys across Arizona (and beyond). We support Sarah's suggestion that each state should take a proactive approach to reducing the possibility of convicting innocents by implementing safeguards at the front and back-end of the criminal justice process.

In sum, this collection represents some of the foremost controversies in innocence cases in America to date. From real-life case examples and considerations about practicability, to the application of innovative academic theory and front-line research, this edited collection thoughtfully engages with the successes, failures, and frustrations of these controversies. It is a welcome, as well as unique, addition to the literature that engages with the revolutionary Innocence Movement in America that touches our daily lives in the trenches.

*The Arizona Justice Project*
January, 2014

# Acknowledgments

In April, 2002 Ray Milton Krone was the one hundredth person in America to be exonerated by post-conviction DNA testing. His story is pivotal to this edited collection.

The naked body of Kim Ancona was found on the morning of December 29, 1991, on the floor of the men's restroom at the bar she worked at in Phoenix, Arizona. She had been fatally stabbed, and had what appeared to be a bite-mark on her left breast.

Two suspects emerged early on in the police's investigation: Ray Krone and an unknown Indian male. Friends and colleagues reported that Kim and Ray were romantically involved and that on the night of her death she had told a friend "Ray" was going to help her close the bar. Others told police there had been problems with American Indian males in the area. A note suspiciously dropped at the crime scene also described an "Indian" as a potential suspect.

Police visited Ray and observed he had crooked teeth. They asked him to bite into a Styrofoam plate, purchased from a convenience store, so that a cast of his teeth could be made and compared with the bite-mark on Ancona's breast. Subsequently, the state criminologist reported Ray's dentition was "consistent with" the bite-mark on Ancona. Soon after, Ray was charged with Ancona's murder. Until that moment, Ray had a clean criminal record and proud military past. The media dubbed him the "Snaggletooth Killer."

The bite-mark was the focal point of the prosecution's case against Ray at his trial in 1992. The state presented a renowned expert in forensic odontology, who testified that Ray's dentition "matched" the bite-mark on Ancona, and presented a videotape to demonstrate the "match." The state also presented evidence that Ray and Ancona were romantically linked. Ray steadfastly denied he had killed Ancona, and that they were romantically involved or that he helped her close the bar on the night of her murder. His defense, however, struggled to overcome the state expert's bite-mark "match," due to a lack of resources and availability of alternative scientific opinion from a comparable expert. In 1991, DNA tests were not conclusive enough to include or exclude Ray as the killer. Ray was convicted of first degree murder and sentenced to death. In 1995, his conviction and sentence were overturned by the Arizona Supreme Court because the expert's videotape had not been disclosed to the defense until the eve of trial.

Ray was re-tried in 1996. The state's case was essentially the same, but the defense presented a far more robust case. This time, four nationally recognized experts rebutted the state's theory that Ray's dentition "matched" the bite-mark on Ancona. In addition, the hair evidence now pointed away from Ray. Seventeen hairs had been found on Ancona's body and none of them matched Ray. Three, however, were Mongoloid. Crucially, DNA testing now established that blood found on the inside pocket flap of Ancona's jeans belonged to someone with a genotype different from both Ray and Ancona. Research indicated that the reported genotype was very popular in the American Indian population. A poly-marker test also revealed that a genetic profile found at the crime scene did not belong to Ray or Ancona. Still, despite all of this fresh evidence in Ray's favor he was convicted again. This time, however, due to the lingering doubts of the trial judge, he was sentenced to life imprisonment.

In 2001, Ray's defense requested DNA testing on biological material present on Ancona's bra, jeans, and tank top. One year later, the results came back. None of the biological material on the items matched Ray's DNA. Several of the items did, however, contain DNA that matched a man named Kenneth Phillips, who was on the FBI database and had an extensive criminal record. He was also an Indian. Ray's legal team interviewed Phillips at the Arizona prison where he was incarcerated. Within hours, they had elicited from Phillips what appeared to be admissions of guilt. Phillips reported that he had woken the morning after the murder with blood on his jeans and shoes, and that when he saw news reports on television he hoped he hadn't committed the crime.

Based on the DNA testing results and Phillips' admissions, Ray Krone walked free on April 8, 2002. Shortly after, additional DNA testing officially exonerated him. The blood found on Ancona's jeans and panties matched Phillips, as did multiple fingerprints lifted from the crime scene. The Snaggletooth Killer was a myth.

Ray Krone's story both inspired this edited collection and my academic career. In 2007, the Arizona Justice Project entrusted me to build a "post-mortem" of Ray's case, which could be used to teach how and why innocent people are convicted of crimes they didn't commit, and I have been hooked on the "controversies" of these cases ever since. I owe a great deal to the folks at the Arizona Justice Project, who continue to feed me with research projects, sounding-boards, and friendship. In particular, I must thank Debbie Hill, Donna Toland, and the sorely-missed Mark Hummels, who mentored me from the start; and Carrie Sperling, Katherine Puzauskas, Andrew Hacker, and Lindsay Herf, who continue to work with me now. The chair of the Arizona Justice Project—Larry Hammond—deserves my special thanks. To be in the same room as Larry is to be inspired. Larry gave me a chance to shine, and I will never forget that.

Next, I must thank the people who brought this collection to life. I am in awe at the awesome caliber of people who have contributed chapters to this collection. Not only have they served up fantastic contributions, but they have also offered great patience, understanding, and humor along the way. I am also very conscious that many of them have done this while actually dealing hands-on with the very "controversies in innocence cases in America." we all discuss. I salute their commitment, enthusiasm, and intellect.

I must also thank those people at my academic home—Birmingham City University—who have supported me both substantively and administratively to deliver this edited collection. My colleagues in the Centre for American Legal Studies—Dr. Jon Yorke, Dr. Anne Richardson-Oakes, Dr. Haydn Davies, and Professor Julian Killingley—have provided outstanding academic support, as always. Professor Alex Kendall, Professor Rosemary Evans, Professor Fiona Church, Ian Fox-Williams, and Sonya Smith have all contributed to providing me with a research and teaching framework that I could work productively within. Professor Meryl Thomas, Jill Molloy, Scarlett McArdle, and Lauren Haddock have also taken the time to discuss this collection with me.

A bundle of student research assistants have also made this collection possible. Daniel Gough, Amna Nazir, Alice Storey, Richard Hammond, Katie Mustard, and Logan Mussman all have energy and intelligence in abundance. They will all succeed handsomely. I am particularly thankful to Daniel and Amna for their spectacular Bluebook skills and ability to turn around projects in super-fast time frames. I hope they have found our working together as rewarding as I have.

I am also indebted to the excellent staff at Ashgate Publishing. Alison Kirk, Sarah Horsley, Elaine Couper, Alex Papworth, and Celia Barlow have been on hand to field my rookie questions and offer support 24/7. I have greatly appreciated their experience, encouragement, and attention to detail throughout.

Finally, I must thank my family. My mother and father—Christine and Paul—have spoiled me with love and encouragement from day one. They have also provided incredibly generous funding arrangements. I owe them everything. My grandparents—Nanny Sylvia, Nanny Vera, Granddad Jack, and my greatly missed Granddad Lenny—have shown me equal devotion. I understand my Nanny Irene, who I never had the pleasure of meeting, would have been just the same. Any success I have is no doubt a consequence of their collective support and inspiring work ethic. I hope I have and continue to make you all proud.

Sarah Lucy Cooper

# List of Abbreviations

| | |
|---|---|
| AALS | Association of American Law Schools |
| ABA | American Bar Association |
| ACLU | American Civil Liberties Union |
| AEDPA | Anti-Terrorism and Effective Death Penalty Act |
| AK | Alaska |
| AL | Alabama |
| AR | Arkansas |
| ATF | Avery Task Force |
| AZ | Arizona |
| CA | California |
| CCFAJ | California Commission on the Fair Administration of Justice |
| CIP | Conviction Integrity Program, New York |
| CO | Colorado |
| CODIS | Combined DNA Index System |
| CT | Connecticut |
| D | Democrat |
| DA | District Attorney |
| D.C | District of Columbia |
| DE | Delaware |
| DNA | Deoxyribonucleic Acid |
| DOJ | United States Department of Justice |
| FIC | Florida Innocence Commission |
| FL | Florida |
| FOIA | Freedom of Information Act |
| FY | Fiscal Year |
| GA | Georgia |
| GAO | General Accounting Office |
| HI | Hawaii |
| IA | Iowa |
| IAC | Ineffective Assistance of Counsel |
| ICITAP | International Criminal Investigative Training Assistance Program |
| ICVA | Innocence Commission for Virginia |
| ID | Idaho |
| IL | Illinois |
| IN | Indiana |
| INCLE | International Narcotics Control and Law Enforcement |
| IPA | Innocence Protection Act |
| KS | Kansas |
| KY | Kentucky |
| LA | Louisiana |
| MA | Massachusetts |
| MD | Maryland |
| ME | Maine |
| MI | Michigan |
| MN | Minnesota |

| | |
|---|---|
| MO | Missouri |
| MS | Mississippi |
| MT | Montana |
| NAACP | National Association for the Advancement of Colored People |
| NAS | National Academy of Sciences |
| NC | North Carolina |
| NCAIC | North Carolina Actual Innocence Commission |
| NCIIC | North Carolina Innocence Inquiry Commission |
| NCSC | National Center for State Courts |
| ND | North Dakota |
| NE | Nebraska |
| NH | New Hampshire |
| NJ | New Jersey |
| NM | New Mexico |
| NV | Nevada |
| NY | New York |
| OCJ | Oklahoma Justice Commission |
| OH | Ohio |
| OIP | Ohio Innocence Project |
| OJP | Office of Justice Programs |
| OK | Oklahoma |
| OPDAT | Office of Overseas Prosecutorial Development Assistance and Training |
| OR | Oregon |
| OSBI | Oklahoma State Bureau of Investigation |
| PA | Pennsylvania |
| R | Republican |
| RI | Rhode Island |
| SC | South Carolina |
| SD | South Dakota |
| TCAP | Timothy Cole Advisory Panel on Wrongful Convictions |
| TCJIU | Texas Criminal Justice Integrity Unit |
| TN | Tennessee |
| TX | Texas |
| UK | United Kingdom |
| US | United States |
| USA | United States of America |
| USSC | United States Supreme Court |
| UT | Utah |
| VA | Virginia |
| VT | Vermont |
| WA | Washington |
| WI | Wisconsin |
| WV | West Virginia |
| WY | Wyoming |

*Dedication: For you—to the end of the world.*

# PART I
# The Rise of the Innocence Movement in America

# Chapter 1
# Innocence Found: The New Revolution in American Criminal Justice

Keith A. Findley

## Introduction: The Discovery of Innocence

The Innocence Movement that began to emerge in the 1990s—which some have described as an "innocence revolution,"[1] or the "new civil rights movement"[2]—has been the most dramatic development in the criminal justice world since the Warren Court's Due Process Revolution of the 1960s. Larry Golden and I, elsewhere,[3] and Jackie McMurtrie in Chapter 2 of this edited collection,[4] among others, have sketched the history of the Innocence Movement and the Innocence Network. This chapter builds on that historical framework, putting into context the Innocence Movement's impact and significance. The chapter examines the lessons learned from wrongful convictions exposed by the Innocence Movement, and explores the Movement's methods and successes and failures at translating those lessons into meaningful reforms. And it places all of this in the broader context of the American criminal justice system.

Throughout most of the history of the American criminal justice system, observers have by and large shared the quaint notion that the justice system did all it could to protect against wrongful conviction of the innocent. The common wisdom was that, while occasional error is inevitable in any human system, such errors in criminal cases were rare, aberrational, and not worthy of serious concern. That sentiment was expressed perhaps most famously and colorfully by Judge Learned Hand, who wrote in 1923: "Our dangers do not lie in too little tenderness to the accused. Our procedure has been always haunted by the ghost of the innocent man convicted. It is an unreal dream."[5] Of similar sentiment, a prosecutor in Worcester County, Massachusetts, as quoted by Yale Professor Edwin Borchard in 1932, declared: "Innocent men are never convicted. Don't worry about it. … It is a physical impossibility."[6]

Decades later, former Attorney General Edwin Meese under President Ronald Reagan reflected that sentiment when he quipped: "But the thing is, you don't have many suspects who are innocent of a crime. That's contradictory. If a person is innocent of crime, then he is not a suspect."[7] Even into the late 1980s and early 1990s, skeptics dismissed the seriousness of the problem of wrongful convictions and the need for reform to prevent wrongful convictions. Former prosecutor and current Michigan Supreme Court Justice Stephen Markman—along with former prosecutor, federal court judge, and now law professor Paul Cassell,

---

1 *See* Keith A. Findley, *Defining Innocence*, 74 Albany L. Rev. 1157, 1157 (2010/11); Lawrence C. Marshall, *The Innocence Revolution and the Death Penalty*, 1 Ohio St. J. Crim. L. 573, 573–4 (2004); Daniel S. Medwed, *Emotionally Charged: The Prosecutorial Charging Decision and the Innocence Revolution*, 31 Cardozo L. Rev. 2187, 2188 (2010); Samuel R. Gross et al., *Exonerations in the United States 1989 Through 2003*, 95 J. Crim. L. & Criminology 523, 523 (2005).

2 *See* Findley, *supra*, at 1157; Daniel S. Medwed, *Innocentrism*, 2008 U. Ill. L. Rev. 1549, 1550 (2008); Robert Carl Schehr, *The Criminal Cases Review Commission as a State Strategic Selection Mechanism*, 42 Am. Crim. L. Rev. 1289, 1302 (2005).

3 Larry Golden & Keith A. Findley, *The Innocence Movement, the Innocence Network, and Policy Reform*, *in* Making Justice: The Innocence Challenge to Criminal Justice Policy and Practice (Marvin Zalman & Julia L. Carrano, eds 2013).

4 Jacqueline McMurtrie, *The Innocence Network: From Beginning to Branding*, Chapter 2, this volume.

5 United States v. Garsson, 291 F. 646, 649 (D.C.N.Y. 1923).

6 Edwin M. Borchard with E. Russell Lutz, Convicting the Innocent: Errors of Criminal Justice vii (1970).

7 Daniel Givelber, *Meaningless Acquittals, Meaningful Convictions: Do We Reliably Acquit the Innocent?*, 49 Rutgers L. Rev. 1317, 1328 & n.34 (1997) (quoting Reagan Seeks Judges with "Traditional Approach," U.S. News & World Rep., Oct. 14, 1985, at 67 (interview with Edwin Meese, Attorney General)).

for example—wrote in 1988 that the risk of executing an innocent person "is too small to be a significant factor in the debate over the death penalty."[8] As Justice O'Connor put it in her 1993 concurring opinion in *Herrera v. Collins*, "Our society has a high degree of confidence in its criminal trials, in no small part because the Constitution offers unparalleled protections against convicting the innocent."[9]

Forensic DNA technology, developed in the mid-1980s, shattered that perception of virtual infallibility—exposing the reality that error in the criminal justice system is systemic, not just freakishly rare or merely episodic. As DNA's potential began to be recognized and utilized, it soon began to prove innocence (as well as guilt) to a degree of scientific certainty that was unprecedented in the criminal justice system, and at rates never before imagined. In 1989, David Vasquez and Gary Dotson became the first Americans convicted of serious crimes to be exonerated by post-conviction DNA testing. The governor of Virginia granted Vasquez a pardon at the joint request of the prosecution and defense when DNA testing on crime scene evidence linked the rape and murder to another man who had committed two other murders.[10] For Dotson, DNA testing did what the victim's recantation could not—proved that Dotson did not rape 16-year-old Cathleen Crowell, on July 9, 1977, in Homewood, Illinois.[11] A third DNA exoneration followed in 1990, and then two more in 1991. More exonerations followed, swiftly and in increasing numbers. As the number of innocence advocacy organizations in America grew each year, as DNA technology advanced, and as awareness of the problem of wrongful convictions increased, the number of DNA exonerations grew steadily after 1992, peaking at 25 exonerations in 2002. And all of this was happening in the most serious cases—almost exclusively rape and murder cases—because those were uniquely the cases with biological evidence that could produce DNA profiles.

Despite predictions that the rate of post-conviction DNA exonerations would begin to dwindle as DNA testing was completed in cases where DNA had not been available when the defendant was convicted, the number of exonerations each year in America has remained fairly constant, ranging between 13 (in 2004) and 23 in (2009). As of August 2013, the total number of known DNA exonerations of wrongly convicted individuals in America had risen to 311.[12]

The DNA exonerations revolutionized perceptions of the criminal justice system. Media accounts of innocent men and women filled the newspapers and airwaves. Scholars began churning out analyses of the flaws in the system highlighted by such cases. No longer was the system deemed virtually infallible; beginning in the early 1990s, "innocence consciousness" replaced the myth of infallibility.[13]

Innocence consciousness in turn led to the discovery of more innocents. The remarkable success of DNA in exonerating the wrongly convicted quickly led to efforts to re-examine other cases where there was no DNA (although this scrutiny was still almost entirely limited to serious felonies; to date very little attention is paid to, and very little is known about, factual error in minor cases).[14] As increasing numbers of post-conviction litigators began looking for new evidence of innocence in a wider range of cases, the number of non-DNA exonerations also began to swell. Innocence consciousness was in full bloom.

Although it is difficult to catalogue or count all non-DNA exonerations—there is no official government record of exonerations—in 2012 the University of Michigan Law School and the Center on Wrongful

8 Stephen J. Markman & Paul G. Cassell, *Comment, Protecting the Innocent: A Response to the Bedau-Radelet Study*, 41 Stan. L. Rev. 121, 121 (1988).

9 Herrera v. Collins, 506 U.S. 390, 420 (1993) (O'Connor, J., concurring).

10 *Know the Cases, David Vasquez*, Innocence Project, http://www.innocenceproject.org/Content/David_Vasquez.php (last visited July 30, 2013).

11 *Know the Cases, Gary Dotson*, Innocence Project, http://www.innocenceproject.org/Content/Gary_Dotson.php (last visited July 30, 2013).

12 *Know the Cases*, Innocence Project, http://www.innocenceproject.org/know/Browse-Profiles.php (last visited July 24, 2013).

13 Marvin Zalman, *An Integrated Justice Model of Wrongful Convictions*, 74 Albany L. Rev. 1465, 1468 (2010–11). Zalman defines "innocence consciousness" as "the idea that innocent people are convicted in sufficiently large numbers as a result of systemic justice system problems to require efforts to exonerate them, and to advance structural reforms to reduce such errors in the first place." *Id.*

14 Samuel R. Gross & Barbara O'Brien, *Frequency and Predictors of False Conviction: Why We Know So Little, and New Data on Capital Cases*, 5 J. Empirical Legal Stud. 927, 931–2, 940–42 (2008); Alexandra Natapoff, *Misdemeanors*, 85 S. Cal. L. Rev. 1313 (2012).

Convictions at the Northwestern University School of Law jointly launched a National Registry of Exonerations. The Registry attempts to locate and list all exonerations regardless of whether DNA evidence was the basis for exoneration. As of July 2013, the National Registry counted a total of 1,175 known exonerations in America since 1989.[15]

**Part I: The Birth of a Movement**

Although not the first American organization devoted to exonerating the wrongly convicted (Centurion Ministries in Princeton, New Jersey, founded in 1983, can make that claim),[16] the Innocence Project in New York City, affiliated with the Cardozo Law School at Yeshiva University, was the first to fully seize upon DNA technology as a tool for exonerating the innocent. Attorneys Barry Scheck and Peter Neufeld founded the Innocence Project in 1992 and quickly set about using DNA to prove innocence, to advance their vision for a network of innocence organizations in every American state, and to lay the foundation for the Innocence Movement. In their influential book, *Actual Innocence*, Scheck and Neufeld, joined by New York Times writer Jim Dwyer, called for changes in the American criminal justice system, including "[c]reat[ing] and fund[ing] Innocence Projects at law schools that will represent clients in DNA and non-DNA cases."[17]

By the time they had made that call, others had already begun following their lead, forming innocence organizations in a handful of states, including Washington (1997),[18] Wisconsin (1998),[19] Arizona (1998),[20] Illinois (1998 and 1999),[21] and California (1999).[22] While the Innocence Project provided critical assistance to each of these early projects as they formed, these projects developed independently and organically, shaping themselves to fit local opportunities and needs. While each project was unique, they all remained faithful to the common goals of providing *pro bono* investigative and legal assistance to the wrongly convicted and working to prevent the conditions that created such wrongful convictions. Many projects followed the model set by the Innocence Project of affiliating with a law school (or in the case of the Medill project, a journalism school) as in-house clinical programs—that is, projects sponsored by and housed in a law school (or journalism school) with the bulk of the case work handled by students supervised largely by university faculty.[23] But not all followed that pattern, and as the number of projects began to grow, they organized themselves in increasingly diverse ways, including as independent non-profit organizations, undergraduate criminal justice programs,

15 *About the Registry*, The National Registry of Exonerations, https://www.law.umich.edu/special/exoneration/Pages/About-Us.aspx (last visited July 25, 2013).

16 *About Us*, Centurion Ministries, http://www.centurionministries.org/about/ (last visited July 24, 2013).

17 Barry Scheck, Peter Neufeld, & Jim Dwyer, Actual Innocence: Five Days to Execution and Other Dispatches from the Wrongly Convicted 260 (2000).

18 The Innocence Project Northwest at the University of Washington School of Law was founded in 1997, initially as a volunteer effort. *Innocence Project Northwest (IPNW) Clinic*, School of Law, University of Washington, http://www.law.washington.edu/Clinics/IPNW/IPNWClinic.aspx (last visited July 24, 2013).

19 The Wisconsin Innocence Project at the University of Wisconsin Law School was founded in 1998. Steven Elbow, *Law Prof Committed to Freeing Wrongly Convicted Inmates*, The Capital Times (July 24, 2011, 6:00 AM), *available at* http://host.madison.com/news/local/crime_and_courts/blog/article_a6e254b6-b4b1-11e0-b06f-001cc4c03286.html.

20 The Arizona Justice Project in Phoenix was created in 1998. Arizona Justice Project, http://www.azjusticeproject.org/ (last visited July 25, 2013).

21 At Northwestern University in Illinois, the School of Law created the Center on Wrongful Convictions in 1998. *Bluhm Legal Clinic, Center on Wrongful Convictions*, Northwestern Law, http://www.law.northwestern.edu/legalclinic/wrongfulconvictions/ (last visited July 24, 2013); and the Medill School of Journalism created the Medill Innocence Project (later renamed the Medill Justice Project) in 1999. Rafi Letzter, *Medill Justice Project Director Explains Name Change*, The Daily Northwestern (Feb. 7, 2013), *available at* http://dailynorthwestern.com/2013/02/07/blogs/medill-justice-project-director-explains-name-change/.

22 The California Innocence Project at California Western School of Law was founded in 1999. California Innocence Project, http://californiainnocenceproject.org/ (last visited July 24, 2013).

23 Keith A. Findley, *The Pedagogy of Innocence: Reflections on the Role of Innocence Projects in Clinical Legal Education*, 13 Clinical L. Rev. 231 (2006).

volunteer or *pro bono* associations of attorneys or law firms, and units within public defender offices, as well as through various degrees of affiliation with law schools.[24]

By the early 2000s, the growing number of such projects began organizing an Innocence Network, bringing together the various organizations devoted to exonerating the innocent and reforming the system to improve its fact-finding reliability. As Jackie McMurtrie describes in more detail in Chapter 2, in 2003 the projects formed a steering committee to organize as a network, and in 2005 the projects elected a Board of Directors, formally launching the Innocence Network. As its website now expresses, the Network's mission is two-fold: "The Innocence Network is an affiliation of organizations dedicated to providing pro bono legal and investigative services to individuals seeking to prove innocence of crimes for which they have been convicted and working to redress the causes of wrongful convictions."[25]

As of 2013, the Innocence Network had hired a small support staff, and had grown to include 65 member projects in the United States, Canada, the United Kingdom, Ireland, Australia, New Zealand, the Netherlands, and France.[26] More projects are seeking to join the Network on a regular basis, including projects in countries not already represented in the Network. By the end of 2012, this growth continued to reflect diversity in the organizational nature of the projects as well: 34 percent were non-profit organizations affiliated with a law school; 27 percent were wholly law school based (that is, not separate non-profit organizations); 20 percent were non-profit organizations with no affiliation; 10 percent were affiliated with a public defender's office; 7 percent were non-profit organizations affiliated with a non-law educational institution; and 2 percent were *pro bono* sections of a law firm.[27]

Throughout all this growth, the Innocence Network has remained committed to remedying individual instances of wrongful conviction and to reforming the system to reduce the risks of such errors. The Innocence Project has developed a sophisticated policy unit that leads much of the policy work underlying the Innocence Movement. Many of the other projects in the Network are similarly engaged in policy reform work, often with the assistance of the Innocence Project. And the Innocence Network itself engages directly in policy work as well, largely through its Committee on Amicus and Policies, which is most notably engaged in an active practice of filing *amicus curiae* briefs in cases that address issues related to wrongful convictions.[28] In sum, the Innocence Movement is simultaneously animated by and instrumental in creating the innocence consciousness that is reshaping attitudes about the criminal justice system.

## Part II: Innocence and the Supreme Court

Slowly and sporadically innocence consciousness is beginning to make its way into judicial opinions, including opinions of the United States Supreme Court. In 2002, the Court in *Atkins v. Virginia* ruled that executing the mentally retarded is unconstitutional, in part because the reduced capacity of mentally retarded defendants increases the risk of wrongful conviction.[29] The Court stated that it "cannot ignore the fact that in recent years a disturbing number of inmates on death row have been exonerated."[30] Four years later, in his dissenting opinion in *Kansas v. Marsh*—a case that addressed decisional rules governing capital cases, but not a claim of actual innocence—Justice Souter wrote that, "[t]oday, a new body of fact must be accounted for in deciding what, in practical terms, the Eighth Amendment guarantees should tolerate, for the period starting in 1989 has seen repeated exonerations of convicts under death sentences, in numbers never imagined

---

24 Jan Stiglitz, Justin Brooks & Tara Shulman, *The Hurricane Meets the Paper Chase: Innocence Projects' New Emerging Role in Clinical Legal Education*, 38 Cal. W. L. Rev. 413 (2002); 2012 Innocence Network Annual Report Summary (on file with the author).

25 The Innocence Network, www.innocencenetwork.org (last visited July 24, 2013).

26 *See Innocence Network Member Organizations*, The Innocence Network, http://www.innocencenetwork.org/members (last visited July 31, 2013).

27 2012 Innocence Network Annual Report Summary (on file with the author).

28 *Brief Bank*, The Innocence Network, http://www.innocencenetwork.org/resources/brief-bank (last visited July 29, 2013).

29 Atkins v. Virginia, 536 U.S. 304 (2002).

30 *Id.* at 321.

before the development of DNA tests."[31] And in 2008, in *Kennedy v. Louisiana*, the Court held that the Eighth Amendment prohibits "the death penalty for the rape of a child where the crime did not result, and was not intended to result, in death of the victim."[32] Citing research on wrongful convictions, the Court reasoned, in part, that "[t]he problem of unreliable, induced, and even imagined child testimony means there is a 'special risk of wrongful execution' in some child rape cases."[33]

The Court has also displayed innocence consciousness in matters beyond those limited to capital cases. In *House v. Bell*, in 2006, the Court took innocence concerns seriously when it held that House had made a sufficient showing of innocence so that he should be permitted to pursue habeas corpus relief despite procedural defaults that otherwise would have barred his claims. (House had been sentenced to death, but the case did not turn on that fact and its rationale was not limited to capital cases.)[34] In 2009, in *Corley v. United States*, while reaffirming the rules limiting the admissibility of some custodial interrogations, the Court cited the "mounting empirical evidence that [police interrogation] pressures can induce a frighteningly high percentage of people to confess to crimes they never committed."[35] In *Melendez-Diaz v. Massachusetts*, the Court observed that "discredited forensics" have contributed to a significant proportion of the known wrongful convictions.[36] Citing an amicus brief filed by the Innocence Network and the cases in which forensic fraud has produced wrongful convictions, the Court held that the Confrontation Clause requires that the state introduce forensic science evidence through live testimony subject to cross-examination rather than by simply presenting the court with a certified written report from a lab analyst.[37]

The Court's response to the evidence of wrongful convictions has by no means been consistent or uniformly sympathetic though. Some cases reveal a Court that remains resistant to the notion of error in the criminal justice system. For example, in 1993 in *Herrera v. Collins*—decided just as the Innocence Movement was beginning to take shape—the Court infamously declared that, in most cases, a showing of "actual innocence" does not state a freestanding due process claim entitling a defendant to relief from his conviction and death sentence in federal habeas corpus proceedings.[38] More recently, in *District Attorney's Office for the Third Judicial District v. Osborne*, the Court found no due process violation in Alaska's refusal to provide post-conviction DNA testing, even though the state conceded that the testing in that case had the potential to conclusively prove actual innocence.[39] And in *Cavazos v. Smith*,[40] a case involving a conviction based on a shaken baby syndrome theory, the Court re-enforced a particularly crabbed application of a reviewing court's authority under the Due Process Clause to review the sufficiency of the evidence to support a conviction.[41] In *Cavazos*, the Court reversed a grant of habeas corpus relief by the Ninth Circuit Court of Appeals in a case that rested almost entirely upon medical experts whose opinions had largely been exposed as novel at best, if not entirely baseless. The majority, in a *per curiam* opinion, wrote: "Doubts about whether Smith is in fact guilty are understandable. But it is not the job of this Court, and was not that of the Ninth Circuit, to decide whether the State's theory was correct."[42] In dissent, Justice Ginsburg, joined by Justices Breyer and Sotomayor, would have given Smith's claim of innocence greater play, observing that "[w]hat is now known about shaken baby syndrome (SBS) casts grave doubt on the charge leveled against Smith."[43]

---

31 Kansas v. Marsh, 548 U.S. 163, 207–8 (2006) (Souter, J., dissenting). Justice Souter's dissent provoked an angry rejoinder from Justice Scalia challenging Souter's assertion that false convictions had become a problem for the system.

32 Kennedy v. Louisiana, 554 U.S. 407, 443 (2008).

33 *Id.* at 443 (quoting *Atkins*, 536 U.S.).

34 House v. Bell, 547 U.S. 518 (2006). The Court's decision referenced an *amicus curiae* brief filed by the Innocence Project. *Id.* at 529.

35 Corley v. United States, 129 S. Ct. 1558, 1570 (2009).

36 Melendez-Diaz v. Massachusetts, 129 S. Ct. 2527, 2537 (2009). *See also* Bullcoming v. New Mexico, 131 S. Ct. 2705 (2011); *but see* Williams v. Illinois, 132 S. Ct. 2221(2012).

37 *Melendez-Diaz* 129 S. Ct. at 2536–7.

38 Herrera v. Collins, 506 U.S. 390, 400 (1993).

39 Dist. Attorney's Office for the Third Judicial Dist. v. Osborne, 129 S. Ct. 2308, 2322 (2009).

40 Cavazos v. Smith, 132 S. Ct. 2 (2011).

41 The Court applied a particularly hands-off approach to the due process standard first enunciated in Jackson v. Virginia, 443 U.S. 307 (1979).

42 *Cavazos*, 132 S. Ct. at 7.

43 *Id.* at 9 (Ginsburg, J., dissenting).

In *Perry v. New Hampshire*,[44] the Court addressed for the first time in 35 years the standards for admissibility of eyewitness identification evidence. Because eyewitness error had been shown to be the leading contributor to wrongful convictions—present in approximately 75 percent of all cases where post-conviction DNA testing proved innocence—innocence advocates hoped the Court would take the opportunity to reshape the law to reflect the teachings of these cases and the advances in social science research about mistaken identifications.[45] Instead, the Court left existing standards in place and even narrowed the due process protections against bad eyewitness evidence, declaring that the Due Process Clause does nothing to protect against admissibility of mistaken eyewitness evidence unless police errors or misconduct tainted the identification.

The majority's decision provoked a dissent from Justice Sotomayor in which she, unlike the majority, directly acknowledged the lessons about eyewitness error from the innocence cases. Justice Sotomayor wrote:

> The empirical evidence demonstrates that eyewitness misidentification is "the single greatest cause of wrongful convictions in this country." Researchers have found that a staggering 76% of the first 250 convictions overturned due to DNA evidence since 1989 involved eyewitness misidentification. Study after study demonstrates that eyewitness recollections are highly susceptible to distortion by postevent information or social cues; that jurors routinely overestimate the accuracy of eyewitness identifications; that jurors place the greatest weight on eyewitness confidence in assessing identifications even though confidence is a poor gauge of accuracy; and that suggestiveness can stem from sources beyond police-orchestrated procedures. The majority today nevertheless adopts an artificially narrow conception of the dangers of suggestive identifications at a time when our concerns should have deepened.[46]

## Part III: Shifting Paradigms

In other arenas, growing innocence consciousness is playing an even more significant role in a broad range of policy initiatives and has begun to reshape the American criminal justice system. Proposals for significant systemic reforms have emerged (and some have been adopted) involving preservation of and post-conviction access to DNA evidence, eyewitness identification procedures, prosecutorial ethics, and electronic recording of custodial interrogations of suspects. New attention has focused on the unreliability of jailhouse informant ("snitch") testimony. Serious concern has surfaced about forensic science evidence, culminating with the game-changing National Academy of Sciences (NAS) report in February 2009, which starkly concluded that: "[w]ith the exception of nuclear DNA analysis, … no forensic method has been rigorously shown to have the capacity to consistently, and with a high degree of certainty, demonstrate a connection between evidence and a specific individual or source."[47] All of these re-examinations of fundamental aspects of the criminal justice system emerged from the lessons learned from the innocence cases.

Before addressing some of these specific reforms, however, it is important to place all of this in a fuller context within the American criminal justice system. The story of the Innocence Movement is even broader than suggested by these remarkable policy developments, for the innocence cases have begun to shape not only new understandings of specific types of evidence or discrete aspects of the criminal justice system, but also to create new criminal justice system models and debates about the goals and effects of the criminal justice system itself. In a sense, the Innocence Movement began to replace old understandings of criminal justice issues left in the wake of the Warren Court Revolution of the 1960s.

The Supreme Court, led by Chief Justice Earl Warren from 1953 to 1969, dramatically expanded the rights of criminal defendants, beginning in the early 1960s. The Warren Court focused on *procedural* rights designed to protect criminal defendants, whether guilty or innocent. In essence, the Court imposed a constitutional code

---

44 Perry v. New Hampshire, 132 S. Ct. 716 (2012).

45 Brandon L. Garrett, Convicting the Innocent: Where Criminal Prosecutions Go Wrong 9, 48, 279 (2011).

46 *Perry*, 132 S. Ct., at 738–9 (Sotomayor, J., dissenting) (footnotes omitted).

47 National Research Council, National Academy of Sciences, Strengthening Forensic Science in the United States: A Path Forward 7 (2009).

of procedure on the states by incorporating most of the Bill of Rights, which by their terms are not applicable to the states, into the Fourteenth Amendment's Due Process Clause, which *is* expressly applicable to the states. In *Mapp v. Ohio* (1961)[48] the Court ruled that the Due Process Clause requires the states to adopt the exclusionary rule for Fourth Amendment search and seizure violations. Subsequently, the Court expanded the scope of those Fourth Amendment protections. For example, in *Katz v. United States* (1947)[49] the Court extended the Fourth Amendment to protect reasonable expectations of privacy even absent a physical trespass by police; and in *Terry v. Ohio* (1968)[50] the Court imposed limits on the ability of police to stop and frisk suspects on reasonable suspicion short of probable cause (while still permitting the practice). In *Robinson v. California* (1962)[51] the Court held that the Eighth Amendment's protection against cruel and unusual punishment applies to the states. *Malloy v. Hogan* (1964)[52] held that the Fifth Amendment right against compelled self-incrimination applies to the states. *Pointer v. Texas* (1965)[53] extended the Sixth Amendment confrontation right to the states. *Klopfer v. North Carolina* (1967)[54] applied the Sixth Amendment right to a speedy trial to the states; and *Duncan v. Louisiana* (1968)[55] applied the Sixth Amendment right to trial by an impartial jury to the states. In perhaps its most controversial move in criminal law, the Warren Court in *Miranda v. Arizona* (1966)[56] imposed on states the obligation to warn suspects of their rights emanating from the Fifth Amendment self-incrimination clause before initiating custodial interrogation.

Central to the Warren Court's due process revolution, *Gideon v. Wainwright* (1963)[57] and *Douglas v. California* (1963)[58] sought to give criminal defendants the tools needed to invoke all of these new rights by extending to the states an obligation under the Sixth Amendment to provide counsel at state expense for indigent defendants, both at trial and on appeal. Four years later, *United States v. Wade* (1967)[59] held that the Sixth Amendment right to counsel applies at post-indictment live-person eyewitness lineup procedures, extending procedural protections to additional aspects of the police investigation process.

To many observers, however, the Warren Court cases represented more of a bump along the way to conviction than a real revolution; while the Court recognized substantial new rights, subsequent decisions quickly restricted those rights or created exceptions or waiver and consent rules that rendered them frequently of little applicability. Indeed, most of the Warren Court rights were trial rights, yet more than 95 percent of all criminal cases are resolved by plea, not trial.[60] A guilty or no contest plea waives trial rights.

To others, the procedural reforms backfired by making criminal litigation more costly, thereby privileging the wealthy and the savvy—those best positioned to take advantage of the new procedural rights—over the poor and unsophisticated, resulting in greater disparity.[61] As noted, the central component of the Warren Court's reforms was the right to counsel, for realization of all of the other rights depended on counsel's ability to invoke them. But defense counsel in the years since have proved unable or unwilling to aggressively assert those rights because (1) underfunding for the vast majority (the indigent) leaves them incapable of taking on the state[62] and (2) they have learned that cooperating with the prosecution tends to result in better outcomes

48 Mapp v. Ohio, 367 U.S. 643 (1961).

49 Katz v. United States, 389 U.S. 347 (1967).

50 Terry v. Ohio, 392 U.S. 1 (1968).

51 Robinson v. California, 370 U.S. 660 (1962).

52 Malloy v. Hogan, 378 U.S. 1 (1964).

53 Pointer v. Texas, 380 U.S. 400 (1965).

54 Klopfer v. North Carolina, 386 U.S. 213 (1967).

55 Duncan v. Louisiana, 391 U.S. 145 (1968).

56 Miranda v. Arizona, 384 U.S. 436 (1966).

57 Gideon v. Wainwright, 372 U.S 335 (1963).

58 Douglas v. California, 372 U.S. 353 (1963).

59 United States v. Wade, 388 U.S. 218 (1967).

60 George Fisher, Plea Bargaining's Triumph, 223 tbl.9.1 (2003).

61 William J. Stuntz, The Collapse of American Criminal Justice 218 (2011).

62 Darryl K. Brown, *The Decline of Defense Counsel and the Rise of Accuracy in Criminal Adjudication*, 93 Cal. L. Rev. 1585, 1602 (2005); Andrew D. Leipold, *How the Pretrial Process Contributes to Wrongful Convictions*, 42 Am. Crim. L. Rev. 1123, 1127 (2005); Stephen B. Bright, Counsel *for the Poor: The Death Sentence Not for the Worst Crime but for the Worst Lawyer*, 103 Yale L.J. 1835, 1870 (1994); Adele Bernhard, *Effective Assistance of Counsel*, in Wrongly Convicted: Perspectives on Failed Justice 220, 226 (Saundra D. Westervelt & John A. Humphrey eds, 2001).

for their clients.[63] Empirical studies reveal that defense lawyers share with police, prosecutors, and judges a common interest in smooth administrative processing of cases, rather than in adversarial jousting to advance differing interests in due process and crime control.[64] Indeed, even after the Warren Court established new due process rights for criminal cases, those rights have not seriously impeded crime control. Despite all of the Warren Court's new rights, the last 50 years have witnessed an unprecedented increase in prosecutions, convictions, and imprisonment rates in America.[65]

Moreover, as the late Bill Stuntz has observed, the Warren Court procedural rights had another inherent weakness: they shifted the focus of criminal litigation "away from the question of the defendant's guilt or innocence and toward the process by which the defendant was arrested, tried, and convicted."[66] That meant more litigation about procedural matters, and less effort to discover and litigate the truth about guilt or innocence. And indeed the empirical record supports that proposition; while there is on the whole little actual litigation in criminal cases, "what activity there is, at least on the defense side, is primarily procedural: motions practice, not factual investigation."[67]

Because the Warren Court recognized procedural rights that could benefit the guilty as well as the innocent—sometimes preventing the conviction of plainly guilty individuals—the reforms bred a backlash. The new procedural protections promised to make law enforcement more difficult, and to do so by providing pathways to overturn convictions based not on the innocence of the defendant, but on the errors of police and prosecutors. And so the backlash came, beginning in the late 1960s and early 1970s when President Richard Nixon launched his war on crime and crime control became politicized like never before.[68] As the politics began to change, the Supreme Court began narrowing and weakening many of the Warren Court's protections.[69] In the 1980s, President Ronald Reagan escalated the war on crime.[70] Stuntz has summarized it this way: "The upshot was a nationalized and punitive politics of street crime that lasted a generation. ... Thus did Warren-style legal doctrine wind up promoting Reaganite politics."[71]

Reflective of the conflict between the Warren Court Revolution and the law-and-order politics that followed is a deeply entrenched view of competing models of the criminal justice system that has long dominated criminal justice discussions. In the early 1960s, Herbert Packer introduced two competing models of criminal justice—the Crime Control Model and the Due Process Model—thereby positing a dichotomy and inherent conflict between society's interest in convicting the guilty and the rights of criminal defendants.[72] The Warren Court's new due process cases reflected enhanced respect for the Due Process Model, while the dominant strain in criminal law, even then and increasingly in the backlash since, has embraced the Crime Control Model.

---

63 F. Andrew Hessick III & Reshma M. Saujanni, *Plea Bargaining and Convicting the Innocent: The Role of the Prosecutor, the Defense Counsel, and the Judge*, 16 B.Y.U. J. Pub. L. 189, 213 (2002); Keith A. Findley & Michael S. Scott, *The Multiple Dimensions of Tunnel Vision in Criminal Cases*, 2006 Wis. L. Rev. 291, 331.

64 Michael McConville & Chester L. Mirsky, *Criminal Defense of the Poor in New York City*, 15 N.Y.U. Rev. L. & Soc. Change 581, 762 (1986–87).

65 *Sourcebook of Criminal Justice Statistics*, University of Albany, School of Criminal Justice, http://www.albany.edu/sourcebook/tost_6.html#6_b (last visited July 26, 2013).

66 Stuntz, *supra* note 61, at 228. *See also* William J. Stuntz, *The Uneasy Relationship Between Criminal Procedure and Criminal Justice*, 107 Yale L.J. 1, 32 (1997).

67 Stuntz, *supra* note 61, at 228.

68 Annual Message to the Congress on the State of the Union, 1 Pub. Papers 8, 12 (Jan. 22, 1970); Katherine Beckett & Theodore Sasson, The Politics of Injustice: Crime and Punishment in America 46 (2d ed. 2004); Michael Flamm, Law and Order: Street Crime, Civil Unrest, and the Crisis of Liberalism in the 1960s 9 (2005).

69 *See* Jerold H. Israel, *Criminal Procedure, the Burger Court, and the Legacy of the Warren Court*, 75 Mich. L. Rev. 1319 (1978); A. Goldberg, *The Burger Court 1971 Term: One Step Forward, Two Steps Backwards?*, 63 J. Crim. L.C. & P.S. 463 (1972).

70 Gerald Shargel, *No Mercy: Ronald Reagan's Tough Legal Legacy*, Slate (June 14, 2004), *available at* http://www.slate.com/articles/news_and_politics/jurisprudence/2004/06/no_mercy.html.

71 Stuntz, *supra* note 61, at 217.

72 Herbert L. Packer, The Limits of the Criminal Sanction 150–73 (1968) [hereinafter Packer, Criminal Sanction]; Herbert L. Packer, *Two Models of the Criminal Process*, 113 U. Pa. L. Rev. 1, 2–68 (1964) [hereinafter Packer, *Two Models*].

According to Packer, the Crime Control Model values repression of crime as the most important function of the criminal justice system. To most effectively repress crime, the Crime Control Model emphasizes efficiency in prosecuting criminal cases. By efficiency, Packer meant the ability to quickly and with finality apprehend, try, convict, and punish a high proportion of criminal offenders. To achieve such efficiency, the system depends on police and prosecutors to quickly resolve questions of factual guilt through informal investigation processes and interrogations with minimal review or oversight by formal adversarial adjudication. As Packer explained, "The model that will operate successfully on these presuppositions must be an administrative, almost a managerial, model. The image that comes to mind is an assembly line or a conveyor belt … ."[73]

The Crime Control Model thus places great confidence in the administrative screening process conducted by police and prosecutors. Once police and prosecutors have screened a case, the system effectively adopts a "presumption of guilt" that permits resolution of most cases by guilty pleas. Packer observed that, "if there is confidence in the reliability of informal administrative fact-finding activities that take place in the early stages of the criminal process, the remaining stages of the process can be relatively perfunctory without any loss in operating efficiency."[74] This model therefore places few restrictions on the administrative fact-finding process, except those restrictions "that enhance reliability, excluding those designed for other purposes."[75]

The Due Process Model, by contrast, is suspicious of the administrative investigative process and skeptical of its capacity to assess guilt accurately without judicial oversight. Moreover, the Due Process Model values individual rights and dignity as well as crime suppression. Accordingly, the Due Process Model rejects informal, administrative fact-finding and favors formal adversarial adjudication. Under this model, there is no legitimate fact-finding until the case is publicly heard and evaluated by an impartial tribunal and the accused has had a full opportunity to challenge the prosecution's case. As its premise, the Due Process Model relies upon a presumption of legal innocence. Hence, as Packer stated, "If the Crime Control Model resembles an assembly line, the Due Process Model looks very much like an obstacle course."[76]

From this brief description it is apparent that the Warren Court criminal procedure cases reflect, to a significant degree, the values of the Due Process Model, while the Nixon/Reagan war on crime embraced the Crime Control Model. More importantly for our purposes, this discussion reflects the dichotomous manner in which criminal justice theorists and policy-makers alike have viewed defendants' rights as being in tension with law and order.

The Innocence Movement has begun to change that dynamic; it has gained much of its traction by implicitly rejecting this dichotomy between the Due Process and Crime Control Models. The Innocence Movement has shown how neither model adequately serves the interests that appear to motivate them. Due Process, alone, as Stuntz argues, diverts attention from substantive justice, and in practice ensures relatively little procedural justice. Crime Control fails to control crime because, as it turns out, its streamlined methods fail the test of effectiveness: they do not reliably sort the guilty from the innocent. They therefore inflict unacceptable injustice on the innocent, while failing to promote public safety by permitting the guilty to go free. And together, they thereby undermine public confidence in the system—which is an essential ingredient in efficient crime control. The result, according to a summary of Stuntz's argument, is that "[t]he Warren Supreme Court's emphasis on procedures, not equity, joined hands with conservative insistence on severe punishment to create a system that is both harsh and ineffective."[77]

The Innocence Movement and the reforms it has generated implicitly build on that criticism, and demonstrate that when applied differently the two value preferences—crime control and due process—can co-exist. In place of the dichotomy between process rights and crime control, the Innocence Movement focuses on values shared by criminal defendants and police and prosecutors alike: the interest in reliably determining guilt and innocence. The Innocence Movement is thus based on what might be viewed as a reliability model, or a substantive justice model, rather than either a Due Process or a Crime Control Model. By focusing on

73 Packer, *Two Models*, at 11.

74 *Id.* at 12.

75 *Id.* at 13.

76 *Id.* at 14.

77 Stuntz, *supra* note 61, jacket cover (summarizing Stuntz's argument).

substantive justice it does not reject due process, but instead emphasizes the procedures best able to achieve accurate factual determinations.[78]

This fundamental value preference lies at the root of the Innocence Movement. While the Innocence Movement is largely perceived as a criminal-defense oriented movement, it openly embraces fundamental crime control values—it focuses on ascertaining factual truth and apprehending the true perpetrator.[79] The innocence literature frequently references the fact that, apart from cases in which there was actually no crime at all, most wrongful convictions also represent a failure to convict the guilty—a failure of crime control. Indeed, innocence advocacy organizations often point out that in more than 40 percent of the DNA exoneration cases, DNA evidence not only freed the innocent but also identified the true perpetrator.[80]

At the same time, the Innocence Movement is making it clear that respect for defendants' rights is in fact an essential part of and consistent with the Crime Control Model—at least to the extent that those rights and procedural protections are designed to enhance reliability. According to Packer, the Crime Control Model can accept some mistakes in determining guilt and innocence, but only "up to the level at which they interfere with the goal of repressing crime, either because too many guilty people are escaping or, more subtly, because general awareness of the unreliability of the process leads to a decrease in the deterrent efficacy of the criminal law."[81]

The wrongful convictions exposed by the Innocence Movement threaten crime control in both of these ways. They remind us that, by convicting the innocent, the system allows the guilty to escape punishment for serious crimes. And the wrongful conviction cases are raising awareness of the fallibility of the system as never before. Faith in the system thus requires—even for those who operate solely from a crime control perspective—renewed attention to protecting against wrongful conviction of the innocent. As long as the Innocence Movement focuses on procedural rights tied directly to achieving accurate results—that is, methods understood as "best practices" for achieving substantive justice—the Innocence Movement offers the opportunity for breaking the logjam created by the competing values underlying traditional notions of procedural due process on the one hand, and law enforcement or crime control on the other.

And indeed, almost all of the reforms emerging from the Innocence Movement—from eyewitness identification reform, to electronic recording of custodial interrogations of suspects, even to enhancing the quality of defense counsel—serve both due process objectives and crime control interests because they improve the reliability of the system.[82] The new innocence paradigm offers a path forward to improving the system on such issues because it is based on shared values.

This fundamental shift—joining the interests of the accused (more accurately, the innocent accused) and law enforcement—can be understood in other ways as well. As noted, the Crime Control Model is premised on a preference for administrative fact-finding centered on police investigations, while the Due Process Model preferences formal adversarial adjudication in open court. The assumption underlying the Due Process Model—and the Warren Court's Due Process Revolution—is that fair treatment is only achieved by adversarial criminal proceedings in which an aggressive defense lawyer invokes available rights and puts the government's case to the test. But because, as the empirical evidence demonstrates, defense lawyers rarely invoke due process rights, conduct independent investigations, file motions to suppress evidence, challenge prosecution-proffered expert testimony, or seek experts of their own, the system is already and inexorably taking on a greater administrative quality. Indeed, the dominant mode of resolving criminal cases today is

---

78 See Keith A. Findley, *Toward a New Paradigm of Criminal Justice: How the Innocence Movement Merges Crime Control and Due Process*, 41 TEX. TECH. L. REV. 133 (2008).

79 *See* D. Michael Risinger & Lesley C. Risinger, Chapter 7, this volume.

80 *See* Findley, *New Paradigm*, *supra* note 78, at 141.

81 Packer, *Two Models*, *supra* note 72, at 15.

82 Not all procedural rights underlying the Packer's Due Process Model or the Warren Court's Due Process revolution, of course, fit within this new paradigm. But that, to some extent, is the point I'm making here. Some procedural rules serve values other than truth-finding, and many of these values are important aspects of the Due Process Model. For example, testimonial privileges and rules that exclude reliable but illegally obtained evidence deliberately sacrifice factual accuracy for the sake of other values. While many in the Innocence Movement are undoubtedly sympathetic to those values and those rules, such rules are not explicitly a part of the Innocence Movement's agenda or a necessary part of the model upon which the innocence reforms are based.

the ultimate of administrative proceedings—the guilty plea. Criminal defendants rarely invoke the most fundamental procedural right, the right to trial itself.

Because the system is becoming increasingly administrative, due process and crime control advocates alike have a shared interest in improving the efficacy of the administrative fact-finding mechanisms. Again, the interests of (innocent) defendants and law enforcement coalesce. If the adversary due process system is not doing much to act as protector of justice, then the focus shifts to increasing the reliability of the administrative processes that produce the facts upon which guilty or no contest pleas are based. Interests align around ensuring that police employ best practices for conducting eyewitness identification procedures, interrogating suspects, questioning witnesses, and obtaining forensic science evidence. Focus on administrative processes also argues for increased checks and balances within the investigative and prosecutorial process (such as separating more clearly the roles of investigation and prosecution, and reviewing or limiting the use of jailhouse snitches), and more expansive criminal discovery.[83] Darryl Brown thus contends that these new administrative mechanisms for ensuring reliability have greater potential for protecting the rights of innocent defendants than the politically unrealistic hope of adequately funding defense counsel to fight prosecutors in adversary litigation.[84]

Thus, it is not surprising that police and prosecutors, along with victims' advocates and judges, are joining innocence advocates in reform efforts to improve the reliability of the criminal justice system—to better protect the innocent and convict the guilty. These efforts are most visible in the work of innocence commissions, criminal justice study commissions,[85] or other similar bodies that have been formed in states such as North Carolina,[86] Virginia,[87] Wisconsin,[88] Illinois,[89] California,[90] Pennsylvania,[91] and Florida,[92] among others. Typically composed of representatives from all perspectives in the criminal justice system, these organizations—some with more success than others—are finding common ground in efforts to improve the functioning of the criminal justice system, implicitly replacing any distinction between the Crime Control and Due Process Models with a model that emphasizes best practices. Such efforts have increasingly become a hallmark of the Innocence Movement.[93]

## Part IV: The Imprint of Innocence in Criminal Justice Policy

The result is a policy agenda focused on improving the processes for gathering, assessing, and testing (both before and at trial) the facts relied upon to charge and prosecute individuals in criminal cases. Studies of DNA exonerations have consistently identified the same cluster of factors that contribute to wrongful convictions.[94] As noted, these include eyewitness error, false confessions, jailhouse snitch or informant testimony and other

83 See Mary Prosser, *Reforming Criminal Discovery: Why Old Objections Must Yield to New Realities*, 2006 Wis. L. Rev. 541.

84 Darryl K. Brown, *The Decline of Defense Counsel and the Rise of Accuracy in Criminal Adjudication*, 93 Cal. L. Rev. 1585, 1590–91 (2005).

85 See Keith A. Findley, *Learning from Our Mistakes: A Criminal Justice Commission to Study Wrongful Convictions*, 38 Cal. Western L. Rev. 333 (2002).

86 See Christine C. Mumma, *The North Carolina Actual Innocence Commission: Uncommon Perspectives Joined by a Common Cause*, 52 Drake L. Rev. 647 (2004).

87 Jon B. Gould, The Innocence Commission: Preventing Wrongful Convictions and Restoring the Criminal Justice System (2008).

88 *See* Katherine R. Kruse, *Instituting Innocence Reform: Wisconsin's New Governance Experiment*, 2006 Wis. L. Rev. 645; *Wisconsin Criminal Justice Study Commission*, University of Wisconsin Law School, http://law.wisc.edu/fjr/clinicals/ip/wcjsc/index.html (last updated Oct. 11, 2011).

89 State of Illinois, Report of the Governor's Commission on Capital Punishment (2002).

90 California Commission on the Fair Administration of Justice, www.ccfaj.org (last visited July 29, 2013).

91 General Assembly of the Commonwealth of Pennsylvania, Joint State Government Commission, Report of the Advisory Committee on Wrongful Convictions (2011).

92 Florida Innocence Commission, Final Report to the Supreme Court of Florida (2012).

93 For an overview of American Innocence Commissions *see* Sarah Cooper, Chapter 11, this volume.

94 *See* Findley & Scott, *supra* note 63, at 292; Garrett, *supra* note 45, at 76; Gross et al., *supra* note 1, at 543–4.

types of perjury, police and prosecutorial misconduct, flawed or fraudulent forensic science, inadequate defense counsel, and tunnel vision.[95] Reforms to redress each of these problems are aimed at enhancing the reliability of the process.

*Eyewitness Identifications*[96]

Considerable work has been done on eyewitness identification reform. Researchers have found that not only is eyewitness error the leading contributor to wrongful convictions, present in more than three-quarters of the DNA exonerations, but also that the methods police use to collect identification evidence can and do contribute significantly to the rate of error. The reforms to address this problem break down generally into two categories: those designed to prevent mistakes during the pre-trial identification process; and those designed to permit fact-finders to more effectively evaluate the reliability of eyewitness evidence offered at trial, such as reforming standards for admissibility of eyewitness evidence and expert testimony on eyewitness perception and memory.[97] The specific reforms are too numerous and complex to address here;[98] it is enough to observe here that police practices are indeed changing, at least in some jurisdictions, in response to this reliability challenge. Legislation has been adopted in a number of states that requires or encourages law enforcement agencies to adopt "best practices" based on social science research.[99] Even in the absence of legislation, a few state attorneys general are mandating or recommending revised procedures designed to minimize eyewitness error,[100] and countless other individual law enforcement agencies around the country are voluntarily adopting the new evidence-based best practices.[101] The vast majority of states and police agencies still have not adopted the new procedures, but change is coming, and is gradually being accepted by law enforcement.[102]

Courts in a number of jurisdictions are also taking note of the new reliability challenges to old eyewitness identification standards and methods, even if the majority of the United States Supreme Court has not done so yet.[103] Numerous state courts are revising admissibility standards to more accurately reflect what social psychology teaches about identification evidence,[104] and to begin to open the door to expert testimony about eyewitness evidence.[105] Most courts remain stuck in outmoded assumptions about eyewitness evidence, but again, change is beginning to occur in ways previously thought impossible.

---

95 *See* Samuel R. Gross, *Convicting the Innocent*, 4 Ann. Rev. L. & Soc. 173, 186 (2008).

96 For a more detailed consideration of eyewitness misidentification *see* Jules Epstein, Chapter 3, this volume.

97 Timothy P. O'Toole & Giovanna Shay, Manson v. Brathwaite *Revisited: Towards a New Rule of Decision for Due Process Challenges to Eyewitnesses Identification Procedures*, 4 Val. L. Rev. 109, 113–15 (2006); Gary L. Wells, *Eyewitness Identification: Systemic Reforms*, 2006 Wis. L. Rev. 615, 616–17.

98 For an overview of those reforms, *see* Reform of Eyewitness Identification Procedures (Brian L. Cutler ed. 2013).

99 *See, e.g.*, N.C. Gen. Stat. §§ 15A-284.52(b)(2); Ohio R.C. § 2933.83; Wis. Stat. § 175.50.

100 *See, e.g.*, Letter from John F. Farmer, Jr., Attorney General, State of N.J., to New Jersey County Prosecutors, Police Chiefs & Law Enforcement Chief Executives (Apr. 18, 2001), *available at* http:// www.state.nj.us/lps/dcj/agguide/photoid.pdf (last visited July 31, 2013); State of Wisconsin, Office of the Attorney General, Model Policy and Procedure for Eyewitness Identification (2010), *available at* http://www.doj.state.wi.us/sites/default/files/2009-news/eyewitness-public-20091105.pdf (last visited July 31, 2013).

101 *See* Wells, *supra* note 97, at 642–3.

102 *See* David A. Harris, Failed Evidence: Why Law Enforcement Resists Science (2012).

103 *See* Perry v. New Hampshire, 132 S. Ct. 716 (2012).

104 *See, e.g.*, State v. Lawson, 291 P.3d 673 (Or. 2012); State v. Henderson, 27 A.3d 872 (N.J. 2011); State v. Dubose, 699 N.W.2d 582 (Wis. 2005); State v. Ledbetter, 881 A.2d 290 (Conn. 2005); Brodes v. State, 615 S.E.2d 766 (Ga. 2005); State v. Hunt, 69 P.3d 571, 576 (Kan. 2003); Commonwealth v. Johnson, 650 N.E.2d 1257 (Mass. 1995); State v. Ramirez, 817 P.2d 774 (Utah 1991).

105 Saul Kassin et al., *On the "General Acceptance" of Eyewitness Testimony Research: A New Survey of the Experts*, 56 Am. Psychologist 405 (May 2001); Michael R. Leippe, *The Case for Expert Testimony About Eyewitness Memory*, 1 Psychol. Pub. Pol'y & L. 909, 911 (1995); Steven D. Penrod & Brian Cutler, *Preventing Mistaken Convictions in Eyewitness Identification Trials: The Case Against Traditional Safeguards*, in Psychology and Law: The State of the Discipline 89, 112–15 (Ronald Roesch et al. eds, 1999).

### *False Confessions*[106]

Progress has been made in terms of addressing false confessions as well. Electronic recording of interrogations is the most widely recommended reform for guarding against false confessions.[107] Electronic recording protects the innocent by deterring police coercion and by making a record for fact-finders when police push too hard or supply the details of a purported confession. Electronic recording aids fact-finders by providing a clear record to resolve otherwise insoluble swearing contests between interrogators and suspects about what happened and what was said in the interrogation room. At the same time, electronic recording serves law enforcement—and hence crime control—directly by protecting police from spurious claims of coercion in the interrogation room, and by providing powerful evidence of guilt when defendants voluntarily confess on tape. By reducing litigable issues, electronic recording directly improves the efficacy and efficiency of the administrative processing of criminal cases.

For these reasons, police across the country are beginning to adopt electronic recording voluntarily.[108] A growing number of states now require electronic recording of at least some interrogations by statute, and the supreme courts in at least five other states have mandated or encouraged recording.[109] Because electronic recording so clearly benefits both the innocent accused and the prosecution, it is a prime example of the type of reliability-based reform that underlies the innocence paradigm. Here again, much more work remains to be done, but the trajectory is clear; electronic recording is the future.

### *Flawed Forensic Science*

Brandon Garrett's detailed analysis of the DNA exoneration cases found that forensic evidence was presented in 74 percent of the first 185 cases in which trial records are available; and in 61 percent of the cases in which a forensic analyst testified for the prosecution, the testimony was invalid.[110] While a serious problem, forensic science, because it has traditionally been so aligned with law enforcement and largely unavailable to the defense, has proven highly resistant to reform. Yet here again, the innocence frame has made some inroads. In part, in response to concerns about wrongful convictions, the NAS, at the request of the United

---

106 For a more detailed consideration of false confessions see Deborah Davies, Richard Leo, & Michael J. Williams, Chapter 4, this volume.

107 *See* Steven A. Drizin & Marissa J. Reich, *Heeding the Lessons of History: The Need for Mandatory Recording of Police Interrogations to Accurately Assess the Reliability and Voluntariness of Confessions*, 52 DRAKE L. REV. 619, 620 (2004); Gail Johnson, *False Confessions and Fundamental Fairness: The Need for Electronic Recording of Custodial Interrogations*, 6 B.U. PUB. INT. L.J. 719, 735 (1997); Thomas P. Sullivan, *Federal Law Enforcement Should Record Custodial Interrogations*, CHAMPION, Apr. 2007, 8, at 8–9.

108 Thomas P. Sullivan, *Electronic Recording of Custodial Interrogations: Everybody Wins*, 95 J. CRIM. L. & CRIMINOLOGY 1127, 1128 (2005). According to Sullivan, as of 2005, more than 300 local police and sheriff's departments in 43 states had adopted a policy of electronic recording. *Id.* Since then several more states have mandated or established statewide policies of electronic recording. *Id.*

109 *See* D.C. CODE ANN. § 5-116.01 (LexisNexis Supp. 2007) (requiring police to record all custodial investigations); 725 ILL. COMP. STAT. ANN. 5/103-2.1 (West 2006) (same); ME. REV. STAT. ANN. tit. 25, § 2803-B (2007) (mandating policy of recording "interviews of suspects in serious crimes"); N.M. STAT. § 29-1-16 (Supp. 2006) (requiring police to record all custodial investigations); N.C. GEN. STAT. § 15A-211 (2007) (requiring complete electronic recording of custodial interrogations in homicide cases); TEX. CODE CRIM. PROC. ANN. art. 38.22, § 3 (Vernon Supp. 2007) (rendering unrecorded oral statements inadmissible); WIS. STAT. §§ 968.073, 938.195 (2005) (declaring it to be state policy that police must electronically record all custodial interrogations in felony cases and in all juvenile cases whenever feasible); Stephan v. State, 711 P.2d 1156, 1158 (Alaska 1985) (mandating electronic recording); Commonwealth v. DiGiambattista, 813 N.E.2d 516, 535 (Mass. 2004) (allowing defense to point out state's failure to record interrogation and calling unrecorded admissions "less reliable"); State v. Scales, 518 N.W.2d 587, 592 (Minn. 1994) (mandating electronic recording); State v. Cook, 847 A.2d 530, 547 (N.J. 2004) (establishing a committee to study and make recommendations on the use of electronic recording); *In re* Jerrel C.J., 699 N.W.2d 110, 123 (Wis. 2005) (mandating electronic recording of all custodial interrogations of juveniles); Van Smith, *Roll the Tape*, Apr. 16, 2008, http://www.citypaper.com/news/story.asp?id=15588 (reporting that electronic recording legislation is on the Maryland governor's desk for his signature, and that the governor was considering it and had supported it while it was in the legislature).

110 GARRETT, *supra* note 45, at 89–90.

States Congress, undertook an in-depth study of the state of forensic sciences in America, leading to its 2009 report, *Strengthening Forensic Science in the United States: A Path Forward*.[111] The report exposed serious weaknesses in the scientific foundation for most forensic methods (other than DNA) and called for widespread reforms—beginning with the creation of a National Institute of Forensic Sciences, which would establish and enforce best practices for forensic science professionals and laboratories; establish standards for mandatory accreditation of laboratories and certification of forensic scientists; promote research and training; establish standard terminology to be used in forensic science reports and testimony; and facilitate the independence of crime laboratories by moving them from the administrative control of law enforcement agencies and prosecutors, among other things.[112]

Until recently, however, relatively little has been done to implement the recommendations in that report.[113] Not eager to create a new federal administrative agency, Congress has balked at creating the National Institute of Forensic Sciences. And most of the NAS Report's other recommendations are dependent on the creation of that institute, so little progress has been made on improving forensic science evidence.

But things appear to be changing. Forensic sciences are receiving scrutiny like never before in scholarly work and even some judicial opinions; and in February 2013, the Department of Justice and the National Institute of Standards and Technology in the Department of Commerce announced that they would be partnering to form a National Commission on Forensic Science.[114] The objective of the Commission is to effectuate many of the recommendations of the NAS Report.

At the state level, substantive reforms are beginning to emerge. In North Carolina, for example, the legislature enacted The Forensic Science Act of 2011, which creates a Forensic Science Advisory board to regulate accreditation of laboratories and certification of analysts.[115] In Mississippi, new legislation in 2011 moved the state medical examiner's office into the University of Mississippi and created a Medical Examiner Advisory Board.[116] In Maryland, the legislature moved the state's accreditation regulation authority to an independent agency, the Department of Health.[117] In 2013, Texas expanded the scope and jurisdiction of the Texas Forensic Science Commission to help it better regulate forensic sciences in that state.[118] Texas also passed a law providing that evidence offered to contradict scientific evidence that had been presented at trial can be the basis for granting an application for a writ of habeas corpus.[119]

### *Post-Conviction Access to DNA Evidence*

Perhaps the most complete success the Innocence Movement can claim on the policy front is the enactment, as a direct response to the DNA exonerations, of statutes in every state and the federal government providing at least some measure of access to post-conviction DNA testing when it might prove innocence. Such statutes were virtually unheard of until innocence organizations and others began using DNA to prove innocence in serious cases. In 2004, Congress passed and President George Bush signed into law the Innocence Protection Act, which was part of a larger compromise bill known as the Justice for All Act.[120] For innocence purposes, the Act was important for setting a model that states could follow by, among other things, requiring law

---

111 National Research Council, National Academy of Sciences, Strengthening Forensic Science in the United States: A Path Forward 7 (2009).

112 *Id.* at 19–33.

113 *See Four Years On, No Action on NAS Forensic Science Report; Across the Nation, Crime Lab Scandals Abound*, National Association of Criminal Defense Lawyers (NACDL) (Feb. 15, 2013), http://www.nacdl.org/NewsReleases.aspx?id=26459.

114 Erin Murphy, *Physician Heal Thyself: Whither the Police and Prosecutor in the Tale of Forensic Science Gone Wrong?*, 91 Tex. L. Rev. 101, 101 (2013). That Commission was formed, and members were officially appointed, in January 2014. Press Release, U.S. Dept. of Justice (Jan. 10, 2014), *available at* http://www.justice.gov/opa/pr/2014/January/14-at-029.html (last visited January 24, 2014).

115 N.C. H.B. 27 / S.L. 2011-19.

116 Miss. S.B. 2435 (2011).

117 Md. H.B. 1294 (2012).

118 Tex. S.B. 1238 (2013).

119 Tex. S.B. 344 (2013).

120 Justice for All Act, Pub. L. No. 108-405, 108th Cong. tit. 4 (2004).

enforcement to preserve biological evidence for post-conviction DNA testing, and permitting access to that evidence after conviction for DNA testing when it might prove innocence. Importantly, the Act also included the Kirk Bloodsworth Post-Conviction DNA Testing Grant Program, which provides money to states for post-conviction DNA testing; and the Paul Coverdell Forensic Science Improvement Grant Program, which provides money to state forensic science laboratories and requires states to create independent entities to review allegations of negligence or misconduct in the laboratories.[121]

To one degree or another, all 50 states have now followed suit by passing post-conviction DNA testing statutes. When Oklahoma adopted its post-conviction DNA testing statute on May 24, 2013, it marked the first time that all 50 states and the federal government provided a statutory right to post-conviction DNA testing.[122] While that reflected a remarkable measure of success for the Innocence Movement, the success was not quite as complete as it might seem. Although all states now have post-conviction DNA testing statutes, many of those statutes are limited in significant ways. Some limit the availability of DNA to specified types of cases, impose onerous burdens on applicants, or deny access to individuals who confessed or pled guilty, despite the fact that approximately 30 percent of the DNA exoneration cases involved false confessions or admissions or a guilty plea.[123] Even this most basic of innocence reforms remains incomplete.

## Part V: Innocence and the Death Penalty

Innocence consciousness and the Innocence Movement have also dramatically affected criminal justice policy debates on at least one issue not directly related to improving the reliability of the system. Despite the undeniable impact of the Innocence Movement on that issue, it is one that the Innocence Movement as a whole does not explicitly identify as part of its policy agenda. That issue is the death penalty.

It is widely recognized that new concern about innocence has dramatically altered the debate and attitudes about the death penalty in America since the 1990s. Most death penalty scholars credit the rise of innocence consciousness as uniquely transformative in its effect on attitudes—and policies—about the death penalty. As Frank Baumgartner and his colleagues have observed, "The new focus on innocence has generated public doubt, official caution, powerful individual stories of exoneration, and fewer death sentences, all in a self-perpetuating cycle."[124] Baumgartner et al. argue, based on their "detailed analysis of the rise of the innocence frame," "that this new frame is (1) unprecedented in its strength compared with previous understandings of the issue, (2) powerful in its effects on public opinion as well as on policy outputs, and (3) *more* powerful in these effects even than underlying social trends, such as the murder rate or other reasonable rival explanations."[125]

In 1993, Kirk Bloodsworth in Maryland became the first person who had been sentenced to death to be exonerated by DNA evidence.[126] Others followed, until today a total of 18 people have been exonerated from death row by DNA.[127] Here again, however, DNA tells only part of the story. Looking beyond the DNA cases, according to the Death Penalty Information Center, altogether since 1973 more than 140 people sentenced to die have been exonerated—meaning their convictions were not only reversed, but they were also subsequently acquitted or fully set free from the conviction and charges.[128] An exhaustive study by James Liebman and his

121 *Id.*

122 *Post-Conviction DNA Testing Laws Enacted in All 50 States*, Santa Clara Law (May 30, 2013, 2:24 PM), http://law.scu.edu/northern-california-innocence-project/post-conviction-dna-testing-laws-enacted-in-all-50-states/.

123 *Access to Post-Conviction DNA Testing*, Innocence Project, http://www.innocenceproject.org/Content/Access_To_PostConviction_DNA_Testing.php (last visited July 31, 2013).

124 Frank R. Baumgartner, Suzanna L. De Boef & Amber E. Boydstun, The Decline of the Death Penalty and the Discovery of Innocence 10 (2008).

125 *Id.* at 14 (emphasis in original).

126 *Know the Cases, Kirk Bloodsworth*, Innocence Project, http://www.innocenceproject.org/Content/Kirk_Bloodsworth.php (last visited July 30, 2013).

127 *The Innocent and the Death Penalty*, Innocence Project, http://www.innocenceproject.org/Content/The_Innocent_and_the_Death_Penalty.php (last visited July 30, 2013).

128 *Innocence and the Death Penalty*, Death Penalty Information Center, http://www.deathpenaltyinfo.org/innocence-and-death-penalty (last visited July 30, 2013).

colleagues found that in all capital cases in the United States between 1973 and 1995, a full two-thirds (68 percent) of the convictions or death sentences in America were reversed at some point in the review process because of serious trial court error.[129] In 7 percent of those cases on retrial the defendant was found not guilty of the offense for which he had previously been sentenced to die.[130]

While the death penalty is still entrenched in many American states, shifts in public attitudes and policy are apparent. The number of death sentences imposed in the first decade of the twenty-first century was half the number imposed in the previous decade.[131] From 1976, when the United States Supreme Court permitted resumption of capital punishment in America,[132] through the mid-1990s—before the Innocence Movement gained full traction—use of and support for the death penalty grew significantly.[133] In the mid-1990s, public opinion polls revealed that about 80 percent—peaking at 86 percent in 1995—of the population in America favored capital punishment for persons convicted of murder.[134] In the mid-1990s, however, those trends began to reverse. By 2006, support for the death penalty had fallen to 70 percent and even lower—around 47 percent—when responders are asked to choose between execution and an alternative severe sanction, such as life in prison without parole.[135] By 2004, the number of death sentences imposed had dropped to 125, down from 314 in 1994.[136] Perhaps most telling, between 2007 and 2012, six states—New Jersey (2007), New York (2007), New Mexico (2009), Illinois (2011), Connecticut (2012), and Maryland (2013)—abolished the death penalty, reducing the number of states with capital punishment from 38 to 32.[137]

The reasons for these shifts are complex, but innocence consciousness is widely credited as the most influential factor. As one indicator of the impact of the innocence narrative, an analysis by Baumgartner and colleagues of the 3,939 articles on capital punishment appearing in the *New York Times* over a 45-year span beginning in 1960 documents "clear shifts in the framing of capital punishment … from the moral and constitutional frames of the 1960s and 1970s to the innocence frame of the last decade and others in between. Of all the frames, the innocence frame is the single most powerful in terms of amount of attention … ."[138] Consistent with that observation, James Unnever and Francis Cullen's review of polling data found that those who believe an innocent person has been executed are less likely to support capital punishment, and 75 percent of Americans in 2003 believed that an innocent person had been executed within the past five years.[139]

Despite the profound effect that innocence has had on the death penalty, it is an issue with which the innocence community has engaged cautiously. And interestingly, even while acknowledging the impact that innocence has had on reshaping attitudes about capital punishment, the anti-death penalty community has for its part responded somewhat cautiously to the Innocence Movement. To some, the focus on innocence diminishes the value of "vindicat[ing] of constitutional rights *per se*"; threatens to undermine the traditional role of defense counsel as a zealous advocate for the guilty and innocent alike; and actually runs the risk of legitimizing the death penalty by improving the reliability, and hence confidence in, its administration.[140]

Reflecting the sensitive and complex nature of the issues surrounding the death penalty, the Innocence Network—the umbrella affiliation of innocence advocacy organizations—has no express policy on capital punishment. The Innocence Project—the first and most influential of the Network's member organizations—takes a middle position, reflecting concern about capital punishment but carefully limiting

129 James S. Liebman et al., *Capital Attrition: Error Rates in Capital Cases, 1973–1995*, 78 Tex. L. Rev. 1839, 1854 (2000).

130 *Id.* at 1852.

131 Baumgartner et al., *supra* note 124, at 5.

132 *See* Gregg v. Georgia, 4428 U.S. 153 (1976).

133 Baumgartner et al., *supra* note 124, at 7.

134 *Id.* at 7, 173, 174.

135 *Id.* at 217.

136 *Id.* at 7–8.

137 *States With and Without the Death Penalty*, Death Penalty Information Center, http://www.deathpenaltyinfo.org/states-and-without-death-penalty (last visited July 30, 2013).

138 Baumgartner et al., *supra* note 124, at 18; *see also id. at* 103-27.

139 James D. Unnever & Francis T. Cullen, *Executing the Innocent and Support for Capital Punishment: Implications for Public Policy*, 4 Criminology & Pub. Pol'y 3 (2005).

140 Carol S. Steiker & Jordan M. Steiker, *The Seduction of Innocence: The Attraction and Limitations of the Focus on Innocence in Capital Punishment Law and Advocacy*, 95 J. Crim. L. & Criminology 587, 609, 618, 622 (2005).

its policy positions to those strictly tied to innocence concerns. Short of advocating abolition, the Innocence Project's web page explains: "The Innocence Project supports a moratorium on capital punishment while the causes of wrongful convictions are fully identified and remedied. This has been the Innocence Project's position since our inception in 1992, and it is the same position the American Bar Association adopted more than a decade ago."[141]

Other innocence organizations within the Innocence Network take an even more hands-off approach. Some innocence organizations in strongly pro-death penalty states conspicuously take no position at all on the death penalty, so as to avoid derailing their efforts to exonerate the innocent and losing credibility in their communities by being branded as a front for abolitionists. In North Carolina, for example, members of the North Carolina Commission on Actual Innocence declared, as one of their initial steps, that because of "varying viewpoints" about capital punishment and a death penalty moratorium, they had "unanimously agree[d] that the Commission will not take a position on these issues and that individual Commission members will not represent their personal viewpoints on these issues as being shared by other Commission members or the Commission as a whole."[142]

Other innocence organizations, however, have fully embraced abolition of the death penalty as a policy objective. Most notably, the Center on Wrongful Convictions at Northwestern University School of Law in Chicago—one of the most prominent innocence organizations—has made abolition of the death penalty one of its principal objectives. In 1998, the Northwestern University School of Law hosted an influential three-day conference on Wrongful Convictions and the Death Penalty, highlighted by the gathering on stage of 29 men and women who had been sentenced to death, but who had subsequently been exonerated. That emotional presentation galvanized the movement to abolish the death penalty in Illinois. In the late 1990s, then Governor George Ryan—at one time one of the architects of Illinois's death penalty law—became concerned when he learned that 13 people on death row in Illinois had been exonerated during the same period in which 12 people had been executed. Upon realizing this, Ryan intervened to stop the process because the risk of executing an innocent person was simply too great.[143] In 2000, in large part at the urging of professors and students at Northwestern, Governor Ryan declared a moratorium on executions and appointed a bipartisan commission to study flaws in the state's capital punishment system.[144] That commission produced a report recommending 85 reforms to minimize the risks of executing an innocent person.[145] In 2003, on the steps of the Northwestern University School of Law, Governor Ryan announced his decision to grant clemency to all 167 death row inmates in Illinois, granting four outright pardons and commuting the remaining 163 sentences to life terms.[146] In 2011, Illinois became the 16th state in the nation to abolish the death penalty entirely.[147]

## Part V: Conclusion

The imprint of the innocence cases on criminal justice policy is thus real and significant. Considerable reform has occurred, but much more remains to be done to meet the reform objectives of the Innocence Network and its member organizations. While change comes slowly, innocence consciousness has made real substantive change possible in ways not imaginable during the heyday of the war on crime.

---

141 *The Death Penalty*, INNOCENCE PROJECT, http://www.innocenceproject.org/Content/The_Death_Penalty.php (last visited July 30, 2013).

142 Mumma, *supra* note 86, at 655 (quoting N.C. Actual Innocence Comm'n, Mission Statement, Objectives, and Procedures (June 2003)).

143 Rob Warden, *Illinois Death Penalty Reform: How It Happened, What It Promises*, 95 J. CRIM. L. & CRIMINOLOGY 381, 382 (2005).

144 Golden & Findley, *supra* note 3; BAUMGARTNER ET AL., *supra* note 124, at 67.

145 STATE OF ILLINOIS, REPORT OF THE GOVERNOR'S COMMISSION ON CAPITAL PUNISHMENT (2002), *available at* http://illinoismurderindictments.law.northwestern.edu/docs/Illinois_Moratorium_Commission_complete-report.pdf (last visited July 31, 2013).

146 BAUMGARTNER ET AL., *supra* note 124, at 69.

147 John Schwartz, *Illinois Governor Signs Capital Punishment Ban*, N.Y. TIMES, Mar. 9, 2011, *available at* http://www.nytimes.com/2011/03/10/us/10illinois.html?_r=0.

The Innocence Movement built its strength on the powerful narratives generated first by the DNA exonerations, and then additionally by the growing number of exonerations in non-DNA cases. The Innocence Movement used those narratives to reframe the debate in the American criminal justice system away from a contest between due process rights for criminal defendants and crime control interests—a contest that criminal defendants, with no natural constituency, were bound to lose—and toward shared values focused on reliability and efficacy in the processes for sorting the guilty from the innocent.

Although that paradigm cannot resolve all criminal justice debates (or perhaps even most)—such as those relating to fairness and respect for human dignity in matters that do not turn on questions of guilt and innocence—it has made reform possible when it comes to the system's most basic truth-finding functions. While the reform effort is still largely nascent, the prospects for real improvement in the system appear more promising than they have in decades. As Baumgartner and his colleagues put it in the death penalty context, "In this way, the innocence frame is much more than a bit of rhetoric or spin. It is a cultural shift embodied by declining trends in sentencing rates, executions, and public support and by a list of exonerated individuals that continues to grow."[148]

148 Baumgartner et al., *supra* note 124, at 52.

# Chapter 2
# The Innocence Network: From Beginning to Branding

Jacqueline McMurtrie

## Introduction

In a few years, the era of DNA exonerations will come to an end.[1]

Barry Scheck and Peter Neufeld did not predict when they founded the Innocence Project in 1992 that DNA exonerations would continue to exponentially rise and that the Innocence Movement would strengthen and grow based upon the expanding number of DNA exonerations. In 2000, when Scheck, Neufeld and Dwyer published their ground-breaking book *Actual Innocence*,[2] 67 people had been sent to prison and death row for crimes post-conviction DNA testing proved they did not commit.[3] Far from 'coming to an end,' the DNA era has flourished, with the current number of post-conviction DNA exonerations standing at 311.[4]

The importance of DNA in criminal investigations is lauded as the "the single greatest advance in the 'search for truth', and the goal of convicting the guilty and acquitting the innocent, since the advent of cross-examination."[5] The growth in DNA exonerations is in part due to advances in technology which allow forensic analysts to obtain profiles from minute traces of biological material previously untestable because the sample was too small or was degraded.[6] Current STR-DNA technology can obtain profiles from minuscule samples of saliva, semen, sweat, skin cells, and cellular material found in the root of a hair.[7] Those profiles are uploaded into the Combined DNA Index System (CODIS), a vast, computerized state and federal registry containing over 10 million convicted-felon STR-DNA profiles.[8] In 49 percent of the first 300 DNA exonerations, CODIS has identified the true perpetrator after a wrongly convicted prisoner is exonerated.[9]

However, the impetus behind Scheck and Neufeld's representation that the DNA era was coming to an end was to urge projects to investigate cases where the "magic bullet of DNA testing" is not present.[10] They were concerned that thousands of people would remain in prison because "the criminal did not ejaculate, spit, bleed, or shed tissue."[11] And while the Innocence Movement is often associated with genetic testing,

---

1 Barry Scheck, Peter Neufeld & Jim Dwyer, Actual Innocence: When Justice Goes Wrong and How to Make it Right 323 (Reprint 2001).

2 Barry Scheck, Peter Neufeld & Jim Dwyer, Actual Innocence: When Justice Goes Wrong and How to Make it Right 323 (2000).

3 *Id.* at xiv.

4 Innocence Project, http://www.innocenceproject.org/ (last visited Aug. 10, 2013).

5 *People v. Wesley*, 533 N.Y.S.2d 643, *644* (Albany Cnty. Ct. *1988*).

6 *See* Robert Aronson & Jacqueline McMurtrie, *The Use and Misuse of High-Tech Evidence by Prosecutors: Ethical and Evidentiary Issues*, 76(3) Fordham L. Rev. 1453, 1470 n.109 (2007): "The first DNA test, restriction fragment length polymorphism (RFLP), required a relatively large sample of biological material (a minimum of 100,000 cells containing DNA). Forensic analysts had to have a sample of biological material that was at least the size of a quarter. Subsequent development of polymerase chain reaction (PCR) testing of DNA revolutionized DNA testing by allowing samples of DNA contained in biological evidence to be copied without affecting the original sample. The PCR amplification technique can be used to reproduce millions of copies of the DNA contained in a few, for example, 50–100, cells."

7 U.S Department of Justice, *Using DNA to Solve Cold Cases*, National Criminal Justice Reference Service, https://www.ncjrs.gov/pdffiles1/nij/194197.pdf (last visited May 5, 2013).

8 *FBI CODIS–NDIS Statistics*, Federal Bureau of Investigation, http://www.fbi.gov/about-us/lab/biometric-analysis/codis/ndis-statistics (last visited Feb. 25, 2013).

9 *Innocence By the Numbers: The First 300*, Innocence Project in Print 8(1) (Innocence Project), Winter 2012, *available at* http://www.innocenceproject.org/docs/ipw2012/numbers.php.

10 Scheck, Neufeld & Dwyer, *supra* note 1, at 323.

11 *Id.*

it remains true that non-DNA evidence forms the basis for the majority of exonerations achieved in the United States. The National Registry of Exonerations, a joint project of the University of Michigan School of Law and Northwestern University School of Law, provides detailed information about 1,106 exonerations occurring in the United States from 1989 to the present.[12] Only 349 of the 1,106 exonerations involve DNA evidence.[13] Factors contributing to wrongful conviction vary depending upon the type of crime, and include mistaken eyewitness identification, perjury or false accusation, false confession, false or misleading forensic evidence, and official misconduct.[14]

To address the need for representation of innocent prisoners, among *Actual Innocence*'s "Short List of Reforms" was a recommendation to create and fund "Innocence Projects at law schools to represent clients in DNA and non-DNA cases" through an Innocence Network.[15] This chapter focuses upon the nonprofit organizations responding to Scheck, Neufeld, and Dwyer's call to action. Part I discusses the formation and history of the first innocence projects in the United States. Part II describes the expansion of innocence organizations and the mobilization of their efforts into the Innocence Network. It discusses the growth of the Network, the current structure of its member organizations, and the identity and governance challenges that accompany the Network expansion. Part III reviews the limited research on innocence organizations and Part IV explores literature in nonprofit branding and governance to provide an initial point of inquiry for the Network to identify and move forward its social mission. The chapter concludes with recommendations drawn from the interdisciplinary research.

## Part I: The Early Projects: Centurion and the Innocence Project

Centurion Ministries, Inc. was the first organization formed to redress the causes of wrongful convictions. It was founded in 1983 under the leadership of James C. McCloskey, and the majority of its cases are non-DNA cases involving intensive fact investigation.[16] McCloskey named the organization in honor of the Roman centurion who proclaimed while standing at the foot of the cross during Christ's crucifixion: "Surely, this one is innocent."[17] Centurion Ministries has succeeded in freeing 50 individuals from prison.[18] It considers cases of factual innocence, which can be established through DNA or non-DNA evidence, where the sentence was life (15-year minimum to serve before parole eligibility) or death.[19]As is true of most innocence organizations, Centurion does not review cases of accidental death, self-defense, or cases where the defendant had any involvement whatsoever in the crime for which he/she was convicted.[20]

The Innocence Project, founded in 1992 by Barry C. Scheck and Peter J. Neufeld at the Benjamin N. Cardozo School of Law, dedicates its efforts to individuals whose innocence can be proven through DNA testing.[21] Scheck and Neufeld were colleagues at the Legal Aid Society in the late 1970s, honing their skills in the Bronx Courthouse and developing an expertise in forensic evidence.[22] Although they have become renowned for their success in using post-conviction DNA evidence, their first exoneration was obtained through more conventional means. In 1987, Scheck and Neufeld took on the appeal of Marion Coakley, who

12 National Registry of Exonerations, http://www.exonerationregistry.org (last visited May 5, 2013).

13 *Id.* The number of exonerations involving DNA is larger than the Innocence Project database because it includes cases where DNA testing was conducted but the results were not central to establishing innocence.

14 *Key Figures and Tables*, National Registry of Exonerations, http://www.law.umich.edu/special/exoneration/Documents/exonerations_us_1989_2012_key_figures.pdf (last visited Feb. 25, 2013).

15 Scheck, Neufeld & Dwyer, *supra* note 2, at 260.

16 *About Us*, Centurion Ministries, http://www.centurionministries.org/about/ (last visited Feb. 25, 2013).

17 *About Us: 1980–1989*, Centurion Ministries, http://www.centurionministries.org/about/history/1980s.php (last visited Feb. 25, 2013).

18 *Seeking Freedom for the Innocent in Prison*, Centurion Ministries, Nov. 2012, *available at* http://www.centurionministries.org/about/newsletter/centurion-ministries-newsletter-november-2012.pdf.

19 *Case Submission Guidelines*, Centurion Ministries, http://www.centurionministries.org/faq/how-to-submit-a-case-to-cm-revised.pdf (last visited Feb. 25, 2013).

20 Id.

21 Innocence Project, http://www.innocenceproject.org/ (last visited Feb. 25, 2013).

22 Scheck, Neufeld & Dwyer, *supra* note 2, at 6–7.

was convicted of a brutal rape and robbery. They believed that the relatively new technology of DNA typing could help prove Coakley's innocence.[23] However, because the biological sample was too small, the evidence could not be tested using existing technology. Instead, Coakley was freed when conventional serology excluded him as the perpetrator, and through the discovery of other exculpatory evidence.[24] The investigation made Scheck and Neufeld realize the potential of DNA forensic testing to exonerate those who had been wrongly convicted. They closely followed the case of Gary Dotson, who in 1989 was the first person to be exonerated through post-conviction DNA testing, and founded the Innocence Project in the spring of 1992.[25]

## Part II: The Establishment and Expansion of the Innocence Network

The concept of an "Innocence Network" was first brought to public attention in November of 1998, at a three-day conference on Wrongful Convictions and the Death Penalty.[26] Nearly 30 exonerated former death row prisoners and over 1,000 lawyers, academics, and activists come together at Northwestern University School of Law in a gathering widely covered by the media.[27] The emotional centerpiece of the event was the introduction of 29 individuals, who one by one marched across the stage of a large auditorium, gave their names, described the crimes they had been wrongly convicted of, the length of their incarceration, and repeated a variation on a simple refrain.[28] Delbert Tibbs's statement was as follows: "The state of Florida sought to kill me for a murder I did not commit. I was sentenced to death in 1974 and finally released in 1982. Had the state of Florida gotten its way, I would be dead today."[29] In addition to the panel of death row survivors, the conference also featured sessions on flawed forensics, investigative techniques, DNA evidence and the effects of incarceration.[30]

However, a small conference workshop called "The Innocence Network" was the session legal experts contemporaneously noted could provide the "most tangible legacy of the conference."[31] During the session, law schools were exhorted to harness the power of a "mother lode of volunteers: law students who ... are dying for a practical, real-life experience" to investigate prisoners' claims of innocence.[32] The Innocence Project at Cardozo Law School was cited as a model of how law schools could train students to uncover new evidence that would lead to freeing people wrongly convicted of murders or other crimes.[33]

At the time of the conference, the Innocence Project Northwest at the University of Washington School of Law had already followed Cardozo's example.[34] Early advocates of an 'innocence network' recognized that policy reform, as well as client representation, was needed to advance the movement. They called upon university law and journalism schools to not only volunteer the investigative and legal tools needed to reexamine selected cases, but to also pool resources and create a database identifying dishonest police officers or prosecutors.[35] During the next two years, law schools and journalism schools founded the Center

---

23 Elisabeth Salemme, *Innocence Project Marks 15th Year*, TIME, June 3, 2007, *available at* http://www.time.com/time/nation/article/0,8599,1628477,00.html.

24 SCHECK, NEUFELD & DWYER, *supra* note 2, at 33–4.

25 Salemme, *supra* note 23.

26 David E. Rovella, *Law Schools Urged to Take Death Cases*, NAT'L L.J., 7 December, 1998, at A9.

27 Don Terry, *Survivors Make the Case Against Death Row*, N.Y. TIMES, Nov. 16, 1988, at A14.

28 Henry Weinstein, *Death Penalty Foes Focus Effort on the Innocent*, L.A. TIMES, Nov. 16, 1998, at A1.

29 Mitchell Zuckoff, *Death-Row Survivors Tell How Justice Errs Conference Puts Death Penalty on Trial*, BOSTON GLOBE, Nov. 16, 1998, at A1.

30 Rovella, *supra* note 26.

31 *Id.*

32 *Id.*

33 Andrew Stern, *Death Penalty Foes Seek Network To Find Wrongful Convictions*, HOUS. CHRON., Nov. 14, 1998, at A6.

34 Rovella, *supra* note 26.

35 Stern, *supra* note 33.

on Wrongful Convictions,[36] Wisconsin Innocence Project;[37] California Innocence Project,[38] and Medill Justice Project.[39]

*A Network Organizes: 2000 to 2005*

Building upon the legacy of the Wrongful Convictions and the Death Penalty conference and the momentum gained through exposure of wrongful convictions in the news and popular media,[40] the first Innocence Network Workshop was held in 2000 at Northwestern University.[41] Representatives of ten programs attended and the annual Innocence Network conference was launched.[42] At the 2003 Innocence Network conference in New Orleans, an *ad hoc* committee met and decided to form a national Innocence Network steering committee to discuss a permanent governance structure for the Network and offer continuing advice and direction to Network members.[43] By this time, over 25 groups had organized to investigate claims of wrongful conviction.[44]

In 2004 and 2005, the steering committee convened to explore the purpose of the affiliation. There was some question about whether the Network would be limited to an advisory function, or whether it would provide members with direction and services. The potential objectives of a collective enterprise included: facilitating communications among members; stimulating the development of new projects; organizing and implementing national initiatives; determining and enforcing Network membership; sharing materials; and facilitating case conferencing. The challenge of governing a network, where members were only loosely affiliated and quite different from one another—in terms of structures, methodologies, funding level, and even purpose—was recognized.[45]

In 2005, the directors of the existing innocence organizations met at the Innocence Network conference in Washington, DC to vote on the steering committee proposals. The steering committee recommended that the entity be called "The Innocence Network," having rejected National Innocence Network because of the membership of non-United States projects. It proposed that the Network be governed by an elected Board of Directors, comprising 18 members, who would serve staggered three-year terms, without term limits. Board members would have to be a part of a member network project or organization. However, the directors would serve as individuals rather than representatives of projects, thereby allowing a project to have more than one member on the Board. The Board would be required to meet at least twice a year, once at the annual conference and once in the fall. The steering committee recommended forming committees on: Amicus Policies, Communications, National Conference, Membership, and New Projects.[46] The project directors voted in favor of the steering committee's proposals and the Innocence Network was officially inaugurated.[47] The following describes the composition of the first Network Board and the unique governance and membership structures of the Innocence Network.

---

36 Northwestern Law Center on Wrongful Convictions, http://www.law.northwestern.edu/wrongfulconvictions/ (last visited Feb. 25, 2013).

37 *Faculty Profile: John Pray*, University of Wisconsin School of Law, http://law.wisc.edu/profiles/japray@wisc.edu (last visited Feb. 25, 2013).

38 California Innocence Project, http://californiainnocenceproject.org/ (last visited Feb. 25, 2013).

39 Alison Flowers, *The Medill Innocence Project to Change Name to The Medill Justice Project*, Medill Justice Project, http://www.medilljusticeproject.org/2012/12/20/the-medill-innocence-project-to-change-name-to-the-medill-justice-project (last visited Feb. 25, 2013).

40 Marvin Zalman, An Integrated Justice Model of Wrongful Convictions, 74 Alb. L. Rev. 1465 (2011).

41 The conference topics were: Investigating Potential Wrongful Convictions; DNA Testing: Getting It and Using It; Creating a Distance Course on Wrongful Convictions; Screening Cases; Legislative Reform; Media Relations; and Litigation. Innocence Network Workshop, Northwestern University School of Law, Dec. 1–3, 2000 (on file with author).

42 *Innocence Network History*, Innocence Network, http://www.innocencenetwork.org/history (last visited May 11, 2013).

43 (Cookie Ridolfi & Theresa Newman, personal correspondence, memorandum, Apr. 16, 2003).

44 *Id.*

45 *Id.*

46 (Theresa Newman, personal correspondence, memorandum, Mar. 27, 2005).

47 *Innocence Network History*, *supra* note 42.

*Network Board*

Candidates for the 2006–07 Board of Directors were presented as a slate: Shawn Armbrust (Mid-Atlantic Innocence Project); Erika Applebaum (Minnesota Innocence Project); Justin Brooks (California Innocence Project); Jennifer Chunias (New England Innocence Project); Maddy deLone (Innocence Project); Keith Findley (Wisconsin Innocence Project); Jackie McMurtrie (Innocence Project Northwest); Daniel S. Medwed (Rocky Mountain Innocence Center); Bill Moushey (Innocence Institute of Point Park University); Theresa Newman (North Carolina Center on Actual Innocence); John Pray (Wisconsin Innocence Project); Cookie Ridolfi (Northern California Innocence Project); Lon Rose (Association in Defence of the Wrongly Convicted); Barry Scheck (Innocence Project); Robert Schehr (Northern Arizona Justice Project); Rob Warden (Center on Wrongful Convictions); and Lynne Weathered (Griffith University Innocence Project).[48] These individuals agreed to serve a one-year term to develop the details of the Network operation, with the rotating election cycle to begin in 2006.[49]

*Network Membership*

Although the innocence movement has been described as the "new civil rights movement,"[50] its membership and governance structures are uniquely different from civil rights organizations. The National Association for the Advancement of Colored People (NAACP), founded in 1909, is the USA's oldest and largest civil rights organization.[51] Its mission is to ensure the political, educational, social, and economic equality of rights and to eliminate race-based discrimination.[52] The NAACP's beginnings were humble; its national office was a small two-room suite of offices in New York with borrowed furniture and one typewriter.[53] Early on, the NAACP focused on a national campaign to expand and strengthen its membership base and, along with it, to generate revenue from accompanying dues and contributions.[54] Currently, the NAACP has over 2,000 local branches nationwide, with more than half a million members and supporters.[55]

The Network, unlike the NAACP, does not operate as a national organization with branch affiliates. Instead, each member project is its own independent entity. Moreover, membership is not offered to individuals, but is limited to organizations meeting the Network's membership criteria. Organizations are eligible for Network membership if they provide *pro bono* legal and/or investigative services to individuals seeking to prove their innocence of crimes for which they have been convicted.[56] Although certain prosecutors' offices have established units to investigate innocence claims,[57] the prosecutor agencies are precluded from joining the Network because of the potential conflicts of interest with other Network members and their clients.[58]

Organizations may apply for membership if they are tax-exempt nonprofit organizations; projects or programs housed within, or sponsored by, other nonprofit organizations—including, programs based at educational institutions; units of attorneys and/or investigators within a governmental agency devoted to the representation of indigent persons ("defender organizations"); coalitions of individuals/organizations within

---

48 (Theresa Newman, personal correspondence, email, Mar. 6, 2006).

49 *Id.*

50 *See* Daniel S. Medwed, *Innocentrism*, 2008 U. Ill. L. Rev. 1549 (2008); Keith A. Findley, *The Pedagogy of Innocence: Reflections on the Role of Innocence Projects in Clinical Legal Education*, 13 Clinical L. Rev. 231 (2006); Robert Carl Schehr, *The Criminal Cases Review Commission as a State Strategic Selection Mechanism*, 42 Am. Crim. L. Rev. 1289 (2005).

51 NAACP, http://www.naacp.org/ (last visited May 5, 2013).

52 *NAACP: Our Mission*, NAACP, http://www.naacp.org/pages/our-mission (last visited May 5, 2013).

53 Patricia Sullivan, Lift Every Voice: The NAACP and the Making of the Civil Rights Movement 17 (2009).

54 *Id.* at 58–9.

55 *NAACP: 100 Years of History*, NAACP, http://www.naacp.org/pages/naacp-history (last visited Feb. 25, 2013).

56 *Innocence Network Membership Guidelines*, Innocence Network, http://www.innocencenetwork.org/resources/membership-materials/membership-guidelines (last visited Feb. 25, 2013).

57 Stuart Pfeifer, *O.C. Pioneering A D.A.-Defender Project on DNA Law*, L.A. Times, July 28, 2000, http://articles.latimes.com/2000/jul/28/news/mn-60702; Mike Ware, *Dallas County Conviction Integrity Unit and the Importance of Getting It Right the First Time*, 56 N.Y.L. Sch. L. Rev. 1033 (2012).

58 *Innocence Network Membership Guidelines*, *supra* note 56.

a given geographic area, whether or not they have formal tax-exempt status, provided that at least one of the participating organizations is nonprofit (for example, a program in which volunteer private attorneys supervise law students on *pro bono* litigation in exchange for academic credit from the students' host university); or law firms that commit substantial *pro bono* resources (e.g. an "innocence project unit") to individuals seeking to prove their innocence.[59]

Only organizations that devote substantial resources towards representing convicted persons with "claims of innocence" can join the Network. The term "wrongly convicted" is used interchangeably within the Network with "claim of innocence" to describe individuals who claim they did not have any level of involvement in the crime. "Substantial resources" means the following: organizations, entities, or coalitions with at least one half-time staff person devoted to such representation or securing representation from qualified attorneys (which may include other administrative/coordination work of the program, in addition to casework); projects based at educational institutions, provided that the host institution has committed a substantial portion of at least one faculty member's time to supervise students on clinical work and oversee the program; the commitment of all or a substantial portion of at least one staff member's time within a defender organization (or its equivalent, among several staff persons) to such representation; and any other group or coalition the Membership Committee concludes devotes consistent and substantial resources to such representation, even if in a form that differs from the other entities described in this section.[60]

*Network Expansion: 2005–2010*

Twenty-one members were admitted to the Network at the first Board of Directors meeting in April 2005.[61] These organizations applied for founding member status, based upon the provision of legal and/or investigative services for at least 18 months prior to the meeting. After 2005, organizations meeting the Network membership criteria have become provisional members and are granted access to member resources and services. After at least 18 months, and upon a favorable vote of the voting membership of the Network, provisional members become full voting Network members.[62] Only full, non-provisional members of the Network may elect Board members, serve on the Board, and vote on matters of policy or governance at the annual project directors meeting.[63]

The Network experienced a tremendous growth from 2006 to 2010, with the addition of 33 member organizations.[64] It added several committees, including: Exonoree Support, Victims, Bibliography, International, and Ethics and Standards.[65] The Ethics and Standards Committee was formed to provide projects with guidance on issues such as conflicts of interest, the formation of attorney/client relationships, and ethical obligations existing prior to the entry of a legal services agreement between attorney and client.[66]

An infusion of funding from the federal government, beginning with the 2004 passage of the Justice for All Act,[67] contributed to the further expansion of innocence organizations. The Act contained a provision, the Kirk Bloodsworth Post-Conviction DNA Testing Program, to help states pay the cost of post-conviction DNA testing.[68] In order to receive funding, states were required to have reasonable procedures for post-conviction DNA testing and for evidence preservation.[69] Kirk Bloodsworth, after whom the provision was

59 *Id.*

60 *Id.*

61 *Innocence Network History*, *supra* note 42.

62 *Innocence Network Membership Guidelines*, *supra* note 56 at 1(f).

63 *Id.* at 1(g); (Theresa Newman, personal correspondence, Feb. 20, 2005).

64 *Innocence Network History*, *supra* note 42.

65 (Shawn Armbrust, personal communication, email, Nov. 18, 2006; Keith A. Findley, personal communication, email, Apr. 10, 2010).

66 Findley, *supra* note 65.

67 PL 108-405, 2004 HR 5107.

68 *Aid for the Innocent*, Times Picayune, Nov. 11, 2004 at 6.

69 *Id.*

named, was convicted in 1984 of the rape and murder of a young girl in Maryland.[70] Bloodsworth served nine years on death row before post-conviction DNA testing proved he did not commit the crimes and implicated another man.[71] Another federal program, the Wrongful Conviction Review Grant, began providing funding in 2009 to ensure that defendants with post-conviction claims of innocence receive high-quality and efficient representation.[72] Numerous innocence organizations enhanced their caseloads and representation of the wrongly convicted as a result of these two federally funded programs, leading to the exoneration of innocent clients and, in some cases, the identification of the actual perpetrators.[73]

*Network: 2010 to Present*

As of May, 2013 there were 65 Network member projects, with 56 based in the United States.[74] Alabama, Colorado, New Jersey, Oregon, and Tennessee do not have a member project. Two projects, the Center on Wrongful Convictions and the Innocence Project, review cases throughout the United States, but most projects limit their advocacy to the geographic location of the organization.[75] The following describes the Network's efforts, since 2010, to expand its outreach to international organizations; develop and adopt an Ethics and Best Practices Guide (leading to a decision to no longer have journalism member projects); hire its first staff (the Innocence Network Unit); and begin the process of strategic planning.

*International Outreach*

In April of 2011, the Ohio Innocence Project hosted the annual Network conference, which was the first to focus upon the phenomenon of wrongful conviction of the innocent in the international arena. The conference brought together selected scholars, lawyers, and exonerees from around the world to interact and learn from one another and to galvanize the innocence movement into a unified international human rights movement.[76]

*Ethics and Best Practices*

In 2011, the Network adopted an Ethics and Best Practices Guide, addressing attorney–client relationships, case management systems, conflicts of interest, student representation, witness interviews, media requests, malpractice insurance, and client compensation claims. Network applicants must comply with the Ethics and Best Practices standards to join the organization. Existing members were required to demonstrate and certify compliance with the Ethics and Best Practices standards by the end of 2011. Projects are advised to consult with local experts and resources when creating policies, procedures, and documentation in order to adhere to state, local, and other professional rules of conduct and also to meet the needs of each individual project member.[77]

The Ethics and Best Practices Guide addresses concerns and goals relevant to all Network members. Innocence organizations receive an overwhelming number of applications for assistance, which must be screened and evaluated. Determining when an attorney–client relationship is formed and what duties are owed

70 Lolita C. Baldor, *Congress Makes Progress on DNA Bill Death Row, Rape Cases to Get Faster Access*, St. Paul Pioneer Press, Oct. 5, 2003 at 3.

71 *Id.*

72 *Bureau of Justice Assistance Issues Grants Notice to Provide High Quality, Efficient Representation for Defendants in Post-Conviction Claims of Innocence*, US Federal News, Jan. 5, 2010.

73 *2014 Appropriations Commerce, Justice, Science Before the House Appropriations Subcommittee on Commerce, Justice, Science and Related Agencies* (2013) (statement of Katie Monroe, Senior Advocate for National Partnerships, Innocence Project Department of Justice).

74 *Innocence Network Members*, Innocence Network, http://www.innocencenetwork.org/members (last visited May12, 2013).

75 *Id.*

76 *University of Cincinnati College of Law: 2011 Innocence Network Conference: An International Exploration of Wrongful Conviction*, University of Cincinnati College of Law, http://www.law.uc.edu/institutes-centers/ohio-innocence-project/2011-Innocence-Network-Conference (last visited Feb. 25, 2013).

77 (Keith A. Findley, personal communication, email, Nov. 12, 2011).

an applicant prior to the formation of an attorney–client relationship are critical assessments in the process. During the course of a case investigation, an innocence organization may uncover additional incriminating evidence against the defendant. However, an attorney must adhere to the ethical obligations owed to the applicant or client and not disclose the damaging information.

It is well established that attorneys, under the governing rules of professional ethics, owe clients a duty of confidentiality and a duty of loyalty. Moreover, attorneys are bound not to disclose communications a prospective client makes to the attorney for purposes of determining whether to undertake representation.[78] The duty of loyalty is "one of the core values of the legal profession, perhaps equal in importance with maintaining confidentiality and diligently or zealously working to advance a client's interests."[79] The duties of confidentiality and loyalty prohibit an attorney, or those working on the attorney's behalf, from disclosing client information or using that information to the disadvantage of the client.

*Journalism Projects*

The Network requirement that members adhere to Ethics and Best Practices Guide standards brought to the forefront issues raised by the different missions of journalism and advocacy organizations. Although journalism projects play an important role in the exoneration movement, they do not provide legal representation to clients, or support services to exonerees. Investigative journalism is at its best when maintaining its objective enterprise of seeking out the truth. Journalists pursuing this mission have done remarkable work uncovering wrongful convictions. Warden[80] describes the influence of Professor David Protess, whose students at Northwestern University's Medill School of Journalism were instrumental in exonerating seven prisoners, including three who were under sentence of death in Illinois.[81] However, journalists do not owe a duty of confidentiality or a duty of loyalty to the individuals whose cases they profile. As a consequence, journalism projects cannot comply with the Network's Ethics and Best Practices Standards. In 2013, the Network limited its membership to advocacy organizations providing legal and investigative organizations and exoneree support organizations.[82] The Medill Innocence Project at the Northwestern School of Journalism changed its name to the Medill Justice Project and hopes to launch a national network for journalism-based projects that investigate potentially wrongful convictions.[83]

*Support Staff and Strategic Planning*

In 2011, a donor approached the Network to explore the possibility of providing the organization with significant funding.[84] Discussions among the Board of Directors, facilitated by the Network President, determined that prospective funding could best be used to create Network staff positions. In 2012, the Network hired its first Innocence Network Coordinator. The Coordinator is tasked with providing administrative support to the Network activities; assisting in the development of a long-term strategic plan for the Network; consulting with individual organizations to strengthen their infrastructure and resources; coordinating strategies for casework and collaboration across projects; and overseeing the membership and quality control functions of the Network Board. In the same year, the Network hired additional members of the Network Support Unit: an Innocence Network Associate, a Shaken Baby Syndrome Litigation Fellow, and an Innocence Network

78 Ellen Yankiver Suni, *Ethical Issues for Innocence Projects: An Initial Primer*, 70 U. Mo-Kan. City L. Rev. 921 (2002).

79 In re Katz, 981 A.2d 1133, 1147 (Del. 2009), quoting Geoffrey C. Hazard, Jr. & W. William Hodes, *The Law of Lawyering* § 10.1:3 (3d ed. Supp. 2004).

80 Rob Warden, *The Revolutionary Role of Journalism in Identifying and Rectifying Wrongful Convictions*, 70 U. Mo-Kan. City L. Rev. 803 (2002).

81 Protess retired from Northwestern University when an investigation was conducted into tactics used by his students, allegations that he cooperated with the defense lawyers (abrogating a journalistic privilege to resist subpoenas), and whether he altered an email to cover up that cooperation. *See* David Carr & John Schwartz, *A Watchdog Professor, Now Defending Himself*, N.Y. Times, June 18, 2011, at A1.

82 *Innocence Network Membership Guidelines*, *supra* note 56.

83 Flowers, *supra* note 39.

84 (Keith A. Findley, personal communication, email, May 3, 2011).

Development Associate. Although the Innocence Support Unit takes its policy direction from the Network Board of Directors, it reports administratively to the Executive Director of the Innocence Project. In the fall of 2012, the Network began a strategic planning process at its Board meeting.[85]

*Current Structure of Member Projects*

Innocence Network projects have varying forms of structure and governance.[86] Some are independent non-project organizations dedicated to investigation and litigation of innocence claims;[87] while others are independent nonprofits devoted to exoneree support services.[88] A number of projects are divisions of a state public defender office.[89] A few are housed in undergraduate institutions.[90] Given the early influence of the Innocence Project law school clinic model, it is not surprising that a substantial majority of Network members are housed within, or affiliated with, law schools.[91]

## Part III: Research By and About Innocence Organizations

To date, research on innocence organizations has primarily focused on the pedagogy of teaching an innocence clinic in a law school or undergraduate setting. Stiglitz, Brooks, and Shulman,[92] Medwed,[93] and Findley[94] write about the benefits and challenges of operating an innocence clinic in a law school. Ricciardelli, Bell, and Clow[95] examine the value of having undergraduate students participate in an innocence practicum. Brooks,[96] Acker and Redlich,[97] and Mourer[98] recently published textbooks on wrongful conviction and a guide for law students working in an innocence program.

There is little empirical research identifying variables that contribute to, or hinder, an innocence organization's ability to achieve its outcomes, or examining how innocence organizations go about collecting and analyzing data to better understand achievements and report their findings. This type of outcome

85 (Meredith Kennedy, personal communication, email, Oct. 19, 2012).

86 *Innocence Network Members*, *supra* note 74.

87 *See, e.g.*, Alaska Innocence Project, The Exoneration Initiative, Georgia Innocence Project, Innocence Project of Florida, Innocence Project of Iowa, Minnesota Innocence Project, Mississippi Innocence Project, Montana Innocence Project, New England Innocence Project, New Orleans Innocence Project, North Carolina Center on Actual Innocence, and Rocky Mountain Innocence Center.

88 *See, e.g.*, Life After Innocence, Resurrection After Exoneration, and Witness to Innocence.

89 *See, e.g.*, Office of the Public Defender, State of Delaware; Kentucky Innocence Project Committee for Public Counsel Services; Office of the Ohio Public Defender and Reinvestigation Project and Connecticut Innocence Project (which is housed in a law firm).

90 *See, e.g.*, The Arizona Innocence Project, Idaho Innocence Project, and Illinois Innocence Project.

91 *See, e.g.*, Arizona Justice Project, California Innocence Project, The Duke Center for Criminal Justice and Professional Responsibility, Innocence and Justice Project at the University of New Mexico School of Law, Innocence Project, Innocence Project Arkansas, Innocence Project Northwest, Innocence Project of Texas, Michigan Innocence Clinic, Mid-Atlantic Innocence Project, Midwestern Innocence Project, Northern California Innocence Project, Pace Post-Conviction Project, Oklahoma Innocence Project, Pennsylvania Innocence Project, Texas Center for Actual Innocence, Thomas M. Cooley Law School Innocence Project, University of Miami Law Innocence Clinic, Wake Forest University Law School and Innocence and Justice Clinic and Wisconsin Innocence Project, Wrongful Conviction Clinic.

92 Jan Stiglitz, Justin Brooks & Tara Shulman, *The Hurricane Meets the Paper Chase: Innocence Projects New Emerging Role in Clinical Legal Education*, 38 Cal. W. L. Rev. 413 (2002).

93 Daniel S. Medwed, *Actual Innocents: Considerations in Selecting Cases for a New Innocence Project*, 81 Neb. L. Rev. 1097 (2003).

94 Findley, *supra* note 50.

95 Rose Ricciardelli, James G. Bell & Kimberley A. Clow, *"Now I See It For What It Really Is": The Impact Of Participation In An Innocence Project Practicum On Criminology Students*, 75 Alb. L. Rev. 1439 (2012).

96 Justin Brooks, Wrongful Convictions: Cases and Materials (2011).

97 James R. Acker & Alison D. Redlich, Wrongful Conviction: Law, Science, and Policy (2011).

98 Sarah A. Mourer, Working in Innocence Programs: Everything You Always Wanted to Know About Innocence Work but Were Afraid to Ask (2013).

measurement has proved productive in other nonprofit enterprises. Morley, Vinson, and Hatry[99] surveyed nonprofit organizations to assess their use of outcome measurements to improve client services and support other activities such as marketing or fundraising. They acknowledge that the capacity to perform reasonably valid outcome measurement remains a major issue for many private nonprofit service organizations, but conclude that the rewards of having useful outcome information helps improve client services to clients and is well worth the effort. Krieger's[100] study is one of the only published articles to undertake a survey of outcome measurement of innocence organizations, and provides a limited amount of information about those efforts.

*Law School Pedagogy*

Findley[101] describes the history of clinical legal education in the United States and the importance of the 1992 publication of the American Bar Association's MacCrate Report. The report identified fundamental lawyering skills and professional values law students ought to possess upon graduation. These include problem solving, legal analysis and reasoning, legal research, factual investigation, communication, counseling, negotiation, litigation and alternative dispute resolution procedures, organization and management of legal work, and resolution of ethical dilemmas. In the same year, the American Association of Law Schools Committee on the Future of the In-House Clinic identified nine goals of clinical education. Building on the MacCrate Report's list of fundamental skills and values, it added goals reflecting clinical education's unique capacity to teach students about legal analysis and problem solving in an unstructured environment, experiential learning, working collaboratively, and the application of doctrine in the real world.

Stiglitz, Brooks, and Shulman[102] provide a blueprint for creating a law school innocence clinic. They discuss issues regarding course content; whether to accept non-DNA as well as DNA cases; open intake versus closed intake (i.e., continual acceptance of cases versus fixed number); credit hours, grading versus a credit/no-credit course; number of students and faculty–student ratio; faculty versus non-faculty supervision; student selection; and physical plant needs. Stiglitz, Brooks, and Shulman note that the course content for an innocence clinic will be driven by the needs of the project's projected casework. The curriculum should involve a combination of substantive and skills topics necessary to work effectively on the cases. It will generally include classes providing students with an understanding of the law and procedures governing post-conviction practice; 'firm meetings' in which students present their cases to their classmates; and experiential learning opportunities provided by videos, guest speakers, and field trips to prisons, crime labs, and courthouses.

Findley[103] engages in a thoughtful analysis of the pedagogical challenges and benefits of innocence program clinics. He addresses Medwed's[104] concern that the size, complexity, and unpredictability of innocence cases pose challenges to clinical teaching methodology, making it difficult, and perhaps impossible, to allow law students to take ownership of the cases and to gain the benefits of nondirective clinical supervision. In addition, the cases often span years and have enormous stakes for the client. Findley provides guidance on how to overcome these challenges through: immersion (requiring a substantial time commitment from students): strategies for making big cases smaller (compartmentalization, connection, collaboration, and continuity); and offering students a variety of cases and problems. Findley provides concrete examples of the successful implementation of these strategies at the Wisconsin Innocence Project. He concludes that innocence clinics provide an effective means for "teaching about the importance of and how to work with facts, about the

---

99 Elaine Morley, Elisa Vinson & Harry P. Hatry, *Outcome Measurement in Nonprofit Organizations: Current Practices and Recommendations*. Washington, DC: Independent Sector (2001), *available at* http://www.iyi.org/resources/mentor/pdf/Outcome_Measurement.pdf.

100 Steven A. Krieger, *Why Our Justice System Convicts Innocent People, and the Challenges Faced by Innocence Project Trying to Exonerate Them*, 14 New Crim. L. Rev. 333 (2011).

101 Findley, *supra* note 50.

102 Stiglitz, *supra* note 92.

103 Findley, *supra* note 50.

104 Medwed, *supra* note 93.

importance of being thorough and skeptical, about professional ethics and values, about fostering a capacity for critical reflection about doctrine and the criminal justice system, and, ultimately, about judgment."[105]

The pedagogical value of law school innocence clinics is not without its critics. Smith[106] expresses a general concern that focusing on defending innocent clients detracts from other more pressing problems in our criminal justice system. She notes that the United States sentencing structure is the harshest and most punitive in the world and that the impact of mass incarceration disproportionally falls upon communities of color. Smith worries that law students will come away from their innocence clinic experience believing they can have a career where they represent only factually innocent people, and ambivalent about working with clients who are not "deserving" of representation.[107] She concludes that the dominance of the innocence movement in legal education raises important political, moral, and educational questions in a time where so many are locked up and abandoned without representation.[108]

*Undergraduate Pedagogy*

Ricciardelli, Bell, and Clow[109] examine the educational value of engaging undergraduate students in innocence work. They report on a pilot project at a small Canadian university giving undergraduate criminology students the opportunity to review claims of wrongful conviction to fulfill their senior practicum requirement. Eight students were selected to participate each term. The university provided a supervisor to assist students in the review process and a guidebook containing information on how to review case files, prepare memorandums and case summaries, keep records, and adhere to confidentiality standards. The academic component of the practicum involved lectures on the criminal trial and appeal process and on legislation governing the post-conviction review process. The practice component involved reading police and forensic evidence reports, witness statements, and trial transcripts; locating and obtaining legal documents; interviewing past legal counsel, witnesses, the applicant, and the applicant's family members; and assessing new evidence. Students were required to complete weekly progress reports, submit a preliminary summary of their case mid-semester, a final summary at the end of the semester, and, if appropriate, present their case orally to a panel of lawyers at the innocence program's head office. Students were assessed on a "pass or fail" basis.

The study found that the innocence practicum had a positive influence on students. Although learning more about wrongful conviction reduced the students' faith in the criminal justice system, it demonstrated that they could make a positive difference in the lives of others and provided them with a sense of empowerment and achievement, as well as the opportunity to put theory into practice. Ricciardelli, Bell, and Clow conclude that the multitude of benefits for students, as well as for the individuals they assisted, support the establishment of innocence practicums in more undergraduate programs.

*Outcome Measurement Research*

Outcomes sought by Network members, although they may vary from project to project, are identifiable. Member projects provide *pro bono* legal and investigative services to individuals seeking to prove they are innocent of crimes for which they have been convicted, work to redress the causes of wrongful convictions, and support exonerees.[110] Outcome measurement, which involves the "identification of outcomes; development of appropriate outcome indicators and data collection procedures; data analysis to better understand organization achievements; and user-friendly, regular reporting of the findings,"[111] is a little-studied area in innocence organizations.

---

105 Findley, *supra* note 50 at 278.

106 Abbe Smith, *In Praise of the Guilty Project: A Criminal Defense Lawyer's Growing Anxiety about Innocence Projects*, 13 U. PA. J. L. & SOC. CHANGE 315 (2010).

107 *Id.* at 327.

108 *Id.* at 329.

109 Ricciardelli, *supra* note 95.

110 *See Innocence Network*, INNOCENCE NETWORK, http://www.innocencenetwork.org/ (last visited Feb. 23, 2013).

111 Morley, Vinson & Hatry, *supra* note 99 at 5.

An interview study conducted by Krieger[112] reports results from interviews of 22 innocence organizations across the United States. Projects provided information about finances; numbers, and types of staff and volunteers; time distribution per task; age of the innocence organization; number of cases undergoing an intensive review; and state characteristics (total population, prisoner population, and state revenues). Krieger drew two conclusions from information gathered during the interviews: (1) a medium level of resources can achieve success equal to or greater than the success of projects with more resources; and (2) increasing the resources beyond the medium level did not necessarily correlate to greater success for the particular project.[113] He proposes the following baseline model for projects: an annual budget of $225,000, four paid staffers, and no more than 40 volunteers, located in a state with a high population and high revenue, with approximately 15 percent of the project's time spent on initial review and in-depth investigation of at least 50 cases a year.[114]

Outcome measurement analysis of innocence organizations is hampered by the uncertainty inherent in a project's advocacy and policy work. Garrett[115] notes that exonerations come about as a "fragile product of scientific and social serendipity."[116] Certain factors, which are outside of a project's control, play an important role in determining whether it can succeed in its mission to free innocent prisoners. These factors, which vary from jurisdiction to jurisdiction, include: prisoners' awareness of the project and their capacity to complete an application for assistance; the preservation of biological evidence gathered in the case, and the conditions under which it was preserved or contaminated; prosecutor amenability to re-examining cases; state procedural bars to re-opening a case; and the court's receptiveness to innocence claims. Policy reforms are equally dependent upon circumstances outside the control of the innocence organization, including the composition of a state's legislative and executive body and each branch's willingness to acknowledge the problem of wrongful convictions. Still, much could be gained by engaging in empirical research about outcome measurements of member projects to improve delivery of their services and to document progress being made towards exonerating innocent prisoners, policy reforms to decrease the error in the criminal justice system, and providing clients support after exoneration.

## Part IV: The Network Future: Branding and Governance

Scientific research and scholarship on the causes of wrongful conviction and associated reforms is too voluminous to summarize in this chapter. Additionally, a rich volume of literature describes individual and collective cases of exoneration.[117] The scientific research, combined with captivating narratives about the tragedy of wrongful conviction, has brought about an unprecedented level of reform in the United States criminal justice system.[118]

At present, there is an absence of research on the Network entity. This is an opportune time for it to examine the issues it faces as an organization. The Network is at a critical juncture in its development, with the recent hiring of a Support Unit and the launching of a strategic planning process. It is not the first collective enterprise to face the growing pains of identity and governance as it expands and can draw from the developing body of research exploring the role of "branding" in nonprofit organizations, including coalitions, to advance long-term social goals. There is also a wealth of literature on collaborative governance. An examination of the interdisciplinary research in nonprofit marketing and governance can provide a beginning framework for the Network's development of a branding strategy and the strengthening of its governance structure.

---

112 Krieger, *supra* note 100, at 333.

113 *Id.* at 334.

114 *Id.* at 397.

115 Brandon L. Garrett, *Innocence, Harmless Error, and Federal Wrongful Conviction Law*, Wis. L. Rev. 35 (2005).

116 *Id.* at 110.

117 *See, e.g.*, Scheck, Neufeld & Dwyer, *supra* note 2. John Grisham, The Innocent Man: Murder and Injustice in a Small Town (2006). Jennifer Thompson-Cannino, Ronald Cotton & Erin Torneo, Picking Cotton: Our Memoir of Injustice and Redemption (2009)

118 *See, e.g.*, Brandon L. Garrett, Convicting the Innocent: Where Criminal Prosecutions Go Wrong (2005). Keith A. Findley, *Defining Innocence*, 74(3) Alb. L. Rev. *1157 (2012); Zalman, supra note 40.*

*Developing a Network Brand*

Branding strategies, which were usually synonymous with trademarks and trade symbols, have been used since the end of the nineteenth century by for-profit corporations as a powerful marketing tool.[119] A brand does not simply encompass the name, logo or trademark of a corporation. Instead it is defined as a complex matrix of meanings hat create a psychological construct in the minds of those who are aware of the brand.[120] In the for-profit world, brands become an expressive part of a consumer's identity and philosophy. Katyal[121] writes that brands offer "individuals a way to express certain identities, preferences, and passions symbolically: some wear Adidas and Nike shoes because they favor an active, athletic, physically competitive lifestyle, along with the philosophy of competitive living; others dress themselves in Prada's subtle shades to suggest a demure, classic, sophisticated presence ... ."[122] Corporate marketing campaigns strive to create a "total brand experience" to imbed and manage these psychological associations in the minds and hearts of consumers.

The role of brand in the nonprofit sector began to be explored in the late 1990s. Richie, Swami, and Weinberg[123] published a seminal work on nonprofit brands emphasizing both the internal role of a nonprofit brand and the "multiple publics" (clients, donors, volunteers, and government) nonprofit brands address. Voeth and Herbst's[124] empirical research focuses upon development of a nonprofit brand as a fundraising tool. Kylander and Stone[125] move beyond the narrow construct of revenue to explore the wider, strategic roles brands can play in driving broad, long-term social goals while strengthening internal identity, cohesion, and capacity.[126] They discuss the recent engagement of several large nonprofits, such as the Bill and Melinda Gates Foundation, in rebranding strategies that do not include fundraising targets. In this new regime, brands are viewed as leverage for the nonprofit organization to engage in greater public discourse and as a catalyst to advance the organization's social mission.

Development of a Network brand is complicated by many factors. First, the Network must explicitly identify its own *raison d'être*, separate from the mission of its member organizations. Brands have been described as the "very soul or essence"[127] of an organization. Currently, the Network identifies itself as an "affiliation"[128] of member projects which are independently dedicated to specific outcomes: exonerations, policy reform, and exoneree support. The generic description of "affiliation" does not express the Network's philosophy or mission. Thus, the Network must determine its goals, separate from its members, to develop a branding strategy.

The Network's philosophy can be inferred from its creation of committees on amicus and policies, international efforts, membership, and ethics and best practices. These suggest a mission to shape the law through amici briefs and public policy through policy statements; expand the Innocence Movement outside the United States; and oversee the quality of work engaged in by its members. The Innocence Network Coordinator job description also supports an inference that the Network's purpose is to further the above goals. The Coordinator was hired to strengthen the infrastructure and resources of member organizations; coordinate strategies for casework and collaboration across projects; and oversee the membership and quality

---

119 Sonia K. Katyal, *Stealth Marketing and Antibranding: The Love that Dare Not Speak Its Name*, 58 BUFF. L. REV. 795 (2010).

120 *Id.* at 796–802.

121 *Id.*

122 *Id.* at 797.

123 Robin J.B. Richie, Sanjeev Swami & Charles B. Weinberg, *A Brand New World for Nonprofits*, 4 INT'L J. NONPROFIT & VOLUNTARY SECTOR MARKETING 29 (1999).

124 Markus Voeth & Uta Herbst, *The Concept of Brand Personality As an Instrument for Advanced Non-Profit Branding: An Empirical Analysis*, 19 J. NONPROFIT & PUB. SECTOR MARKETING 71 (2008).

125 Nathaniel Kylander & Christopher Stone, *The Role of Brand in the Nonprofit Sector*, STANFORD SOC. INNOVATION REV., Spring, 35–41 (2012).

126 *Id.* at 37.

127 *Id.*

128 *See* INNOCENCE NETWORK, *http://www.innocencenetwork.org/* (last visited May 10, 2013) ("The Innocence Network is an affiliation of organizations dedicated to providing pro bono legal and investigative services to individuals seeking to prove innocence of crimes for which they have been convicted and working to redress the causes of wrongful convictions.").

control functions of the Network Board. However, the Network must explicitly set forth its own mission; undertaking a strategic planning process will assist in defining the Network philosophy and brand.

Second, the Network's development of a brand is complicated by its relationship with the Innocence Project, one of its member organizations. The Innocence Project, which has engaged a brand consultant,[129] is widely recognized and associated with exonerations and policy reform. In contrast, the name "Innocence Network" does not convey the powerful psychological association required to implement an effective branding strategy. Although trademarks are not the only component of a brand, they do play a role in the development of a branding strategy. "Innocence Network" is not trademarked, whereas "Innocence Project" received a trademark license in 2004.[130] The Innocence Project provides a free license to Network members, with the requirement that the organizations use their geographic or other qualifiers in their names (i.e., Innocence Project of Texas, Cooley Innocence Project, Midwest Innocence Project).[131] To protect its trademark, the Innocence Project recently filed a complaint against the Family Innocence Project, alleging that its use of the mark is likely to cause confusion or mistake, or to deceive, and constitutes trademark infringement under federal and state law.[132]

Network projects using the "Innocence Project" mark certainly benefit from an association with the Innocence Project. However, there is a tremendous amount of confusion about the relationship between the Network, its member projects, and the Innocence Project. The confusion exists even among those working in the innocence movement. As an example, Centurion Ministries, a 501(c)(3) organization, is not a member of the Innocence Network. In explaining why it is a different entity, it erroneously states "[t]he name *Innocence Project* (IP) has come to mean those law school pro bono clinics working with the New York Innocence Project. On the whole, they work on wrongful convictions that rely on DNA results to prove innocence."[133] In fact, Network members are independent of the Innocence Project. Nor are they all law school clinics. And, the majority of projects affiliated with the Network accept non-DNA cases.[134]

The public confusion about the relationship between the Network, its members, and the Innocence Project is cultivated by the media. As an example, the Innocence Project Northwest has been referred to as a "branch" of the Innocence Project.[135] Moreover, the media often credits the Innocence Project with DNA exonerations achieved through the advocacy of other Network members.[136] Statements to the media by the Innocence Project have fostered that misconception. A *New York Times* op-ed relays: "Barry Scheck, the co-founder of the Innocence Project, told me that the group has gotten 300 people exonerated, mostly by using sophisticated DNA testing."[137] Barry Scheck and a colleague write in their own opinion piece: "The Innocence Project has identified the real perpetrator in more than 100 of its nearly 300 DNA exonerations nationwide."[138] However, the Innocence Project has not represented, or assisted, the 300 individuals exonerated though post-conviction DNA testing.[139] Confusion engendered about the relationship between the Innocence Project, Network

---

129 *Our Clients*, Simon Does, http://simondoes.com/our-work/identity/the-innocence-project-brand-identity (last visited May 11, 2013).

130 INNOCENCE PROJECT, Registration No. 2,852,350.

131 (Madeline DeLone, personal communication, email, Mar. 15, 2013).

132 Innocence Project, Inc., The v. Family Innocence Project, Inc. (2012). No. 0:12cv02174 (D. Minn. Sept. 5, 2012).

133 *FAQs*, Centurion Ministries, http://www.centurionministries.org/faq/ (last visited Feb. 25, 2013).

134 *See Innocence Network Members*, Innocence Network http://www.innocencenetwork.org/members (last visited May 10, 2013) (listing types of cases—DNA and non-DNA—accepted by member projects).

135 Sarah Freishtat, *Innocent But Locked Up for 17 Years, Man Hopes for Compensation*, Seattle Times, Feb. 17, 2013, at B1.

136 *See, e.g.*, Keith Eldridge, *Exonerated Convicts Ask Washington to Pay Up for Lost Time*, KOMO News, http://www.komonews.com/news/local/Exonerated-convicts-ask-Washington-to-pay-up-for-lost-time-190303061.html (crediting the Innocence Project with exonerations obtained by the Innocence Project Northwest).

137 Joe Nocera, Op-Ed., *A Texas Prosecutor Faces Justice*, N.Y. Times, Nov. 13, 2012, at A27.

138 Barry C. Scheck & Karen A. Newirth, Op-Ed., *The Case for "Blind" Lineups*, L.A. Times, Sept. 17, 2012, http://articles.latimes.com/2012/sep/17/opinion/la-oe-scheck-photo-lineups-20120917.

139 *See Know the Case: Browse Profiles*, Innocence Project, http://www.innocenceproject.org/know/Browse-Profiles.php (last visited May 11, 2013) (providing information about DNA cases, including name of organization involved in obtaining exoneration).

members, and the Network impacts the latter's ability to strengthen its internal identity, create organization cohesion, and build capacity.

The Network could benefit from examining studies of coalitions comprised of member organizations with varying resources and capacities. Kylander and Stone[140] report that nonprofit leaders in such coalitions often worry that the collective identity will overshadow their own brand, and a number of coalitions have collapsed because of this concern. They conclude that the concept of "brand affinity" is particularly important in coalitions where many nonprofits join together in a common cause with its own image and identity. Brand affinity means the brand is a good team player, works well alongside other brands, shares space and credit generously, and promotes collective over individual interests. Kylander and Stone then discuss an example of a successful coalition—The TckTckTck campaign—which advocates for global climate action. Here, the brand of each individual organization remained prominent in the collective brand. Each organization retains its own identity and logo, "a flotilla of ships with distinct brand flags"[141] which unites the different groups.[142] To engage in a successful branding strategy, the Network must develop a plan of action in which its members promote collective, over individual interests in order to enhance the Network's operational capacity and drive its social impact.[143]

*Network Governance: Lessons Learned from Collaborative Governance*

As noted above, the Network is a unique collective enterprise. Member organizations are independent entities; they are not branches, affiliates, or franchises of the Network. The Network is a collective body, made up of organizations with independent purposes and structures. It is governed by a Board comprised of 21 individuals, drawn from the 'stakeholders', i.e., member projects. Each Board member has a loyalty to his or her organization, as well as to the Network.

A study of collaborative governance research can assist the Network in moving forward as an enterprise composed of independent stakeholders. Ansell and Gash[144] define collaborative governance as:

> A governing arrangement where one or more public agencies directly engage non-state stakeholders in a collective decision-making process that is formal, consensus-oriented, and deliberative and that aims to make or implement public policy or manage public programs or assets.[145]

There are differences between the collaborative governance model and the Network governance structure. The Network is not a union of public and private actors working collectively in distinctive ways to establish laws and rules for the provision of public goods. However, the Network endeavors to engage stakeholders in a consensus-oriented and deliberative decision making process and can draw from the lessons learned from collaborative governance to strengthen its own enterprise.

Ansell and Gash's meta-analytical study of the existing literature on collaborative governance identifies variables which influence whether or not this mode of governance will produce success. These variables include: (1) prior history of conflict or cooperation, (2) incentives for stakeholders to participate, (3) power and resources imbalance, (4) leadership, and (5) institutional design. They also identify factors crucial to the collaborative process itself. Those include face-to-face dialogue, trust building, and the development of commitment and shared understanding. Ansell and Gash advance a 10-point collaborative governance contingency model for practitioners and researchers.[146] Several points in Ansell and Gash's model can be used by the Network to analyze and assess the success of its governance and identify areas of future research.

---

140 Kylander & Stone, *supra* note 125.

141 *Id.* at 41.

142 *See, e.g.*, TCKTCKTCK, http://tcktcktck.org/ (last visited Apr. 4, 2013).

143 Kylander& Stone, *supra* note 125.

144 Chris Ansell & Allison Gash, *Collaborative Governance in Theory and Practice*, 18 J. PUBLIC ADMIN. RESEARCH & THEORY 543 (2007).

145 *Id.* at 544.

146 *Id.* at 551–61.

*Power and Resource Imbalances*

Ansell and Gash conclude that resource and power imbalances between stakeholders are a commonly noted problem in collaborative governance. If stakeholders do not have the capacity, organization, status, or resources to participate on equal footing, the collaborative governance process will be thwarted. Power and resource imbalances exist in the Network's collective enterprise. One of its members, the Innocence Project, has grown from a law school clinic into an organization with an over $16 million budget[147] and more than 70 staff.[148] Other projects struggle to obtain the resources needed to keep their doors open[149] and a number of start-up projects have closed. In 2005, an article on the proliferation of innocence efforts reported that the Palmetto Project was underfunded and operated with an all-volunteer staff of lawyers, paralegals, and investigators.[150] The Palmetto Innocence Project is no longer a member of the Network.[151]

Ansell and Gash, after reviewing literature discussing the range of strategies that can be used to empower weaker or underrepresented groups, draw the following conclusion:

> (1) If there are significant power/resource imbalances between stakeholders, such that important stakeholders cannot participate in a meaningful way, then effective collaborative governance requires a commitment to a positive strategy of empowerment and representation of weaker or disadvantaged stakeholders.[152]

The Network's commitment to empowerment and representation of disadvantaged members is evidenced through its hiring of an Innocence Network Development Associate. This person is charged with overseeing and assisting individual Network projects to meet their fundraising goals and, in coordination with the Innocence Project, develop strategies for supporting Network activities. The Network will need to continue to identify and implement strategies to empower members with fewer resources to develop and flourish and to ensure that these members have meaningful representation on the Board.

*Incentives to Participate*

Ansell and Gash report that incentives to participate in the collaborative process depend in part upon whether stakeholders expect it will yield meaningful results, particularly when weighed against the time and energy required by the process. Incentives to participate increase when stakeholders see a direct relationship between their participation and concrete, tangible, effectual policy outcomes, and when they perceive that cooperation from other stakeholders is essential to achieving their goals. Ansell and Gash propose the following addition to the contingency model:

> (2) If alternative venues exist where stakeholders can pursue their goals unilaterally, the collaborative governance will only work if stakeholders perceive themselves to be highly interdependent.[153]

Participation in the Network offers unique benefits to its members that are not available in alternative forums. First, as discussed above, only Network members are given a limited license to use the "Innocence Project" mark in their organization's title. Second, member organizations are able to call upon the Network Support Unit for assistance with management and organizational development, fundraising, and litigation in selected types of cases. Third, Network members can join list-serves, which provide project directors, litigators, and

---

147 The Innocence Project Annual Report 2011 (Innocence Project), *available at* http://www.innocenceproject.org/ar2011/contents.php.

148 *Innocence Project Staff*, Innocence Project, http://www.innocenceproject.org/about/Staff-Directory.php (last visited May 5, 2013).

149 Amanda Bohman, *Alaska Innocence Project Has Lots of Cases, Limited Resources*, Anchorage Daily News, Jan. 11, 2011, *available at* http://www.adn.com/2011/01/10/1641320/alaska-innocence-project-has-lots.html#storylink=cpy.

150 *Innocence Projects Multiply*, Charlotte Observer, Jan. 16, 2005 at 4.

151 *Innocence Network Members*, *supra* note 74.

152 Ansell & Gash, *supra* note 144, at 551–2.

153 *Id.* at 553–4.

clinic professors the opportunity to discuss issues of importance. Finally, members can access an intranet website to obtain confidential documents for case litigation. These types of benefits are not available in alternative venues and provide incentives for stakeholders to join and remain in the Network. Creating a continued sense of interdependence among the member organizations will strengthen the Network enterprise.

## Part V: Conclusion

When *Actual Innocence* was published in 2000, there were few organized efforts dedicated to freeing prisoners convicted of crimes they did not commit and reforming the criminal justice system to decrease the number of wrongful convictions. The Innocence Network has grown from a handful of organizations to 65 members working throughout the world to remedy miscarriages of justice in the United States. The efforts of member organizations has already had a transformative effect on the lives of exonerees and their families, the criminal justice system, and the development of attorneys and students who engage in innocence advocacy and reform. The Network is well positioned to use its existing strengths to explore the strategic role that brand can play in driving its social goals and to enhance its internal cohesion, identity, and capacity. It can do so by working to empower member organizations with fewer resources and creating and augmenting incentives for innocence organizations to participate in the collective enterprise.

# PART II
# How Are Innocent People Convicted? Common Causes of Wrongful Convictions

# Chapter 3
# Eyewitnesses and Erroneous Convictions: An American Conundrum

Jules Epstein

## Introduction

Eyewitness error is not as "American as apple pie," as the phenomenon of mistaken identification knows no borders and has been recognized as a problem in many nations.[1] Yet in America the phenomenon has been prevalent and chronic, with study after study confirming the problem: for at least the past century, whenever there have been criminal trials in America there have been erroneous identifications by eyewitnesses, and the United States Supreme Court seemingly acknowledged this in the late 1960s and early 1970s when it began to impose constitutional limits on eyewitness procedures and evidence. Today, it is clear that where there are proven wrongful convictions, mistaken identification is a root cause in roughly 75 percent of those cases.[2]

The dimensions of this problem have not been offset by consistent system responses. The underpinnings of law, both in federal and state courts, are built upon an acceptance of eyewitness testimony as reliable and trustworthy and upon a willingness to trust fact-finder (juror) intuition in ascertaining whether any particular witness is correct. This is coupled with an ill-informed public (from which jurors are drawn) where beliefs on eyewitness reliability often are demonstrably erroneous. Finally, because of the principles of "federalism,"[3] there is no mandate for uniformity in the collection or use of identification evidence, and the result is a hodge-podge of system approaches to the use of eyewitness evidence in court.

Part I of this chapter will assess the history of mistaken identification in the US, and the recognition arising from early DNA exonerations of eyewitness fallibility as a severe concern in criminal justice. Part II summarizes the explosion of scientific research that has addressed causes of such error. In Part III, the response of courts to eyewitness testimony and error is surveyed and assessed. Part IV addresses proposed "systems" responses and the current developments in law and policy that seek to remedy or ameliorate this problem. The Conclusion, in Part V, is less than optimistic—the criminal trial process in the US offers no consistent and reliable solution to the problem of mistaken identification.

---

1 *See, e.g.*, Canadian Department of Justice, Report on the Prevention of Miscarriages of Justice, *available at* http://www.justice.gc.ca/eng/dept-min/pub/pmj-pej/pmj-pej.pdf; Finlo Rohrer, *The Problem With Eyewitnesses*, BBC News (Aug. 24, 2005), http://news.bbc.co.uk/2/hi/uk_news/4177082.stm; Devlin Committee Report: Report of the Committee on Evidence of Identification in Criminal Cases, 1976 Cmnd. 338, 134/135;Tim Coates, The Strange Story of Adolf Beck (2001) (1999); Michael C. Bromby et al., *An Examination of Criminal Jury Directions in Relation to Eyewitness Identification in Commonwealth Jurisdictions*, 36 Common L. World Rev. 303, 303–6 (2007); *SIT Seeks to set free man Arrested on Mistaken Identity*, Express News Service (India), (May 12, 2009), http://www.expressindia.com/latest-news/sit-seeks-to-set-free-man-arrested-on-mistaken-identity/457795.

2 *Eyewitness Misidentification*, The Innocence Project, http://www.innocenceproject.org/understand/Eyewitness-Misidentification.php (last visited Aug. 10, 2013).

3 "Federalism" is the governing principle allocating power between the United States Government and the governments of the 50 states. *See, e.g.*, Setser v. United States, 132 S. Ct. 1463, 1471 (U.S. 2012) ("In our American system of dual sovereignty, each sovereign—whether the Federal Government or a State—is responsible for the administration of [its own] criminal justice system.") (internal quotations and citation omitted).

**Part I: A History of Mistaken Identification in America**

It is impossible to determine the number of wrongful identifications and resulting wrongful convictions in the United States. There is no precise counting of cases where eyewitness evidence is the sole or primary proof against an accused, and only a rough estimate of some 80,000 such prosecutions per year.[4] If the error rate is 0.5 percent, there are 400 wrongful convictions annually; and there is little reason to set the threshold this low.[5] As well, *proving* that a conviction was wrongful requires available contradictory evidence and, except in DNA cases, that proof is often unavailable. Nonetheless, a starting point for assessing the dimensions of this problem is found in the retrospective analyses of proved wrongful convictions—time and again, those are found to have been caused by eyewitness error in roughly half to as many as 79 percent of the studied cases.[6]

At least as telling as the numbers are the recurring stories of mistaken identification. Borchard's *Convicting the Innocent* tells of one instance in 1913 where 17 victims of fraud identified Herbert Andrews as the perpetrator, only to have the frauds continue after Andrews' conviction and imprisonment. When the true perpetrator was caught, the prosecutor observed that:

> I wondered how so many persons could have sworn that the innocent man was the one that had cashed the bad checks. The two men were as dissimilar in appearance as could be. There was [sic] several inches difference in height and there wasn't a similarity about them.[7]

Barely one decade later, then law professor and subsequently United States Supreme Court Justice Felix Frankfurter called into question the conviction of Sacco and Vanzetti, two Italian-born anarchists charged with robbery and murder. In *The Case of Sacco and Vanzetti*,[8] Frankfurter wrote "[w]hat is the worth of identification testimony, even when uncontradicted[,]"[9] emphasizing a lengthy history of mistaken identifications and quoting at length from a Boston psychiatrist's 1926 letter to the editor describing at least one of the trial identifications as "psychologically impossible."[10] Much of the book, intended for "laymen," was devoted to debunking the eyewitness testimony and emphasizing "all the grave hazards due to the frailties and fallibilities of human observation and memory."[11]

Recurrences of the phenomenon of mistaken identification were periodically given great public exposure. In the late 1970s, it was the case of Father Pagano, a priest accused of having committed seven armed

---

4 Alvin G. Goldstein et al., *Frequency of Eyewitness Identification in Criminal Cases: A Survey of Prosecutors*, 27 Bull. Psychonomic Soc'y 71, 73 (1989).

5 *See* D. Michael Risinger, *Innocents Convicted: An Empirically Justified Factual Wrongful Conviction Rate*, 97 J. Crim. L. & Criminology 761 (2007) (Professor Risinger has estimated "a minimum factually wrongful conviction rate for capital rape-murder in the 1980s: 3.3 %"). *See also* Brian L. Cutler & Steven D. Penrod, Mistaken Identification: The Eyewitness, Psychology, and the Law 7–8 (1995) (Estimates by Professors Cutler and Penrod put the error rate at close to 0.5 percent, or 4,500 of the 1 million convictions a year.). *But see* Ronald J. Allen & Larry Lauden, *Why Do We Convict as Many Innocent People as We Do?: Deadly Dilemmas*, 41 Tex. Tech L. Rev. 65, 71 (2008) (positing "an error rate of .008371, .84 %, or 8.4 out of 1000 convictions").

6 *See, e.g.*, Edwin M. Borchard, Convicting the Innocent (1932); Hugo A. Bedau & Michael L. Radelet, *Miscarriages of Justice in Potentially Capital Cases*, 40 Stan. L. Rev. 21 (1987); Brandon Garrett, *Judging Innocence*, 108 Colum. L. Rev. 55, 78 (2008) ("The overwhelming number of convictions of the innocent involved eyewitness identification – 158 of 200 cases (79%).").

7 Borchard, *supra* note 6, at 5.

8 Felix Frankfurter, *The Case of Sacco and Vanzetti*, Atl. Monthly, 1927. Frankfurter's book was not an academic tome of restricted circulation; rather, it was published first in the *Atlantic Monthly* magazine and has been described as a "hugely significant moment in the public history" of this case that "sparked a growing focus" on the trial. Moshik Temkin, The Sacco-Vanzetti Affair: America on Trial 30–31 (2009).

9 Frankfurter, *supra*, at 30.

10 *Id.* at 14 (quoting letter of Dr. Morton Prince, published in the *Boston Herald*, October 30, 1926).

11 *Id.* at 24. Frankfurter went on to write about how "[a]ll the identifying witnesses were speaking from casual observation of men they had never seen before, men of foreign race, under circumstances of unusual confusion." *Id.* at 31.

robberies in which the description was of a "gentleman bandit." Charges were withdrawn only when another man confessed to the crimes.[12]

It was the DNA exonerations, however, that brought the most compelling stories of wrongful conviction to light.[13] With some irony, the recounting of the role of eyewitness error in wrongful convictions can be traced, first, to a June, 1996 National Institute of Justice (NIJ) publication, *Convicted by Juries, Exonerated by Science.*[14] A study of 28 cases (27 trial convictions, one guilty plea) where DNA later exonerated the convicted defendant, it highlighted the role of eyewitness error:

> All cases, except for homicides, involved victim identification both prior to and at trial. Many cases also had additional eyewitness identification, either placing the defendant with the victim or near the crime scene (e.g., in *Bloodsworth*, five witnesses testified that they had seen the defendant with the 9-year-old victim on the day of the murder).[15]

In its chapter titled "Policy Implications," the report went further:

> In the majority of the cases, given the absence of DNA evidence at the trial, eyewitness testimony was the most compelling evidence. Clearly, however, those eyewitness identifications were wrong ... This points conclusively to the need in the legal system for improved criteria for evaluating the reliability of eyewitness identification.[16]

Yet perhaps its most persuasive portion was the recounting of the 28 cases.[17] Included among them is one that has received great prominence, and given impetus to eyewitness reform—the wrongful conviction of Ronald Cotton.

Cotton was accused and convicted of the rape of Jennifer Thompson, then a college student who was assaulted in her apartment late at night. Although she was not wearing eyeglasses and the lighting was dim, her convincing and heartfelt identification of Cotton was believed, leading to his conviction and imprisonment.

Once in jail, Cotton heard of another inmate who had admitted to the Thompson rape, and when he won a new trial arranged to have that inmate, Bobby Poole, brought to court. Thompson viewed him but reaffirmed her identification of Cotton as the perpetrator, and he was again convicted. DNA testing years later showed Cotton to be innocent, and confirmed that Poole was indeed the rapist. The fallibility of eyewitness testimony and the malleability of memory could not be clearer, as here a crime victim had seen the scientifically proven perpetrator but instead saw Cotton's face as that of her assailant.[18]

This is not the only powerful account of eyewitness error; nor is it the only one to be spread beyond the NIJ report. Kirk Bloodsworth's account—that of the first death row-sentenced inmate to be exonerated by DNA—was retold in a powerful book;[19] and Darryl Hunt's exoneration in a case where eyewitness error played a prominent role was retold in an award-winning documentary.[20] But because Jennifer Thompson began advocating for eyewitness reform with a crime victim's voice and poignancy, the Ronald Cotton story had an added dimension and a powerful impact on the public discourse.

This chapter cannot leave the "stories" of DNA exoneration and eyewitness error without discussing one more of the more than 280 exonerations, that of John White. White, accused of rape, was placed in a

12 Noah A. Clements, *Flipping a Coin: A Solution for the Inherent Unreliability of Eyewitness Identification Testimony*, 40 Ind. L. Rev. 271, 275 (2007).

13 These can be found collected in numerous sources, the most prominent of which are Brandon Garrett, Convicting the Innocent, ch. 3 "Eyewitness Misidentifications" (2011). *See also*, *Eyewitness Misidentification*, *supra* note 2.

14 U.S. Dep't of Justice, Convicted by Juries, Exonerated by Science: Case Studies in the Use of DNA Evidence to Establish Innocence After Trial (1996), *available at* https://www.ncjrs.gov/pdffiles/dnaevid.pdf.

15 *Id.* at 15.

16 *Id.* at 24.

17 *Id.* at 43–4.

18 Jennifer Thompson-Cannino et al., Picking Cotton: Our Memoir of Injustice and Redemption, 43–4 (2009).

19 Tim Junkin, Bloodsworth: The true story of one man's Triumph over Injustice (2005).

20 The Trials of Darryl Hunt (2006).

live-person line-up with "fillers" chosen from among others in the local jail. Identified again in the line-up, he was convicted and imprisoned until DNA established his innocence and proved that another person in the line-up, placed there serendipitously, was the actual perpetrator. His was the first known exoneration case where a crime victim saw the real perpetrator in a line-up but picked another person.[21] In an analysis of this phenomenon, Professor Gary Wells, among the leading researchers in eyewitness psychology in the world, explained that:

> [t]he witness had already identified John White from a photographic lineup. And, John White was the only person who was in both the photographic lineup and the live lineup.
>
> Hence, what we have here, I believe, is a strong example of how a mistaken identification from one procedure (a photo lineup) is repeated in the next procedure (a live lineup) even though the real perpetrator is clearly present in the second procedure. Repeating the same mistake can occur for several reasons. One possibility is that the initial mistaken identification changed the memory of the witness; in effect John White's face "became" her memory of the attacker and the face of Parham no longer existed once she mistakenly identified John White. Another possibility is that she approached the live lineup with one goal in mind—find the man she had identified from the photos. Perhaps she never really looked at Parham because she quickly saw the man she identified from photos and did not need to look further.[22]

Figure 3.1 shows the photograph of the line-up. Mr. White is in the middle; the actual perpetrator, dissimilar in appearance, is on the far right.

**Figure 3.1 The mistaken identification of John Jerome White**

21 *Know the Cases*, The Innocence Project, http://www.innocenceproject.org/Content/John_Jerome_White.php (last visited Aug. 10, 2013).

22 *The Mistaken Identification of John Jerome White*, Iowa State University, http://www.psychology.iastate.edu/~glwells/The_Misidentification_of_John_White.pdf (last visited Aug., 10, 2013).

The exoneration stories received extensive coverage. One thousand or more print media articles addressed this issue between 1996 and 2012.[23]

To an extent, more than a century of court decisions in the United States have also echoed the refrain of eyewitness unreliability. As early as 1839, a court wrote that:

> No one, however, of professional experience in trials at law, who has had opportunities of observing the errors which witnesses, of the best character, innocently fall into in delivering their testimony, not only of long past, but of recent transactions, will be willing to say that any evidence, from whatever witness it may come, may not be founded in some mistake. On the subject of the identity of persons, instances have occurred of the most surprising description. They have occurred in relation to brute animals, as well as to men.[24]

In 1858, the Illinois Supreme Court ordered a new trial because the identification witnesses "might have been mistaken in their identity[,]"[25] an action repeated in a 1926 New York state case where the court questioned the reliability of the identification evidence.[26] In a homicide trial in the late 1800s, the jury was instructed that "[q]uestions, concerning the identity of persons, animals and vehicles are liable to confusion, uncertainty and mistake[,]"[27] and in 1967 the United States Supreme Court penned its famous lines emphasizing the "vagaries of eyewitness identification."[28] Albeit in a dissenting opinion, this was restated forcefully in 1981 by an appellate court judge: "Many experts have concluded that convictions based solely on one eyewitness' identification represent conceivably the greatest single threat to the achievement of our ideal that no innocent men shall be punished."[29]

**Part II: Scientific Research and Developments**

What is the science that explains eyewitness error and about which so many jurors (and jurists) remain unaware? It is a body of research so well-developed that one court recently[30] described it as the "gold

23 A June 14, 2012 search of the LEXIS "News, All (English Full text) database" with parameters "dna w/18 eyewitness w/22 exonera! and date aft 1/1/1996" produced 929 results.

24 *In re* of Williams, 1839 U.S. Dist. LEXIS 3, 17–18 (E.D. Pa. 1839).

25 Lincoln v. People, 20 Ill. 364 (Ill. 1858). The Illinois Supreme Court continued its adherence to this approach through at least 1948: "We find the law to be that where witnesses may be mistaken in identifying the accused and an alibi is proved by other witnesses who give their residence and occupation, so that the truth or falsity of their testimony may be inquired into on another trial, the court will take this into consideration and will give the accused the benefit of a second trial." People v. Grizzel, 46 N.E.2d 78, 81–2 (Ill. 1943). Two years later, however, this principle was narrowed if not repudiated: "The testimony of one witness as to identification, if positive and the witness credible, is sufficient to convict even though the testimony is contradicted by the accused." People v. Vaughn, 61 N.E.2d 546, 548 (Ill. 1945). As is discussed, *infra*, the general approach to eyewitness testimony in the twentieth and now twenty-first centuries is that it is solely for a jury to decide whether an eyewitness is credible, and such a determination will not be reviewed on appeal.

26 People v. Klvana, 150 N.E. 523, 524 (N.Y. 1926) (rejecting as adequate a witness' positive identification testimony that was subsequently "modified by saying that 'he looks like him'"). *But see* People v. Seppi, 221 N.Y. 62, 68 (N.Y. 1917) (taking the more commonly held position that "[w]here a witness positively identifies a defendant as the man who committed a crime, the weight of the evidence of identification is for the jury unless it is incredible as a matter of law").

27 Commonwealth v. Clemmer, 190 Pa. 202, 221 (Pa. 1899).

28 United States v. Wade, 338 U.S. 218, 228 (1967) ("the vagaries of eyewitness identification are well-known; the annals of criminal law are rife with instances of mistaken identification").

29 United States v. Butler, 205 U.S. App. D.C. 19, 636 F.2d 727 (D.C. Cir. 1980) (Bazelon, J. dissenting), cert. denied, 451 U.S. 1019, 69 L. Ed. 2d 392, 101 S. Ct. 3010 (1981).

30 The body of research on eyewitness memory and performance numbers more than 2,000 peer-reviewed research articles and extends back at least 30 years. Representative summaries of the research and the current state of knowledge are found in State v. Henderson, 27 A.3d 872, 894–908 (N.J. 2011); Dan Simon, In Doubt: The Psychology of the Criminal Justice Process, ch. 3 (2012); Elizabeth F. Loftus et al., Eyewitness Testimony: Civil and Criminal (4th ed. 2007); and Jules Epstein, *The Great Engine that Couldn't: Science, Mistaken Identity, and the Limits of Cross-Examination*, 36 Stetson L. Rev. 727 (2007). The following summary draws on these sources.

standard in terms of the applicability of social science research to the law."[31] Its fundamental precept is that the mind does not record images like a video camera, but instead is malleable, with the potential for erroneous input and/or malleability at each of three stages: encoding (the original act of perception); retention (the storage of the memory); and retrieval (when the memory must be called upon, whether in an interview, an identification procedure, or in courtroom testimony).

At the acquisition stage, the ability to clearly observe detail may be impacted by a variety of factors—stress, the presence of a weapon, whether a perpetrator was wearing a hat, and the difference in race between criminal and victim or witness.[32] The retention stage—when the memory of the incident is being stored—can be impacted by post-event information. This can include questions by investigators that suggest a fact, e.g., "did the robber have a moustache," or by exposure to external information such as seeing a face in a newspaper photograph or hearing someone say "I think it was Jack who did the robbery."[33] Finally, when the witness is asked to "retrieve" the event, for example at a line-up or for interviews or court testimony, the conduct of police, lawyers, or judges may unintentionally alter memory or confirm a flawed recollection. This may occur through suggestion, as when an investigator says "look at the line-up again, especially at person number 3"; through flawed instructions such as "can you pick the person in the line-up," and through confirmatory feedback such as "well done" after a witness does select a suspect.[34]

For clarity, factors that may adversely affect eyewitness accuracy have been denominated "estimator" and "system" variables.[35] The former term includes those factors attendant to the crime, the criminal and the observer—duration, race, the presence of a weapon, levels of stress, degree of attention, lighting—which may affect perception and memory but the impact of which can only be estimated; and the latter references the responsive mechanisms of the "system"—the police interview, line-up instructions, blind or non-blind administration—that can be controlled and the impact of which can more readily be quantified. What is clear is that in the often-traumatic and abbreviated circumstances of a criminal episode, each of these factors may cause a witness to fail to perceive salient details, to have the memory altered while in "storage," or to have that memory distorted or changed during the retrieval activities.

These factors affect what the eyewitness claims. Additional research has addressed how that testimony is viewed. Even with proof of mistaken identifications, there remains a powerful misapprehension of the durability of memory. Put most simply, laypersons (and often judges)[36] have had and continue to have an a-scientific trust in eyewitness memory, one that distorts trial verdicts and contributes to wrongful convictions (and, as is discussed *infra*, the judicial system has failed to adequately respond to).

Part of this is a by-product of both scientific and popular understanding of memory as immutable and retrievable. In *Memory: Fragments of a Modern History*,[37] Professor Alison Winter chronicles a century of mistaken understanding of memory as an intact, unmalleable construct—be it from experiments in "truth serum"[38] to the treatment of those traumatized by war[39] and the conceptualization of "flashbulb memories"[40] and on to the movements endorsing "recovered memory," particularly for victims (or possible victims) of childhood abuse.[41] Throughout the book, Winter shows how these beliefs pervaded both medical and scientific

31 *Henderson*, 27 A.3d at 916.

32 The research on the potency of each of these factors is substantial, and is documented in various books, most significantly Loftus et al., *supra*, note 30. A more succinct summary of the studies is found in *Henderson*, 27 A.3d at 904–8.

33 *Henderson*, 27 A.3d at 894–5; Elizabeth F. Loftus & John C. Palmer, *Reconstruction of Automobile Destruction: An Example of the Interaction Between Language and Memory*, 13 J. Verbal Learning & Verbal Behav. 585, 586 (1974).

34 *Henderson*, 27 A.3d at 896–904.

35 The terms "estimator" and "systems" variables were developed by eyewitness researcher Professor Gary Wells. *Applied Eyewitness-Testimony Research: System Variables and Estimator Variables*, 36 J. of Personality & Soc. Psychol. 1546 (1978).

36 *See infra* note 42.

37 Alison Winter, Memory: Fragments of a Modern History (2012).

38 *Id.* ch. 2.

39 *Id.* ch. 3.

40 *Id.* ch. 7.

41 *Id.* ch. 8.

communities and the popular imagination, and even finds a substantial fascination with the purported capacity to 'remember' past lives.[42]

The persistence of these misinformed beliefs about memory has been well-documented. In *Juror Understanding of Eyewitness Testimony: A Survey of 1000 Potential Jurors in the District of Columbia*, a 2004 survey of adults eligible for jury service confirmed a significant 'disconnect' between scientific research and layperson beliefs.[43] The findings included the following:

- Juror misunderstandings of memory in general: Almost two-thirds of the respondents (66 percent) thought the statement "I never forget a face" applied "very well" or "fairly well" to them.[44]
- Weapon focus: 37 percent thought the presence of a weapon would make a witness' memory for event details more reliable, while 33 percent believed that a weapon either would have no effect or were not sure of what effect a weapon would have.[45]
- The impact of violence and/or stress: 39 percent concluded that when an event is violent it makes a witness' memory for details more reliable, while 33 percent responded that this either would have no effect or that they were not sure of what effect violence during the commission of the crime would have.[46]
- Duration of the incident: Over 40 percent thought that witnesses were able to accurately estimate how long a crime occurred (and thus how long the opportunity to see who the criminal was) or were not sure whether such estimates were accurate. Almost 25 percent believed that eyewitnesses normally underestimate an event's duration.[47]

These were not the only conflicts between lay beliefs and the findings of eyewitness researchers. Few prospective jurors understood that there is at best only a slight correlation between confidence and accuracy; nearly half thought racial differences between the witness and the perpetrator had no impact on accuracy; and further results showed the respondents' unfamiliarity with problems of suggestivity in show-up and line-up procedures. [48]

The results of this survey are not idiosyncratic. A 2011 study,[49] surveying over 1,800 persons in America, had similar and significant findings as to eyewitness reliability: "63.0% agreed that 'human memory works like a video camera, accurately recording the events we see and hear so that we can review and inspect them later.'… 47.6% agreed that 'once you have experienced an event and formed a memory of it, that memory does not change.'"[50] Other surveys report similar findings,[51] and some courts have drawn the same conclusion.[52]

42 *Id.* ch. 5.

43 Elizabeth F. Loftus et al., *Juror Understanding of Eyewitness Testimony: A Survey of 1000 Potential Jurors in the District of Columbia*, 1 (2004).

44 *Id.* at 6.

45 *Id.* at 8.

46 *Id.* at 9.

47 *Id.* at 11.

48 *Id.* at 13–20.

49 Daniel J. Simons, *What People Believe about How Memory Works: A Representative Survey of the U.S. Population*, PLOS ONE, Aug. 3 (2011).

50 *Id.*

51 J. Don Read & Sarah L. Desmarais, *Expert Psychology Testimony on Eyewitness Identification: A Matter of Common Sense? in* EXPERT TESTIMONY ON THE PSYCHOLOGY OF EYEWITNESS IDENTIFICATION (Brian Cutler ed., 2009). The knowledge deficit is not limited to lay jurors, as many judges have similar beliefs. *See, e.g.*, Richard A. Wise & Martin A. Safer, *What US Judges Know and Believe about Eyewitness Testimony*, 18 (4) APPLIED COGNITIVE PSYCHOL. 427–43 (2004).

52 State v. Clopten, 223 P.3d 1103, 1108 (Utah 2009): "[T]here is little doubt that juries are generally unaware of these deficiencies in human perception and memory and thus give great weight to eyewitness identifications. Indeed, juries seemed to be swayed the most by the confidence of an eyewitness, even though such confidence correlates only weakly with accuracy." *See also*, Tillman v. State, 354 S.W.3d 425, 442 (Tex. Crim. App. 2011) (citing to expert testimony that "research reveals that jurors do not understand eyewitness identification completely and do not know how to apply what they do know to a particular case"); *Henderson*, 27 A.3d at 911 (studies "reveal generally that people do not intuitively understand all of the relevant scientific findings [and as] a result, there is a need to promote greater juror understanding of those issues").

The determinations of eyewitness accuracy (often confused by jurors with eyewitness sincerity) are made by fact-finders who are often either uninformed or operating under substantial misapprehension of how memory and recall work. It is in this context that the response of the United States judiciary to the risk of eyewitness error must be assessed.

## Part III: The Vagaries and Failings of the Judicial Response to Eyewitness Fallibility

Because of the federal/state dichotomy[53] in the criminal justice system in the United States, it is impossible to describe a uniform system of laws governing eyewitness identification and its use in criminal prosecutions. What is clear, however, is that in general what can be described as the "default" principle is to admit eyewitness evidence and leave it to lay jurors to determine its value and strength. This is confirmed when analyzing the normative approach, across jurisdictions, to the many issues and procedures that arise in identification-based prosecutions.

### *Legal Framework and Appellate Review*

First is the uniform acceptance of eyewitness testimony, even that of questionable validity, to be sufficient in and of itself to support a conviction and the concomitant unwillingness (if not outright impermissibility) for a reviewing appellate court to overturn a guilty verdict in such cases. Reviewing courts do not re-weigh witness credibility, instead analyzing a case for its evidentiary sufficiency, i.e., whether there is any evidence in the trial record that a *jury could have found* to be true and that establishes each element (constituent part) of the criminal offense(s) charged.[54] In the eyewitness context, that involves a single inquiry—whether there was a statement identifying the accused as the criminal who perpetrated the offense, regardless of what contradictory evidence is of record and how the identifying witness' credibility and/or accuracy were impeached.

Illustrative in the identification context is the case of *Brown v. Davis*.[55] The facts show how questionable the identification testimony was, and the absence of *any* corroboration:

> Although the victim knew the appellant over a period of years and saw him daily, and clearly saw the intruder in her lighted living room on the night of the attack, she did not give his name to Detective Moore when he first interviewed her on February 17. She described a man eleven years younger than Brown and wearing a one inch beard. Apparently, sometime later, she informed the police that "my granddaughter thinks [Franklin Long] is the attacker." Not until March 3, 1981, after a $2,500 reward had been offered, did the victim by written statement positively identify McKinley Brown as the attacker. The victim's panties and dress, as well as the belt, prophylactic, and Brown's hair samples, were sent to the Federal Bureau of Investigation for examination, but neither the laboratory results nor any physical evidence connecting the appellant to the crime were produced at trial.[56]

Countering the identification evidence, Brown offered evidence of alibi and the more general defense, one acknowledged by the appellate court that "judged by any standard, Brown was not a plausible candidate to commit this attack."[57]

Notwithstanding this paucity of convincing evidence, the appellate court had no choice but to affirm the conviction:

---

53 *See supra* note 3.

54 Under the due process guarantee of the United States Constitution, "[t]he evidence is sufficient to support a conviction whenever, after viewing the evidence in the light most favorable to the prosecution, any rational trier of fact could have found the essential elements of the crime beyond a reasonable doubt." Parker v. Matthews, 132 S. Ct. 2148, 2152 (U.S. 2012) (internal quotations and citation omitted).

55 Brown v. Davis, 752 F.2d 1142, 1146 (6th Cir. Tenn. 1985).

56 *Id.* at 1144.

57 *Id.* at 1145.

> There is nothing in the victim's initial statement to the police or in her trial testimony that makes her identification of Brown impossible. The jury saw and heard the victim and her alleged assailant and they may have believed that the victim could not quickly bring herself to name Brown because he had always been nice and respectful to her and she knew that she had been under sedation and might be confused. Conceivably, she may have been puzzling over the circumstances and events of the attack but, with the passage of time and the improvement in her health, her mind gradually became clearer and she may have realized that she had been right all along—that it was Brown indeed who had attacked her.
>
> ...
>
> We have carefully considered the victim's failure to promptly name Brown as her assailant and the discrepancies in her identification. Only when the record evidence cannot reasonably support a finding of guilt beyond a reasonable doubt can we hold that there has been a constitutional denial of due process. The defense had every opportunity to cross-examine and impeach the victim's credibility. The issue of credibility, the demeanor of the parties, and the weighing of the evidence were properly for the jury. We perceive no constitutional error.[58]

*Brown* is not an isolated holding but instead is reflective of the general "near-total deference" accorded to jury decisions.[59] What it shows is that a jury's erroneous determination at trial, without some other error in the proceedings, insulates a wrongful conviction from review and the remedy of a new trial or outright release from prison.

The sufficiency test is that used after conviction, on appellate review. Thus, attention should be paid to the pre-trial and trial processes in identification cases to assess whether they offer sufficient protections against wrongful conviction. For the most part they do not.

### *The Pre-Trial Process and "Suppression"*

The starting point in this assessment is the potential for suppression, a pre-trial determination that identification evidence should not be admitted at all in the prosecution's case. The availability of this remedy grew out of a larger movement, sometimes called the Warren Court's "revolution" in criminal procedure.[60] Applying both specific provisions of the Constitution's Bill of Rights and the more general guarantee of "due process," the Court identified constitutional rules for interrogation and for police-conducted eyewitness identification procedures.

The latter began with a focus on the post-indictment right to counsel guaranteed by the United States Constitution. Because there is the right to counsel at all "critical stages" of the criminal process after formal charges are brought (up to and through trial, sentencing, and appeal), the absence of counsel at a post-charging line-up was held to require automatic exclusion of this "out-of-court"[61] identification.[62] Yet even when such an exclusion was mandated, this did not prevent the witness from identifying the suspect in court, as long as it could be shown that the in-court testimony was sufficiently independent of the unconstitutional pre-trial procedure or, as the Court described it, "[w]hether, granting establishment of the primary illegality, the

58 *Id.* at 1146–7.

59 Ash v. Marshall, 2010 U.S. Dist. LEXIS 41488 (C.D. Cal. Mar. 26, 2010) ("The jury resolved the issue of Alcazar's credibility in favor of a verdict of guilt, and that determination is entitled to near-total deference under Jackson'").

60 Brandon Garrett, *Aggregation in Criminal Law*, 95 Calif. L. Rev. 383, 450 (2007) ("the Warren Court's due process 'revolution' created a series of individual procedural rights").

61 The term "out of court" refers to any circumstance prior to trial where the witness sees a suspect (or a photo or other image of a suspect) and identifies her/him as the perpetrator. "In-court" identifications are those occurring at trial, where the witness directly states that a person in the courtroom is the criminal.

62 *See e.g.*, Gilbert v. California, 388 U.S. 263 (U.S. 1967); *Wade*, 388 U.S.

evidence to which instant objection is made has been come at by exploitation of that illegality or instead by means sufficiently distinguishable to be purged of the primary taint."[63]

These rights, albeit important, play a minor role in eyewitness suppression litigation. Counsel is easily provided at post-charging line-ups, and unless the initial stop or arrest of the suspect is without sufficient cause, the out of court identification will not be deemed unlawful and inadmissible.

Instead, the primary protection developed as part of the Warren Court "revolution" was a Due Process analysis. Evolving over a several year period, the test that the Court finally settled on had two primary concerns: was the police-conducted identification process "suggestive," i.e., did it impermissibly prompt the witness to identify the suspect; and, if suggestivity was present, was the ultimate identification nonetheless "reliable," i.e., was the person's statement of "that's the guy/woman" a result of the eyewitness' pre-existing memory of the features seen at the crime rather than a prompted memory created by the suggestive process.[64]

How was reliability to be measured? The Court identified those factors to be considered in its "totality" assessment: (1) the opportunity of the witness to view the criminal at the time of the crime; (2) the witness' degree of attention; (3) the accuracy of his prior description of the criminal; (4) the level of certainty demonstrated by the witness at the confrontation; and (5) the length of time between the crime and the confrontation.[65]

What can be said with certainty is that the test as designed is neither scientific[66] nor rigorous and instead fails to ensure that only truly reliable identifications are admitted at trial. This test was developed before the "explosion" in eyewitness psychology research and is contrary to science in its own terms; fails to consider the myriad factors now known to contribute to mistaken identifications; and erroneously presumes that suggestivity and reliability are distinct phenomena with no overlap or interplay.[67] Indeed, a handful of states have developed more stringent criteria, but the national model is that developed by the United States Supreme Court.[68]

Three points confirm that the test is not rigorous, and readily permits unreliable identification evidence to reach a jury for weighing. First, in finding an identification to be reliable, a judge need not conclude that it is actually reliable, but instead that it has potential reliability sufficient for a jury to weigh it.[69] Second, there are numerous decisions showing that even the briefest opportunity to observe at the crime scene will

---

63 *Wade*, 388 U.S. at 241 (internal quotations and citation omitted). The Court applied essentially the same test when the initial identification procedure was then outgrowth of an unlawful search and seizure, one that violated the Fourth Amendment to the Constitution: the out-of-court was automatically suppressed, while an in-court identification would be barred only if it was not independent of the initial procedure. United States v. Crews, 445 U.S. 463 (1980).

64 Neil v. Biggers, 409 U.S. 188 (1972); Manson v. Braithwaite, 432 U.S. 98 (1976).

65 Gottschalk v Benson, 409 U.S. 63, 199–200 (1972).

66 In Perry v. New Hampshire, 132 U.S. S. Ct. 716 (2012), the Court was urged by various amici curiae to reconsider the various reliability criteria and bring them into line with current scientific knowledge. (*See, e.g.*, Brief for Amicus Curiae American Psychological Association in Support of Petitioner (No. 10-8974)). (The Court took no such step, instead endorsing its 1970s criteria and keeping the decision focused on the narrow claim presented, whether suppression was an option when the initial identification was the result of private party conduct rather than a police-created procedure. The Court limited suppression to "state action," again narrowing the remedies available when unreliable identification evidence is offered at trial.)

67 Critiques of the "reliability" test are found in Gary L. Wells & Deah S. Quinlivan, *Suggestive Eyewitness Identification Procedures and the Supreme Court's Reliability Test in Light of Eyewitness Science: 30 Years Later*, 33 LAW & HUM. BEHAV. 1–24 (2009); Richard A. Wise et al., *How to Analyze the Accuracy of Eyewitness Testimony in a Criminal Case*, 42 CONN. L. REV. 435 (2009); Timothy O'Toole & Giovanna Shay, *Manson v. Braithwaite Revisited: Towards a New rule of Decision for Due Process Challenges to Eyewitness Identification Procedures*, 41 VAL. U. L. REV. 109 (2006); Margery Malkin Koosed, *Reforming Eyewitness Identification Law and Practices to Protect the Innocent*, 42 CREIGHTON L. REV. 595 (2009); Margery Malkin Koosed, *The Proposed Innocence Protection Act Won't—Unless it also Curbs Mistaken*, 63 OHIO ST. L. J. 263, 276–8 (2002).

68 Those states are Utah (State v. Ramirez, 817 P.2d 774, 780 (Utah 1991)); Kansas (State v. Hunt, 69 P.3d 571, 577 (Kan. 2003)); Massachusetts (Commonwealth v. Martin, 850 N.E.2d 555, 560 (Mass. 2006)); New York (People v. Duuvon, 571 N.E.2d 654, 657 (N.Y. App. 1991)); Wisconsin (State v. Dubose, 699 N.W.2d 582, 584–5 (Wisc. 2005)); and New Jersey (27 A.3d 872, 878 (N.J. 2011)).

69 Jules Epstein, *Irreparable Misidentifications and Reliability: Reassessing the Threshold for Admissibility of Eyewitness Identification*, 58 VILL. L. REV. 69 (2013).

be deemed sufficient to support a reliability finding, again making the test largely toothless.[70] Finally, the DNA exoneration cases (with proven unreliable identifications) show that the suppression remedy was no protection at all. A study of the first 250 DNA exonerations by Professor Brandon Garrett showed that, of the 190 in which eyewitness testimony was core proof, of the 39 who challenged the denial of suppression on appeal (claiming suggestivity in the identification process), none had relief granted.[71] The suppression tool exists, but it rarely results in exclusion, making the suppression court's "gatekeeper" role an empty one.[72]

*The Trial Process: Hearsay and Cross-Examination*

The trial process cannot be said to successfully screen out "bad" identifications from "good" ones or to ensure verdict accuracy. Rules of evidence permit testimony about any out-of-court identifications as "substantive" evidence, i.e., evidence a jury may use as proof to convict. The Federal Rules of Evidence (and many state evidence codes) exclude from the ban on hearsay a statement that "identifies a person as someone the declarant perceived earlier"[73] as long as the declarant (the person who originally made the identification) testifies at trial. The rationale is that the earlier identification is more reliable because it was made under "less suggestive conditions" than the in-court identification.[74] This ignores the acceptance of "suggestive" identifications inherent in the suppression rules, and in no way requires a jury to be told about in-court suggestivity. What this means is that a witness' claim of "that's the criminal," made at a suggestive confrontation, is not only admissible (even where the witness now says "I was wrong") but is stand-alone evidence of guilt.

The trust in eyewitness claims is not offset by the "weapons" in the defense counsel's arsenal, not even that of cross-examination. The right to approach and question an identifying witness in an adversarial manner is a core right in the American trial scheme, one adopted from the practice as originated in England[75] and hailed as the "greatest legal engine ever invented for the discovery of truth."[76]

The limits of cross-examination derive, first, from the nature of this form of witness interrogation: its historic genesis is in exposing lies, not honestly held mistakes. Its inutility in eyewitness identification trials is well documented.[77] Mock jury studies have shown, for example, "there was no significant difference in the results obtained by the tyros and those obtained by the pros" when the skill of the cross-examiner was the variable tested.[78] An even more problematic result was obtained when the variable was not attorney skill but eyewitness capacity—when a mock crime scenario was presented to "jurors," a 72 percent conviction rate

70 *See, e.g.*, State v. Mitchell, 127 Conn. App. 526, 735–6, 16 A.3d 730 (2011) ("[e]ven if the victim only saw the defendant's face for a second, as the defendant suggests, that is still sufficient to support the court's finding that the victim had a substantial opportunity to view the defendant"); State v. McCarthy, 105 Conn. App. 596, 939 A.2d 1195, 1203 (2008) (few seconds, chaotic conditions, from 300 feet away); State v. Lopez, 289 Conn. 779, 911 A. 2d 1099 (2007) (saw masked attacker for 2–3 seconds); State v. Ledbetter, 275 Conn. 534, 577, 881 A.2d 290, 317 (2005) (few seconds during struggle with two culprits); State v. Morgan, 274 Conn. 790, 877 A. 2d 739 (2005) (briefly saw face as robber came in and pulled down mask); State v. Vega, 13 Conn. App. 438, 443–4, 537 A.2d 505, 508 (1988) (officer's view and night-time pursuit of burglar); State v. Ledbetter, 185 Conn. 607, 615, 441 A.2d 595, 600 (1981) (glance was 15–20 seconds); State v. Salgado, 974 P.2d 661 (N.M. 1999) (10-second viewing of shooter, in the evening, sufficient); McElrath v. Commonwealth, 592 A.2d 740, 743 (Pa. Super. Ct. 1991) (5-second viewing in gunpoint robbery sufficient).

71 Garrett, *supra* note 13, at 187.

72 As the New Jersey Supreme Court reported in 2011, with the exception of one case reversed on appeal, we have found no reported Appellate Division decision since 1977 that reversed a conviction because the trial court failed to suppress identification evidence. *Henderson*, 27 A.3d at 919 n9.

73 Rule 801(d)(1)(C), Federal Rules of Evidence (2011).

74 *Id.*, *in* Advisory Committee Notes.

75 John H. Langbein, The Origins of Adversary Criminal Trial (2003).

76 California v. Green, 399 U.S. 149, 158 (1970) (quoting John H. Wigmore, 5 Evidence § 1367, at 29 (3d ed., 1940)).

77 *See* Epstein, *supra* note 30, at 770–74.

78 R.C.L. Lindsay et al., *Mock-Juror Belief of Accurate and Inaccurate Eyewitnesses: A Replication and Extension*, 13 Law & Hum. Behav. 333 (1989).

based on eyewitness identification dropped only four percentage points when the facts were altered to include the partial blindness of the witness.[79]

Finally, a skilled cross-examination that identifies the system and estimator variables present in the case may inadvertently reinforce juror misperceptions. For example, despite consistent findings that the presence of a weapon may distract the witness/victim and direct his/her attention away from the perpetrator's face,[80] many laypersons believe that the presence of a weapon *enhances* attention and reliability.[81] Thus, a skilled cross-examination, derived from reliable science, risks enforcing erroneous beliefs and making the eyewitness seem more reliable.[82]

*Expert Witnesses*

One move toward increased juror understanding of the frailties of eyewitness evidence has been the trend, since the early 1980s, to permit expert testimony in identification cases.[83] While most jurisdictions now permit such evidence to explain the science of memory and recall but *not* to comment on whether a particular eyewitness is mistaken, a handful still bar it categorically; and in those where the evidence is allowed it is at the discretion of the trial judge, whose decision to bar such testimony will be affirmed on appeal if there is a conviction unless there has been an "abuse of discretion."[84] The importance of expert assistance to jurors cannot be minimized; but, given the low number of available expert witnesses as measured against the cost of such testimony and the high number of trials involving identification evidence, expert testimony is not a system-wide remedy for the problem of eyewitness error.

*Jury Instructions*

The last potential tool for educating jurors and reducing the risk of mistaken identification convictions is the jury instruction, the process at a trial's conclusion where the trial judge informs jurors of the controlling principles of law. Beyond the overarching concern of whether any instruction at the end of trial (and delivered often in a monotone from written text) can correct impressions developed during trial,[85] the particular forms of eyewitness evidence instructions also call into question their utility, especially in light of the reality that "juries are generally unaware of [the] deficiencies in human perception and memory."[86]

79 E.F. Loftus, *Reconstructive Memory: The Incredible Eyewitness*, 8 Psychol. Today 116 (1974). Later studies with similar scenarios had lower rates, but still showed juror belief even when the witness was discredited. Cutler & Penrod, *supra* note 5, at 194–5.

80 Nancy M. Steblay, *A Meta-Analytic Review of the Weapon Focus Effect*, 16 Law & Hum. Behav. 413, 415–17 (1992).

81 In a study of 1,000 jury-service-eligible adults in the Washington, DC area, 37 percent of the respondents actually thought the presence of a weapon would make a witness' memory for event details more reliable, while 33 percent thought that the presence of a weapon either would have no effect or were not sure of what effect a weapon would have. Loftus et al., *supra* note 43.

82 This example does not stand in isolation. Laypersons similarly assume that the stress of an event may actually enhance accuracy (Loftus et al., *id.*), while studies confirm stress and violence as factors that degrade eyewitness reliability. Charles A. Morgan III et al., *Accuracy of Eyewitness Memory for Persons Encountered During Exposure to Highly Intense Stress*, 27 Int'l J.L. & Psychiatry 265 (2004); Kenneth A. Deffenbacher et al., *A Meta-Analytic Review of the Effects of High Stress on Eyewitness Memory*, 28 Law & Hum. Behav. 687, 687–99 (2004).

83 The history and governing law regarding expert evidence in eyewitness cases is detailed in Jules Epstein, *Expert Testimony: Legal Standards for Admissibility*, *in* Cutler, *supra* note 51, at 76–9.

84 *Id.*, summarizing the many grounds used by appellate courts to find that exclusion of expert testimony was not an abuse of discretion.

85 Instructions at trial's end have a diminished ability to inform juror understanding and increase sensitivity. Gabriella Ramirez et al., *Judges' Cautionary Instructions on Eyewitness Testimony*, 14 Am. J. Forensic Psychol. 31, 45 (1996).

86 *Clopten*, 223 P.3d.

Not all states require such instructions, and some bar them categorically as an improper comment on evidence.[87] In those federal and state courts that mandate an eyewitness "cautionary" instruction, it is often generic, telling jurors nothing more than "testimony of witnesses as to identity must be received with caution and scrutinized with care."[88] The instructions often derive from cases decided years or even decades before the explosion in eyewitness psychology research.[89] Finally, because some courts impose narrowing triggering conditions as a prerequisite to making the instruction available, in many identification cases not even the generic language will be provided. These circumstances, largely without scientific foundation or validity, include "where no corroboration of the testimony exists, or where the witness' memory has faded by the time of trial, or where there was a limited opportunity for observation."[90]

This is not to say that no jury instruction is adequate, or that no courts give focused and informative charges.[91] A small but significant movement in that direction is apparent, with the Hawaii[92] and New Jersey[93] Supreme Courts recently mandating the use of science-based, detailed instructions in eyewitness identification trials. Yet the generic instructions so often used, and the risk that they can actually reinforce jurors' mistaken beliefs about eyewitness reliability,[94] show that a blanket notion that having *some* instruction provides a

---

87 *See, e.g.*, Conley v. State 607 S.W.2d 328, 330 (Ark. 1980); Lewis v. State, 363 N.E.2d 1230, 1231 (Ind. 1977); Roberson v. State, 852 S.W.2d 508, 511 (Tex. Crim. App. 1993) ("a charge on mistaken identity is an improper comment on the weight of the evidence and should not be given").

88 United States v. Angiulo, 897 F.2d 1169, 1205 n.19 (1st Cir. 1990), quoting and citing approvingly United States v. Kavanagh, 572 F.2d 9, 11 (1st Cir. 1978). *See* the much-heralded "Telfaire" instruction, cited by numerous courts as a model; Christian Sheehan, *Making the Jurors the "Experts": The Case for Eyewitness Identification Jury Instructions*, 52 B.C. L. Rev. 651, 673 (Mar., 2011) offers little more. It tells jurors that identification must be proved beyond a reasonable doubt, that identification is dependent upon the opportunity and capacity of the witness to observe, and without guidance asks jurors to be "satisfied that the identification made by the witness subsequent to the offense was the product of [the witness'] own recollection." United States v. Telfaire, 469 F.2d 552, 558 (C.C.D. D.C. 1972).

89 Pennsylvania, for example, uses a jury instruction developed in the 1950s. Commonwealth v. Ali, 10 A.3d 282, 303 (Pa. 2010) (affirming that the cautionary instruction to be provided in eyewitness cases is that found in Commonwealth v. Kloiber, 106 A.2d 820 (Pa. 1954)). The "Kloiber" instruction requires caution only in cases of witness uncertainty or limited opportunity to observe, and has no play when various estimator variables are present: "where the witness is not in a position to clearly observe the assailant, or he is not positive as to identity, or his positive statements as to identity are weakened by qualification or by failure to identify defendant on one or more prior occasions, the accuracy of the identification is so doubtful that the Court should warn the jury that the testimony as to identity must be received with caution." *Kloiber*, 106 A.2d at 826–7.

90 Heath v. Hill, 2009 U.S. Dist. LEXIS 124624 *32 (D. Or. Nov. 17, 2009) (internal quotation and citation omitted).

91 *See, e.g.*, United States v. Jones, 762 F. Supp. 2d 270, 278 n.5 (D. Mass. 2010) (detailing the supplemental instruction provided at trial that emphasized problems with cross-racial identification and the potential degrading impact on eyewitness reliability occasioned by the stress of a criminal act).

92 In State v. Cabagbag, 2012 Haw. LEXIS 165 (Haw. 2012), the Hawaii Supreme Court mandated, prospectively, that "when eyewitness identification is central to the case, circuit courts must give a specific jury instruction upon the request of the defendant to focus the jury's attention on the trustworthiness of the identification." The approved instruction includes some estimator variables, particularly stress and own-race bias, and the Hawaii Court encouraged "modification of this instruction or the development of other related instructions [… and referred] this instruction to the Committee on Pattern Criminal Jury Instructions for future comments, suggestions, and any recommended modifications." *Id.* at 36–7.

93 In *Henderson*, 27 A.3d at 924, the New Jersey Supreme Court held that enhanced instructions be given to guide juries about the various factors that may affect the reliability of an identification in a particular case. Those instructions are to be included in the court's comprehensive jury charge at the close of evidence. In addition, instructions may be given during trial if warranted. For example, if evidence of heightened stress emerges during important testimony, a party may ask the court to instruct the jury midtrial about that variable and its effect on memory. Those instructions were promulgated in July, 2012. http://www.judiciary.state.nj.us/pressrel/2012/jury_instruction.pdf.

94 *See, e.g.*, Commonwealth v. Santoli, 680 N.E.2d 1116, 1121 (Mass. 1997) (changing state's eyewitness instruction regarding a witness' confidence in the identification because "there is significant doubt about whether there is any correlation between a witness's confidence in her identification and the accuracy of her recollection"); Sheehan, *supra* note 88, at 679 ("instructions can aggravate error by reinforcing erroneous assumptions about eyewitnesses"). The risk of juror misunderstanding as a result of a scientific jury instructions is demonstrated in the Telfaire charge itself, which advises jurors that "you must consider the credibility of each identification witness in the same way as any other witness, consider whether he is truthful … " Telfaire, 469 F.2d at 559. Rarely is truthfulness (credibility) the issue in an eyewitness case, as

meaningful tool for the assessment of eyewitness testimony is mistaken and contradicted by substantial research.[95]

If this analysis of the limits of the criminal court trial to weed out mistaken identifications is correct, then US complacent reliance on its system of justice as the "best in the world"[96] is put to the lie when the subject is eyewitness evidence. The trial of the case is "too little, too late" to protect against erroneous identifications, at least as currently practiced in many if not most jurisdictions. Where there is movement, however, is in the pre-trial investigation stage, with law enforcement evidence collection improvements beginning to take hold.

## Part IV: System Responses: Law Enforcement Initiatives

In the years since the publication of *Convicted by Juries, Exonerated by Science*,[97] the arena in which science has been brought to bear and where reform has shown some chance of reducing mistaken identifications has been in police practices. As a sequel to that publication, the National Institute of Justice convened a "technical working group" on eyewitness identification that ultimately produced *Eyewitness Evidence: A Guide for Law Enforcement*.[98] Not a mandate, it was nonetheless intended to provide "rigorous criteria for handling eyewitness evidence that are as demanding as those governing the handling of physical trace evidence."[99]

Although only a "guide," the publication represented a beginning in encouraging science-based police practices. Still not embraced by legislative, executive or judicial mandate in all (or even most) jurisdictions, they represent the beginning of a movement to improve identification-evidence gathering. Changes have come from within the law enforcement community,[100] from legislatures, government agencies in New Jersey and

---

the witness testifies without malice or corrupt motive; rather, the issue is that of an honest mistake. A jury instruction that redirects the focus to honesty (credibility) focuses jurors on the wrong issue.

95 Jennifer L. Devenport et al., *Effectiveness of Traditional Safeguards Against Erroneous Conviction Arising from Mistaken Eyewitness Identification*, *in* Cutler, *supra* note 51, at 63–4, conclude after surveying juror instruction efficacy research that "judicial cautionary instructions, in their present state, may be an ineffective safeguard against erroneous convictions resulting from mistaken eyewitness identifications, and, at best, their effectiveness is questionable ... [R] esearch suggests that the cautionary instructions currently relied on by the courts...either have no effect or enhance juror skepticism rather than juror sensitization ...".

An additional concern is the stilted language of many jury instructions. *See* Dennis J. Devine et al., *Jury Decision Making: 45 Years of Empirical Research on Deliberating Groups*, 7 Psych. Pub. Pol. & L. 622, 667 (2001) ("It is clear from 20 years of research that jurors have difficulty wading through the technical jargon, convoluted logic, and stilted structure that characterize many pattern instructions."); J. Brittany Cross, *Juror Incomprehension: Advocating for a Holistic Reform of Jury Instructions*, 98 Ky. L.J. 355 (2009/10); Molly Armour, *Comment: Dazed and Confused: The Need for a Legislative Solution to the Constitutional Problem of Juror Incomprehension*, 17 Temp. Pol. & Civ. Rts. L. Rev. 641, 642 (2007); American Bar Association, Principles for Juries & Jury Trials Principle 14 (a) (discussing how pattern jury instructions are "typically drawn from case law or statutes that lay jurors are not familiar with and which they do not understand"), *available at* http://www.americanbar.org/content/dam/aba/migrated/juryprojectstandards/principles.authcheckdam.pdf.

96 A 1999 survey conducted by the American Bar Association found that 80 percent of all respondents either strongly agree or agree, based on a five-point scale, that "in spite of its problems, the American justice system is still the best in the world." *See, American Bar Association Report on Perceptions of the U.S. Justice System*, 62 Alb. L. Rev. 1307, 1308.

97 U.S. Dep't of Justice, *supra* note 14

98 U.S. Dep't of Justice, *Eyewitness Evidence: A Guide for Law Enforcement* (1999), *available at* https://www.ncjrs.gov/pdffiles1/nij/178240.pdf.

99 *Id.* at 2.

100 Mark Hansen, *Show Me Your ID: Cops and Courts Update their Thinking on Using Eyewitnesses*, 98 A.B.A.J. 18 (2012). Reforms include the issuance of "model" policies by the International Association of Chiefs of Police and the Commission on Accreditation for Law Enforcement Agencies. Val Van Brocklin, *Defending Your Lineup in Court*, Officer.com (Jul. 19, 2011), http://www.officer.com/article/10300765/defending-your-lineup-in-court.

Vermont[101] and courts[102] to mandate better practices in eyewitness cases, particularly in witness interviewing and identification procedures. In particular, several states have laws mandating specific identification procedures such as pre-line-up warnings,[103] or requiring police departments to develop such policies. These include Connecticut, Illinois, Maryland, North Carolina, Ohio, Virginia, West Virginia, and Wisconsin. Texas passed legislation requiring police departments to adopt their own policies or a "model" developed by the Law Enforcement Management Institute of Texas.[104] These reforms include double-blind[105] administration of identification procedures and the use of sequential rather than simultaneous line-ups and/or photo arrays,[106] with hundreds of individual police districts and two states—New Jersey and North Carolina—either requiring these procedures or stating a strong preference for their use.[107]

Nonetheless, this is cause for, at best, modest optimism. It remains the case that "there is wide variability among and within the almost 20,000 law enforcement departments nationwide as to which identification procedures they use and how they conduct them."[108] Perhaps more significantly, there still remains vocal and vociferous opposition among some prosecutor and victims' rights advocates to legislating such reforms, describing them as "designed solely to benefit criminal defendants"[109] and sometimes challenging whether the exonerations actually involve cases of innocence.[110] So, notwithstanding progress within law enforcement, it is not uniform or necessarily widespread.

---

101 *See, e.g.*, *Attorney General Guidelines for Preparing and Conducting Photo and Live Lineup Identification Procedures*, Office of the New Jersey Attorney General (Apr. 18, 2001), *available at* http://www.state.nj.us/lps/dcj/agguide/photoid.pdf; Beth Schuster, *Police Lineups: Making Eyewitness Identification More Reliable*, 258 Nat'l Inst. Just. J. (2007), *available at* http://www.nij.gov/journals/258/police-lineups.html; Vermont Dep't of Public Safety Law Enforcement Advisory Board, Summary Report (2011), *available at* http://www.leg.state.vt.us/reports/2012ExternalReports/277888.pdf (proposing a model eyewitness policy for police departments).

102 Massachusetts Supreme Judicial Court designed a "protocol" for conducting photo arrays and explained that it "expect[s] such protocols to be used in the future." Commonwealth v. Silva-Santiago, 906 N.E.2d 299 (Mass. 2009). That same Court, however, declined to impose a requirement that identification arrays be "sequential" rather than simultaneous. Commonwealth v. Walker, 953 N.E.2d 195, 207 (Mass. 2011). The New Jersey Supreme Court imposed a requirement in 2012 that identification procedures be recorded, preferably electronically. *See Rule 3:11—Record of an Out-of-Court Identification Procedure*, New Jersey Courts, http://www.judiciary.state.nj.us/pressrel/2012/new_rule.pdf (last visited Aug., 10, 2012).

103 For example, Illinois law requires that the line-up be photographed and that the witness be instructed that "[t]he suspect might not be in the lineup or photo spread and the eyewitness is not obligated to make an identification." 725 ILCS 5/107A-5. Ohio requires the police investigator to "inform … the eyewitness that a photograph of the alleged perpetrator of the offense may or may not be included in the photographs the eyewitness is about to see and that the administrator does not know which, if any, of the folders contains the photograph of the alleged perpetrator." ORC Ann. 2933.83.

104 Tex. Code Crim. Proc. art. 38.20.

105 The term "double-blind" refers to the identification process where neither the witness nor the process administrator knows which person in the line-up or array is the suspect.

106 A "sequential" presentation is one where the witness is shown one photo or one suspect at a time, while in a "simultaneous" presentation all six photographs or line-up members are viewed together, permitting comparisons between and among the participants. Schuster, *supra* note 101.

107 *Id.* Page 3.

108 Simon, *supra* note 30. A survey of police departments, reported in 2013, confirms that "most police agencies have not fully implemented all of the recommendations from the NIJ Guide." Police Executive Research Forum, A NATIONAL SURVEY OF EYEWITNESS IDENTIFICATION PROCEDURES IN LAW ENFORCEMENT AGENCIES, vii (2013), http://policeforum.org/library/eyewitness-identification/NIJEyewitnessReport.pdf

109 *See, e.g.*, Independent Report of Law Enforcement and Victim Representative Members of the Advisory Committee on Wrongful Convictions (2011), *available at* http://webcache.googleusercontent.com/search?q=cache:http://www.phila.gov/districtattorney/pdfs/Law_Enforcement_Report.pdf. This "independent report was a response to proposals for reform practices in eyewitness and interrogation processes in Pennsylvania. Report of the Advisory Commission on Wrongful Convictions (2011), *available at* http://jsg.legis.state.pa.us/resources/documents/ftp/documents/9-15-11%20rpt%20-%20Wrongful%20Convictions.pdf.

110 *Id.* at 11–13.

## Part V: Conclusion

Substantial research confirms that "people do not perform well at distinguishing between accurate and inaccurate identifications."[111] Yet American law proceeds from the opposite stance, that identification evidence is "significant evidence [but] … still only evidence, and … not a factor that goes to the very heart—the 'integrity'—of the adversary process."[112] That there is a greater awareness of the risk of mistaken identification cannot be denied; but the disconnect between science and a trust in the jury system of determining witness accuracy will likely continue to result in cases of wrongful conviction.

111 Simon, *supra* note 30, at 151.

112 Watkins v. Sowders, 449 U.S. 341, 348 (U.S. 1981).

Chapter 4

# Disputed Interrogation Techniques in America: True and False Confessions and the Estimation and Valuation of Type I and II Errors

Deborah Davis, Richard A. Leo, Michael J. Williams

## Introduction

On March 22, 2007 Mario Mathews was brought to a police station, where he was accused of molesting his niece, and interrogated for slightly less than one hour.[1] The interrogation was not physically coercive and did not include the full armament of persuasive interrogation techniques taught and used pervasively throughout America. No one would look at the recorded interrogation and come to the conclusion that it was coerced, or that Mario Matthews' confession was false. And yet it *was* false.

Mario Mathews languished in jail for over two years until his case came to trial. The victim took the stand, and was asked the standard question of whether the man who molested her was in the courtroom. But, contrary to the expectations of all who watched, she said "No." The District Attorney (DA) reminded her that she had said it was her uncle, Mario Mathews, who had molested her, whereupon she replied that this was correct. But she had two Uncle Mario Mathews, and it was the other who had molested her. In this very dramatic way, a false confession that would otherwise never have been recognized as such came to light.

Nothing about Mathews' case fit the "profile" of a suspect vulnerable to false confession, or of interrogation tactics likely to elicit one. Had his innocence not been revealed so definitively by the victim herself in open court, he would almost certainly have served many more years in prison for the crime he didn't commit. Mario Mathews was very lucky that evidence of any kind existed to prove him innocent. But how many others have offered false confessions that cannot later be identified? Was Mathews' false confession an exceptionally rare reaction to police interrogation, or is the potential for interrogation-induced false confessions much higher than one might expect? Do false confessions occur in response to milder interrogations, and in more normal suspects, than commonly assumed? Is the rate at which interrogation-induced false confessions occur an acceptable cost of obtaining true confessions from the guilty? Or, should reforms be enacted to minimize the rate of false confessions, even at the cost of some true confessions?

This chapter addresses each of these issues. In the process, we consider how assumptions regarding the prevalence of false confessions affect reactions to those claiming to have falsely confessed as they proceed through the judicial process. We further consider how differences in the weight given to Type I errors (elicitation of false confessions) versus Type II errors (failure to elicit true confessions) have fueled controversy regarding whether and what reforms of interrogation practices are needed.

## Part I: The Problem of False Confession

The phenomenon of false confession has had a long and often notorious history in America. Documented interrogation-induced false confessions began to appear as long ago as the Salem witch trials of 1692, when roughly 50 people falsely confessed to witchcraft. Psychologists began to take note in the early 1900s,

1 California v. Mario Stevens Mathews (2008). Case No. FVA-700214a.

when Hugo Munsterberg published his classic work *On the Witness Stand,*[2] which reviewed a number of documented cases of false confession and discussed potential causes.

Many early false confessions were obtained through extreme forms of physical and psychological coercion. Indeed, colloquially referred to as the "third degree," such extreme interrogation practices were rampant in American police interrogation through the late nineteenth century and well into the first three decades of the twentieth.[3] But the extremity of third degree abuse led to widespread public protests, and to official investigation and condemnation in media, government, and United States Supreme Court decisions supporting the exclusion of coerced confessions from trial evidence. In response, police interrogators developed strategies to address the twin issues of (1) how to minimize the occurrence of false confessions, and (2) how to maintain the admissibility of interrogation-induced confessions into trial evidence. In the process, however, they also developed extreme overconfidence in the ability of their new methods to elicit only true confessions (while avoiding false confessions altogether), which has contributed strongly to the widespread belief among law enforcement, prosecutors, and even the judiciary that false confessions are extraordinarily rare. Interrogation researchers, however, have widely argued that false confessions do not appear to be rare at all, and are likely to be much more common than intuition would suggest.

The new methods developed in the 1930s and beyond were less physically coercive and eschewed explicit psychologically coercive threats, and therefore appeared less likely to elicit false confessions. Nonetheless, they remained psychologically coercive, and therefore still sufficiently potent to elicit false confessions from the innocent. Faced with the new reality that confessions extracted through third degree practices would not likely be admissible evidence against the defendant, interrogators turned to strategies of psychological manipulation and trickery still practiced today in the United States, and condoned by the courts. Interrogation methods, as they evolved during the 1930s forward, were formalized in a series of interrogation manuals published beginning in the 1940s. The most prominent method, the Reid 9-Step Method, was developed largely by John Reid and Fred Inbau, and has been taught widely throughout the world by John Reid Associates,[4] and formally described in an interrogation manual now in its 5th edition.[5]

The new psychological methods of interrogation were purportedly firmly based in science, and designed to produce reliable results. The Inbau et al. manual, for example, claimed that, if acting according to their protocol, the interrogator would be able to clearly distinguish guilty from innocent suspects prior to the interrogation through the use of scientific behavioral lie detection techniques.[6] Thereby, only the guilty would be subject to interrogation. The interrogation techniques would then elicit true confessions from the guilty at a high rate, while avoiding false confessions altogether. Based on this reasoning, Reid trainers and manuals made two claims still prevalent today: that those using their method do not interrogate innocent people; and that even if an innocent person were to be mistakenly interrogated, their methods would not induce an innocent person to falsely confess. Instances of false confession were attributed to improper deviation from the recommended techniques.

The perception of minimal risk of false confession among interrogators seems to fit with common intuitions, as reflected in surveys of laypersons[7] and in case law and trial rulings among the judiciary.[8] That is, both populations appear to overestimate the effectiveness of behavioral lie detection methods, and to

2 H. Munsterberg, On the Witness Stand: Essays on Psychology and Crime (1908).

3 R.A. Leo, Police Interrogation and American Justice (2008).

4 John E. Reid & Associates, http://www.reid.com (last visited June 12, 2013).

5 F.E. Inbau et al., Criminal Interrogation and Confessions (5th ed., 2013).

6 *Id.*

7 I. Blandon-Gitlin, K. Sperry & R. Leo, *Jurors Believe Interrogation Tactics Are Not Likely to Elicit False Confessions: Will Expert Witness Testimony Inform Them Otherwise?*, 17(3) Psychol., Crime & L. 239 (2011); M. Costanzo, N. Shaked-Schroer & K. Vinson, *Juror Beliefs About Police Interrogations, False Confessions, and Expert Testimony*, 7(2) J. Empir. L. Stud. 231 (2010); R.A. Leo & B. Liu, *What Do Potential Jurors Know About Police Interrogation Techniques and False Confessions?*, 27 Behav. Sci. & L. 381 (2009).

8 D. Davis & R.A. Leo, *Commentary: Overcoming Judicial Preferences for Person- Versus Situation-Based Analyses of Interrogation-Induced Confessions*, 38(2) J. Am. Acad. Psychiatry & L. 187 (2010); C. Watson, K.J. Weiss & C. Pouncey, *False Confessions, Expert Testimony, and Admissibility*, 38(2) J. Am. Acad. Psychiatry & L. 174 (2010).

underestimate the extent to which the psychological trickery and manipulation of common interrogation tactics can elicit false confessions from normal persons suffering no mental disability or defect.

Nevertheless, documented false confessions have continued to appear throughout the twentieth century and into the first decades of the twenty-first. As late as this decade, false confession remains among the most prominent causes of wrongful conviction of the innocent. Systematic analyses of causes of wrongful conviction have shown that from 14 percent to over 60 percent of those proven to have been wrongfully convicted falsely confessed. Others falsely pled guilty, or were implicated by false confessions given by others.[9] Additional studies have identified samples of false confessors (including those whose cases were dismissed before trial),[10] and a large number of individual false confessors continue to be identified through pre-trial disproof of their confessions or through post-conviction exoneration. Though the retarded, mentally ill, or very young are disproportionately represented among false confessors, the majority are normal, and suffer no discernible mental defect.

Supplementing these real-life instances of false confession is a growing body of laboratory studies disputing both claims of interrogation trainers. Studies addressing the effectiveness of strategies intended to differentiate guilty from innocent suspects prior to interrogation have thoroughly debunked the methods as unscientific and ineffective, and instead have shown training in such methods to reduce accuracy.[11] Moreover, both children and adults have been led to confess falsely to various non-criminal offenses via use of standard interrogation practices. Though clearly not as serious as the heinous alleged murders, rapes, and other violent crimes of the documented real-life false confessors, participants in laboratory studies have falsely confessed to offenses as serious as academic cheating (which is known to carry the possible penalty of expulsion from their universities), and have falsely confessed under conditions carrying financial or other undesirable consequences. Depending upon the interrogation tactics used and the nature of the offense, as many as 40 percent to 100 percent of participants in laboratory studies have falsely confessed.[12]

Such findings from field and laboratory have led many interrogation scholars to argue that false confessions are not likely to be rare at all, and that the commonly taught methods of interrogation (even if done according to protocol) can and do elicit false confessions from the innocent. Accordingly, they have widely called for reforms in interrogation strategies to curtail the specific practices most strongly implicated as promoting false confession. Though many such reforms have long since been instituted in parts of Europe and Canada, American interrogators and courts have been slow to follow. The community of interrogators (particularly interrogation trainers) has denied the magnitude of the problem and made almost no changes to their methods. Similarly, the judiciary continues to view interrogation practices that are strongly implicated in promoting false confession as acceptable: as reflected in trial court rulings, appellate decisions, and resistance to expert testimony on the reality and causes of false confession.

This discord between interrogation scholars and law enforcement and the judiciary has its roots in conflicting values and assumptions. First is the fundamental difference in estimation of the frequency of false confession, particularly among mentally "normal" suspects. Second is the value to be placed upon false confession and its role in conviction of the innocent, versus on failure to extract a confession from the guilty and the risk they will go free. We first consider the issue of the rate of false confession, and how assumptions regarding this base rate affect the false confessor from interrogation through post-conviction appeals.

## Part II: The Issue of Base Rates: Why Is It Important?

Medical students are commonly admonished to "Think horses, not zebras!" when attempting to diagnose a patient's illness. Such advice reflects the assumption that what is most commonly true is also most likely to be

9 *See* Leo, *supra* note 3; S.M. Kassin et al., *Police-Induced Confessions: Risk Factors and Recommendations*, 34(1) Law & Hum. Behav. 3, 8 (2010); B.L. Garrett, Convicting The Innocent: Where Criminal Prosecutions Go Wrong (2011) for reviews.

10 S. Drizin & R.A. Leo, *The Problem of False Confessions in the Post-DNA World*, 82 N.C. L. Rev. 891 (2004).

11 *See* A. Vrij, Detecting Lies and Deceit: Pitfalls and Opportunities (2008) for a review.

12 *See* Kassin et al., *supra* note 9, at 8–12 for review.

true in a particular instance: i.e., what is most commonly the cause of a patient's symptoms is more likely to be this patient's illness than any other candidate illness. The corollary, of course, is that if something is almost never true, it is also highly unlikely to be true in a particular instance. Or, if false confessions almost never happen, it is highly unlikely that this suspect falsely confessed. This reasoning is, in a nutshell, why the issue of the base rate at which false confessions occur (i.e., the percentage of all interrogation-induced confessions that are false) is so important, and why it is also so hotly debated.

Assumptions regarding base rates for the occurrence of false confession are vital to the reactions of the attorneys or judges who must present or decide motions to suppress an allegedly involuntary confession or to admit expert testimony on the topic (or specific parts of such testimony)—and those of jurors who must decide the ultimate issue of whether the confession was or was not true. Yet two problems arise: one entailing the accuracy and appropriateness of the specific presumed base rates; and the other regarding their relevance to the issue in question.

In the sections to come, we first discuss the issue of the base rate of false confession itself. We address the difficulties in establishing accurate base rates, and the nature and outcomes of previous attempts to do so. We then argue that the potential for interrogation-induced confession is often underestimated, in part because the focus is typically upon the overall rate of false confession among all interrogated rather than upon the appropriate base rate for the specific circumstances of the suspect, interrogation, and confession in question.

We then turn to the question of when base rates are or are not relevant for the issue at hand. While we agree that base rates are a relevant consideration for determination of the validity of a confession, and that they may be relevant (though less directly) for determination of the voluntariness of the confession, we suggest they are *not* likewise relevant for the issue of whether expert testimony on the existence and causes of false confession should or should not be admitted into evidence.

## Part III: Can We Establish Base Rates of Interrogation-Induced False Confessions?

One cannot disagree with the contention that knowing the base rate at which false confessions occur is relevant to the issue of whether a specific defendant falsely confessed. However, there is disagreement both on whether one can establish this base rate at all, and on what specific base rate is relevant (for example, must it be specific to the type of interrogation strategies deployed, the type of crime at issue, defendants' specific characteristics, etc.).

### *The Problem of Ground Truth (Actual Guilt or Innocence)*

The first point of contention regards the criteria for establishing base rates. Many interrogation scholars have argued that an overall base rate of interrogation-induced false confession cannot be reliably established, for several reasons. The most important (and the most difficult) of these is the necessity to know the ground truth of whether the confessor did or did not actually commit the crime. Definitive evidence is exceedingly rare, and therefore other criteria have been offered and dismissed as inadequate.

*Jury verdicts as ground truth?*
Some have suggested that jury verdicts, though imperfect, should be considered indices of ground truth. Indeed, some have claimed that it would be easy to establish such base rates via jury verdicts. Even if valid, however, jury verdicts would provide a base rate only for disputed confessions at trial. Moreover, jury verdicts are clearly unreliable tests of the validity of a confession, as indicated by a conviction rate of 73–81 percent of false confessors whose cases were tried by juries,[13] and by a variety of data suggesting widespread inability

13 R. Leo & R. Ofshe, *The Consequences of False Confessions: Deprivations of Liberty and Miscarriages of Justice in the Age of Psychological Interrogation*, 88 J. Crim. L. & Criminology 429, 483 (1998); See also Drizin & Leo, *supra* note 10, at 960.

among laypersons, legal professionals, and juries to recognize coercion or to distinguish between true and false confessions.[14]

The inability to distinguish true from false confessions is due to problems with both the availability and interpretation of evidence.[15] The confession itself may corrupt the truth-seeking process. It impacts the extent of police investigation of the crime, in that police tend to stop the investigation when a suspect confesses and may fail to search for other suspects or further investigate to verify or dispute the confession. Moreover, evidence necessary to understand the suspect's decision to confess may never be collected or presented to others. The physical and psychological state of the confessor is crucial, but may not be assessed, recorded, or presented to prosecutors, judges, or juries. The interrogation itself is often unrecorded, leaving only the written or recorded confession (or reports of the confession by law enforcement) as evidence.

If evidence is available, its implications may not be understood. Prosecutors, judges, and juries are not sufficiently (if at all) aware of such issues as what characteristics of the person or their condition at the time of interrogation matter and how; the nature of interrogation practices and how and why they can elicit false confessions; or how the content of confessions can be contaminated and shaped by the interrogator to appear as if the suspect must have committed the crime.[16]

Crucially, none are aware of the impact of the confession on how other evidence is perceived. Expectations of guilt created by a confession have been shown to impact the reports of forensic experts such as fingerprint[17] or polygraph examiners,[18] as well as witness reports such as eyewitness identification of the perpetrator.[19]

Jurors' own perceptions of the strength and meaning of all other evidence can likewise be altered by the fact of the confession.[20] Nor are attorneys exempt. Exonerating evidence, for example, is often dismissed as inadequate by prosecutors and others. Many defendants in proven cases of wrongful conviction were excluded by DNA, some even before trial, but were nevertheless prosecuted and convicted.[21] The DNA exclusions were reinterpreted to fit the presumption of guilt created by the false confession: for example, to suggest that the defendant did not personally rape a victim, but rather was present and conspired with the actual rapist. Similarly, inculpating evidence appears stronger when there has been a confession: a phenomenon referred to as "corroboration inflation."[22] Together, such findings clearly indicate that the fact of a defendant's confession alters perceptions of other evidence among the professionals who provide evidence to juries and among the jurors who must judge the confession in the context of that evidence.

Research has also demonstrated that neither law enforcement nor laypersons can distinguish true from false verbal confessions.[23] In part, this is due to a general reliance on incorrect verbal and nonverbal indicators of deception. Perhaps in greater part it is due to the content of the confessions themselves. If taken by a skilled interrogator, a confession is a very carefully constructed attempt to persuade, not an uncontaminated item of evidence.

---

14 *See* S.M Kassin, *Why Confessions Trump Innocence*, 67 Am. Psychol. 431, 436 (2012).

15 See D. Davis & R. Leo, *To Walk in their Shoes: The Problem of Missing, Misunderstood and Misinterpreted Context in Judging Criminal Confessions*, 46 New Eng. L. Rev. 4 (2012).

16 Blandon-Gitlin et al., *supra* note 7; D.E. Chojnacki, M.D. Cicchini & L.T. White, *An Empirical Basis for the Admission of Expert Testimony on False Confessions*, 40 Ari. St. L.J. 1 (2008). See Constanzo et al., *supra* note 7; L.A. Henkel, K.A.J Coffman & E.M. Dailey, *A Survey of People's Attitudes and Beliefs about False Confessions*, 26 Behav. Sci. & L. 584 (2008); Davis & Leo, *supra* note 15.

17 *See, e.g.*, I.E. Dror & D. Charlton, *Why Experts Make Errors*, 56 J. Forensic Ident. 600, 605–8 (2006).

18 *See, e.g.*, E. Elaad, A. Ginton & G. Ben-Shakhar, *The Effects of Prior Expectations and Outcome Knowledge on Polygraph Examiners' Decisions*, 7 J. Behav. Decision Making 279 (1994).

19 *See, e.g.*, L.E. Hasel & S.M. Kassin, *On the Presumption of Evidentiary Independence: Can Confessions Corrupt Eyewitness Identifications?* 20 Psychol. Sci. 122 (2009). *See* S.M. Kassin, I.E. Dror & J. Kukucka, *The Forensic Confirmation Bias: Problems, Perspectives, and Proposed Solutions*, 2 J. Applied Res. Memory Cognition 42 (2013) for review.

20 Hasel & Kassin, *supra*.

21 Center On Wrongful Convictions, Other Convictions in the Face of Exculpatory DNA (2010); K.A. Findley & M.S. Scott, *The Multiple Dimensions of Tunnel Vision in Criminal Cases*, 40 Wis. L. Rev. 14 (2006); Garrett, *supra* note 9; A. Martin, *The Prosecution's Case Against DNA.*, N.Y. Times, Nov. 27, 2011 (Magazine), at p. MM44.

22 *See* Kassin, *supra* note 14.

23 *See* Kassin et al., *supra* note 9; Kassin, *supra* note 14; Vrij, *supra* note 11 for reviews.

Interrogators attempt to ensure that the written or recorded confession presented to prosecutors, judges and juries includes elements that will appear as if the suspect would not (and could not) have included them if innocent: such as a detailed story of what happened and why, crime knowledge only the true perpetrator could have known; emotional expressions such as guilt and remorse; and explicit statements that the confession was given voluntarily.[24] In some cases, the suspect may have been led to reenact the crime on video. Unfortunately, a large number of proven false confessions have contained all such elements, including knowledge only the perpetrator should have had. But police can convey such knowledge to suspects through mechanisms such as showing them crime scene photos, telling them what other witnesses have said, contradicting suspects' accounts during the interrogation by contrasting them with known evidence, and others. Many a false confessor has been undone by the inclusion of such "misleading specialized knowledge"[25] in the confession. None, from prosecution through appeal, are likely to believe the confession to be false.

Such problems with interpretation of the confession and other evidence, among many others, impede recognition of false confessions when they occur.[26] As Kassin put it, sometimes "confessions trump innocence."[27] They affect judgments by all who know of them, and affect the defendant's outcomes from investigation through post-conviction appeal. Police tend to drop the investigation, leaving potentially exonerating evidence unexplored. The defendant is inevitably charged with the crime, and even defense attorneys tend to disbelieve their clients' retractions and claims of innocence—often encouraging them to plead guilty rather than face almost certain conviction at trial. Analysis of Innocence Project data, for example, showed that exonerees who had falsely confessed were four times as likely to have pled guilty compared to others who had not.[28]

Confessions tend to have greater impact on jury verdicts than other powerful forms of evidence, even if there is reason to discount their validity: such as when the confession is elicited via a coercive interrogation; from a person with psychological illness or severe interrogation-induced stress; or from an informant given an incentive to implicate the defendant. Even judges fail to discount coerced confessions, and thus it is not surprising that few are suppressed as involuntary before trial; nor are many coercive interrogations viewed as sufficient to reverse convictions upon appeal.[29] Clearly, jury verdicts, and even appellate decisions, cannot be regarded as reliable indices of ground truth.

### *Other Indices of Ground Truth are Inconsistently Available*

Though jury verdicts are multiply flawed as indices of ground truth, they are at least consistently available for confessions disputed at trial. In other circumstances there is no clearly imaginable index consistently available. The thoroughness of investigation as well as the forms of evidence available between cases varies widely, making reliable assessments of ground truth unavailable. Moreover, police agencies do not keep records of the number of interrogations, the frequency of confession, or the portion deemed false. Rarely is definitive evidence available. No method has yet been identified for objective determination of ground truth in all cases.

### *Self-Reported False Confessions*

A different source of estimates of the base rate of false confessions has been surveys in which participants are asked whether they had ever been interrogated by police, and, if so, whether they had ever offered true or false confessions. Gudjonsson et al., for example, reported rates of false confession across seven European countries of 13.8 percent overall: ranging from as low as 10.6 percent in Lithuania to as high as 19 percent in

---

24 *See* Leo, *supra* note 3.

25 *Id.*

26 *See* D. Davis & R. Leo, *Interrogation-Regulatory Decline: Ego Depletion, Failures of Self-Regulation and the Decision to Confess*, 18 *Psych., Pub. Pol'y & Law* 673 (2012); Kassin, *supra* note 14 for reviews.

27 *See* Kassin, *supra* note 14.

28 A.D Redlich, *False Confessions and False Guilty Pleas: Similarities and Differences, in* Interrogations and Confessions: Current Research, Practice, and Policy (G.D. Lassiter & C. Meissner eds., 2010).

29 *See* Davis & Leo, *supra* note 8; Davis & Leo, *supra* note 15; Kassin, *supra* note 14; Leo, *supra* note 3.

Russia.[30] Gudjonsson and his colleagues have conducted a number of other such studies in Europe, identifying a number of personal characteristics associated with the rate of reported false confession.[31] Moreover, Redlich and colleagues have conducted such a survey in the United States, focusing only on the mentally ill.[32] They obtained rates of false confession ranging across states from 9 to 28 percent and of false guilty pleas from 27 to 41 percent. Ignoring the methodological maxim that self-reported data cannot be assumed to be trustworthy, the fact remains that the survey populations in both Europe and America are not representative. Interrogation procedures among European nations are—by design—dissimilar from their American counterparts. Those in many jurisdictions have been reformed to avoid aspects of the Reid Method most strongly implicated in elicitation of false confessions, and therefore surveys of their populations are arguably likely to underestimate the rate of false confessions in America.[33] Nor are rates among the mentally ill likely to be representative of the general American population of interrogated suspects.

### *The Problem of Multiple Base Rates*

Even if the problem of ground truth could be solved, an overall base rate would not be relevant to a specific case. An overall rate of false confession cannot predict the rate for particular circumstances of interrogation for special categories of vulnerable individuals, such as the young or the retarded, those interrogated in a specific jurisdiction or by a specific interrogator, or among particular populations—such as those who dispute the validity of their confessions. Nor can an overall base rate be applied to a case entailing a specific combination of such factors.

Scientific studies of interrogation have revealed associations between personal characteristics, features of the interrogation, and the likelihood of false confession. These include personal characteristics such as youth, mental defects such as retardation or mental illness, personality characteristics associated with suggestibility, a history of difficult life experiences, and others.[34] Similarly, a number of interrogation tactics taught by Reid Associates and others have been shown to increase the rate of both true and false confession, as have excessively long length and other features associated with discomfort.[35]

Even innocence itself has been shown to pose some risk, in part due to misperception of the risks of interrogation, and hence greater willingness to submit to questioning, trust in law enforcement, and willingness to cooperate with police requests. Moreover, innocents often see less risk in falsely confessing, believing that they will soon be proven innocent by further investigation.[36] Considering that a given case of alleged false confession entails an amalgam of the aforementioned factors, to estimate the likelihood that a given confession is false would require knowledge of (a) the base rate of false confession among each class of suspects and circumstances; and (b) how those factors tend to affect (interact with) one another: data that is clearly unavailable and unobtainable with presently conceived methods.

---

30 G.H. Gudjonsson, J.F. Sigurdsson & I.D. Sigfusdottir, *Interrogation and False Confessions among Adolescents in Seven European Countries: What Background and Psychological Variables Best Discriminate Between False Confessors and Non-False Confessors?* 15 Psychol., Crime & Law 711 (2009).

31 *Id.*

32 A.D. Redlich, A. Summers & S. Hoover, *Self-Reported False Confessions and False Guilty Pleas among Offenders with Mental Illness*, 34 Law & Hum. Behav. 79 (2010).

33 R. Bull & S. Soukara, *Four Studies of What Really Happens in Police Interviews*, *in* Police Interrogations and False Confessions: Current Research, Practice, and Policy Recommendations 81–95 (G.D. Lassiter & C.A. Meissner, eds., 2010).

34 *See* G.H. Gudjonsson, The Psychology of Interrogations and Confessions: A Handbook (2003); G.H. Gudjonsson, *The Psychology of False Confessions: A Review of the Current Evidence*, *in* Lassiter & Meissner (2010), *supra*; Kassin et al., *supra* note 9; J. Owen-Kostelnik, N. Reppucci & J. Meyer, *Testimony and Interrogation of Minors: Assumptions about Maturity and Morality,* 61 Am. Psychol. 286 (2006); A.D. Redlich, R. Kulish & H.J Steadman, *Comparing True and False Confessions among Persons with Serious Mental Illness,* 17 Psychol. Pub. Pol'y & L. 394 (2011); G.H. Gudjonsson et al., *False Confessions to Police and their Relationship with Conduct Disorder, ADHD, and Life Adversity*, 52(6) Personality & Ind. Diff. 696 (2012) for reviews.

35 *See* Leo, *supra* note 3; *See* Kassin et al., *supra* note 9; Davis & Leo, *supra* note 15.

36 *See* Kassin, *supra* note 14; J.T. Perillo & S.M. Kassin, *Inside Interrogation: The Lie, the Bluff, and False Confessions*, 35 Law & Hum. Behav. 327 (2011).

**Part IV: Are False Confessions Much More Common than Assumed?**

There are (at least) eight reasons why false confessions are likely more common than might be assumed.

*1. Interrogators Interrogate More Innocent Suspects Than Claimed*

The debate about the base rate of false confessions necessarily focuses upon populations of those who are interrogated. The most fundamental way to ensure a low base rate of false confessions would be for law enforcement agencies to interrogate only guilty suspects. Indeed, a co-author of the predominant Inbau et al. interrogation manual[37] has claimed that "we don't interrogate innocent people."[38] For law enforcement agencies to make good on that promise would require them to have 100 percent accuracy in their a priori knowledge of suspects' guilt.[39] Unfortunately, such accuracy is not only unrealistic, but also is not supported by the empirical literature.[40] Considering that law enforcement personnel cannot be certain of suspects' guilt prior to interrogation, by default some innocent suspects are interrogated. In other words, if there is no compelling evidence against a given suspect prior to her/his interrogation (other than stereotypes about who commits certain crimes, etc.) the potential for a false confession is much higher than if compelling evidence is available.

*2. Innocents Are More Likely to Submit to Interrogation*

That police inadvertently interrogate the innocent is made worse by the second reason why false confessions are likely to be more common than might be assumed: that the innocent are less likely than the guilty to protect themselves by invoking their Miranda rights.[41] Those who resist confessing by invoking Miranda are more likely to have had experience with the legal system (i.e., to have been questioned regarding, and/or convicted of, previous crimes). Therefore, the guilty who choose to remain silent cannot falsely confess. In contrast, innocent people are at risk due, in part, to their willingness to be interrogated. Furthermore, there have been cases where innocent suspects have falsely confessed to crimes based upon their naïve assumptions that evidence will exculpate them.[42] Upon realization that evidence will not necessarily exculpate them, it is logical for such false confessors to retract their confessions. Of course, this suggests the base rate of false confessions will likely be higher among cases where defendants have retracted their confessions.

*3. The Rising Tide of DNA Exonerations*

Exonerations continue to escalate in cases involving DNA evidence, but—obviously—such exonerations can only occur in cases for which DNA evidence is available. Considering that such evidence is available only in select cases, those exonerations represent only a portion of the prevalence of false confessions.

*4. Plea Bargains by Innocents Should be Considered False Confessions*

Considering the cost of going to trial, and/or the likelihood of being convicted due to confession evidence, defendants often accept plea bargains.[43] Approximately 95 percent of all convictions are settled by plea bargains.[44] Therefore, cases that go to trial represent only a small portion of total cases in which false confessions are alleged. In other words, interrogations induce false confessions at a given rate, but only some

---

37 F.E. Inbau et al., Criminal Interrogation and Confessions (4th ed., 2001); Inbau et al., *supra* note 5.

38 S.M. Kassin & G.H. Gudjonsson, *The Psychology of Confession Evidence: A Review of the Literature and Issues*, 5 Psychol. Sci. in the Pub. Int. 35, 36 (2004).

39 *See* Gudjonsson (2010), *supra* note 34.

40 *See* Vrij, *supra* note 11 for review.

41 *See* Kassin, *supra* note 14, at 434.

42 Kassin, *supra* note 14.

43 *See* Redlich, *supra* note 28.

44 *Id.*

of those are retracted, and fewer still refuse plea bargains and persist to trial. That distillation process strongly suggests (or virtually ensures) that the base rate of false confessions among trial cases is higher than for those resolved without trial.

### *5. False Confession is Not Necessarily Irrational: The Power of Interrogation Strategies to Persuade*

More than 100 years of social science evidence attests to the power of influence techniques used in contemporary American interrogations to induce individuals to comply with requests.[45] The unfounded assumption that false confession base rates are low relies, in part, on the perceptions that false confession is an extreme act against one's self-interest; and that such self-betrayal is recognized by the false confessor prior to the confession. However, interrogation consists of a large armament of scientifically tested and supported influence strategies applied to convince suspects that confession is affirmatively in their best long-term interests.[46] Given that interrogation tactics are inherently deceptive—suspects are faced with (a) making a decision based upon false information that was (b) presented by an authority figure, who is (c) in a better position than they to know the consequences of their refusal to confess, and who (d) maintains that he is trying to help the suspect—the decision to confess can appear to the accused to be a rational choice.

A variety of evidence from reports of confessors (both true and false) has shown that many believe that they will be let go without consequences once they confess.[47] Others can also recognize and be persuaded by the implied messages of the interrogation that confession is best. Our own research has shown that after exposure to only five–seven pages of transcribed interrogations incorporating common techniques many observers recommend false confession as the best option for an innocent suspect (compared to refusing to talk further or talking but continuing to deny culpability). Depending upon the nature of the criminal charges and interrogation tactics, from 16 percent to over 70 percent recommend that false confession is the best way for the innocent suspect to avoid being charged with a crime at all, being convicted if charged, or to get the least serious charges.[48]

Essentially, interrogation conducted as American trainers and manuals recommend is a masterful con job that misleads the suspect with respect to the motives and feelings of the interrogator, the nature of the evidence against the suspect, the options available to the suspect, and the implications of confession versus denial. The principles of influence are the same as those employed by influence professionals of all stripes, and work very effectively to persuade: in this case to trick the suspect into thinking the worst thing he can do is actually the best.

### *6. Stereotype Threat and Vulnerability*

Some categories of people are more vulnerable to the interrogator's trickery than one would expect. Most can readily believe that the mentally ill or retarded, children and teenagers, or those severely mentally or physically distressed can be more susceptible to interrogative influence—though the vulnerability of such persons is often underestimated by judges and juries. But other groups can be more vulnerable due to different mechanisms.

Interrogation strategies create the impression that confession is best through a largely two-pronged strategy. First, the suspect is to be persuaded that he cannot successfully convince either his interrogators or prosecutors, or judges and juries that he is innocent. This is done largely through stating with conviction

---

45 D. Davis, *Selling Confession, the Interrogator, the Con Man, and their Weapons of Influence*, 16(1) Wis. Defender 1 (2008); D. Davis, *Lies, Damned Lies, and the Path from Police Interrogation to Wrongful Conviction*, in The Scientist and the Humanist: A Festschrift in Honor of Elliot Aronson (M.H. Gonzales, C. Tavris & J. Aronson, eds., 2010); D. Davis & W.T. O'Donohue, *The Road to Perdition: "Extreme Influence" Tactics in the Interrogation Room*, in Handbook of Forensic Psychology (W.T. O'Donohue & E. Levensky, eds., 2004).

46 *See* Davis 2008, 2010, *supra* note 45; Davis & O'Donohue, *supra* note 45 for reviews.

47 *See* Kassin et al., *supra* note 9.

48 D. Davis, R.A. Leo & W.C. Follette, *Selling Confession: Setting the Stage with the "Sympathetic Detective" with a Time-Limited Offer*, 26 J. Contemp. Crim. Just. 441 (2010); J.G. Villalobos, M.J. Williams & D. Davis, *Self-Regulation and the Perceived Wisdom of a False Confession to Murder*, Soc'y for Personality & Soc. Psychol. (Jan. 2013).

that the evidence clearly indicates the suspect is guilty, and then confronting him with some of that evidence: whether actual evidence or false claims of evidence against him. Once this sense of hopelessness is established, a variety of further tactics are deployed to convince the suspect that confession is the best remaining option to minimize the consequences of being firmly implicated as the perpetrator.[49]

Indeed, Mario Mathews experienced just such a process. The detective repeatedly claimed to have evidence against him—some of it clearly false. He told Mathews:

> It was you. All the physical evidence I've read, or all the physical evidence I sent to the crime lab, comes back to you. And when I showed her the picture, she said "That's the person." You kind of stand out. "That's the person right there." "Are you positive?" "That's him. That's who did all that stuff to me, multiple times." That's why I went to the judge ... Good enough for me ... .

These claims were clearly sufficient to induce hopelessness in Mathews, who responded, "So, I don't have no way ... I don't have no way!"[50]

Some groups of suspects—such as Mathews—are particularly vulnerable to both prongs of this approach, simply because they realize that their personal characteristics are stereotypically associated with commission of the class of crime in question. They are more likely to assume others will believe them guilty because of who they are, and therefore become hopeless more easily. And, because the increased anxiety and worry caused by awareness of this "stereotype threat"[51] leads them to experience increased cognitive load, they are less able to critically analyze what interrogators are telling them, to remember information that would suggest confession is unwise, and to think clearly; and therefore they are more susceptible to the tactics designed to convince them confession is wise.[52]

Those susceptible to this process include such suspects as minority persons accused of violent crime, stepfathers, foster parents, priests, or homosexual men accused of child sexual abuse, prior offenders, and others. It is our belief, for example, that there are many false confessors who, like Mario Mathews, falsely confess to child sexual abuse or other offenses where a seemingly credible witness is the only evidence because they are firmly convinced they will not be believed, and there is no available evidence to effectively counter the witness. They are likely to do so in interrogations far less seemingly coercive or powerful than those intuition would suggest are necessary to induce a false confession—or may take a plea bargain whether they did or did not falsely confess—simply because they are already convinced before they enter the interrogation or courtroom that no one is going to believe them.

Our research has shown, for example, that 26–77 percent of observers recommend false confession for an innocent child abuse suspect for the purposes of minimizing the likelihood of being charged at all, being convicted, or to minimize the seriousness of charges if any are filed. In explaining their choices, participants predominantly stated that no one would believe he didn't do it, given the little girl's claims, and that it was better to tell a seemingly less culpable story than to just be thought a liar.[53] It is difficult to know how many such false confessors are serving time for crimes they didn't commit. They will not be exonerated like those for whom DNA or other evidence can eventually be found. And, as with Mario Mathews, their false confessions will go unnoticed and unrecognized, even if challenged, precisely because they can neither produce exonerating evidence nor convince others that the interrogation was sufficiently coercive to induce a false confession.

---

49 *See* Davis 2010, *supra* note 45 for review.

50 Interrogation transcript 72–3 (interview by Detective Cunningham with Mario Mathews, 3/22/07, Case 930607346 Rialto, CA Police Dep't).

51 C. Steele, Whistling Vivaldi: How Stereotypes Affect Us and What We Can Do (2011).

52 *See* Davis & Leo, *supra* note 26; Villalobos et al., *supra* note 48.

53 *See* Davis et al., *supra* note 48.

### *7. Cultural Sources of Vulnerability*

A related issue concerns vulnerability to interrogation tactics resulting from cultural differences. Such cultural vulnerabilities derive from three considerations. First, cultural differences exist in due process rights, and suspects' understanding and/or belief of what they are told in interrogation may be affected by expectations based on their culture of origin. Second, perceived consequences of failure to comply with police demands can be affected by culture of origin-based expectations and/or by perceived personal vulnerabilities such as immigration status. The person may falsely confess to avoid feared consequences of noncompliance. Finally, language barriers can compromise understanding, enhance anxiety, and impose increased cognitive load on the suspect, rendering him more vulnerable to stress-induced false confession as well as false confession resulting from misunderstanding of the consequences.[54] Immigrants and minority groups for whom English is a second language are interrogated frequently, and therefore may enhance the base rate of false confession.

### *8. The Power of Distress to Provoke Confession*

A common theme among those subjected to the pressure cooker of the interrogation room is that they confessed merely to escape an intolerable situation. The phenomenon of "temporal discounting" long established in the broader psychological literature refers to the tendency to react more strongly to immediate rewards and punishments than to those anticipated in the future.[55] Even though a suspect may recognize probable negative outcomes of confession, he may be unable to endure further interrogation. If he fails to recognize that he can terminate the interrogation through invoking his right to remain silent, confession may be seen as the only way to get away.

Most recognize that this process may occur. But there exists significant misunderstanding of both the multiple effects of distress that can create vulnerability to confession and the degree of distress necessary to trigger such effects. Davis and Leo[56] coined the term "Interrogation-Related Regulatory Decline" to refer to the decline in self-regulatory functions resulting from multiple forces surrounding and during interrogation. The person's ability to control impulses (such as the impulse to escape the interrogation), emotions, and thinking can be impaired during interrogation because of stressors prior to interrogation (such as distress surrounding the crime, fatigue, sleep-deprivation, drug use or withdrawal, and others) or during it (such as escalating fatigue, emotions such as fear and embarrassment, aversive interrogation tactics, glucose depletion, and many others).[57]

Though research has shown that control of impulses and emotion as well as of rational thinking and decision making can be impaired by very brief and seemingly mild prior efforts or stressors, judges and jurors have shown a tendency to severely underestimate the impact of stress on behavior in interrogation. Judges have ruled many known false confessions taken in highly stressful and lengthy interrogations as voluntary, and juries have convicted the defendants—even though the interrogations may have lasted for many hours (or even across days), and even though the suspect may have been impaired by alcohol, sleep deprivation, and other physical stressors. Such reactions reflect inaccurate assumptions that a person should be able to resist falsely confessing almost notwithstanding the level of his distress, and that if he does not, the confession must be both voluntary and true.

Two considerations suggest that stress-induced false confession is more common than might be expected. First is the body of literature on self-regulation failure showing that stressors that would not be given a second thought by judges and juries considering the issue of false confession have led to significant declines in impulse control, emotion regulation, and rational thinking.[58] Second is the fact that there are strong individual

---

54 S. Berk-Seligson, Coerced Confessions: The Discourse of Bilingual Police Interrogations (Language, Power, and Social Process) (2009).

55 S. Madon et al., *Temporal Discounting: The Differential Effect of Proximal and Distal Consequences on Confession Decisions*, 36 Law & Hum. Behav. 13 (2012).

56 Davis & Leo, *supra* note 15.

57 *See id.* for review.

58 *See id.*

differences in distress intolerance, such that some people will find lower levels of distress sufficient to lead them to confess just to escape the circumstances of the interrogation.[59]

## Part V: Valuation of Type I And II Errors: Implications for Estimation of and Reactions to Base Rates

Given the myriad problems with establishing agreed-upon estimates of relevant rates of false confession, this issue has devolved into an unresolved persistent conflict of assumptions between those aligned with defense versus prosecution. Among prosecutors and law enforcement (who clearly place greater value on eliciting confessions from the guilty, compared to protecting against false confessions from the innocent), widespread claims of low base rates have provided apparent justification for (a) discounting claims of false or coerced confession; (b) disallowing expert testimony on the topic; and/or (c) resisting calls for reform of interrogation practices. Defense attorneys and others placing relatively greater value on avoidance of false confessions and wrongful imprisonment have, instead, widely claimed higher rates of false confession in support of the opposite.

### *Involuntary or False Confession and the Role of Expert Testimony*

Those of us who testify or offer Continuing Legal Education seminars on the topic of interrogation-induced false confessions are almost universally confronted with the issue of how often such (presumably) rare events occur. In our own experience, this issue is almost universally raised by prosecutors upon cross-examination, either in trial, in pre-trial suppression hearings, or in hearings to determine the admissibility of expert testimony on false confessions—and in the proffered prosecution and defense motions and subsequent judicial rulings. The prosecutor may be targeting several purposes by raising the issue. (S)he may be attempting to convince the jury that the defendant's claim of false confession is implausible, both directly and by undermining the significance of the expert testimony on the existence and causes of false confession. (S)he may be attempting to undermine claims of involuntary confession by arguing that because false confessions are exceedingly rare the normal person clearly has sufficient capacity to resist interrogation, thereby also rendering involuntary confessions exceedingly rare. Or, (s)he may attempt to prevent the admission of expert testimony on false confession by claiming that because false confessions are so rare, expert testimony will be a waste of time, prejudicial, and not probative.

Finally, (s)he may attempt to limit the scope of expert testimony, if it is admitted. In this regard, even *misunderstanding* of base rates can be important. For example, to support claims of the reality of false confession in criminal cases (versus laboratory studies), experts on interrogation-induced false confession often cite studies of wrongful conviction showing that for 14 percent to over 60 percent of these cases false confessions or false guilty pleas were implicated as causes of the wrongful conviction.[60] Prosecutors often object to such data, mischaracterizing it as suggesting that the base rate of false confession is what is being presented. In other words, the prosecution mischaracterizes a statistic that represents the percent of wrongful convictions in which false confessions were presented as evidence as a claim regarding the base rate of false confession (among all those interrogated or tried for a crime).

Such misinterpretation is not infrequently the basis of a judicial ruling to exclude mention of studies of wrongful conviction on the grounds that it is inappropriately suggesting to the jury that the likelihood that the person in question falsely confessed or was misidentified is as high as 14–60 percent. Such misunderstandings often persist despite detailed explanations of the difference between the statistics among those wrongfully convicted and base rate statistics among the population of all confessions.

We suggest that use of base rate arguments for any of the above purposes is inappropriate and misleading. While it is true that in order to evaluate a specific claim of false confessions it is important to know if such phenomena are one-in-a-million occurrences or if they are relatively commonplace, the inability to establish

59 W.C. Follette, D. Davis & R.A. Leo, *Mental Health Status and Vulnerability to Interrogative Influence*, 22(3) Crim. Just. 42 (2007).

60 *See* Kassin et al., *supra* note 9 and Leo, *supra* note 3 for reviews.

a relevant base rate should not be reason to discount claims of false confession or to exclude expert testimony to explain the conditions under which they are more likely to occur.

*Relevance and the Issue of Multiple Base Rates*

All concerned would agree that there is no one base rate of false confession, as discussed earlier. This multiple base rate assumption is the basis, for example, for suppression rulings in which the judge determines whether to admit a confession into evidence or exclude it. If taken from a sufficiently vulnerable individual or via sufficiently coercive strategies and circumstances, the confession would be excluded precisely because the risk of false confession would be deemed unacceptably high *in those circumstances.* Strikingly, it appears more common that expert testimony is allowed for suppression hearings than for trial (particularly in some jurisdictions): though, in both cases, the issues of the vulnerability of the individual and the forces of influence in the interrogation are at issue.

This divergence in admissibility of experts for suppression hearings versus trial may reflect two distinct base rate assumptions. First, the judiciary may, as a whole, view the potential for undue coercion and *involuntary* confession as much higher than that for *false* confession. If police interrogate innocent and guilty persons similarly, *and* many more of those interrogated are guilty than innocent, it would certainly be true that the potential for coerced involuntary confessions is higher than that of false confessions.

Second, it may reflect assumptions among the judiciary that whereas the base rate of false confession among those high in vulnerability (such as the young, mentally ill, or mentally deficient) may be significant, it is vanishingly small among mentally able adults. This seems likely, in that while expert testimony regarding both the suspect's vulnerabilities *and* characteristics of the interrogation itself are commonly admitted in suppression hearings, it is often the case that only expert testimony regarding suspect vulnerabilities is admitted at trial.[61] Strangely, while the view that base rates of false confession are higher among vulnerable individuals is pervasive, prosecutors and some judges are much more reluctant to consider the multiple base rates applicable to interrogations of varying characteristics.

*Should Experts Testify About Rare Phenomena?*

The underlying commonality to arguments to exclude expert testimony based on the presumed rarity of false confessions is the notion that experts should not testify about the existence and causes of rare phenomena.

Assuming for the moment that false confessions are rare, that assertion does not negate—but instead reinforces—the notion that they indeed occur. Similarly, rare events happen daily: individuals win jackpots; they are afflicted with rare diseases (e.g., Huntington's, mesothelioma); and they commit rare crimes such as cannibalism. Rarity is not synonymous with implausibility. Consider that the odds of an American home getting damaged by fire in a given year are 1 in 309,[62] a base rate much lower than the roughly 5 percent police estimate as the percent of confessions they take that are false.[63] Yet, virtually every single American homeowner carries insurance against such a rare calamity. Among the millions of American homes there are many fires each year, though the percent of all homes experiencing fires is very low. Should the homeowner be unable to buy fire insurance because fire is rare? Similarly, should defendants be deprived of a comprehensive defense even if false confessions are rare?

Expert testimony may also offer benefit to the broader justice system in addition to that to the individual defendant. In addition to affording adequate defense for alleged false confessors, judicial decisions to include expert testimony regarding false confessions may have the ancillary benefit of enhancing the effectiveness of policing. That is, if expert testimony on false confessions is more readily admitted in court, it will include

61 There are other reasons for such differences in admission of expert testimony: such as the view that the existence and causes of false confession are within the common knowledge of the jury, or exclusion based on perceived inadequacy of the science underlying the testimony; *see* Watson et al., *supra* note 8.

62 M. Ahrens (2011), *Home Structure Fires*. National Fire Protection Association: Quincy, MA., *available at* http://saferinsulation.greensciencepolicy.org/wp-content/uploads/2012/12/Home-structure-fires-NFPA.pdf.

63 Kassin et al., *supra* note 9.

coverage of the role of common police interrogation techniques in producing false confessions. Arguably, this exposure might motivate law enforcement agencies to be all the more likely to enact reforms to prevent false confessions. To that end, judicial understanding of the likelihood of false confessions—and their subsequent allowance of expert testimony on that topic—will advance the laudable, ethical mission that is the bedrock of both law enforcement and the judiciary: to hold responsible the guilty, and to exculpate the innocent.

## Part VI: Base Rates and the Issue of Interrogation Reform

All would agree that false confessions among innocent suspects are counterproductive. They terminate investigations that might otherwise locate the guilty party. They give the guilty party the opportunity to commit other crimes. They lead to terrible outcomes—in some cases even death—for the false confessor. And, they waste public resources through investigation, prosecution, and incarceration of the false confessor. Clearly it is to the benefit of all to prevent them.

Attraction to and pursuit of this clear benefit may be dimmed, however, by the prospect that interrogation reforms likely to reduce the incidence of false confession would also reduce that of true confessions. Particularly if one assumes that false confession is a very rare phenomenon, this price may seem too steep. Adding to this source of resistance is the heavy investment of interrogation training organizations in their methods. Reid Associates and Wicklander-Zulawski have together arguably directly or indirectly (via their trainees training others in their organizations) trained most American law enforcement (and even corporate) interrogators. Their insistent public claims regarding the effectiveness of their methods in avoiding interrogating innocent suspects altogether, while extracting true confessions from the guilty, have widely enhanced confidence among law enforcement personnel, and indirectly among the judiciary, that false confessions are extremely unlikely—and, in addition, have made any admission that the methods are in any way flawed very difficult.

Research has clearly indicated, however, that these claims are only partially true. The methods are effective at eliciting confessions. But the methods for detecting deception and selecting only the guilty for interrogation are pseudoscientific and inaccurate. Thus, innocents are, indeed, interrogated and put at risk.[64] Moreover, this risk is unnecessarily high.

It is not the case that one must sacrifice true confessions to reduce the rate of false confession. Reforms in some Canadian jurisdictions and in England and other parts of Europe, for example, have eliminated some practices posing risks for false confession while maintaining the rate at which confessions are obtained.[65] While these reforms have entailed shifting from emphasis on interrogation (to obtain a confession) to emphasis on "investigative interviewing" (to acquire full and accurate information), many have argued that significant reduction in the rate of false confession can be achieved even with modifications within Reid-like methods.[66] In particular, by limiting the allowable length of interrogation, forbidding presentation of false evidence against the suspect (e.g., false claims to have eyewitnesses, fingerprints, DNA, or other evidence), eliminating the communication of implied incentives for confession or threats regarding consequences of denial, and by enacting protections for the vulnerable the rate of false confession can be decreased[67]—though no field data currently exists to show that the rate of true confessions can remain unaffected.

---

64 D. Davis & R.A. Leo, *The Problem of Police-Induced False Confession: Sources of Failure in Prevention and Detection*, *in* Handbook of Forensic Sociology and Psychology (S. Morewitz & M. L. Goldstein eds.,2014); *see also* Kassin et al., *supra* note 9; Leo, *supra* note 3; Vrij, *supra* note 11.

65 R. Bull, T. Valentine & T. Williamson, Handbook of Psychology of Investigative Interviewing: Current Developments and Future Directions (2009). *See* Kassin et al., *supra* note 9; T. Williamson, B. Milne & S.P. Savage, International Developments in Investigative Interviewing (2009).

66 *See* Kassin et al., *supra* note 9 for review.

67 *Id.*

**Part VII: Conclusions**

Whether rare or common, interrogation-induced false confessions indisputably do occur in startling numbers. However, the issues of whether the phenomenon is indeed relatively rare or common and of how to address interrogation and confession in law enforcement and the courts remain controversial in America. Persistent belief in the rarity of interrogation-induced false confession appears to fuel resistance to interrogation reforms and to introduction of expert testimony on false confession in American courts.

Interrogation scholars are amassing a steadily increasing body of laboratory research and documented cases of false confession to lend support to claims that false confessions occur more frequently than commonly assumed, and to identify interrogation techniques that increase the rate at which false confessions are elicited. This body of scholarship has led interrogators to soften their claims somewhat, and to recommend some changes in their strategies. The latest edition of the prominent Inbau et al. interrogation manual,[68] for example, has included greater discussion of the possibility of false confession, as well as a few new recommendations targeted toward minimizing this risk. No real overhaul of core techniques involved in the communication of incentives for confession has yet been attempted, however. Until this occurs, the risk of interrogation-induced false confession will remain relatively unchanged.

---

68 *See* Inbau et al. (2013), *supra* note 37.

# Chapter 5
# Innocence and the Suppression of Exculpatory Evidence by Prosecutors

Lissa Griffin

## Introduction

In its 1963 decision in *Brady v. Maryland*,[1] the United States Supreme Court held that the prosecution has an obligation, under the United States Constitution's Fifth and Fourteenth Amendment Due Process clauses, to provide favorable evidence to the defense, on request, when that evidence is material to guilt or punishment. At the time, *Brady* was heralded as a landmark decision that would even the playing field between prosecution and defense and bring previously undisclosed evidence into the light of the adjudication process. Unfortunately, this promise has not been fulfilled. Prosecutorial suppression of exculpatory evidence has emerged as one of the leading causes of wrongful convictions.[2] The kind of information that frequently results in wrongful convictions—prior misidentifications or identifications of others,[3] leniency deals with witnesses,[4] or faulty forensic science[5]—is often suppressed pretrial and only later discovered—usually serendipitously—after conviction. DNA exonerations of convicted defendants often show that evidence of the identity of the real perpetrator was available to police from the beginning but was never disclosed.[6] Still, innocent defendants continue to be convicted due, in large part, to flaws in *Brady*: when non-disclosure comes to light post-conviction, the courts most often uphold the conviction on the ground that disclosure would not have changed the result of the trial.[7] And, although the United States Supreme Court has charged prosecutors with the consequences of non-disclosure by investigatory agencies like the police,[8] there is still no reliable mechanism for even good faith prosecutors to make sure the police disclose exculpatory evidence to them.[9] Finally, *Brady* has only limited application in the vast majority of American criminal prosecutions—those that result in a guilty plea; and, even where it applies in the trial context, the *Brady* obligation can be easily evaded by prosecutors.

---

1 Brady v. Maryland, 373 U.S. 83, 87 (1963).

2 *See* Bennett L. Gershman, Prosecutorial Misconduct (2d ed., 2007).

3 For a detailed analysis of the relationship between mistaken identification and wrongful convictions see Jules Epstein, Chapter 3, this volume. *See also, Eyewitness Misidentification*, Innocence Project, http://www.innocenceproject.org/understand/Eyewitness-Misidentification.php (last visited Aug., 11 2013) ("Eyewitness misidentification is the single greatest cause of wrongful convictions nationwide, playing a role in nearly 75% of convictions overturned through DNA testing.").

4 *See Informants*, Innocence Project, http://www.innocenceproject.org/understand/Snitches-Informants.php (last visited Aug., 11 2013) ("In more than 15% of wrongful conviction cases overturned through DNA testing, an informant testified against the defendant at the original trial."). *See also* United States v. Bagley, 473 U.S. 667 (1985) ("the possibility of a reward, the size of which is directly related to the Government's success at trial, gave the two witnesses a 'personal stake' in the conviction and an 'incentive['] to testify falsely in order to secure a conviction").

5 *See Government Misconduct*, Innocence Project, http://www.innocenceproject.org/understand/Government-Misconduct.php (last visited Aug., 11, 2013); James S. Liebman et al., *Capital Attrition: Error Rates in Capital Cases, 1973–1995*, 78 Tex. L. Rev. 1839 (2000).

6 *See, e.g.*, Banks v. Reynolds, 54 F.3d 1508 (10th Cir. 1995) (prosecutor failed to disclose that another person had been arrested for the murder as well as eyewitness identification of that other suspect); Bloodsworth v. State, 307 Md. 164 (1986) (ordering a new trial when the prosecution failed to disclose a detective's statement indicating another suspect).

7 *See, e.g.*, Strickler v. Green, 527 U.S. 263 (1999).

8 Kyles v. Whitley, 514 U.S. 419, 437 (1995).

9 See Symposium, *New Perspectives on Brady and Other Disclosure Obligations: Report of the Working Groups on Best Practices*, 31 Cardozo L. Rev. 1962, 2023 (2010).

Yet the steady stream of exonerations and the study of the causes of wrongful convictions has had an impact. Awareness of the major role the prosecutor plays in causing the wrongful conviction of innocent people by withholding exculpatory evidence has led to scholarly and professional efforts that are focusing on changing and formalizing the prosecutor's *Brady* obligations. Recent proposals would reform *Brady* by formalizing it in court rules and checklists—like those used in the UK—that would make the prosecutor's obligations clearer, more transparent, less discretionary and more realistic, and therefore easier to implement and enforce both between prosecutors and police and the prosecution and the defense.

Part I of this chapter discusses the scope of the prosecutor's duty to disclose exculpatory evidence to the defense from the constitutional, common law *Brady* doctrine to legislative and judicial requirements. Part II analyzes the cases involving *Brady* and innocence. It is divided according to the forms of unreliable proof the suppression of which have been shown repeatedly to result in erroneous convictions: faulty eyewitness identification, third-party guilt, misleading or false forensic evidence, false confessions, and unreliable government "snitches." It concludes with a discussion of a recent, high-profile non-disclosure case—the prosecution of US Senator Ted Stevens. Part III surveys and evaluates recent reform efforts. Part IV concludes that the common law development of the *Brady* doctrine has not provided meaningful protection for the innocent, but that recent reform efforts may lead to fewer wrongful convictions resulting from the suppression of evidence of innocence.

## Part I: The Obligation to Disclose

### *Common Law: The Brady Doctrine*

In *Brady v. Maryland*, the United States Supreme Court held that "suppression by the prosecution of evidence favorable to an accused violates due process when the evidence is material to either guilt or punishment, irrespective of the good faith or bad faith of the prosecutor."[10] This so-called *Brady* rule was intended to ensure a fair trial in which all relevant evidence of guilt or innocence is presented to the fact-finder, resulting in a reliable verdict. For the first time, the Court imposed a duty on the prosecutor to investigate, preserve, and disclose favorable information in possession of any member of the prosecution, including the police.[11]

Thus, to establish a *Brady* violation, the defense must show that (1) favorable evidence (2) was suppressed by the prosecution (known to the prosecution but not known to the defense) and that (3) the suppressed evidence was material to guilt or punishment.

### *Favorable Evidence*

Favorable evidence includes both exculpatory and impeachment evidence. Unfortunately, unlike the situation in the UK, where specific "unused evidence" is delineated in checklists, the specific categories of information that must be disclosed are not detailed in the case law, in any of the federal and state statutes, or in any court rules that are intended to effectuate *Brady*'s requirements. Generally, however, exculpatory evidence includes evidence that is inconsistent with a defendant's factual guilt: for example, third-party confessions, witness recantations, eyewitness identifications of another person, or witness descriptions that are inconsistent with the defendant's actual appearance. Forensic evidence that excludes or might exclude the defendant would also be included.[12]

10 *Brady*, 373 U.S. at 87. Brady was found guilty of murder and sentenced to death. He admitted that he took part in the crime, but claimed his partner, Boblit, who was tried separately, was the shooter. Before trial, Brady's attorney specifically requested disclosure of all of Boblit's statements. The prosecutor disclosed several statements, but withheld one—the one in which Boblit had admitted doing the shooting. The Court held that suppression of that statement violated due process and vacated Brady's sentence. It did not vacate his conviction because evidence that Brady had not been the actual shooter did not affect his conviction for murder.

11 *Id.* at 88.

12 *See, e.g.*, Connick v. Thompson, 131 S. Ct. 1350 (2011) (involving suppression of an article of clothing that contained blood stains that were not tested but that would have identified the DNA of the perpetrator).

However, "favorable" does not necessarily include everything that might be helpful to the defense: helpful evidence that is considered neutral rather than favorable need not be disclosed. So, for example, while a ballistics report that shows a defendant's gun was not the murder weapon would be required to be disclosed,[13] a ballistics report that discloses no latent prints of value is considered neutral and is not required to be disclosed, even if it might support a defense that the defendant was not the one who used the gun.[14] Similarly, while a statement by a witness identifying someone else as the perpetrator generally would be required to be disclosed,[15] evidence that an eyewitness could not state whether the defendant was one of the perpetrators is not.[16]

*Brady* requires disclosure of a broad range of impeachment evidence that could be seen to weaken the prosecution's case, including evidence suggesting bias or motive to fabricate (including immunity or leniency deals).[17] Prior inconsistent statements of witnesses must also be disclosed,[18] including prior statements of witnesses failing to identify the defendant or identifying someone else as the perpetrator, where that witness identifies the defendant at trial.[19]

Finally, in many US jurisdictions, favorable evidence need not be disclosed if it is inadmissible. Thus, for example, evidence of the result of a polygraph examination by a government witness need not be disclosed.[20] At the same time, some courts have found a *Brady* violation where suppressed evidence, although inadmissible, would have led to admissible evidence.[21]

*Suppression*

*Brady* requires disclosure of evidence that is "known to the prosecutor but unknown to the defense."[22] Most *Brady* violations involve evidence the prosecutor knowingly withholds. However, there are situations in which the prosecutor does not know of the information because it is held by other law enforcement personnel, like the police, but where that knowledge will be imputed to the prosecution. In that case, the prosecutor is obligated to disclose information about which he should have known.[23]

In *Kyles v. Whitley*, the United States Supreme Court made clear that non-disclosure of exculpatory evidence by the police is imputed to the prosecution even if the police withhold that information from the prosecutor.[24] In *Kyles*, a murder case, the police had withheld several items of exculpatory evidence that indicated that the actual killer had framed the defendant, contradicted the actual killer's claims, and failed to

---

13 *See* Barbee v. Warden, Md. Penitentiary, 331 F.2d 842 (4th Cir. 1964).

14 *See* People v. Penland, 64 Ill. App. 3d 656 (4th Dist. 1978).

15 *See* Bloodsworth v. State, 307 Md. 164 (1986); Bowen v. Maynard, 799 F.2d 593 (10th Cir. 1986); Oklahoma v. Munson, 886 P.2d 999 (Okla. Crim. App. 1994); *ex parte* Brandley, 781 S.W.2d 886 (Tex. Crim. App. 1989).

16 *See* Comm. v. Satterfield, 373 Mass. 109 (1977).

17 *See, e.g.*, Phillips v. Ornoski, 673 F.3d 1168 (9th Cir. 2012) (failure to disclose immunity agreement with key witness).

18 Giglio v. United States, 405 U.S. 150 (1972). *See also* Spicer v. Roxbury Correctional Institution, 194 F.3d 547 (4th Cir. 1999) (prior inconsistent statements by eyewitness); United States v. Isgro, 751 Supp. 846 (C.D. Cal. 1990) (prior sworn testimony of key witness that was contrary to his grand jury testimony).

19 *See* Smith v. Cain, 132 S. Ct. 627 (2012) (reversing a conviction based on failure to disclose that its only eyewitness to the murder initially "could not … supply a description of the perpetrators other than they were black males"). *But see* Moore v. Illinois, 408 US 786 (1972) (non-disclosure of witness's pretrial statement identifying another person as the killer was not material).

20 *See* Wood v. Bartholomew, 516 U.S. 1 (1995). Madsen v. Dormire, 137 F.3d 602 (8th Cir. 1998) (no *Brady* violation based on failure to disclose prosecutor's opinion that his own forensic chemist was incompetent to testify, because that was "not evidence at all"); *but see* Jacobs v. Singletary, 952 F.2d 1282 (11th Cir. 1992) (prosecution must disclose statements of a witness to polygraph examiner that contradict his trial testimony); Carter v. Rafferty, 826 F.2d. 1299 (3rd Cir. 1987) (reports of lie detector test of "important prosecution witness" were material).

21 *See e.g.*, Ellsworth v. Warden, 333 F.3d 1 (1st Cir. 2003); United States v. Gil, 297 F.3d 93, 104 (2d Cir. 2002); *but see* Hoke v. Netherland, 92 F.3d 1350, 1356 n. 3 (4th Cir.1996) (as a matter of law, inadmissible evidence is "immaterial" for *Brady* purposes).

22 *See* United States v. Agurs, 427 U.S. 97 (1976).

23 *See* Kyles v. Whitley, 514 U.S. at 419.

24 *Id.* at 437.

connect the defendant with the crime. The state argued that it should not be charged with the suppression by the police. Nevertheless, the Court held that the "prosecutor has a duty to learn of any favorable evidence known to the others acting on the government's behalf in the case, including the police." The Court assumed that a prosecutor "has the means to discharge the government's *Brady* responsibility" by establishing "procedures and regulations" to ensure a flow of "all relevant information" from the police to the prosecutor's office.[25]

The courts have taken varied approaches to how far to extend this doctrine of imputed knowledge. Clearly, a prosecutor will be deemed to know information within any agency participating in the actual investigation of the case within the prosecutor's jurisdiction.[26] A prosecutor is also charged with knowledge of the contents of the personnel records of law enforcement officers he intends to call as trial witnesses,[27]and of a witness's criminal and prison record—again, within the jurisdiction.[28]

Whether or not the prosecutor knows of exculpatory information, the prosecution has no duty to disclose information that the defense already knows, or with reasonable diligence could discover.[29] Thus, for example, where the criminal record of a prosecution witness or other information is available in a public record, the prosecutor's failure to turn it over is not a *Brady* violation, assuming a reasonable defendant in the exercise of due diligence would have looked for it.[30]

### *Materiality*

*Brady* promised to make the adversary system "less like a sporting event" and more like a search for truth.[31] Theoretically, exculpatory evidence that might never have surfaced would now be revealed and subjected to adversarial testing as part of a fair search for the truth. The prosecutor's superior investigatory resources would level the playing field in the criminal process. This promise has floundered—more than anything else—on *Brady*'s materiality requirement. Non-disclosure of favorable evidence does not result in a *Brady* violation unless the defense establishes that the suppressed evidence was material. "Evidence is 'material' when there is a reasonable probability that, had the evidence been disclosed, the result of the proceeding would have been different." [32]

Since *Brady*, the United States Supreme Court has analyzed the materiality requirement several times, ultimately interpreting it quite narrowly. Thus, in *United States v. Agurs*,[33] a homicide case in which the

---

25 *Id.* at 437–8.

26 *See* Pennsylvania v. Ritchie, 480 U.S. 39, 107 S. Ct. 989, 94 L.Ed.2d 40 (1987) (disclosure of exculpatory evidence held by child welfare agencies); Smith v. Secretary of N.M. Dep't of Corrections, 50 F.3d 801, 824 (10th Cir. 1995); United States v. Wood, 57 F.3d 733 (9th Cir. 1995) ("For *Brady* purposes, the FDA and the prosecutor were one"). *But see* Goff v. Bagley, 601 F.3d 445, 476 (2010) (no obligation to learn of information possessed by government agencies not involved in the investigation or prosecution); United States v. Canniff, 521 F.2d 565, 573 (2d. Cir 1975) (Probation Department is not an arm of the prosecution); United States v. Hutcher, 622 F.2d 1083, 1088 (2d. Cir. 1980) (knowledge of contents of bankruptcy files are not imputed to the prosecution).

27 United States v. Henthorn, 931 F.2d 29 (9th Cir. 1991); United States v. Lacy, 896 F. Supp. 982 (N.D. Cal. 1995).

28 United States v. Santiago (9th Cir. 1995) (Bureau of Prisons records); United States v. Sipe, 388 F.3d 471 (5th Cir. 2004) (criminal history of its witness); People v. Valentin, 1 AD 3d 982 (4th Dep't 2003) (same).

29 *See* United States v. Grossman, 843 F.2d 78, 85 (2d Cir.1988) (no *Brady* violation where government informed defendant that witness's grand jury testimony might be exculpatory); United States v. Bermudez, 526 F.2d 89, 100 (counsel on notice where materials were provided to him in his representation in another case); *but see* United States v. Mahaffy, 693 F.3d 113 (2d. Cir 2012) (prosecution was required to disclose its witness's statement to the Securities and Exchange Commission (SEC) about a conversation with the defendant even though the defendant knew that the conversation had taken place).

30 *See* United States v. Payne, 63 F.3d 1200, 1208 (2d Cir. 1995).

31 William J. Brennan, Jr., *The Criminal Prosecution: Sporting Event or Quest for Truth?*, 68 WASH. U.L.Q. 279 (1990) ("Procedural rules ought to be designed to maximize the chance that the outcome of the trial will be a verdict that is based on what truly occurred, and it would be mere happenstance if the set of rules thus derived bore any resemblance to a set of rules that would ensure fairness in the sporting sense of fair play between counsel—evenly matched legal gladiators.").

32 Kyles v. Whitley, 514 U.S. at 434 ("The question is not whether the defendant would more likely than not have received a different verdict with the evidence, but whether in its absence he received a fair trial, understood as a trial resulting in a verdict worthy of confidence.").

33 United States v. Agurs, 427 U.S.

defendant claimed self-defense, the defendant had not requested and the government had not disclosed clearly exculpatory evidence that would have shown that the deceased had a history of violence, supporting the self-defense claim.[34] The Court prescribed two different materiality tests, depending on whether the defendant had requested the suppressed information, and found the suppressed evidence of the deceased's violent history (which the defense had not explicitly requested) was not material. Later, in *United States v. Bagley*,[35] the Court explicitly held that "exculpatory evidence" includes impeachment evidence. In that case, the defense had requested but the prosecution had failed to disclose prior agreements with government witnesses by which they would be paid if the defendants were convicted. The Court also revisited the issue of materiality in the request–no request context, and adopted a unitary "reasonable probability" standard of materiality for the request, no request, and general request situations.[36]

Later, in *Kyles v. Whitley*,[37] the Court explained that "materiality" does not require that a defendant prove that disclosure of suppressed material would have resulted in his acquittal or that the remaining evidence would have been insufficient. It also made clear that materiality is to be determined by the cumulative impact of all suppressed exculpatory evidence.[38]

Next, in *Strickler v. Greene*, the Court took an extremely constricted view of materiality.[39] In that case, the prosecutor had failed to disclose a series of communications with its star witness that were found in police files after the defendant's conviction, even though the prosecutor's office allegedly complied with its "open file" disclosure policy.[40] The materials documented a course of police–witness interaction through which the witness's initial statement—that she had failed even to notice the defendant or the kidnapping occurring in front of her in a parking lot—gradually changed into dramatic and frightening testimony that included her certain identification of the defendant as the ringleader, her assurance that she had closely witnessed the kidnapping proceed, and her detailed and dramatic recounting of how violent and threatening the whole incident had been.[41] Undisclosed police notes showed that she initially could not identify the victim or the defendant, and that her memory allegedly improved only after several additional sessions with both the police and the victim's boyfriend.[42] Nevertheless, the Court affirmed the conviction upon finding that the undisclosed evidence was not material.[43]

Most recently, in *Smith v. Cain*,[44] the United States Supreme Court held that statements made by a witness to police five days after an alleged murder were material and should have been disclosed. There, as in *Strickler*, the prosecution failed to disclose police notes concerning interviews with the witness who ultimately identified the defendant at trial. Again, these notes revealed prior statements of this witness in which he had explicitly told the police he could not describe the perpetrators other than that they were black males and that he had not been able to see their faces. He also told the police he, "would not know them if [he] saw them" and "could not identify any of the perpetrators of the murder." This information had never been disclosed to the defense,

34 *Id.* at 98–9.

35 United States v. Bagley, 473 U.S. 667 (1985).

36 *Id.* at 682.

37 Kyles v. Whitley, 514 U.S.

38 *Id.* at 454.

39 Strickler v. Greene, 527 U.S. 263, 281 (1999).

40 Some prosecution offices have enacted an "open file" discovery policy, which purports to allow defense access to the entire case file pretrial. However, some prosecutors have used this alleged openness to hide documents that have been removed from the file. *See* Bennett L. Gershman, *Litigating* Brady v. Maryland*: Games Prosecutors Play*, 57 Case W. Res. L. Rev. 531 (2007).

41 *Strickler*, 527 U.S. at 273.

42 *Id.* at 272–4 (observing "petitioner's Brady claim [to] consist of notes taken by Detective Claytor during his interviews with Stoltzfus, and letters written by Stoltzfus to Claytor[,] [claiming] [that] they cast serious doubt on Stoltzfus' confident assertion of her 'exceptionally good memory.'").

43 *Id.* at 296 (concluding that the defendant had "not shown that there is a reasonable probability that his conviction or sentence would have been different had these materials been disclosed").

44 Smith v. Cain, 132 S. Ct.

even though, as the Court noted, it was obviously material. As the Court explained, "[n]o other witnesses and no physical evidence implicated Smith in the crime."[45]

There is a second, important, thread to the court's materiality jurisprudence. "Materiality" is not simply an extremely high harmless error test; it is also the standard by which the police and prosecutor must make their decisions whether to disclose *pretrial.* That is, the same outcome determinative standard governs whether a conviction should be reversed for failure to disclose and whether the prosecutor or police are even required to disclose something in the first place. This test requires even a good-faith prosecutor to "engage in a bizarre kind of anticipatory hindsight review."[46] That review, in turn, requires both the police and prosecution to overcome their own cognitive biases and identify material weaknesses in the case—weaknesses that might result in an acquittal—despite their own decisions to arrest, charge, and prosecute the defendant in the first place. Having done so, they must then continue to prosecute the case.[47]

### *Legislative and Judicial Requirements*

Existing statutory or rule-based requirements are generally modeled on *Brady* and so reflect the same flaws as the common law doctrine itself.

In the federal system, 37 of the 94 federal districts have a relevant local rule, order or procedure governing disclosure of *Brady* material.[48] And where the states are concerned, 33 of 51 state jurisdictions have rules or procedures that codify the *Brady* rule.[49]

### *Guilty Plea and Timing Issues*

Two other significant limitations on disclosure are the restriction of *Brady* to cases that go to trial and the absence of any specific time requirements for *Brady* disclosure. First, at least insofar as impeachment evidence is concerned, *Brady* has been construed by the United States Supreme Court as a right only available to a defendant who goes to trial.[50] That means that in about 95 percent of cases in America—those that result in

---

45 While the state argued that the witness had made other, earlier statements indicating he could identify one of the perpetrators and that he could have made the statements at issue out of fear, the Court made clear that the possibility that the jurors might have disbelieved the suppressed statements was insufficient to sustain confidence in the verdict they reached without knowing anything about them. *Id.* at 630.

46 *See* Alafair S. Burke, *Improving Prosecutorial Decision Making: Some Lessons of Cognitive Science*, 47 William & Mary L. Rev. 1587, 1610, 1612 (2006) ("[C]ompared to a neutral decision maker, the prosecutor will overestimate the strength of the government's case against the defendant and underestimate the potential exculpatory value of the evidence whose disclosure is at issue. As a consequence, the prosecutor will fail to see materiality where it might in fact exist."); Bruce A. Green & Ellen Yaroshefsky, *Prosecutorial Discretion and Post-Conviction Evidence of Innocence*, 6 Ohio St. J. Crim. L. 467, 488 (2009) ("Tunnel vision has had an obvious impact in the pretrial stage: having formed an initial judgment that a particular defendant is guilty of a crime, prosecutors and police will tend to discredit or discount the significance of new exculpatory evidence or fit it into their preexisting theory.").

47 *See* Alafair Burke, *Revisiting Prosecutorial Disclosure*, 84 Ind. L. J. 481, 485, 488 (Apr. 2009).

48 *See, e.g.*, Fed. R. Crim. P. §16; Laural L. Hooper, Jennifer E. Marsh & Brian Yeh, Treatment of Brady v. Maryland Material in United States District and State Courts' Rules, Orders, and Policies, Federal Judicial Center (2007) (hereinafter FJC Report), *available at* http://www.fjc.gov/public/pdf.nsf/lookup/bradyma2.pdf/$file/bradyma2.pdf. This is a compilation of federal and state *Brady* statutes and rules.

49 *Id.* at 12. Twenty-three of the 33 states define the material required to be disclosed in language such as "any material or information which tends to negate the guilt of the accused as to the offense charged or would tend to reduce the accused's punishment therefore." Ten others refer to "exculpatory material." Although five other states use the term "favorable" in describing evidence subject to disclosure, all of them limit this clause with a condition that it must be "material and relevant to the issue of guilt or punishment." Twenty-six states use the terminology of Rule 16, requiring evidence that is "material to the preparation of the defendant's defense." *Id.* at 50–52.

50 *See* United States v. Ruiz, 536 U.S. 622, 631 (2002); Kevin C. McMunigal, *Guilty Pleas, Brady Disclosure, and Wrongful Convictions*, 57 Case W. Res. L. Rev. 651 (Spring 2007). *But see* Tate v. Wood, 963 F.2d 20, 24 (2d Cir. 1992) (*Brady* obligation applies to guilty pleas).

guilty pleas—the prosecution has no duty to disclose impeachment evidence to the defense.[51] In cases where the defendant does go to trial, there is no specific time by which that evidence has to be disclosed. The courts generally hold that prosecutors have met their *Brady* obligations if they produce all material exculpatory information at a point before trial that allows the defense to use it at trial.[52]

## Part II: Brady and Innocence

It is difficult to estimate how many innocent defendants have been convicted because of a prosecutor's suppression of exculpatory evidence. However, according to one study, out of a total of 133 known exoneration cases that have resulted in a written decision, 14, or just over 10 percent, resulted in relief based on *Brady*.[53] A study of all exonerations in Massachusetts revealed that 12 of 33 cases, or over 36 percent involved a *Brady* violation.[54] And it is not disputed that, apart from errors relating to incompetent counsel, the most frequent basis for wrongful convictions has been prosecutorial suppression of exculpatory evidence.[55]

*Brady* violations have been found in cases involving all of the recognized causes of wrongful convictions—mistaken eyewitness identification, faulty science, third party guilt, false confessions, and false testimony by incentivized witnesses ("snitches").

### *Mistaken Identification and Third-Party Guilt*

The cases involving mistaken eyewitness identification—or of a third party's actual guilt—are perhaps the most chilling.[56] In those cases, the suppressed evidence that the eyewitness was wrong runs the gamut from evidence that the police had another suspect or utterly failed to heed clues to another suspect,[57] to an eyewitness's pretrial failure to identify the defendant, to outright identification of another person as the perpetrator.[58] None of this information was revealed.

---

51 Interestingly, in approximately 9 percent of the DNA exonerations—28 out of 311—the defendant had pleaded guilty before being exonerated. http://www.innocenceproject.org/Content/When_the_Innocent_Plead_Guilty.php (last visited Aug., 11, 2013).

52 *See, e.g.*, United States v. Scott, 524 F.2d 465, 467 (5th Cir. 1975); United States v. Brown, 582 F.2d 197, 200 (2d Cir. 1978); Grant v. Alldredge, 498 F.2d 376, 382 & n.7 (2d Cir. 1974); Leka v. Portuondo, 257 F.3d 89, 91, 93–4 (2d Cir. 2001).

53 Brandon Garrett, *Judging Innocence*, 108 Colum. L. Rev. 55, 97 (2008). Indeed, a study of all 5,760 capital convictions in the United States from 1973 to 1995 found that suppression of evidence was responsible for 16 percent of reversals at the state post-conviction stage. *See* James S. Liebman, Jeffrey Fagan & Valerie West, A Broken System: Error Rates in Capital Cases (2000).

54 Stanley Z. Fisher, *Convictions of Innocent Persons in Massachusetts: An Overview*, 12 B.U. Pub. Int. L.J. 1 (2002).

55 *See* Gershman, *supra* note 2; Paul Craig Roberts, *Where's the Justice?*, The Independent Institute (June 25, 2001), http://truthinjustice.org/where-justice.htm; Cynthia E. Jones, *A Reason to Doubt: The Suppression of Evidence and the Inference of Innocence*, 100 J. Crim. L. & Criminology 415 (2010). *See also*, Ken Armstrong & Maurice Possley, *Trial and Error: How Prosecutors Sacrifice Justice to Win*, Chicago Tribune, Jan. 10, 1999, at 1 (since *Brady*, 381 homicide defendants have had convictions reversed because prosecutors either used false evidence or suppressed evidence that suggested the defendant's factual innocence).

56 For a detailed discussion of the connection between mistaken identification and innocence see Epstein, *supra* note 3.

57 *Ex parte* Brandley, 781 S.W.2d (prosecutor suppressed, *inter alia*, evidence placing other suspects at the scene of the crime near the time of the crime); Bowen v. Maynard, 799 F.2d 593 (10th Cir. 1986) (prosecution withheld, *inter alia*, information that the police had considered another individual as a primary initial suspect); State v. Munson, 886 P.2d 999, 1003 (Okla. Crim. App. 1994) (failure to disclose the existence of another suspect with a similar modus operandi who was seen at the scene of the crime); Cook v. State, 940 S.W.2d 623, 625 (Tex. Crim. App. 1996) (failure to disclose the existence of a person who had a motive to kill the victim and had threatened to kill the victim shortly before her death).

58 *See* State v. Thompson, 825 So. 2d 552, 557 (La. Ct. App. 2002) (prosecutors withheld police reports with eyewitness descriptions that did not match the defendant); U.S. *ex rel* Boyd v. Pierce, 2010 WL 3731251 (N.D. Illinois 2010) (*Brady* claim was untimely but showed that prosecutors failed to disclose that, after its witness viewed a line-up containing the defendant, "she told police that he was not the shooter").

Most recently, in *Smith v. Cain*[59] the Supreme Court reversed a conviction on the ground that the prosecution had failed to disclose a police officer's notes of his interview with the only identification witness. These notes revealed that this witness—who positively identified the defendant at trial—had made prior statements to the police in which he admitted he had been unable to see the faces of the perpetrators, could not identify them, and , "would not know them if [he] saw them" and "could not identify any of the perpetrators of the murder."[60]

Similarly blatant is the case of Michael Morton, who was charged and convicted of murdering his wife. There, the prosecution suppressed evidence not only that there had been a third party present on the day of the murder but also that Morton's son had actually witnessed an unknown man enter the home and brutally attack his mother.[61] After 25 years of incarceration, Morton was exonerated and a third party was indicted for the murder.[62]

In *D'Ambrosia v. Bagley*,[63] a murder case, the prosecution suppressed evidence that someone who had been indicted for a rape for which the deceased in this case was a witness (and who was actually guilty of the charged crime) had (1) anonymously called the police and revealed non-public facts; (2) first led the police to suspect the defendant; (3) requested police assistance with an unrelated charge in exchange for his testimony against the defendant; and (4) fabricated a burglary to implicate the defendant in the murder.[64] It also withheld evidence that contradicted its star witness's allegations about where and when the crime had taken place.[65] Another example is *Watkins v. Miller*,[66] a child abduction and murder case, where the prosecution withheld evidence "that another suspect in the case failed a polygraph test; and that investigators received reports of other men who had known [the victim] and who either told others they had killed her or turned up with blood on their clothes the night she disappeared."[67] The police had singled out Watkins as a suspect because of his history of pedophilia and did not investigate further. In addition, the prosecutors also failed to disclose evidence that witnesses had seen the victim being abducted at a time for which Watkins had a solid alibi.[68]

### *Misleading or False Forensics*

The state's suppression of exculpatory forensic evidence has also resulted in conviction of the innocent. For example, in *People v. Descovic*, where the defendant was convicted of murder and rape, the police failed to disclose that a DNA test had excluded the defendant. They also failed to test hair samples that most likely came from the medical examiner but that the prosecutor asserted had come from the defendant.[69] Similarly, in *Connick v. Thompson*, an innocent defendant was convicted where prosecutors suppressed a swatch of the victim's clothing that concededly was stained with the perpetrator's blood, as well as the fact that they had tested the swatch and found the blood to be Type B—a type that the defense could have proven did not match Thompson's Type O blood.[70] Thompson spent 18 years in prison (14 years isolated on death row) for crimes he did not commit.

Similarly, in *State v. Grimes*, a rape case, the prosecution's case rested on the victim's cross-racial identification and the result of hair microscopy. At trial, although the defense presented eight alibi witnesses,

---

59 Smith v. Cain, 132 S. Ct. 627 (2012).

60 *Id.* at 630.

61 *See Know the Cases*, THE INNOCENCE PROJECT, http://www.innocenceproject.org/Content/Michael_Morton.php (last visited Aug. 11, 2013).

62 *See* Brandi Grissom, *Updated: Suspect in Michael Morton Case Arrested*, THE TEXAS TRIBUNE, NOV. 9, 2011, *available at* http://www.texastribune.org/texas-dept-criminal-justice/texas-court-of-criminal-appeals/suspect-arrested-michael-morton-murder/.

63 D'Ambrosia v. Bagley, 527 F.3d 489 (2008).

64 *Id.* at 498–9.

65 *Id.*

66 Watkins v. Miller, 92 F.Supp.2d 824 (2000).

67 *Id.* at 828.

68 *Id.*

69 SNYDER ET AL., REPORT ON THE CONVICTION OF JEFFREY DESKOVIC, PREPARED AT THE REQUEST OF JANET DIFIORE, WESTCHESTER COUNTY DISTRICT ATTORNEY, (June 2007), *available at* http://www.westchesterda.net/Jeffrey%20Deskovic%20Comm%20Rpt.pdf.

70 Connick v. Thompson, 131 S. Ct. 1350, 1371 (2011) (Ginsburg, J., dissenting).

Grimes was convicted.[71] Years later, as a result of a subpoena issued by the North Carolina Actual Innocence Commission, the police produced a suppressed fingerprint card that had originally revealed two fingerprints that did not belong to the defendant.[72] Once disclosed, the prints were used to identify the original suspect in the case as the rapist and Grimes was declared innocent.[73] A final example is *State v. Hobley*,[74] an arson prosecution. There, the case was remanded for an evidentiary hearing to examine the prosecutor's failure to disclose a report that the defendant's fingerprints were *not* on the gasoline can introduced against him at his trial.

### *False Confessions*[75]

While *Brady* does not require disclosure of inculpatory evidence such as a confession, false confession cases are important because in those cases the prosecution can be found to have withheld evidence that shows the confession to be false, either because other evidence contradicts it or because there is evidence that the confession resulted from improper police conduct. Thus, for example, in *People v. Descovic*,[76] the defendant was convicted of the rape and murder of a fellow high school student based largely on his false confession. As the report studying his wrongful conviction concluded, the police "did not take adequate account of his youth, naiveté, inexperience … and psychological vulnerabilities" and deliberately failed to record, or turned off the recorder during, substantial portions of his most inculpatory statements when the police misconduct was most apparent.[77]

### *Impeachment of Prosecution Witnesses*

Suppression of impeachment evidence that results in a wrongful conviction comes in many forms, but there are situations that seem to recur. For example, prosecutors have failed repeatedly to reveal immunity deals with their chief witnesses.[78] In some of these cases, the prosecutors knew about these deals or had personally participated in making them and yet allowed the witnesses to testify that they did not exist.

Another recurring violation is the prosecutor's failure to disclose that a witness whose statements initially were not helpful has been hypnotized before trial, resulting in stronger trial testimony. A good example of such a case is *Emmett v. Ricketts*,[79] where the case depended entirely on one witness, an addicted prostitute who offered her initial statements only after a promise of immunity on a pending charge. When her early statements were proven to be false and inconsistent with the physical evidence, the prosecutors had her hypnotized. Her testimony at trial changed and the defendant was convicted. The prosecution withheld her pre-hypnotic statements, destroyed some of the tapes of the hypnosis sessions, and lied about the disappearance of the tapes. In granting the petition for a writ of habeas corpus, the court concluded that "[t]he prosecutorial

---

71 *See* State v. Grimes, North Carolina Innocence Commission, http://www.innocencecommission-nc.gov/grimes.html (last visited Aug. 11, 2013).

72 *See* Raquel Cohen, *Fingerprints on Fruit Help Exonerate Wrongfully Convicted Man in NC*, California Innocence Project, (Oct. 18, 2012, 9:51 PM), http://www.californiainnocenceproject.org/blog/2012/10/18/fingerprints-on-fruit-help-exonerate-wrongfully-convicted-man-in-nc/.

73 *See North Carolina Man Declared Innocent*, Innocence Project, (Oct. 10, 2012, 12:00 PM), http://www.innocenceproject.org/Content/North_Carolina_Man_Declared_Innocent.php.

74 *See, e.g.*, State v. Hobley, 696 N.E.2d 313, 331 (Ill. 1998).

75 Based on DNA exonerations studied by the Innocence Project, 23 percent of convictions are based on false confessions or admissions. Barry Scheck, Peter Neufeld & Jim Dwyer, Actual Innocence: When Justice Goes Wrong and How to Make it Right 92 (2000).

76 The prosecution also suppressed DNA evidence that excluded the defendant as the murderer. *See* Snyder et al., *supra* note 69.

77 Scheck, Neufeld & Dwyer, *supra* note 75, at 77–88.

78 *See, e.g.*, Phillips v. Ornoski, 673 F.3d 1168 (9th Cir. 2012); Tassin v. Cain, 517 F.3d 770 (5th Cir. 2008); United States v. Butler, 567 F.2d 885 (9th Cir. 1978); Boone v. Paderick, 541 F.2d 447 (4th Cir. 1976).

79 Emmett v. Ricketts, 397 F. Supp. 1025 (N.D. Ga. 1975).

suppression of nearly all evidence concerning [the witness] resulted in a criminal proceeding that bordered on the Kafkaesque … ."[80]

*McMillian v. State* is another wrongful conviction case that resulted from the blatant suppression of evidence that prosecution witnesses were lying. There, the prosecutor withheld, among other things, a tape recording of a plot by a witness to frame the defendant for the murder the witness had committed.[81] Similarly, in *State v. Gell*, a murder case as well, the prosecution withheld a tape of one of the two main prosecution witnesses saying she had to "make up a story."[82] In that case, the prosecution also withheld evidence from 17 witnesses who told investigators they had seen the deceased alive after the date on which the prosecution claimed he had been murdered.[83] These are not simple cases of defective judgment-making, but rather clear cases of prosecutorial misconduct that was not seen—and certainly not prevented—under the current *Brady* regime.

Finally, police witnesses can be impeached like any other witnesses, and frequently the defense will make an application to see a police officer's personnel file to discover evidence for that purpose. A conviction may be reversed where the prosecutor opposes such disclosure, and the file is later determined to contain significant impeachment evidence.[84]

While not a typical innocence case, the well-publicized federal prosecution of US Senator Ted Stevens[85] in Alaska shows just how brazen prosecutorial non-disclosure can be, even in a well-publicized and closely watched case, and may be an impetus for reform that would impact state innocence cases. Ted Stevens, a US Senator from Alaska, was convicted in October 2008 of making false statements on Senate financial disclosure forms. The charges were based on his receipt of and failure to report more than $250,000 worth of renovation and repair services on his part-time residence in Girdwood, Alaska from the VECO Corporation and its owner, Bill Allen, a friend of Stevens. Allen became the chief witness against Stevens. The critical issue at the trial, and Stevens' defense, was that he did not intentionally file false disclosure forms because he and his wife believed that their payments of $160,000 to the contractor they hired covered the entire cost of the renovation, including VECO's services. Exculpatory evidence that supported this defense and established that Stevens was probably innocent was concealed by the prosecution. The trial court found that the team of experienced and highly respected federal prosecutors had violated *Brady* by doctoring documents to redact exculpatory statements, removing a witness from the jurisdiction who had material exculpatory information, failing to turn over clearly exculpatory and inconsistent prior statements, and lying to the court about all that they had done.[86] Ultimately,

---

80 *Id.* at 1048. *See also* Ok. v. Munson (prosecution suppressed evidence of government's witness FBI hypnosis); Jean v. Rice (prosecutor had suppressed "twice-requested" audio recordings and reports of the identifying eyewitness's hypnosis).

81 McMillian v. State, 616 So. 2d 933 (Ala. Crim. App. 1993).

82 State v. Gell, No. 95 CRS 1884, Order (Sup. Ct. Bertie County 2002). *See also*, Killian v. Poole, 282 F.3d 1204 (9th Cir. 2002), where the court reversed the defendant's murder conviction based on the prosecutor's failure to disclose the key prosecution's letter stating that he had lied to convict the defendant.

83 *See Innocence Cases 2004–Present*, Death Penalty Information Center, http://www.deathpenaltyinfo.org/innocence-cases-2004-present (last visited Aug. 11, 2013). In that case, the defendant spent six years in jail, including four years on death row, before he was ultimately acquitted of all counts.

84 *See, e.g.*, Milke v. Ryan, 9th Cir. No. 07-99001, (3/14/13).

85 *See* United States v. Stevens, No. 08-cr-231 (EGS), 2009 WL 6525926 (D.D.C. Apr. 7, 2009). For a discussion of the *Brady* issues in the *Stevens* case, *see* Jones, *supra* note 55.

86 First, a VECO employee, Williams, who supervised the renovation work on Stevens' house and who was interviewed four times pretrial, repeatedly told the prosecutors that after reviewing the Christensen builders' bills, he sent the bills to Allen along with the additional charges for his time and the time of other VECO employees, and that it was his understanding that Allen would add these costs to the Christensen bills before sending the bills to Stevens. After he did poorly on a mock cross-examination on the day of opening statements, the prosecutors sent Williams back to Alaska and never disclosed his prior statements. Second, Bambi Tyree, a child prostitute who had a sexual relationship with Bill Allen, and who had been indicted on drug conspiracy and child-sex trafficking charges, told prosecutors that she had sex with Bill Allen when she was 15 years old and that she had signed a sworn affidavit claiming she did not have sex with Allen at Allen's request. The Stevens prosecutors concealed this information by, *inter alia*, falsely reporting that Allen "never made a false statement under oath and never encouraged others to do so" and stating that they were aware of "no evidence" to support a "suggestion" that Allen asked Tyree to lie.

Even worse was the prosecution's handling of two notes in which Stevens had asked Allen for a bill for VECO's services, clearly key to Stevens' defense. Despite Allen's prior denials, eventually he had remembered receiving the notes

the case was dismissed,[87] and the court appointed a well-known attorney to conduct an investigation into the prosecutors' misconduct.[88] That investigation revealed repeated and knowing *Brady* violations by an entire team of elite, highly sophisticated, well-educated federal prosecutors.[89]

Following the revelations in *Stevens*, one commentator noted "with prosecutors [now] feeling the brunt of the chasm between vague legal rules and lofty ethical obligations –both individually and as representatives of the people—reform may finally be possible."[90]

## Part III: Reform Efforts

The continuing revelation of DNA exonerations may have an impact on disclosure practices in America. Changes in prosecutorial practices, substantial academic attention, professional concern, and legislative action are all increasing and may result in measures that would bring more exculpatory evidence into the light of adversarial testing.

### *Changes in Prosecution Practices*

First, anecdotally, some prosecution offices have moved toward open-file disclosure or at least broadened their voluntary disclosure practices. In open-file disclosure, the prosecution purports to turn its entire file over to the defense after removing attorney work product. While seemingly generous, the danger of this type of disclosure is the representation that the entire file has been turned over, when, unbeknownst to defense counsel, it may not have been disclosed.[91] There is really no way to monitor the good faith of a prosecutor claiming to have turned everything over, much less to know whether the allegedly complete file contains all of the police records. Another danger is that prosecutors will use this method of disclosure to dump large volumes of evidence on the defense that paralyzes defense preparation.[92]

---

and, after the prosecutors put pressure on him, he also suddenly remembered the person who gave him the note had said, "Don't worry about getting a bill. Ted is just covering his ass." The prosecutors never disclosed Allen's recognition of the note or alleged recollection of this statement to the defense. When, at trial, the defense confronted him with it as a recent fabrication, he falsely suggested he had told the prosecution about this conversation earlier, a statement the prosecutors left uncorrected.

87 *Stevens*, 2009 WL 6525926.

88 *See in re* Special Proceedings, Misc. No. 09-0198 (EGS) (D.D.C. 2012) (Report to Hon. Emmet G. Sullivan of Investigation Conducted Pursuant to the Court's Order, dated Apr. 7, 2009). This report concluded that the case was "permeated by the systematic concealment of significant exculpatory evidence which would have independently corroborated [his] defense and his testimony, and seriously damaged the testimony and credibility of the government's key witness." This was found to be willful and intentional on at least one occasion. *Id.*

89 At about this time, other federal prosecutions were subject to publicity based on the government's failure to comply with its disclosure obligations. *See, e.g.*, United States v. Jones, 620 F. Supp. 2d 163 (D. Mass. 2009); United States v. Zhenli Ye Gon, 287 Fed. App. 113 (D.C. Cir. 2008); United States v. Shaygan, 661 F. Supp. 2d 1289 (S.D. Fla. 2009); United States v. Jones, 686 F. Supp. 2d 147, 149 (D. Mass. 2010); Jordan Weissmann, *Prosecutors in Kidnapping Case Rebuked over Brady*, The Blog of Legal Times (June 24, 2009), http://legal-times.typepad.com/blt/2009/06/prosecutors-in-kidnapping-case-rebuked-over-brady.html.

90 *See, e.g.*, Amanda Coyne, *Could Botched Ted Stevens Prosecution Prompt Federal Legal System Reform?*, Alaska Dispatch (Nov. 28, 2011), http://www.alaskadispatch.com/article/could-botched-ted-stevens-prosecution-prompt-federal-legal-system-reform; David Ingram, *Ted Stevens Became a Symbol for Prosecutorial Misconduct*, The Blog of Legal Times (Aug. 10, 2010, 4:22 PM), http://legaltimes.typepad.com/blt/2010/08/ted-stevens-became-a-symbol-for-prosecutorial-misconduct.html; Carrie Johnson, *Court Ruling Reignites Debate Over Sharing Evidence*, NPR (Jan. 12, 2012), *available at* http://www.npr.org/2012/01/12/145102823/court-ruling-reignites-debate-oversharing-evidence.

91 *See* Gershman, *supra* note 40. ("To the extent that an open file policy represents to a defendant that a prosecutor has disclosed everything in her file relevant to the case, it may lull a defendant into believing that he need take no further action to enforce discovery requirements. In such a case, an open file policy may become a trap for the unwary."). *See also* Smith v. Sec'y of N.M. Dep't of Corr., 50 F.3d 801 (10th Cir. 1995) (rejecting state's claim that its open file policy satisfied its *Brady* obligation).

92 *See, e.g.*, United States v. Skilling, 554 F.3d 529, 577 (5th Cir. 2009) (*Brady* violation may occur when "the government 'padded' an open file with pointless or superfluous information to frustrate a defendant's review of the file [or

*Formalizing Brady's Requirements*

Second, legal academics and the profession have taken steps toward *Brady* reform. These efforts have focused on two problems: non-disclosure by police and the difficulty of implementing, and meeting, the materiality test. Accordingly, recommendations have been made to develop standardized procedures and checklists for disclosure and to set a standard for disclosure, irrespective of materiality.

As cases like *Kyles* show, police can easily withhold exculpatory evidence from the prosecution, or even destroy it before it comes to anyone's attention outside the investigating officers. In addition, the police arguably have well-recognized cognitive biases that, without sufficient guidance, can make it extremely difficult for them to pass on information that tends to prove they have investigated the wrong person. As noted above, the *Kyles* doctrine that imputes police suppression to the prosecutors has failed to result in any sort of reliable process by which prosecutors can ensure that the police pass exculpatory information on to them. Prosecutors simply have no reliable way to enforce disclosure by the police to them. While the doctrine is undoubtedly correct, it is simply not consistent with what is really going on.

Several recommendations for change on this front have come from the academy. An excellent example is the report that issued from the Cardozo Law School's symposium, *New Perspectives on Brady*, held in November 2009. This symposium brought together approximately 75 participants: representatives from the profession—prosecutors' offices, defense lawyers, judges, as well as legal academics, cognitive scientists, social psychologists, and medical professionals—and produced several significant recommendations.[93] Among other things, it was the consensus of the working groups at this symposium that "developing constructive and productive relationships with law enforcement can be one of the most difficult aspects of the prosecutor's job."[94] To overcome cultural differences and distrust, the working groups recommended the use of checklists, greater involving of police in discovery proceedings, and prosecutorial certifications of compliance. It also recommended technological improvements, such as updated software with checklists, tasks, deadlines, and completion information, and the use of similar software on smartphones or netbooks.[95]

The ABA has also endorsed modifications in the discovery rules that would formalize obligations and remove some of the discretion from police and prosecutors. And the American College of Trial Lawyers, as long ago as 2003, recommended amending the Federal Rules of Criminal Procedure to require disclosure within 14 days of a request of "all information favorable to the defendant" without a requirement of materiality.[96] In addition, the United States' Attorneys' Manual has undergone recent changes to its disclosure requirements, including requiring disclosure of information "beyond that which is 'material' to guilt."[97]

There is a growing consensus that pretrial disclosure requirements cannot be effectively defined judicially and should be codified. Issues surrounding wrongful convictions may be particularly amenable to legislative response, as demonstrated by the widespread legislative response to post-conviction DNA testing.[98] As a result of the Stevens case, and following Stevens, a bill has been introduced in the United States Senate—The Fairness in Disclosure of Evidence Act of 2012—that would require the government to disclose information

---

by] … [c]reating a voluminous file that is unduly onerous to access … [a]nd it should go without saying that the government may not hide *Brady* material of which it is actually aware in a huge open file in the hope that the defendant will never find it."); United States v. Gil, 297 F.3d 93 (2d Cir.2002) (*Brady* violation where the government included an exculpatory two-page memorandum among voluminous documents on the Friday before a Monday trial); United States v. Salyer, 2010 WL 3036444 (E.D. Cal., Aug. 2, 2010) (government had heightened obligations where it produced "voluminous" discovery to a detained defendant with a small defense team).

93 *See* Symposium, *supra* note 9.

94 New perspectives on Brady and other Disclosure Obligations: Report of the Working Group on Best Practices, 31 Cardozo L. Rev. 1961, 1975 (2010).

95 *Id.* at 2021.

96 Am. Coll. of Trial Lawyers, Proposed Codification of Disclosure of Favorable Information under Federal Rules of Criminal Procedure 11 and 16, 41 Am. Crim. L. Rev. 93, 111 (2004).

97 U.S. Dep't of Justice, U.S. Attorneys' Manual s 9-5.001© 1997.

98 *See* District Attorney's Office for the Third Judicial District et al. v. Osborne, 557 U.S. 52 (2009) ("The elected governments of the States are actively confronting the challenges DNA technology poses to our criminal justice systems … as well as the opportunities it affords. To suddenly constitutionalize this area would short-circuit what looks to be a prompt and considered legislative response.").

(not just admissible evidence) pretrial "that may reasonably appear to be favorable to the defendant."[99] This would effectively do away with the materiality requirement, something also urged by the academy and the bar. In Texas, following the exoneration of Michael Morton,[100] a bill was introduced in the Senate and has been passed by the legislature that requires broad disclosure, including, among other things, the disclosure of "any evidence relevant to the defendant's guilt or punishment." The same bill requires disclosure of the entire investigatory file in the case to the prosecution by any investigative agencies. [101]

In addition, there is a growing recognition that checklists should be developed and used to ensure the free flow of information from the police to prosecutors.[102] These checklists are already in use in the UK for unused evidence, and require disclosure by the police to the prosecution and the prosecution to the defense of a long list of evidence that will not be used by the prosecution in its case. These checklists would be technology based and provided by the prosecutors to the police.[103] They would be filled out in real time, by someone other than the investigating officers, with audits or prosecutorial certifications of compliance and possible mandatory police participation at recommended judicial discovery conferences.[104] Indeed, in 2011, the ABA House of Delegates adopted Resolution 104A, that urges all US courts to adopt a procedure for disseminating "to the prosecution and defense a written checklist delineating in detail the general disclosure obligations of the prosecution under [*Brady*] and its progeny and applicable ethical standards."[105]

*Expanding Ethics Rules*

The ABA has been active on another front: revising the ABA Prosecution and Defense Function Standards. The proposed revision defines disclosable evidence as evidence that is favorable to the defense without regard to its impact on the trial outcome.[106] It also directs prosecutors promptly to seek, identify, ensure

---

99 S. 2197: Fairness in Disclosure of Evidence Act of 2012. *See also* 18 U.S.C. § 3014, Duty to Disclose Favorable Information (proposed by the NACDL).

100 In Morton, the defendant was convicted of murdering his wife. Among other evidence found to have been withheld by the prosecutor was a statement by Morton's son that he saw another man kill his mother at a time when his father was not at home. After the exoneration, a state board of inquiry was convened and the district attorney in the case was indicted. *See* Martha Nell, *Former DA Jailed after Judge Issues Scathing Opinion in Rare Texas Court of Inquiry*, ABA Journal (Apr. 22, 2013), *available at* http://www.abajournal.com/news/article/foermer_da_jailed_after_judge_issues_scathing_opinion_in_rare_texas_court_of_inquiry; Brandi Grissom, *Morton Calls Anderson's Inquiry "Road to Accountability"*, Tex. Trib. (July 2, 2013), *available at* http://www.texastribune.org/2013/02/07/morton-calls-andersons-inquiry-road-accountability/.

101 S.B. No. 1611, *available at* http://www.capitol.state.tx.us/tlodocs/83R/billtext/html/SB01611I.htm (the "Michael Morton Act").

102 102 *See* Symposium, *supra* note 9; Stanley Z. Fisher, *The Prosecutor's Ethical Duty to Seek Exculpatory Evidence in Police Hands: Lessons from England*, 68 Fordham L. Rev. 1379, 1383 (2000). Fisher advocates an English-style legislative solution. *Id.* at 1385. He would achieve this by amending the ABA Model Rules of Professional Conduct and the ABA Standards for the Prosecution Function to articulate and clarify the prosecutor's obligation to get information known to the police by requiring reasonable efforts to ensure that exculpatory evidence is revealed, familiarity with law enforcement record keeping practices, and by helping law enforcement to adopt uniform police reporting practices (e.g., checklists). *Id.* at 1424.

103 *See* Ellen Yaroshefsky, Foreword, *New Perspectives on Brady and Other Disclosure Obligations: What Really Works?*, 31 Cardozo L. Rev. 1943 (2010) (particularly noting the proposal of a *Brady* checklist system that would provide "safety nets to prevent irreparable harm from inevitable human error, and a streamlined and standardized electronic infrastructure … [that provide] better operation of the disclosure process in the criminal justice system").

104 *Id.* at 1957 (recommending greater judicial enforcement of compliance with checklists and disclosure obligations, mandatory judicial reporting of prosecutors to disciplinary committees, vertical case assignments of judges, and prosecutorial certifications of compliance).

105 *See* Am. Bar Ass'n, *Urges Changes to Criminal Trial Court Procedures*, ABA Now, http://www.abanow.org/2011/01/104a/ (adopting, as revised, Resolution 104A).

106 ABA Formal Opinion 09-454 at 11a explains: the Model Rules of Professional Conduct 3.8(d) is more demanding than the constitutional case law, and obligates prosecutors to disclose evidence or information favorable to the defense without regard to the anticipated impact of the evidence or information on a trial's outcome. Thus, the rule mandates that prosecutors avoid the ambiguity of the constitutional direction, and always err on the side of caution. *See* ABA Formal Opinion 09-454, Prosecutor's Duty to Disclose Evidence and Information Favorable to the Defense (July 8, 2009) ("This

the preservation of, and disclose such evidence.[107] Finally, it requires prosecutors to promptly advise other government agencies involved in the case about their own disclosure duties, and to make reasonable efforts to discover such information.[108]

## Part V: Conclusion

The common law development of the *Brady* doctrine has not been successful in providing meaningful protection of the innocent. The doctrine of materiality, the absence of a process for ensuring police disclosure to the prosecution, exclusions for guilty pleas, porous time limitations, and the ease with which disclosure obligations can be evaded are real limitations that too often contribute to conviction of the innocent. Exonerations reveal that prosecutors often possessed and suppressed evidence of the defendant's innocence that was never exposed to adversarial testing but which established the guilt of a third person or substantially impeached the prosecution's proof.

Possible reforms include broader voluntary disclosure by prosecutors; codification of specific disclosure rules, requirements, and checklists; a broader definition of the disclosure obligation without regard to materiality; and clearer and more effective time limits.

ethical duty is separate from disclosure obligations imposed under the Constitution, statutes, procedural rules, court rules, or court orders.").

107 ABA Task Force to Revise the Prosecution and Defense Function, Standards, Prosecution Function, June 2010 draft (on file with author).

108 Standards for Criminal Justice: Prosecution and Defense Function § 3-3.11(a) (3d ed., 1993).

# Chapter 6
# The Two-Legged Stool: The Asymmetry of American Aid for the Rule of Law and the Risk of Wrongful Conviction

Carrie Leonetti

## I. Introduction

> If we are to keep democracy, there must be a commandment:
> Thou shalt not ration justice.
>
> Judge Learned Hand

The past four decades have seen an explosion of international efforts to promote the rule of law. Today, these efforts are part of both bilateral and multilateral assistance strategies designed to support democratic reform, encourage better governance, secure legal empowerment and justice for the poor and traditionally disenfranchised groups, and support post-conflict reconstruction efforts in troubled societies among other objectives.[1] Many of these efforts to promote democracy through legal development have been funded by American Government agencies and foundations. This chapter seeks to evaluate one aspect of the efficacy of those foreign-assistance investments, investments in criminal justice, to engage a comparative dialogue on their relationship to the risk of wrongful convictions in the hope that this dialogue will provoke a broader discussion of reforming America's foreign aid policy.

The thesis of this chapter has both a descriptive and a normative element. The descriptive claim is that the criminal justice component of American foreign rule of law programs is asymmetrical, providing far more assistance to prosecutors and other law enforcement entities than it does to public defenders' offices and the defense bar.[2] The normative claim is that this asymmetry is antithetical to justice and heightens the risk of wrongful convictions abroad.

Part II lays out the first part of this equation, by making the case that American foreign aid for criminal justice asymmetrically favors prosecution and police functions over the defense function.[3] Part III makes the normative claim that this asymmetry is bad. It considers the abstract case for the effective assistance of defense counsel[4] and how adequate funding meshes with the history and rhetoric of the adversarial criminal justice system in the United States. It describes the case law governing the function of defense counsel in America, particularly its role in preventing wrongful convictions,[5] summarizes common examples in which the effective

1 *See* Lelia Mooney et al., *Promoting the Rule of Law Abroad: A Conversation on its Evolution, Setbacks, and Future Challenges*, 44 Int'l Law. 837 (2010).

2 The objective of this chapter is to spawn a normative debate from specific examples. It is only an initial inquiry into an area that calls for a larger empirical study.

3 By *defense function*, this chapter refers to a functional, rather than formal, conception of criminal defense.

4 "Defense counsel" as used herein includes defender offices, criminal-defense attorneys in defender offices, contract attorneys, or attorneys in private practice, whether retained or court appointed.

5 A "wrongful conviction," as used in this chapter, means the conviction of a factually innocent defendant. Within this universe of wrongful convictions are exonerations. An "exoneration," as used in this chapter, occurs when a convicted individual's innocence is later proven (after conviction), usually to the satisfaction of a court or prosecutor. While most exonerations in the past two decades have been done through the use of DNA elimination (e.g., an individual convicted of rape in part because his blood type matches that of the semen taken from the victim, but whose conviction is later

assistance of defense counsel is most important for protecting the innocent, and analyzes the impact that the spread of the Anglo-American adversarial criminal justice framework has had on the importance of the defense function in protecting the innocent globally. Part IV contains ideas for, and obstacles in the way of, improving the American contribution to the rule of law and administration of justice through its foreign aid programs. Part V concludes by offering some final thoughts about reforming the scope and application of American foreign rule of law assistance. The hope is that this preliminary work will inspire further comparative research on the defense function in protecting against wrongful convictions and its relationship to the asymmetrical funding of criminal justice internationally.

## Part II: American Foreign Assistance for "Rule of Law" Programs

Foreign aid comprises approximately 1 percent of the American federal budget. In Fiscal Year (FY) 2011, America appropriated $2,482,100,000 through the State Department and US Aid[6] for foreign investment in democracy, human rights, and governance, $762,200,000 of which was dedicated to initiatives in the "rule of law and human rights." This American rule of law assistance is aimed almost exclusively at helping foreign legal institutions investigate and prosecute crimes.

For example, one of the largest beneficiaries of American bilateral assistance is Palestine. During FY 2004–11, the United States gave the Palestinians $359 million for International Narcotics Control and Law Enforcement (INCLE), as well as almost $105 million in INCLE and security-assistance funds that were reprogrammed to the Palestinian Authority in 2007 and $25 million for counterterrorism training.[7] The assistance was given to Palestinian Authority security forces, ministries, and the "justice system."[8] In April 2012, the Obama Administration notified Congress of its intention to obligate $100 million in INCLE to the Palestinians in FY 2012 and has requested $70 million in INCLE aid for FY 2013.[9] The purpose of this aid is to train and assist security forces, assist prosecutors and criminal investigators, and build courthouses, police stations, and prisons.[10]

Since the 1980s, America has provided "rule of law" assistance to Latin American and Caribbean countries to improve their justice-system institutions.[11] That aid has focused on reforming judicial institutions, the police, and other law enforcement organizations.[12] America has pledged $20 million to El Salvador to help it establish a new police force and police academy.[13] During the period following American military intervention in Panama in December 1989, America gave Panama foreign aid to "reform its criminal justice system," which it defined as developing professional police forces, creating an independent judiciary, and improving prison conditions.[14]

In addition to monetary assistance, the United States Department of Justice (DOJ) has an Office of Overseas Prosecutorial Development Assistance and Training (OPDAT) that sends American legal experts around

---

overturned when more precise DNA analysis excludes him as the source of the semen) In this sense, wrongful convictions are presumably a larger category than exonerations, and exonerations generally are a larger category than DNA exonerations.

6 The American Government delivers more than $58 billion per year in foreign assistance through more than 20 agencies. This chapter is based on data only for the portion of that aid appropriated to the State Department and US Aid, since those two agencies are responsible for the management of most of the rule of law and human-rights portions of that aid, and since they are the agencies for which detailed foreign aid budget data is most readily available.

7 *See* Jim Zanotti, U.S. Foreign Aid to the Palestinians (Congressional Research Service, Aug. 12, 2010) at 3, 6 (on file with author).

8 *See id.* at 4.

9 *See* Jim Zanotti, U.S. Foreign Aid to the Palestinians (Congressional Research Service, June 15, 2012) at 5, 11 (on file with author).

10 *See id.* at 6.

11 *See* U.S. General Accounting Office, Foreign Assistance: U.S. Rule of Law Assistance to Five Latin American Countries (Aug. 1999) [hereinafter GAO Latin America Report], at 1 (on file with author).

12 *See id.*

13 *See* U.S. General Accounting Office, Aid to El Salvador (Sept. 1992), at 1 (on file with author).

14 *See* U.S. General Accounting Office, Aid to Panama: Improving the Criminal Justice System (May 1992), at 1 (on file with author).

the world to work with prosecutors on criminal justice reform, and an International Criminal Investigative Training Assistance Program (ICITAP) to train police forces.[15] In Colombia, for example, ICITAP provides criminalistics and criminal-investigation training and technical assistance to prosecutors, police and other law enforcement organizations, investigative units, and forensics laboratories.[16] In El Salvador, ICITAP helped establish a new police academy, trained academy officials, developed an instructional manual on criminal procedures, and funded a new police forensics laboratory and special units for criminal investigation.[17] In Guatemala, ICITAP is helping to develop the police Criminal Investigative Service, Criminal Investigative School, and forensics laboratory.[18] In 1992, Congress authorized the Executive Branch to begin law enforcement training in Central and Eastern Europe and the former Soviet Union.[19]

In addition to general funding and assistance, America frequently gives prosecutorial and police offices abroad special funding for particular prosecution and investigation programs (e.g., domestic-violence prosecutions and drug-enforcement programs). For example, in Colombia, OPDAT provides assistance to the Office of the Prosecutor General to improve the capabilities of prosecutors.[20] The State Department funds training programs implemented by American law enforcement agencies.[21] In Honduras, ICITAP provided technical assistance to the police, helped revise academy curriculum, funded police investigative training, and helped establish a crime laboratory.[22]

The American Government's overarching interest is assisting countries with security and antiterrorism efforts.[23] The defense of those accused of crimes abroad is, at best, an afterthought. American rule of law assistance supports courts, prosecutors, and law enforcement organizations, but rarely supports criminal defense attorneys, defense investigators and experts, or public-defense agencies. Its priorities are making courts, prosecution services, and policing agencies more competent and efficient. In practical terms, this includes the development of training programs and the improvement of salaries and working conditions for judges, prosecutors, and police.[24]

In August 1991, America appropriated $36 million for a six-year judicial-reform project in Colombia.[25] The goal was to improve the Colombian criminal justice system so that suspected drug traffickers could be prosecuted domestically without extradition to America.[26] The American Government's interest in Colombia's reform of its criminal justice system, however, was limited to assistance aimed at combating drug trafficking and did not extend to any other judicial reforms.[27] The American "technical assistance" included helicopters, trucks, motorcycles, and German shepherds to aid Colombia in its anti-drug efforts.[28]

All of this assistance stands in stark contrast to the funding and training provided to defender offices that handle these same cases. Collette Rausch, the director of the United States Institute of Peace Rule of Law Center of Innovation, has described the rule of law-reform strategies that she has witnessed as "train[ing] some judges and prosecutors, maybe a few defense attorneys for good measure."[29]

---

15 *See* U.S. General Accounting Office, Foreign Assistance: Meeting the Training Needs of Police in New Democracies (Jan. 1993), at 2 (on file with author) [hereinafter GAO Police Training Report].

16 *See* Michael R. Pahl, *Wanted: Criminal Justice—Colombia's Adoption of a Prosecutorial System of Criminal Procedure*, 16 Fordham Int'l L.J. 608, 625 (1993); p. 5.

17 *See* GAO Latin America Report, *supra* note 11, at 5.

18 *See id.*

19 *See* Pub. L. No. 102-511, 106 Stat. 3320, 3329, 3355 (1992).

20 *See id.*

21 *See id.*

22 *See id.*

23 *See* Steven Lee Myers, *United Arab Emirates Shuts Down U.S.-Financed Democracy Group*, N.Y. Times, Apr. 1, 2012, at A11.

24 *See* Thomas Carothers, *The Rule of Law Revival*, 77 Foreign Affairs 95, 99 (1998).

25 *See* Pahl, *supra* note 16, at 625.

26 *See* Juan E. Mendez, Americas Watch Committee, Political Murder and Reform in Colombia: The Violence Continues 111 (1992).

27 *See* Pahl, *supra* note 16, at 625 n.103.

28 *See Fiscala No Tiene Futuro, Por Ahora*, El Tiempo, Aug. 27, 1992, at 3A.

29 Mooney, *supra* note 1, at 849. This chapter is not intended to be a complete comparison of all American foreign aid financing for prosecution versus defense functions for several reasons. First, the detailed and extensive data necessary

The asymmetry of the American foreign aid budget suggests that the Government views the defense as a lesser function within the justice systems of the countries to which it gives rule of law assistance. The result is that the scales of justice in these countries are further tipped in favor of the prosecution in terms of funding, as law enforcement resources far outweigh indigent-defense resources, both in terms of dollars and in-kind resources that are difficult to quantify, such as access to law enforcement resources, crime labs, and expert witnesses.

The emphasis on training for prosecutors, but not defense attorneys, has serious practical implications. For example, an American criminal-defense attorney described recent training at the State Court of Bosnia and Herzegovina for approximately 15 law students from the University of Sarajevo.[30] The students were participating in an exercise involving opening statements in a criminal case, which they had prepared ahead of time. Not only had every student prepared an opening statement for the prosecution, but, when the American judge running the training suggested that someone practice giving an opening statement for the defense, "[e]very one shook their heads no and made faces like no one would want to be on the defense side."[31] The students had received the message of American foreign rule of law assistance, whether intended or not, loud and clear.

## Part III: The Problem with Asymmetry

A criminal justice system, like any "system," is a group of interdependent elements forming a complex whole.[32] The actions of any one component necessarily impact each of the others.[33] The failure of any individual component of the criminal justice system threatens the ability of the entire system to dispense justice.[34] The link between the prosecution and defense functions should be evident to American policy makers, and yet, apparently, it is not. The right to counsel is one of the most sacred principles of the rule of law, yet experience has shown that this celebrated right is not implemented fully in American rule of law programs abroad.

According to the American Bar Association (ABA), the function of defense counsel is as follows:

> (a) Counsel for the accused is an essential component of the administration of criminal justice. A court properly constituted to hear a criminal case must be viewed as a tripartite entity consisting of the judge (and jury, where appropriate), counsel for the prosecution, and counsel for the accused.

---

for a numerical comparison are not available, at least not without an extensive Freedom of Information Act (FOIA) request, since published aid data is not divided into fine enough categories for more than sweeping comparisons. Second, making that comparison in quantitative terms involves difficult methodological questions beyond the scope of a chapter that is intended as a general, universal introduction to the topic. For example, what categories of aid should be compared against defense–attorney funding/training—prosecutor funding/training or funding/training for all law enforcement? Third, the focus of this chapter is on the normative argument that asymmetrical criminal justice aid is bad policy. To the extent that there is any question that America gives more aid, monetary and in kind, to law enforcement than to criminal defense, more detailed empirical research is needed. Nonetheless, even with the basic data available and included in this chapter, the funding, training, and other aid that America provides to foreign prosecutors specifically and law enforcement generally so greatly exceeds aid of any kind for defense attorneys that a detailed breakdown is not necessary to make the case for a more symmetrical approach. In short, if there is any question about the empirical premise of this chapter, if anyone believes that s/he can make the case that American rule of law aid is not disproportionately skewed toward the prosecution, s/he is welcome to try to prove this assumption wrong.

30 In Bosnia and Herzegovina, there are two centers for judicial and prosecutorial training. The primary duties of the centers are to provide regular training to judges and prosecutors.

31 Notes of interview with Robert Rainwater, Rainwater Law Group, Mar. 30, 2012 (on file with author).

32 *See* National Legal Aid and Defender Association (NLADA), Justice Impaired: The Impact of the State of New York's Failure to Effectively Implement the Right to Counsel (Oct. 2007) (on file with author) [hereinafter NLADA NY Report], at 2.

33 *See id.*

34 *See id.*

(b) The basic duty defense counsel owes to the administration of justice and as an officer of the court is to serve as the accused's counselor and advocate with courage and devotion and to render effective, quality representation.[35]

### *A. Constitutional Development*

Constitutions guarantee defendants a host of important rights, including the right to counsel,[36] largely to ensure that the innocent are not wrongly convicted.[37] The right to counsel, exemplified in the Sixth Amendment to the United States Constitution,[38] is the primary safeguard of a defendant's rights within the American criminal justice system.

The assistance of a qualified attorney is essential to assure a defendant a fair trial because "a fair trial is one in which evidence subject to adversarial testing is presented to an impartial tribunal."[39] Adequate representation ensures that all of a defendant's other rights—to be free from compelled self-incrimination, to confront witnesses—are protected.[40] The lack of meaningful access to the right to counsel renders these other rights superfluous and increases the likelihood of their violation.[41] "[A]ccess to counsel's skill and knowledge is necessary to accord defendants the 'ample opportunity to meet the case of the prosecution.'"[42]

---

35 ABA, Standards for Criminal Justice: Providing Defense Services [hereinafter ABA Standards], Standard 4-1.2. The ABA was the first organization to adopt standards relating to the provision of criminal defense services, adopting the first edition of the ABA Standards in 1967. *See* ABA, The Ten Principles of a Public Defense Delivery System (2002), *available at* www.abanet.org/legalservices/downloads/sclaid/10principles.pdf (last visited July 12, 2012) [hereinafter Ten Principles]. Several other American professional organizations have subsequently adopted criminal-defense standards, including the NLADA Performance Guidelines for Criminal Defense Representation (1995), *available at* http://www.nlada.org/Defender/Defender_Standards/Performance_Guidelines (last visited Sept. 27, 2012) [hereinafter NLADA Performance Guidelines]; NLADA Standards for the Administration of Assigned Counsel Systems (1989) [hereinafter NLADA Assigned Counsel Standards]; NLADA Guidelines for Negotiating and Awarding Contracts for Criminal Defense Services (1984) [hereinafter NLADA Contracts Standards]; Institute of Judicial Administration/ABA Juvenile Justice Standards (1979–80); National Study Commission on Defense Services Guidelines for Legal Defense Systems in the United States (1976) [hereinafter NSC Defense Guidelines]; and President's National Advisory Commission on Criminal Justice Standards and Goals, The Defense (1973) [hereinafter NAC Defense Standards]. Collectively, these standards contain the minimum requirements for legal representation for trial and appeal, including for juvenile and capital defendants, but they are directed, for the most part, toward lawyers who provide defense services, not toward governmental officials or policy makers who fund them, either domestically or abroad. *See* Ten Principles, *supra*. As the Introduction to the ABA Standards notes:

"The Defense Function Standards have been drafted and adopted by the ABA in an attempt to ascertain a consensus view of all segments of the criminal justice community about what good, professional practice is and should be. Hence, these are extremely useful standards for consultation by lawyers and judges who want to do "the right thing" or, as important, to avoid doing "the wrong thing."

The sheer volume of all of these standards makes it impracticable for policymakers tasked with appropriating foreign aid funding to wade through them in order to find guidance relevant to their duties. Thus, the standards do not address the particular needs of those who are responsible for funding and reforming criminal justice systems internationally.

36 *See, e.g.*, U.S. Const. amend VI; European Convention on Human Rights, Council of Europe, § I, art. 6 (Nov. 4, 1950).

37 *See* Rodney Uphoff, *Convicting the Innocent: Aberration or Systemic Problem?*, 2006 Wis. L. Rev. 739, 740.

38 The Sixth Amendment reads, in pertinent part: "In all criminal prosecutions, the accused shall enjoy the right … to have the Assistance of Counsel for his defence."

39 Strickland v. Washington, 466 U.S. 668. *See* Report of the Attorney General's Committee on Poverty and the Administration of Federal Criminal Justice 10–11 (1963) ("The proper performance of the defense function is … as vital to the health of the system as the performance of the prosecuting and adjudicatory functions. It follows that insofar as the financial status of the accused impedes vigorous and proper challenges, it constitutes a threat to the viability of the adversary system."); *see also infra* Section III (B) for a more detailed comparison of the aspects of adversarial and inquisitorial criminal justice systems that are most salient for the purpose of this chapter.

40 *See* Lakeside v. Oregon, 435 U.S. 333, 341 (1978) ("[I]n an adversary system of criminal justice, there is no right more essential than the right to the assistance of counsel.").

41 *See* Uphoff, *supra* note 37, at 809.

42 *Strickland*, 466 U.S. 668 (quoting Adams v. United States *ex rel.* McCann, 317 U.S. 269, 275–6 (1942)).

Since 1932, indigent defendants in America have had a due-process right to the assistance of counsel under *Powell v. Alabama*.[43] The United States Supreme Court (USSC), in *Powell*, reasoned:

> The right to be heard would be, in many cases, of little avail if it did not comprehend the right to be heard by counsel. … Left without the aid of counsel he may be put on trial without a proper charge, and convicted upon incompetent evidence, or evidence irrelevant to the issue or otherwise inadmissible. … He requires the guiding hand of counsel at every step in the proceedings against him. Without it, though he be not guilty, he faces the danger of conviction because he does not know how to establish his innocence.[44, 45]

Although the Sixth Amendment does not, in express terms, require the appointment of counsel for those who cannot afford it, the USSC has interpreted its guarantees to establish the contours of publicly financed criminal defense. Fifty years ago, in *Gideon v. Wainwright*,[46] declaring it an "obvious truth" that "lawyers in criminal courts are necessities, not luxuries," the Court determined that the Sixth Amendment required defendants charged with felonies to be provided with appointed legal counsel if they could not afford to retain an attorney.[47] As a result, all criminal defendants in America who have been charged with crimes,

---

43 287 U.S. 45 (1932) (holding that it was a violation of due process for a state court to fail to appoint counsel in a capital case).

44 *Id.* at 68–9.

45 Europe similarly recognizes a fundamental right to counsel for suspects and defendants. In 2003, the European Commission, in an effort to establish minimum procedural safeguards for defendants in criminal proceedings within the European Union, issued a statement declaring that, while all the rights needed to ensure a fair trial were important, some rights were so fundamental that they should be given priority status, and designating the right to legal advice and assistance the first priority. *See Commission Green Paper, Procedural Safeguards for Suspects and Defendants in Criminal Proceedings Throughout the European Union*, at 75, COM (2003) 75 final (Feb. 19, 2003).

In 2008, the European Court of Human Rights, in Salduz v. Turkey, held that Article 6.1 of the European Convention on Human Rights, which sets out the minimum human rights standards for all territory under the auspices of the Council of Europe, required a lawyer to be present from the first time that a suspect was interrogated by police, unless there was good cause to proceed without counsel. *See* Salduz v. Turkey (2008) Eur. Ct. H.R. 1542 (holding that access to a lawyer should be provided beginning with the first police interview of a suspect, unless it could be demonstrated, under the circumstances of the case, that there had been compelling reasons not to do so), *available at* http://www.bailii.org/eu/cases/ECHR/2008/1542.html (last visited July 22, 2012). Individual countries have begun to introduce interrogation reforms to implement the requirements of *Salduz*. For example, France and Scotland have begun the practice of providing counsel in police stations during and even before a suspect's first interrogation. *See* U.S Dep't of Justice, Expert Working Group Report: International Perspectives on Indigent Defense (Sept. 2011), at 21 (on file with author) [hereinafter International Perspectives].

46 372 U.S. 335 (1963) (recognizing that the Sixth Amendment right to counsel included the right to court-appointed counsel for indigent defendants, and holding that it applied to the states by virtue of the Fourteenth Amendment). *Gideon*'s mandate has been consistently extended to any case that may result in a potential loss of liberty, including initial appeals, juvenile-delinquency proceedings, and misdemeanor cases punishable by an actual or suspended jail sentence. *See* Shelton v. Alabama, 535 U.S. 654 (2002) (recognizing that the right to appointed counsel extended to misdemeanors involving suspended sentences); Argersinger v. Hamlin, 407 U.S. 25 (1972) (recognizing that the right to counsel guaranteed by the Sixth Amendment included an indigent defendant's right to court-appointed counsel in any case in which s/he was facing the possibility of incarceration, including misdemeanors); Coleman v. Alabama, 399 U.S. 1 (1970) (recognizing that the constitutional right to appointed counsel applied during preliminary hearings); *in re* Gault, 387 U.S. 1 (1967) (recognizing that the constitutional right to appointed counsel applied during juvenile proceedings that carried the potential for confinement); Douglas v. California, 372 U.S. 353 (1963) (recognizing that the constitutional right to appointed counsel applied during direct appeals).

47 *See Gideon*, 372 U.S. 335 (concluding that "in our adversary system of criminal justice, any person hauled into court, who is too poor to hire a lawyer, cannot be assured a fair trial unless counsel is provided for him"). Gideon was charged with felony burglary. Prior to his trial, he informed the trial court in Florida that he could not afford an attorney and requested that one be appointed to represent him at state expense. The court denied his request, he proceeded to trial *pro se*, and he was found guilty and sentenced to five years in prison. On retrial after the court vacated his uncounseled conviction, with the assistance of defense counsel, the jury found Gideon not guilty after deliberating for only an hour. *See* Anthony Lewis, Gideon's Trumpet 234–50 (1964).

conviction for which could result in incarceration, are constitutionally entitled to legal representation at Government expense.[48]

The USSC has long recognized that the right to counsel includes the right to the effective assistance of counsel and that the core purpose of the right to counsel was "to assure 'Assistance' at trial, when the accused was confronted with both the intricacies of the law and the advocacy of the public prosecutor."[49] In keeping with this guarantee, 30 years ago, in *Strickland v. Washington*, the USSC declared that the right to counsel included some minimum level of quality, explaining: "The right to the effective assistance of counsel is ... the right of the accused to require the prosecution's case to survive the crucible of meaningful adversarial testing."[50] The USSC acknowledged that the obligation of counsel to provide effective assistance imposes "certain basic duties," including: advocating for the defendant's cause, conducting reasonable factual and legal investigations, and bringing to bear the necessary skills and knowledge.[51]

In *Ake v. Oklahoma*,[52] the USSC recognized that "mere access to the courthouse doors does not by itself assure a proper functioning of the adversary process, and that a criminal trial is fundamentally unfair if the State proceeds against an indigent defendant without making certain that he has access to the raw materials integral to the building of an effective defense."[53] This includes adequate access to defense experts. Thus, to ensure that defendants could present their claims fairly within the adversary system, the USSC held that the "basic tools" of an adequate defense had to be provided at state expense for defendants who could not afford them.[54]

### *B. Wrongful Convictions and Situations in Which Effective Assistance Matters Most*

Effective lawyers can protect innocent people from being wrongfully convicted.[55] As former United States Attorney General Janet Reno stated:

> A competent lawyer will skillfully cross-examine a witness and identify and disclose a lie or a mistake. A competent lawyer will pursue weaknesses in the prosecutor's case, both to test the basis for the prosecution and to challenge the prosecutor's ability to meet the standard of proof beyond a reasonable doubt. A competent lawyer will force a prosecutor to take a hard, hard look at the gaps in the evidence. ... A competent lawyer will know how to conduct the necessary investigation so that an innocent defendant is not convicted. ... In the end, a good lawyer is the best defense against wrongful conviction ...[56]

The system assumes that, if the prosecution charges an innocent person with a crime, defense counsel will bring forward the evidence to correct the mistake. As the USSC has noted, the "very premise" of the criminal justice system "is that partisan advocacy on both sides of a case will best promote the ultimate objective that

48 In America, more than 80 percent of felony defendants in state courts and approximately two-thirds of felony defendants in federal court use publicly financed counsel. *See* Caroline Wolf Harlow, U.S. Dep't of Justice, Defense Counsel in Criminal Cases 1 (2000); *see generally* William J. Stuntz, *The Virtues and Vices of the Exclusionary Rule*, 20 Harv. J. L. & Pub. Pol. 443, 452 (1997).

49 United States v. Ash, 413 U.S. 300, 309 (1973).

50 *See Strickland*, 466 U.S. 668.

51 *Id.* at 688–91.

52 470 U.S. 68 (1985) (holding that Ake, an indigent criminal defendant, had a due-process right to the appointment of a defense expert as part of the "basic tools of an adequate defense").

53 *Id.* at 77.

54 *See id.*

55 *See* Office of Justice Programs, U.S. Dep't of Justice, Nat'l Symposium on Indigent Defense: Redefining Leadership For Equal Justice, at 75 (2000) [hereinafter DOJ Indigent Defense]. ("There are many ways that innocent people may be drawn into the criminal justice system ... But there is one overarching way that innocent indigent people can be extricated from the system: by furnishing competent legal representation.").

56 *Id.* at vi–vii.

the guilty be convicted and the innocent go free."[57] Without counsel's competent assistance, few accused people would be capable of mounting a meaningful challenge to the prosecution.[58]

Defense attorneys cannot fulfill their duties unless they function within a system that provides them with necessary support, skills, and resources.[59] When public defense is underfunded, there is a substantially greater risk that defendants will not receive adequate legal representation and that wrongful convictions will occur.

The failure to fund adequately and administer effectively a defense counsel delivery system inevitably results in too few lawyers handling too many cases.[60] Overworked, undertrained defense attorneys do not have the time, skill, or resources to perform the investigation and preparation needed to screen innocent defendants from the system.[61] If defense counsel is so overburdened and under-resourced that s/he cannot put the prosecution to the test, the adversarial system breaks down, and the criminal justice system can no longer be relied upon to produce results that are fair and just.[62] Ineffective or incompetent defense counsel, by failing to investigate, call witnesses, or prepare for trial (due to workload or incompetence), have allowed those who might otherwise have been proven innocent to be sent to prison.

Inadequate counsel has played a significant role in American wrongful conviction cases.[63] The case of Davien Woods exemplifies what can happen when a defense attorney lacks adequate time and skills to be effective. On September 24, 2001, two men accosted a customer at a gas station and stole his car at gunpoint.[64] Three days later, a police officer stopped a speeding car that turned out to have been the one that had been stolen.[65] Woods was a passenger in the car during the stop.[66] The following day, the car's owner picked Woods out of a photo line-up and identified him as one of the carjackers.[67]

State law prohibited the use of photo line-ups when the accused was physically able to participate in an in-person line-up, which Woods had been, but Woods's attorney did nothing to challenge the improper use of the photo line-up or his identification.[68] Even though research demonstrates that eyewitness identifications are often inaccurate,[69] the attorney did not retain an expert on their unreliability.[70]

Prior to trial, Woods told his attorney that his brother and grandmother could testify that he had been sleeping on a pullout bed in his grandmother's living room when thc carjacking occurred.[71] The attorney did not contact either witness and failed to notify the court within the requisite time period that he intended to present an alibi defense.[72] As a result, the alibi witnesses were barred from testifying.[73]

---

57 Herring v. New York, 422 U.S. 853, 862 (1975). *See* Nix v. Williams, 467 U.S. 431, 453 (1984) (admonishing that a criminal conviction had to be the product of an adversarial process, rather than the state's *ex parte* investigation and decision making); Wheat v. United States, 486 U.S. 153, 158 (1988) (explaining that the right to counsel "was designed to assure fairness in the adversary criminal process").

58 *See* Uphoff, *supra* note 37, at 740.

59 *See* American Civil Liberties Union, Faces of Failing Public Defense Systems: Portrait's of Michigan's Constitutional Crisis 7 (2011) (on file with author) [hereinafter ACLU Michigan Report], at 7.

60 *See* NLADA NY Report, *supra* note 32, at 2.

61 *See* Uphoff, *supra* note 37, at 809.

62 *See Strickland*, 466 U.S. at 687.

63 For example, Luis Rojas was convicted of murder in New York when his out-of-state lawyer failed to investigate his alibis. Had he done so, they would have convincingly placed Rojas far from the scene of the crime at the time of commission. *See* Adele Bernhard, *Effective Assistance of Counsel*, *in* Wrongly Convicted: Perspectives On Failed Justice 220, 221–5 (Saundra D. Westervelt & John A. Humphrey eds., 2001).

64 *See* ACLU Michigan Report, *supra* note 59, at 55.

65 *See id.*

66 *See id.*

67 *See id.* at 55–6.

68 *See id.* at 56.

69 *See infra*, Section III B iv.

70 *See* ACLU Michigan Report, *supra* note 59, at 56.

71 *See id.*

72 *See id.* at 55–6.

73 *See id.* at 55. The attorney attempted to call Woods's brother as an alibi witness at trial, but he was precluded from doing so because he had not given the prosecutor and the trial court timely notice of Woods's alibi defense under the local rules of criminal procedure. *See id.* at 56. The attorney later admitted that he was unaware of the time period within which he had to provide notice. *See id.*

Based solely on the illegal identification of him, and in light of Woods's lack of admissible alibi evidence, he was convicted of carjacking, armed robbery, and possession of a firearm.[74] After Woods's conviction, a different individual admitted to having been the carjacker.[75] Woods spent two years in prison before the court vacated his conviction because his attorney had "unequivocally" provided ineffective assistance of counsel (IAC), having failed, among other things, "to move for suppression of identification," "adequately investigate and prepare the case," or "communicate on a regular basis" with Woods.[76]

In the arena of indigent criminal defense, nothing can add value faster than money.[77] Criminal defendants get what they (or the Government) pay for, and a good defense is expensive. Although there are genuine debates about the most efficient ways to organize public defense,[78] money can improve any method of delivering defense services.[79] Exonerating an innocent client requires a great deal of time and resources to investigate, uncover exculpatory evidence, and present it convincingly in court. As the ABA admonishes:

> Defense counsel should conduct a prompt investigation of the circumstances of the case and explore all avenues leading to facts relevant to the merits of the case and the penalty in the event of conviction. The investigation should include efforts to secure information in the possession of the prosecution and law enforcement authorities. The duty to investigate exists regardless of the accused's admissions or statements to defense counsel of facts constituting guilt or the accused's stated desire to plead guilty.[80]

A good defense requires basic items that indigent defenders sometimes lack, like training, support staff, office space, and computers. Without a well-trained, well-funded attorney, an innocent defendant will often find it extremely difficult to prove his/her innocence. In an underfunded system, defense counsel has far too many cases to conduct legal research, interview witnesses, conduct factual investigation, hire experts, file briefs, or perform the other activities that are required to provide a competent defense.[81] Overloaded defenders are forced to triage, recommending quick guilty pleas for some clients to preserve their ability to fight for others. The former are "pleaded out" without having been given the time, effort, or attention necessary for real investigation or legal research. It is possible, in these cases, that plea agreements represented the best possible result for the defendant, but it is also possible that the defendant was innocent and just too frightened, confused, or hopeless to reject the lawyer's recommendation. For these reasons, inept or overburdened lawyers increase the likelihood that innocent defendants will plead or be found guilty.[82] Unfortunately, asymmetrical assistance assures that public defenders remain strapped for resources.

---

74 *See id.* at 55–6.

75 *See id.* at 57. The first carjacker had already pleaded guilty and admitted his involvement prior to Woods's trial. *See id.*

76 *See id.* at 55, 57.

77 *See* Wright, *infra* note 327, at 267.

78 Compare Bob Sablatura, *Study Confirms Money Counts in County's Courts: Those Using Appointed Lawyers Are Twice as Likely to Serve Time*, Hous. Chron., Oct. 17, 1999, at 1 (finding that privately retained attorneys achieved lower conviction rates and sentences than publicly funded attorneys representing clients facing comparable charges) with Hanson et al., Indigent Defenders Get the Job Done and Done Well 103–6 (1992); Matthew Dolan, *New Study Makes Case for Public Defenders*, Virginian-Pilot, Dec. 18, 2001. *See generally* Floyd Feeney & Patrick G. Jackson, *Public Defenders, Assigned Counsel, Retained Counsel: Does the Type of Criminal Defense Counsel Matter?*, 22 Rutgers L.J. 361 (1991) (analyzing the perceptions of judges, attorneys, and defendants regarding the relative quality of the three main types of appointed counsel in the United States).

79 *See* Wright, *infra* note 327, at 221.

80 ABA Standards, *supra* note 35, Standards 4-3.6 & 4-4.1 (a).

81 *See* Uphoff, *supra* note 37, at 754–5, 762; *see generally* ABA Standards, *supra* note 35(setting forth the tasks that defense counsel must perform in order to render competent assistance to a client charged with a crime).

82 *See* Uphoff, *supra* note 37, at 741.

During the past decade, the flood of wrongfully convicted Americans has underscored the importance of providing effective defense services for the indigent.[83] While there are many reasons why the American justice system too often convicts innocent people, inadequate representation often is cited as a significant factor.[84]

In an adversary system, fairness is served if both sides are represented by lawyers who are evenly matched in time, training, experience, and resources. When the defense does not measure up to the prosecution, there is a heightened risk of mistakes.[85] The ABA has suggested that the appropriate measure of health within a criminal justice system is whether each of its branches—courts, prosecutors, and defenders—receives adequate and balanced resources.[86] Giving substantially more funding to prosecutors and law enforcement agencies can unfairly disadvantage already underfunded indigent defense lawyers. A one-sided, untested presentation of the facts compromises reliability and increases the likelihood of error.[87] Applying this measure of success, American foreign aid funding for criminal justice, and the systems that it funds, are failing.

In February 2002, the ABA adopted *Ten Principles of a Public Defense Delivery System*, which "constitute the fundamental criteria to be met for a public defense delivery system to deliver effective and efficient, high quality, ethical, conflict-free representation to accused persons who cannot afford to hire an attorney."[88] The eighth principle addresses parity of defense and prosecution resources:

> There is parity between defense counsel and the prosecution with respect to resources and defense counsel is included as an equal partner in the justice system. There should be parity of workload, salaries and other resources (such as benefits, technology, facilities, legal research, support staff & paralegals, investigators, and access to forensic services and experts) between prosecution and public defense … . No part of the justice system should be expanded or the workload increased without consideration of the impact that expansion will have on the balance and on the other components of the justice system. Public defense should participate as an equal partner in improving the justice system.[89]

The ninth principle recommends: "Defense counsel is provided with and required to attend continuing legal education. Counsel and staff providing defense services should have systematic and comprehensive training … and *at least equal to that received by prosecutors*."[90]

The inequities between prosecution and defense can take several forms, including disparity in the amount and sources of funding, in-kind resources, staffing, and salaries.[91] The failure of defense systems to meet the Ten Principles has a profound effect on individuals who rely upon them. The most common causes of wrongful conviction, like faulty scientific evidence and mistaken eyewitness identifications, are matters that competent defense lawyers can address.[92] Without symmetrical funding and training, however, innocent defendants will be convicted abroad. What follows are situations in which innocent defendants in the United States have been convicted the most often, and an analysis of their relationship to asymmetrical criminal justice funding.

---

83 *See Executive Summary*, in AMERICAN BAR ASSOCIATION ("ABA"), GIDEON'S BROKEN PROMISE: AMERICA'S CONTINUING QUEST FOR EQUAL JUSTICE, A REPORT ON THE AMERICAN BAR ASSOCIATION'S HEARINGS ON THE RIGHT TO COUNSEL IN CRIMINAL PROCEEDINGS (2004) [hereinafter ABA GIDEON'S REPORT], at iv (on file with author).

84 *See* C. RONALD HUFF & ARYE RATNER, CONVICTED BUT INNOCENT: WRONGFUL CONVICTION AND PUBLIC POLICY 76–7 (1996); BARRY SCHECK ET AL., ACTUAL INNOCENCE: FIVE DAYS TO EXECUTION AND OTHER DISPATCHES FROM THE WRONGLY CONVICTED 183–92 (2000); Lefstein, *infra* note 327, at 868.

85 *See* NATIONAL RIGHT TO COUNSEL COMMITTEE, JUSTICE DENIED: AMERICA'S CONTINUING NEGLECT OF OUR CONSTITUTIONAL RIGHT TO COUNSEL (Apr. 2009), at 6 (on file with author) [hereinafter JUSTICE DENIED].

86 *See* The Spangenberg Group, Status of Indigent Defense in New York: A Study for Chief Judge Kaye's Commission on the Future of Indigent Defense Services (June 16, 2006) (on file with author) [hereinafter "Kaye Commission Report"], at 83.

87 *See* Uphoff, *supra* note 37, at 740–41.

88 TEN PRINCIPLES, *supra* note 35.

89 Id.

90 *Id.* (emphasis added). Professional standards typically recommend linking indigent defense training to the level of training available to prosecutors. *See* Scott Wallace & David Carroll, The Implementation and Impact of Indigent Defense Standards 15 (Dec. 2003) (on file with author).

91 *See* JUSTICE DENIED, *supra* note 85, at 61.

92 *See id.* at 47.

*i. Junk science*

Increasing numbers of criminal cases are resolved largely on the basis of forensic sciences like handwriting, ballistics, fingerprint comparison, and DNA analysis.[93] Yet, the data supporting the validity of these techniques, the safeguards against fraud or mistake, the training and supervision of personnel, and the existence and enforcement of sound, standardized procedures are deficient.[94] Tainted or fraudulent science contributed to the wrongful convictions in almost half of the first 225 Innocence Project exonerations in America.[95]

Changing poor forensic practices begins with defense attorneys challenging them and asking courts to compel best practices. In many criminal cases, securing forensic experts to examine and retest evidence, advise counsel, and testify is critical. Defense counsel should have the ability to consult with experts in the forensic disciplines and related scientific fields to identify the scientific limits of the evidence and present the results of independent testing and the testimony of independent experts, if appropriate.

Incompetence-of-counsel cases involving scientific evidence abound. The case of Carl Vinson is one. On January 3, 1986, a man broke into a Detroit home and raped a nine-year-old girl.[96] The girl was initially unable to identify her attacker.[97] Later, her mother suggested to her that her attacker might be Vinson, who was the ex-husband of her former babysitter.[98] Vinson's family insisted that he had been asleep at his mother's house at the time of the rape.[99] The blood cells in the semen that the police had collected from the victim's bed sheets were Type-O, while Vinson's blood type was AB, and there was no other physical evidence linking him to the crime.[100] At trial, the prosecutor claimed that Vinson had a particular physiology that prevented his fingertips from leaving fingerprints and his blood type from being detected in his semen, and that the Type-O blood cells in the semen were the victim's.[101] Although these assertions were false, Vinson's attorney did not attempt to refute them.[102] A recent analysis of Vinson's blood revealed that his blood type could be detected in his semen.[103] This evidence was not introduced at Vinson's trial because his attorney never retained a forensic expert.[104] Vinson was convicted of rape and sentenced to a term of imprisonment of 10–50 years.[105] His motion to vacate his conviction is currently pending.[106]

One of the significant systemic costs of the failure to provide defendants with effective, well-funded counsel with access to expert assistance is the extent to which most forensic evidence goes unchallenged.[107] Inadequate funding for criminal-defense attorneys makes misconduct almost impossible to detect and redress. Without an expert to review or test the findings of the prosecution's expert(s), defendants have no meaningful ability to controvert questionable forensic evidence.[108] Rule of law assistance should, therefore, include

---

93 *See* Taslitz, *Temporal Adversarialism*, *infra* note 332, at 26.

94 *See id.*; *see also* Stanley Cohen, The Wrong Men: Americas Epidemic of Wrongful Death Row Convictions 220 (2003); Paul Giannelli & Emmie West, *Forensic Science: Hair Comparison Evidence*, 37 Crim. L. Bull. 514 (2001); Edward Imwinkelried, *Flawed Expert Testimony: Striking the Right Balance in Admissibility Standards*, 18:1 CRIM. JUST. 29 (Spring 2003). Documented cases of junk science have had some impact on the ease with which American courts admit forensic science testimony. For example, in *Ramirez v. State*, the Florida Supreme Court recently noted the "rising nationwide criticism of forensic evidence" as part of the basis for its decision to exclude the State's proffered expert testimony. 810 So. 2d 836, 853 (Fla. 2001).

95 *See* Scheck et al., *supra* note 84, at 246.

96 *See* ACLU Michigan Report, *supra* note 59, at 43.

97 *See id.*

98 *See id.*

99 *See id.* at 44.

100 *See id.*

101 *See id.*

102 *See id.*

103 *See id.* at 43–4.

104 *See id.* at 43.

105 *See id.* at 44.

106 *See id.* at 45.

107 *See* Uphoff, *supra* note 37, at 786.

108 *See* ABA Standards, *supra* note 35, Standard 5-14, Commentary, at 22 ("The quality of representation at trial … may be excellent and yet unhelpful to the defendant if the defense requires the assistance of a psychiatrist or handwriting expert and no such services are available."); Uphoff, *supra* note 37, at 786. This at least partially explains how a rogue

providing defense attorneys with the resources to obtain the assistance of forensic and scientific experts for confidential consultation and testimony and the use of forensic facilities for independent testing.

*ii. False confessions*

False confessions are another example of why well-trained and well-funded defense attorneys are crucial to preventing the conviction of the innocent. The USSC recognized the important role that counsel can play in averting false confessions in *Miranda v. Arizona*,[109] in which it held that the right to counsel extended to custodial interrogations.

Approximately 27 percent of DNA exonerations in America involved confessions or incriminating statements, and, in many of these cases, the defendants reported either that they had confessed as the result of beatings or that they had never made the statements attributed to them.[110] False confessions result in convictions because of the dramatic impact at trial of a suspect who has admitted his/her guilt to the police,[111] leading scholars to conclude that that "placing a confession before a jury is tantamount to an instruction to convict."[112]

Because of the difficulty in overcoming evidence of a false confession, well-funded, well-trained counsel is crucial. If a defense attorney is overburdened or undertrained, a client who has confessed is the least likely to receive a share of limited time or resources. It also unlikely, in such a case, that counsel will visit the scene of the crime or interview witnesses.[113] Indeed, an unprepared or untrained attorney may be skeptical of a client's claim of innocence and a false confession. Not surprisingly, a defendant represented by a skeptical defense lawyer who does not have the time, training, or resources to investigate a false-confession claim and prepare to litigate it is unlikely to risk a trial.[114]

The case of Eddie Joe Lloyd demonstrates the price that a defendant who falsely confesses can pay if s/he has an ineffective attorney. In October 1984, while Lloyd was involuntarily committed in a psychiatric hospital for a delusional thought and mood disorder, he wrote a letter to the police suggesting that he had information about a highly publicized rape and murder of a 16-year-old girl eight months earlier.[115] Lloyd had previously written letters to the police offering to assist in cases that he had learned about through newspapers or television.[116] The police visited Lloyd at the hospital on at least four separate occasions.[117] They convinced him that if he confessed to the crime and was arrested, he would help them "smoke out" the real perpetrator.[118] They told him confidential details about the crime scene and had him make written and tape-recorded confessions while he was hospitalized.[119]

Lloyd's attorneys never challenged the manner in which the confessions were obtained.[120] They did not have a psychiatric expert evaluate Lloyd's condition to determine the veracity and reliability of his confession.[121] At trial, Lloyd's attorney did not call witnesses, present expert testimony, cross-examine the officer primarily responsible for obtaining Lloyd's confession, or cross-examine the medical examiner, and

---

criminologist like Zain was able to escape detection in the years before his misconduct was uncovered. *See* Giannelli & West, *supra* note 94, at 445–7.

109 384 U.S. 436 (1966).

110 *See* Scheck et al., *supra* note 84, at 120–21; David K. Shipler, *Why Do Innocent People Confess?*, N.Y. Times, Feb. 26, 2012, at SR6.

111 *See* Taslitz, *Temporal Adversarialism*, *infra* note 332, at 23.

112 Richard Ofshe & Richard Leo, *The Decision to Confess Falsely: Rational Choice and Irrational Action*, 74 Denver U. L. Rev. 979, 1118 (1997).

113 *See* Uphoff, *supra* note 37, at 795.

114 *See id.*

115 *See* ACLU Michigan Report, *supra* note 59, at 23–4.

116 *See id.* at 24.

117 *See id.*

118 Id.

119 *See id.* at 23–4.

120 *See id.* at 23. Lloyd's attorneys also neglected to have the biological evidence that the police had collected at the crime scene analyzed. *See id.* They did not seek funding for experts to analyze the blood, hair, semen, or fingernail scrapings collected by police investigators at the crime scene. *See id.* at 24.

121 *See id.* at 24.

he gave a five-minute summation.[122] The jury convicted Lloyd of first-degree murder after less than an hour of deliberation.[123] Subsequent DNA analysis revealed that Lloyd could not have been the perpetrator, but only after Lloyd served 17 years in prison.[124]

*iii. Snitches*

In a 2005 study, the Center on Wrongful Convictions found that false or misleading informant testimony was responsible for 38 wrongful convictions in capital cases in America. Nonetheless, law enforcement agencies continue to rely heavily on witnesses cooperating in exchange for leniency, despite their strong incentives to lie and the lack of systemic competency in verifying the veracity of their claims.[125]

The case of Rodney Hubbard demonstrates what can happen when a jailhouse snitch and an ineffective defense attorney collide. On March 4, 1999, Raymondo Davis's body was found in an alley near Hubbard's house.[126] Davis had been shot in the back.[127] Investigators found no bullets, blood, or weapon at the crime scene.[128] Several neighborhood residents identified another local drug dealer, "Detroit Mike," as the killer, but the police did not pursue him as a suspect.[129] Instead, little happened in the case until July 2004, when the police received a letter from a jail inmate who was facing a lengthy sentence as a habitual offender.[130] The inmate claimed that Hubbard, who was incarcerated in the same jail on an unrelated charge, had confessed to murder.[131] The inmate subsequently provided an illicit recording of an unidentified man admitting that he had killed someone named "Edward" by shooting him in the chest and claimed that the man was Hubbard.[132] The inmate later received a significantly reduced sentence.[133] Hubbard's court-appointed lawyer did almost nothing to investigate the charges or prepare for trial.[134] Despite Hubbard's consistent claim that the voice on the tape was not his, his attorney did not retain a voice expert to analyze it.[135] He made no attempt to locate and interview Detroit Mike or the confidential informants who claimed to have been present when he shot Davis.[136] He also made no attempt to locate or interview witnesses who could have discredited the testimony of the jailhouse snitch, including two other inmates who had told the police that the snitch had stated that he would do whatever it took to "free himself up" and that he was "going to testify on Rodney Hubbard, because Rodney was trying to mess up a case he was on."[137] Hubbard was convicted of Davis's murder and sentenced to life in prison.[138] Although a voice-identification expert has since concluded that Hubbard's voice was not that of the man on the tape, he remains in prison.[139]

The case of Kenneth Wyniemko is an example of what can happen when the unchallenged testimony of a snitch and an attorney's failure to challenge bad forensic science combine. In July 1994, a woman was raped in her home.[140] She described the rapist as 20 to 25 years old, 6′ to 6′2″, and 200 to 225 pounds.[141] Although

---

122 *See id.*
123 *See id.*
124 *See id.* at 25.
125 *See id.*
126 *See* ACLU Michigan Report, *supra* note 59, at 15.
127 *See id.*
128 *See id.*
129 *See id.*
130 *See id.*
131 *See id.* at 16.
132 *See id.*
133 *See id.*
134 *See id.* at 17.
135 *See id.*
136 *See id.*
137 Id.
138 *See id.* at 15–17.
139 *See id.* at 17.
140 *See id.* at 59.
141 *See id.*

he had a nylon stocking over his head and had blindfolded her, she stated that she had glimpsed his face and assisted in creating a composite sketch.[142]

At the time of the rape, Wyniemko was 43 years old, 5′11″, and weighed 198 pounds, although he bore some resemblance to the victim's sketch.[143] There was no physical evidence tying him to the crime.[144] On the contrary, an analysis of the semen on the victim's sheets revealed that the semen contained Type-A blood cells, while Wyniemko was Type-O.[145] Because there was no physical evidence, the prosecution was built around a jailhouse snitch, who testified that Wyniemko had confessed to him while awaiting trial.[146] Wyniemko's attorney did not ask to have the semen stains on the victim's underwear analyzed or the stains on the sheet subjected to DNA analysis; nor did he retain a defense expert for independent DNA testing.[147] The attorney also failed to establish that the snitch had only agreed to testify against Wyniemko after the lead detective and prosecutor had told him that "he would never see the light of day" if he did not.[148] Wyniemko was convicted of rape and sentenced to 40–60 years in prison.[149] Subsequent DNA analysis established that Wyniemko could not have been the rapist, and Wyniemko was released after nine years in prison.[150]

Hubbard's and Wyniemko's cases are not anomalous. In one highly publicized debacle, in 2000, a drug task force arrested dozens of individuals in a housing project in Hearne, Texas, based on information from a single, mentally ill informant who fabricated the evidence in an attempt to snitch his way out of burglary charges.[151] While many of the charges were ultimately dismissed, several defendants had already been convicted after pleading guilty, before the prosecution divulged the problems with its star witness's credibility. Erma Faye Stewart, a 30-year-old, single mother of two, was one of the defendants in the Hearne drug sweep.[152] In jail, with no one to care for her two young children, she panicked.[153] Though she maintained her innocence, her court-appointed lawyer told her to plead guilty in exchange for a sentence of 10 years' probation.[154] After a month in jail, Stewart relented and agreed to plead guilty to felony drug trafficking.[155]

*iv. Eyewitness identification*

An Innocence Project estimate shows that around 75 percent of thc now over 300 DNA exonerations in America involved eyewitness misidentification.[156] In case after case, DNA analysis has proven what cognitive scientists had long been trying to tell police and prosecutors: that eyewitness identification is inherently unreliable and frequently inaccurate. This is why attorney competence is particularly important in cases involving eyewitness identification.

The case of Edward George Carter is one example of what can happen when there is an asymmetry of attorney time, experience, and resources combined with an inaccurate eyewitness. On October 24, 1974, a student at Wayne State University in Detroit was sexually assaulted and robbed.[157] Although the victim was initially unable to identify her assailant, she later identified Carter from a photo line-up that contained multiple photos of him, and from an in-person line-up consisting of Carter and several others who bore no resemblance

---

142 *See id.*

143 *See id.*

144 *See id.* at 59–60.

145 *See id.* at 60.

146 *See id.*

147 *See id.* at 59–61.

148 *Id.* at 61.

149 *See id.*

150 *See id.*

151 *See* Alexandra Natapoff, Snitching: Criminal Informants and the Erosion of American Justice (2009).

152 *See* Michelle Alexander, *Go to Trial: Crash the Justice System*, N.Y. Times, Mar. 11, 2012, at SR5.

153 *See id.*

154 *See id.*

155 *See id.*

156 *See Eyewitness Misidentification*, Innocence Project, http://www.innocenceproject.org/understand/Eyewitness-Misidentification.php (last visited August 21, 2013).

157 *See* ACLU Michigan Report, *supra* note 59, at 11.

to him.[158] The victim's identifications were the only evidence against Carter.[159] Two university employees who had seen a suspicious young man in the hallways immediately prior to the assault did not identify Carter. The fingerprints, semen, and seminal fluid collected at the scene and from the victim did not match Carter, who had an alibi.[160] Carter's public defender, who had been practicing law for 18 months, met with Carter only twice—at his preliminary hearing and the day before trial.[161] Without the necessary training, time, or resources, Carter's attorney failed to adequately investigate, challenge the suggestive line-ups, or otherwise mount an effective defense.[162] She did not retain an expert on the unreliability of eyewitness identifications, request discovery of the analysis of the fingerprints found at the crime scene, or provide timely notice of Carter's alibi witness, which prevented him from presenting it to the jury.[163] After a trial that lasted only a few hours, Carter was convicted of aggravated rape and armed robbery and sentenced to life imprisonment.[164] Carter was exonerated, after 35 years in prison, when the crime-scene fingerprints were determined to match those of a sex offender who had been convicted of a number of very similar armed rapes around the same time, two of them on the Wayne State campus.[165]

The case of Alphonso Sones, Sr. is another example. On August 26, 2002, a man brandishing a butcher knife robbed a gas station.[166] According to two gas-station employees, the man was in his mid-forties, dark-skinned, had facial hair, and was wearing blue sweatpants and a white T-shirt.[167] Several days later, police stopped Sones, who was walking down the street wearing blue pants and a white T-shirt.[168] The officers searched him, his car, and his girlfriend's house, but did not find the $400 that was taken in the robbery or the butcher knife that had been used.[169] Sones was picked out of a six-person line-up in which he was one of only two men who matched the eyewitnesses' description of the robber.[170] The faulty line-up identification was the only evidence against Sones.[171] Sones's attorney met with him only once prior to his trial and pressured him to plead guilty.[172] When Sones refused, he obtained a continuance on the eve of trial to retain an expert on the unreliability of eyewitness identification, but then failed actually to retain one before the second trial date.[173] When the court denied his request for a second continuance, he made no opening statement and called no witnesses.[174] Sones was convicted and sentenced to 22–36 years in prison.[175]

*v. Cross-examination*

It is an oft-quoted axiom that cross-examination is the greatest engine for discovering the truth.[176] Undoubtedly, cross-examination is a powerful weapon when wielded by a well-prepared, skilled practitioner.[177] Without proper training and preparation, however, an unskilled advocate will find it exceedingly difficult to conduct an effective cross-examination, and even a well-intentioned defense lawyer may be unable to undermine effectively the testimony of an incredible prosecution witness.[178]

---

158 *See id.*
159 *See id.*
160 *See id.*
161 *See id.* at 12.
162 *See id.* at 10–12.
163 *See id.* at 12.
164 *See id.* at 10–12.
165 *See id.* at 12–13.
166 *See id.* at 35.
167 *See id.*
168 *See id.* at 36.
169 *See id.*
170 *See id.*
171 *See id.* at 35–6.
172 *See id.* at 36.
173 *See id.* at 35–7.
174 *See id.* at 37.
175 *See id.* at 35, 37.
176 *See* John Henry Wigmore, Evidence in Trials at Common Law 1367 (James H. Chadbourn ed., 1974).
177 *See* Uphoff, *supra* note 37, at 787.
178 *See id.*

The now famous case of Ronald Williamson[179] is an example of the consequences of ill-equipped defense counsel. Williamson's attorney was a sole practitioner appointed to defend him in his capital murder case.[180] He was paid a total of $3,200.[181] The attorney did not retain an investigator or any experts, and failed to investigate Williamson's extensive psychiatric history, despite having been told about it.[182] Had he done so, he would have discovered that Williamson had a long history of delusional mental illness that left him with a distorted perception of reality.[183] Williamson was convicted of capital murder and sentenced to death largely on the basis of a "dream confession" that he recounted to the police, the testimony of a jailhouse informant, and questionable forensic hair-analysis evidence, the credibility of which his attorney did essentially nothing to challenge.[184] Defense counsel failed to elicit Williamson's mental-health history or the fact that another man had confessed to the crime on cross-examination.[185] Five days before Williamson was scheduled to be executed, a federal court stayed his execution and subsequently overturned his conviction because of the ineffectiveness of his counsel's assistance.[186] While Williamson was awaiting retrial, DNA analysis exonerated him.[187]

*vi. Plea bargaining*

The threat of long sentences persuades many defendants to plead guilty and negotiate a lesser sentence.[188] As a result, criminal cases increasingly are no longer decided on the basis of a traditional "full" trial.[189] In common law and increasingly in civil law systems, the great majority of cases are resolved without trial, usually through a guilty plea or its equivalent.[190]

This system of plea and sentence bargaining is already heavily rigged against the accused.[191] It is critical for defense counsel to accurately size up a case and give good legal advice to the defendant about whether to go to trial. Defendants who reject plea offers typically do so hoping to get a better deal nearer to or at trial.[192] For a defendant with inadequate representation, by contrast, it is much harder to resist the pressure to plead guilty in exchange for a reduced sentence.

Even in cases in which a guilty plea is in the defendant's best interest, his/her attorney must adequately prepare to negotiate the terms. It is particularly important that the defense attorney have a reliable factual basis on which s/he can rely in the bargaining process. Otherwise, the outcome of the bargaining process depends not on considerations of fairness and justice, but solely on the distribution of power between the parties and/or their relative skills at gambling.[193]

---

179 *See* Williamson v. Ward, 110 F.3d 1508 (10th Cir. 1997). Williamson's case was profiled in John Grisham, The Innocent Man (2006) and Scheck et al., *supra* note 84, at 163–203.

180 *See Williamson*, 110 F.3d, at 1510–12.

181 *See id.* at 1522. Williamson's attorney spent a total of 14 hours working on trial motions and 43.5 hours preparing for a capital murder trial that lasted 45 hours. *See id.* at 1512.

182 *See id.* at 1513.

183 *See id.* at 1514–16, 1519.

184 *See id.* at 1510.

185 *See id.* at 1512, 1520–21.

186 *See* Williamson v. Reynolds, 904 F. Supp. 1529, 1576 (E.D. Okla. 1995).

187 *See* Scheck et al., *supra* note 84. There is nothing to suggest that ineffective assistance of counsel like Williamson received occurs any less often in less serious cases; on the contrary, capital defendants in America have likely been exonerated largely because of the *better* representation that they tend to receive.

188 *See* Nathan Gorenstein, *"Mandatory Minimum" Laws Can Mean Grossly Disparate Sentences for Gun Crimes*, Phila. Inquirer, Feb. 7, 2012.

189 *See* Heike Jung, *Nothing But the Truth? Some Facts, Impressions and Confessions about Truth in Criminal Procedure*, in 1 The Trial on Trial 147, 155 (Antony Duff et al., eds., 2004).

190 *See* Thomas Weigend, *The Decay of the Inquisitorial Ideal: Plea Bargaining Invades German Criminal Procedure*, *in* Crime, Procedure and Evidence in a Comparative and International Context: Essays in Honour of Professor Mirjan Damaska 39, 41 (John Jackson et al., eds., 2008).

191 *See* Mary Prosser, *Reforming Criminal Discovery*, 2006 Wis. L. Rev. 541, 560 (2006) (describing the disparate power between the prosecution and the defense throughout the plea bargaining process).

192 *See* Gorenstein, *supra* note 188.

193 *See* Thomas Weigend, *Should We Search for the Truth, and Who Should Do It?*, 36 N.C.J. Int'l L. & Com. Reg. 389, 411 (2011) [hereinafter Weigend, *Truth*]; cf. Albert W. Alschuler, *The Defense Attorney's Role in Plea*

Defendants with lawyers lacking the time or the resources to provide an adequate defense, especially those who are innocent, are likely to suffer significantly.[194] These defendants have only one viable option: accept the plea offer.[195] Many innocent defendants succumb to the pressure to plead guilty, especially when their attorneys are unprepared to defend them at trial.[196] According to the Innocence Project, just less than 10 percent of the defendants who have been exonerated by DNA in America pleaded guilty.[197]

The USSC, in a pair of companion cases in its 2011–12 term, recognized the important role that competent defense attorneys play in plea bargaining, holding that defendants have a constitutional right to the effective assistance of counsel during plea negotiations.[198] The Court based its holding, in part, on the "central role plea bargaining takes in securing convictions and determining sentences," noting: "In today's criminal justice system, the negotiation of a plea bargain, rather than the unfolding of a trial, is almost always the critical point for a defendant."[199]

---

*Bargaining*, 84 YALE L.J. 1179, 1249–53 (1975) [hereinafter Alschuler, *Defense Attorney's Role*] (discussing public defenders' use of coordinated refusals to plead guilty as a "strike" against blanket prosecutorial decisions with which they disagreed).

194 *See* Uphoff, *supra* note 37, at 763.

195 *See id.* The other option that these defendants face is to risk a more severe sentence, and often additional counts and charges—*see* Bordenkircher v. Hayes, 434 U.S. 357, 359, 364 (1978) (holding that it was constitutionally permissible for a prosecutor to threaten to bring significantly enhanced charges as a means of inducing Hayes to plead guilty)—by going to trial with a lawyer who is unprepared to do so. *See* Uphoff, *supra* note 37, at 763. Realistically, however, this option is meaningless if counsel's lack of preparation renders him/her unable to subject the Government's case to meaningful adversarial testing. *See id.*

196 For some reason, American judges and prosecutors often cling to the myth that an innocent defendant would never plead guilty. *See* Uphoff, *supra* note 37, at 798. As Justice Scalia recently proclaimed: "There is nothing in our system that encourages or even allows an innocent person to—to plead guilty." United States v. Ruiz, 536 U.S. 622 (2002), Transcript of Oral Argument at 26. Contrary to Justice Scalia's proclamation, however, the USSC has recognized the right of a defendant who maintains innocence nonetheless to enter a guilty plea out of a strategic calculation that the risks of going to trial are too high. *See* North Carolina v. Alford, 400 U.S. 25 (1970); *see generally* CAROLINE WOLF HARLOW, DEFENSE COUNSEL IN CRIMINAL CASES 8 (2000) (reporting that 17 percent of state inmates and 5 percent of federal inmates enter either *Alford* or no contest pleas).

The state charged Terry Alford with murder. *See Alford*, 400 U.S. 25. Pursuant to the state law in effect at the time, he was eligible for a death sentence only if he demanded a jury trial. *See id.* On the advice of his lawyer, Alford pleaded guilty to murder, thereby waiving his right to trial by jury but, at the same time, declared: "I pleaded guilty on second degree murder because they said there is too much evidence, but I ain't shot no man, but I take the fault for the other man … I just pleaded guilty because they said if I didn't they would gas me for it, and that is all." *Id.* The USSC held that the trial court could accept Alford's guilty plea despite his continued claim of innocence. *See id.* at 37 ("An individual accused of crime may voluntarily, knowingly, and understandingly consent to the imposition of a prison sentence even if he is unwilling or unable to admit his participation in the acts constituting the crime."). *See generally* Jenny McEwan, *Ritual, Fairness and Truth: The Adversarial and Inquisitorial Models of Criminal Trial*, in 1 THE TRIAL ON TRIAL, *supra* note 189, at 58 ("Truth is here subservient to defendant autonomy, or the appearance of it."). Compare Albert W. Alschuler, *Straining at Gnats and Swallowing Camels: The Selective Morality of Professor Bibas*, 88 CORNELL L. REV. 1412, 1412 (2003) (arguing that *Alford* pleas are a clear violation of due process) with Albert W. Alschuler, *The Changing Plea Bargaining Debate*, 69 CAL. L. REV. 652 (1981) (arguing that *Alford* pleas, but not all guilty pleas, should be discontinued).

197 *See When the Innocent Plead Guilty*, INNOCENCE PROJECT, http://www.innocenceproject.org/Content/When_the_Innocent_Plead_Guilty.php (last visited August 21, 2013).

198 *See* Missouri v. Frye, 132 S. Ct. 1399 (2012) (holding that Frye had the right to effective assistance of counsel during plea negotiations and that his right was violated when he missed his chance to accept a favorable plea offer because his lawyer failed to relay the offer to him); Lafler v. Cooper, 132 S. Ct. 1376, 1387 (2012) (holding that the remedy for the ineffective assistance of counsel in plea negotiations was to impose "the sentence [that] he or others in his position would have received in the ordinary course, absent the failings of counsel"). After the state's plea offers expired, Frye pleaded guilty (without a plea deal) and received a substantially longer sentence than the one that the state, unbeknownst to him, had previously offered. Reversing Frye's sentence, the Court held that "as a general rule, defense counsel has the duty to communicate formal offers from the prosecution to accept a plea on terms and conditions that may be favorable to the accused." Lafler's attorney reported a favorable plea offer to him, but erroneously advised him to reject it. After Lafler rejected the plea offer, he had a "full and fair trial before a jury." After the jury convicted him, he received a harsher sentence than the one that prosecutors had offered in the rejected plea deal. The Court held that the Sixth Amendment entitled Lafler to the more favorable sentence that he was denied due to his counsel's bad advice.

199 *Frye*, 566 U.S. at 1407.

*C. The Spread of Adversarial Criminal Justice*

There are two main approaches to criminal procedure in most of the world: the inquisitorial and the accusatorial.[200] The comparison between the two systems, while imperfect, helps to illustrate the relationship

200 *See* Craig M. Bradley, *The Convergence of the Continental and the Common Law Model of Criminal Procedure*, 7 CRIM. L.F. 471, 471 (1996) [hereinafter Bradley, *Convergence*]; Elaine E. Sward, *Values, Ideology, and the Evolution of the Adversary System*, 64 IND. L.J. 301, 312 (1989). Although the distinction between "adversarial" and "inquisitorial" systems can be imprecise and value-laden—see, e.g., Abraham Goldstein, *Reflections on Two Models: Inquisitorial Themes in American Criminal Procedure*, 26 STAN. L. REV. 1009, 1018 (1974) ("Americans tend to equate inquisitorial systems with coercive interrogation, unbridled search, and unduly efficient crime control.")—this chapter employs them in their most basic and descriptive sense. *See generally* MARY ANN GLENDON ET AL., COMPARATIVE LEGAL TRADITIONS 180 (1985), to contrast the current features of Anglo-American criminal procedure (extensive and largely unreviewable prosecutorial discretion, independent defense investigation, public trials by lay juries, the hearsay rule and other exclusionary rules, cross-examination, plea bargaining and the guilty plea) with the current features of criminal procedure observed in most of continental Europe (compulsory prosecution, professional decision makers, judicial investigation and interrogation of witnesses, the written dossier, the written verdict with justification), not in the normative senses in which they are sometimes used ("adversarial" denoting a system that respects a defendant's procedural rights and obtains a truer outcome and "inquisitorial" denoting an authoritarian lack of respect for these values). *See, e.g.*, Lawrence J. Fassler, *The Italian Penal Procedure Code: An Adversarial System of Criminal Procedure in Continental Europe*, 29 COLUM. J. TRANAT'L L. 245 (1991). In this chapter, therefore, "adversarial" refers to systems, like those in the United States and the United Kingdom, in which the parties (prosecution and defense) have the responsibility of presenting evidence and the judicial role is restricted to hearing cases as a neutral arbiter. "Inquisitorial" refers to systems, such as those traditionally found in continental Europe, in which the judge(s) or magistrate(s) bear the responsibility for gathering evidence and deciding the case's outcome.

Of course, one must be cautious in generalizing about the procedures of "inquisitorial" and "adversarial" systems, respectively, two categories with as much variance within as between them. *See* CRIMINAL PROCEDURE SYSTEMS IN THE EUROPEAN COMMUNITY (Christine Van den Wyngaert et al., eds., 1993) [hereinafter CRIMINAL PROCEDURE SYSTEMS]; BARTON L. INGRAHAM, THE STRUCTURE OF CRIMINAL PROCEDURE 30–32 (1987); Craig M. Bradley, *The Emerging International Consensus as to Criminal Procedure Rules*, 14 MICH. J. INT'L L. 171, 219–20 (1993) [hereinafter Bradley, *Emerging Consensus*]. The purpose of this chapter, however, is not to provide a thorough or nuanced comparison of various legal traditions. The description of the inquisitorial–adversarial dichotomy laid out in this chapter is important not for its complexity or even its accuracy, but rather for the following reason: America is disproportionately funding police and prosecutorial agencies at the exact moment that the role of defense counsel is becoming much more important throughout the world. It is the expanding and often novel concept of a vigorous, independent defense on which the system relies to screen out the innocent that is the point of the comparisons made here. For that reason, the chapter relies on these categorical generalizations of "adversarial" and "inquisitorial." Thus, for the purpose of this chapter, the concentration of prosecutorial and adjudicative powers in the same person is the quintessence of the inquisitorial scheme. *See* Ennio Amodio & Eugenio Selvaggi, *An Accusatorial System in a Civil Law Country: The 1988 Italian Code of Criminal Procedure*, 62 TEMPLE L. REV. 1211 (1989). For analyses of the procedure and rules of evidence of the different international criminal jurisdictions based on the dichotomy of the adversarial and the inquisitorial, *see, e.g.*, RENE DAVID & JOHN E. C. BRIERLEY, MAJOR LEGAL SYSTEMS IN THE WORLD TODAY (3d ed., 1985); JOHN H. LANGBEIN, COMPARATIVE CRIMINAL PROCEDURE: GERMANY (1977); Guillaume Champy, *Inquisitoire-Accusatoire devant les jurisdictions penales internationales*, 68 INT'L REV. PENAL L. 149 (1997); Nancy Amoury Combs, *Copping a Plea to Genocide: The Plea Bargaining of International Crimes*, 151 U. PA. L. REV. 1 (2002); Richard S. Frase, *Comparative Criminal Justice as a Guide to American Law Reform: How Do the French Do It, How Can We Find Out, and Why Should We Care?*, 78 CAL. L. REV. 539 (1990); Richard S. Frase & Thomas Weigend, *German Criminal Justice as a Guide to American Law Reform: Similar Problems, Better Solutions?*, 18 B.C. INT'L & COMP. L. REV. 317 (1995); Richard May & Marieke Wierda, *Trends in International Criminal Evidence: Nuremberg, Tokyo, The Hague, and Arusha*, 37 COLUM. J. TRANSNAT'L. L. 725 (1999); Daryl A. Mundis, *From "Common Law" Towards "Civil Law": The Evolution of the ICTY Rules of Procedure and Evidence*, 14 LEIDEN J. INT'L L. 367 (2001); Vladimir Tochilovsky, *Rules of Procedure for the International Criminal Court: Problems to Address in Light of the Experience of the* Ad Hoc *Tribunals*, 46 NETH. INT'L L. REV. 343 (1999). For studies of other models and categories that have been used for analyzing different types of criminal procedure, *see, e.g.*, HERBERT L. PACKER, THE LIMITS OF THE CRIMINAL SANCTION 149–246 (1968); Peter Arenella, *Rethinking the Functions of Criminal Procedure: The Warren and Burger Courts' Competing Ideologies*, 72 GEO. L.J. 183 (1983); Mirjan Damaska, *Models of Criminal Procedure*, 51 ZBORNIK (COLLECTED PAPERS OF ZAGREB LAW SCHOOL) 477 (2001); John Griffiths, *Ideology in Criminal Procedure, or a Third "Model" of the Criminal Process*, 79 YALE L.J. 359 (1970); Erik G. Luna, *The Models of Criminal Procedure*, 2 BUFF. CRIM. L. REV. 389 *(1999)*. The grafting of adversarial elements onto an inquisitorial system raises interesting questions and issues in itself, but such is beyond the scope of this chapter, as is the relative merits of the two systems.

between the system of criminal adjudication that a society uses and the importance of competent defense counsel therein.

The American criminal justice system, like those of the United Kingdom,[201] Canada, and Australia, is primarily accusatorial, pitting the State against accused defendants.[202] The inquisitorial system,[203] which evolved primarily in continental Europe, has historically been the norm throughout much of the rest of the world.[204] Theorists have argued that adversarial presentation and argument are the best way to arrive at the truth.[205]

At the same time that the American government has been engaging in the asymmetrical assistance of international law enforcement entities, it has also been encouraging countries with inquisitorial traditions (or no functioning criminal justice traditions) to adopt at least elements of adversarialism, such as prosecutorial discretion, independent defense investigation, rules of evidence, cross-examination, plea bargaining, and guilty pleas. Many individuals in newly industrializing societies are obliged to buy into this model if their countries are to receive help from the institutions of global neoliberalism.[206]

*Inquisitorial systems*

Inquisitorial proceedings are relatively informal and non-confrontational.[207] The judge is primarily responsible for gathering the evidence.[208] Counsel for the parties play a very minor role in the conduct of the trial.[209] They do not present their own witnesses; they generally do not interview witnesses in advance.[210] The judges call the witnesses, determine the order of the trial, and conduct most of the examinations, with counsel relegated

201 The British system is similar to the American system in certain respects, including the use of juries in fact-finding; the general prohibition of introducing a defendant's prior convictions as evidence of guilt; an adversarial trial with a less active judge; the exclusion of evidence the admission of which is unfair to the defendant; and the conclusive effect of a defendant's guilty plea. *See, e.g.*, R. v. Gerald Gall, [1990] 90 Crim. App. 64, 68–9 (Eng.) (discussing and applying the evidentiary exclusionary rule); *cf.* Fed. R. Evid. 403 & 404.

202 *See* Bradley, *Convergence*, *supra* note 200, at 471–2. The term "primarily" is necessary because some English and American developments, such as the requirement that exculpatory evidence be handed over to the defense, *see, e.g.*, United States v. Bagley, 473 U.S. 667 (1985), and, in some states, extensive reciprocal defense discovery obligations, have a more inquisitorial nature. *See* Bradley, *Convergence*, *supra* note 200, at 482. Older features of the Anglo-American system, such as "an organized police force and overt acceptance of police power to detain and interrogate in order to generate evidence against the suspect," also originated in inquisitorial systems. Nico Jorg et al., *Are Inquisitorial and Adversarial Systems Converging?*, in Criminal Justice in Europe: A Comparative Study 48 (Phil Fennell, et al., eds., 1995) [hereinafter Jorg et al., *Converging*]. *See* Goldstein, *supra* note 200, at 1018.

203 While "civil law" and "inquisitorial" are not synonymous, civil law systems have traditionally had inquisitorial systems of adjudication, while common law systems have traditionally had adversarial systems of adjudication. *See* Sward, *supra* note 200, at 314 n.57.

204 *See* Saks, *Accuracy v. Advocacy: Expert Testimony Before the Bench*, Tech. Rev., Aug.–Sept. 1987, at 42, 43; Sward, *supra* note 200, at 301; *see generally* A. Engelmann, History Of Continental Civil Procedure (1927).

205 *See* Jerome Frank, Courts On Trial: Myth And Reality In American Justice 80 (1949) (arguing that the adversary system is the best system for discovering the truth); Stephan Landsman, The Adversary System: A Description And Defense 36 (1984) (arguing that the adversary system is the most likely to reach a just result); Freedman, *Judge Frankel's Search for Truth*, 123 U. Pa. L. Rev. 1060, 1065 (1975) (arguing that parties to an adversary system have the best information and motivation to present the best case); David Luban, *Calming the Hearse Horse: A Philosophical Research Program for Legal Ethics*, 40 Md. L. Rev. 451, 468–9 (1981) (arguing that the adversary system does the best job of getting at the truth).

206 *See* William E. Scheuerman, *Globalization and the Fate of Law*, *in* Recrafting the Rule of Law (David Dyzenhaus ed., 1999), at 243–66.

207 *See* Bradley, *Convergence*, *supra* note 200, at 471; James W. Diehm, *The Introduction of Jury Trials and Adversarial Elements into the Former Soviet Union and Other Inquisitorial Countries*, 11 J. Transnat'l L. & Pol'y 1, 6–7 (2001). In Germany, for example, the average trial for minor criminal offenses takes approximately two hours and, for more serious cases, approximately one day. *See* Langbein, *supra* note 200at 77.

208 *See* Sward, *supra* note 200, at 313.

209 *See* Jacqueline Hodgson, French Criminal Justice: A Comparative Account of the Investigation and Prosecution of Crime in France 101,105 (2005).

210 *See* Mirjan Damaska, *Presentation of Evidence and Factfinding Precision*, 123 U. Pa. L. Rev. 1083 (1975), at 1088–9; Langbein, *infra* note 254, at 826–30.

to a limited role in questioning witnesses.[211] If experts are needed, the judges designate and initially examine them in a way that is designed to produce balanced, rather than biased, testimony.[212]

The judge has a relatively free hand in pursuing investigations and is not confined to considering only the parties' interests and arguments.[213] Since there is no independent fact-finder[214] and judges control the questioning, there are few rules of evidence, and courts may rely on hearsay.[215] As described by John Merryman in his primer on civil law:

> The examining judge controls the nature and scope of [the pre-trial phase of the criminal process]. He is expected to investigate the matter thoroughly and to prepare a complete written record, so that by the time the examining stage is complete, all the relevant evidence is in the record. If the examining judge concludes that a crime was committed and that the accused is the perpetrator, the case then goes to trial. If he decides that no crime was committed or that the crime was not committed by the accused, the matter does not go to trial.[216]

Because judges are professionally trained to present and examine both sides of each case, the quality of legal representation, though not inconsequential, is not as crucial as in an adversarial system.[217] The judge and prosecutor are trusted to protect the rights of the accused—in fact, the prosecutor has a duty to present exculpatory and mitigating evidence, which lessens the need for a vigorous independent defense.[218] As a result, inquisitorial systems have traditionally been characterized by a less-than-aggressive defense bar, which features few, if any, professional groups with an interest in uncovering wrongful convictions.[219]

*Adversarial Systems*

Adversarial systems, by contrast, are formal, legalistic, and rights driven, with complex rules and procedures. Adversarial systems emphasize formal legal contestation, in which disputants readily invoke legal rights, duties, and procedural requirements, backed by recourse to litigation and judicial review.[220]

Adversarial legal processes are party driven and participatory. The defining feature of an adversarial system is that the party and attorney, knowing the case and motivated solely by the client's best interests, make the strategic decision of what evidence to seek and present, given limited time and resources.[221]

The fact-finder knows little about the litigation until trial, when the parties present their cases.[222] The judge is, for the most part, passive and becomes involved only to rule on objections, motions, or other legal issues

---

211 *See* Ingraham, *supra* note 200, at 27–30; Langbein, *supra* note 200, at 13–32, 38; Cliff Roberson & Dilip K. Das, An Introduction to Comparative Legal Models of Criminal Justice 120, 110 (2008); Frase & Weigend, *supra* note 200, at 342–4; Langbein, *infra* note 254, at 828.

212 *See* Langbein, *supra* note 200, at 75–6; Bradley, *Convergence*, *supra* note 200, at 472. In Germany, for example, only one expert is chosen per field, and the court selects this expert. *See* Langbein, *infra* note 254, at 839–41.

213 *See* Sward, *supra* note 200, at 315.

214 Germany is to some extent an exception to this general principle, as it uses lay judges. For a more detailed discussion, *see* Craig Bradley, *The Exclusionary Rule in Germany*, 96 Harv. L. Rev. 1032, 1063 (1983) [hereinafter Bradley, *Exclusionary Rule*].

215 *See* Criminal Procedure Systems, *supra* note 200, at 147 (noting that, in Germany, there are, in principle, no rules of evidence); Bradley, *Convergence*, *supra* note 200, at 471; Frase, *supra* note 200, at 677–8 (explaining that, in France, the trial procedures and evidentiary rules are more relaxed than in the United States).

216 John Henry Merryman, The Civil Law Tradition 129 (2d ed. 1985).

217 *See* Craig M. Bradley, Criminal Procedure: A Worldwide Study xviii–xix (2d ed. 2007).

218 *See* Luna & Wade, *infra* note 258, at 1484.

219 *See id.* at 1484, 1490.

220 *See* Robert A. Kagan, *Adversarial Legalism: Tamed or Still Wild?*, 2 N.Y.U. J. Legis. & Pub. Pol'y 217, 220 (1998–99) (arguing that adversarial legalism must be understood as a distinctively American "mode of government," a fragmented, party-centered alternative to Western European-style bureaucratic centralization).

221 *See* Gerald Walpin, *America's Adversarial and Jury Systems: More Likely to Do Justice*, 26 Harv. J.L. & Pub. Pol'y 175, 183 (2003), at 177–8.

222 *See* Sward, *supra* note 200, at 312. The requirement that the finder of fact know nothing about the case until the parties present their evidence stems from concerns with impartiality and implicit bias. *See id.* at 313. Adversary theorists worry that a judge who has taken an active role in the development of the case might pre-decide the case and, consciously or not, stop looking for evidence or argument contrary to that preordained conclusion. *See, e.g.*, Damaska, *Presentation*

that the attorneys raise.[223] From this clash of interests and arguments before a neutral umpire, truth is supposed to emerge and justice be done.[224]

Underlying this adversary theory are the assumptions that the litigants will do a better job of gathering all available evidence and formulating the arguments therefrom because their personal investment in the dispute provides the best incentive for them to do so,[225] and that the disputants have roughly equal power, status, and resources.[226] When these assumptions hold true, adversary theory dictates that the party on whose side the facts and the law fall, rather than the party with the better lawyer, will emerge victorious.[227] A problem arises, which adversary theorists tend to ignore, when the parties are unequal in resources or skill.[228] If the assumption of roughly equal power fails, so does the adversary system.[229] Rather than healthy competition producing the results of the trial, other, less legitimate factors determine the outcome.[230]

*Adversarial criminal justice*

The adversarial model of criminal justice starts with a police investigation that is openly not neutral, but rather, at least after it has focused on a suspect, aimed at collecting evidence that will prove that suspect's guilt.[231] The parties to the ensuing criminal litigation, the prosecution and the accused, direct the subsequent investigation and trial. The prosecutor gathers and presents evidence to prove the defendant's guilt, and the defendant may respond by rebutting the prosecution's evidence and presenting proof of innocence.

The defendant, through counsel, is entitled to challenge the prosecution's case, conduct independent investigation, and cross-examine accusers.[232] Every piece of the government's case, which is vigorously presented by the prosecutor, is supposed to be contested with equal vigor by the defense lawyer, with only the fittest evidence surviving.[233]

One premise behind adversarial criminal justice is that the clash between partisan advocates produces reliable, accurate results—that it is more likely to bring out "the truth."[234] Proponents of the system claim that the self-interests of the prosecutor and the defendant will move each party to do everything in its power to collect and present favorable evidence.[235] This "battle model" of criminal justice assumes that the truth will be uncovered and justice achieved through a contest between adversaries, the prosecution and defense, as the fact-finder sifts through opposing stories.[236] For proponents of adversarialism, the procedure of proof is a proxy for the substance of guilt. In other words, the more proof that there is against a defendant, the less likely

---

*supra* note 210, at 1091–2, 1105; Lon L. Fuller, *The Adversary System*, in TALKS ON AMERICAN LAW (H. Berman ed., 1961); *see generally* John Thibaut et al., *Adversary Presentation and Bias in Legal Decisionmaking*, 86 HARV. L. REV. 386 (1972) (attempting to test scientifically the cognitive biases and relative truth-finding abilities of adversarial and inquisitorial systems). For a critique of Thibaut's methodology, *see* Damaska, *Presentation*, *supra* note 210.

223 *See* Diehm, *supra* note 207, at 6.

224 *See* Stephan Landsman, *A Brief Survey of the Development of the Adversary System*, 44 OHIO ST. L.J. 714 (1983).

225 *See* LANDSMAN, *supra* note 205, at 713, 715; Sward, *supra* note 200, at 310. In addition to this incentive-based benefit, some have argued that party control causes participants to view the process as more fair. *See* EDGAR ALLAN LIND & TOM R. TYLER, THE SOCIAL PSYCHOLOGY OF PROCEDURAL JUSTICE 208 (1988).

226 *See* FRANCIS PAKES, COMPARATIVE CRIMINAL JUSTICE 50–59 (2004); Michael Dominic Meuti, *Legalistic Individualism: An Alternative Analysis of Kagan's Adversarial Legalism*, 27 HASTINGS INT'L & COMP. L. REV. 319, 338 (2004), at 340; Weigend, *Truth*, *supra* note 193, at 406.

227 *See* Meuti, *supra*, at 340.

228 *See* Sward, *supra* note 200, at 312.

229 *See* Meuti, *supra* note 226, at 347.

230 *See id.*

231 *See* Bradley, *Convergence*, *supra* note 200, at 471.

232 *See* MERRYMAN, *supra* note 216, at 130–31; Michael Louis Corrado, *The Future of Adversarial Systems*, 35 N.C.J. INT'L L. & COM. REG. 285, 289 (2010).

233 *See* Bradley, *Convergence*, *supra* note 200, at 473.

234 *See* Weigend, *Truth*, *supra* note 193, at 407; *see, e.g.*, Herring v. New York, 422 U.S. 853, 862 (1975) ("The very premise of our adversary system of criminal justice is that partisan advocacy on both sides of a case will best promote the ultimate objective that the guilty be convicted and the innocent go free.").

235 *See* Mirjan Damaska, *Evidentiary Barriers to Conviction and Two Models of Criminal Procedure: A Comparative Study*, 121 U. PA. L. REV. 506, 563 (1973).

236 *See* Luna & Wade, *infra* note 258, at 1466.

it is that s/he is innocent. In theory, if the adversarial system works as it should, the innocent defendant will be acquitted.[237] This theory persists even though, in reality, defendants lacking adequate means for mounting a full defense often feel constrained to negotiate a guilty plea.[238]

If an adversarial system is to function properly, competent defense lawyers are necessary to scrutinize and challenge the police investigation, the credibility of the evidence, and the prosecution's theory of the case.[239] Conversely, if a defendant does not have a vigorous advocate who is prepared to examine the evidence solely from his/her point of view, there is a greater chance that an innocent person may be convicted simply because, on the most obvious view of the evidence, s/he appeared to be the likeliest suspect.[240]

Justice can be achieved in an adversarial system only if the lawyers representing the parties are of equal ability and have equal resources.[241] Frequently, it is only through the efforts of defense investigators or experts that defense counsel uncovers the weaknesses of the prosecution's case or finds the proof that reveals the defendant's innocence.[242] The right to call defense witnesses, for example, is of little value without the assistance of counsel with the time to locate, interview, and subpoena those witnesses.[243]

Although, in principle, the prosecution and defense are supposed to stand equal before the law, in practice, the prosecution typically has greater resources than the defense, including a professional police force to carry out investigations and a department of prosecutors who are paid better than their counterparts in court-appointed defense.[244] The defendant, by contrast, is likely to be represented by a court-appointed attorney or public defender with fewer investigative resources, a relatively larger workload, and relatively smaller compensation.[245] These indigent defendants in asymmetrically and underfunded defense systems get underrepresented by inept or overworked lawyers with little time to do more than just plea bargain.[246] This is because the only alternative, in an adversarial system, to a trial with unequal arms is plea bargaining, negotiating the "truth."[247]

Regardless of guilt or innocence, most defendants are unwilling to take the risk of being found guilty, and the vast majority of cases in adversarial criminal justice systems are resolved without a trial.[248] For example, even though plea bargaining ostensibly does not exist in the United Kingdom, guilty pleas brokered by prosecutors constitute a high proportion of criminal actions in England and Wales.[249]

The weaker the prosecution's case, the more likely it is that a favorable bargain will be offered to the defendant.[250] Because "weakness" in the prosecution's case correlates with the innocence of the defendant, innocent defendants will, on average, be pressured more strongly than guilty ones to plead guilty by highly

237 *See* Uphoff, *supra* note 37, at 740, 767.

238 *See* Weigend, *Truth*, *supra* note 193, at 406–7; *supra* Section III (A) (vi).

239 *See* McMann v. Richardson, 397 U.S. 759 (1970), at 771 n.14.

240 *See* Bradley, *Convergence*, *supra* note 200, at 472.

241 *See* Diehm, *supra* note 207, at 7–8.

242 *See* Uphoff, *supra* note 37, at 747.

243 *See id.* at 780.

244 *See* Bradley, *Convergence*, *supra* note 200, at 473; Weigend, *Truth*, *supra* note 193, at 412.

245 *See id.*

246 *See* Uphoff, *supra* note 37, at 754–5.

247 *See* Jorg et al., *Converging*, *supra* note 202, at 48.

248 For example, the National Center for State Courts (NCSC) found that, in the 13 American jurisdictions it surveyed, the percentage of felony cases resolved by jury trail ranged from a low of 2.1 in Texas to a high of 6.9 in Alaska. *See* Jeffrey Abramson, We, The Jury 298 (1994).

249 In the United Kingdom, defendants can receive discounts in sentences for early pleas, and sentences are generally reduced by a third if defendants plead guilty at the first hearing. In 2004, two-thirds of all cases before Crown courts and three-quarters of all cases before magistrates' courts were resolved by guilty pleas. *See* Luna & Wade, *infra* note 258, at 1461; Uphoff, supra note 37, at 753.

250 *See* Bradley, *Convergence*, *supra* note 200, at 474.

favorable plea offers.[251] Extensive plea bargaining produces an approximation of events, and it is rare for a judicial authority to challenge the agreed-upon assertions.[252]

Recently, the differences between the Anglo-American and continental systems have begun to diminish.[253] David Nelken has suggested that globalization is pushing other nations toward legal convergence on the Anglo-American model of criminal adjudication.[254] There is a clear international trend toward an expansion of adversarial elements at the expense of "pure" inquisitorial systems.[255] In Europe, "the traditional distinction [between adversarial and inquisitorial] is tending to blur," as individual nations "bring their laws and regulations more closely into line with what are now common European principles."[256] Civil law nations are increasingly adopting at least some of the traditional components of an adversarial system, and the Anglo-American model of party-led negotiated justice is becoming the worldwide norm, even in continental Europe.[257]

---

251 *See id.* By contrast, guilty defendants are more likely to benefit from a system that incentivizes plea bargaining, reaping the benefit of a plea discount at sentencing without suffering any prejudice from the limited representation that they receive. *See* Ralph Adam Fine, Escape of the Guilty 42, 48–50 (1986) (discussing examples of what he describes as guilty defendants receiving undeserved leniency); Uphoff, *supra* note 37, at 763.

252 *See id.*

253 *See* Bradley, *Convergence*, *supra* note 200, at 474. On the convergence between America and Germany, *see* Frase & Weigend, *supra* note 200; *see also* Craig Bradley, The Failure of the Criminal Procedure Revolution 95–143 (1993) (discussing how various common law and civil law countries are moving toward an American-style, rights-oriented approach to rules governing criminal investigation).

254 *See* David Nelken, *Signaling Conformity: Changing Norms in Japan and China*, 27 Mich. J. Intl. L. 933 (2006); *see also* Bradley, *Convergence*, *supra* note 200, at 474 ("The differences between the Anglo-American and the continental system have begun to diminish."); Mary C. Daly, *Some Thoughts on the Differences in Criminal Trials in the Civil and Common Law Legal Systems*, 2 J. Inst. Study Legal Ethics 65, 65 (1999) ("[The civil and common law legal systems] are separately undergoing a remarkable transformation in which the influence of each on the other is substantial."); Matthew T. King, *Security, Scale, Form and Function: The Search for Truth and the Exclusion of Evidence in Adversarial and Inquisitorial Systems*, 12 Int'l Legal Persp. 185, 193–207 (2002); John H. Langbein, *The German Advantage in Civil Procedure*, 52 U. Chi. L. Rev. 823, 842 (1985); *see generally*, Weigend, *supra* note 190. *But see* Pierre Legrand, *European Legal Systems Are Not Converging*, 45 Int'l & Comp. L.Q. 52, 61–2 (1996).

255 *See* Weigend, *Truth*, *supra* note 193, at 404.

256 Committee of Ministers of the Council of Europe, *The Role of Public Prosecution in the Criminal Justice System, Recommendation 19 and Explanatory Memorandum*, at 2 (2000), *available at* http://www.venice.coe.int/site/main/texts/JD_docs/rec(2000)19_E.pdf (last visited Jan. 26, 2012).

257 *See* Maria Rosaria Ferrarese, Le Istituzioni della Globalizzazione (2000); Wolf Heydebrand, *From Globalisation of Law to Law under Globalisation, in* Adapting Legal Cultures (David Nelken & Johannes Feest, eds., 2001), at 117–37; Weigend, *Truth*, *supra* note 193, at 404. One important factor in the advance of adversarial elements is the influence of international human rights instruments, most importantly the International Covenant on Civil and Political Rights (ICCPR) and, in Europe, the European Convention for the Protection of Human Rights and Fundamental Freedoms (ECHR). *See* ICCPR, G.A. Res. 2200A (XXI), U.N. Doc. A/RES/art. 14 (Mar. 24, 1976); Convention for the Protection of Human Rights and Fundamental Freedoms (CPHRFF), art. 6, June 1, 2010, Eur. Ct. H.R. These instruments contain specific provisions on the rights of criminal suspects and defendants, *see* ICCPR, G.A. Res. 2200A (XXI), U.N. Doc. A/RES/art. 14 (Mar. 24, 1976); CPHRFF, art. 6, June 1, 2010, Eur. Ct. H.R., and they have been shaped by Anglo-American legal thinking. *See* Weigend, *Truth*, *supra* note 193, at 405. Although these instruments do not prescribe a certain trial mode, they emphasize the right to conduct an active defense, *see* ICCPR, G.A. Res. 2200A (XXI), U.N. Doc. A/RES/art. 14(3)(b),(d) (Mar. 24, 1976); CPHRFF, art. 6(3)(b)–(c), June 1, 2010, Eur. Ct. H.R. (requiring that defendants be afforded sufficient time to prepare their defense, the right to be present at trial, and the right to choose or have assigned a defense lawyer), and provide for the defendant's right to confront adverse witnesses. *See* ICCPR, G.A. Res. 2200A (XXI), U.N. Doc. A/RES/art. 14(3) (March 24, 1976) ("In the determination of any criminal charge against him, everyone shall be entitled to the following minimum guarantees, in full equality … to examine, or have examined, the witnesses against him and to obtain the attendance and examination of witnesses on his behalf under the same conditions as witnesses against him."). In Europe, the jurisprudence of the European Court of Human Rights has encouraged (or even demanded that) the states that are parties to the ECHR adapt their procedural arrangements to the demands of the Convention. *See* Weigend, *Truth*, *supra* note 193, at 405–6. The court's emphasis, *inter alia*, on the defendant's confrontation right—*see, e.g.*, Unterpertinger v. Austria 110 (No. 9120/80), Eur. Ct. H.R. (ser. A) P ¶ 28–30 (1986); Doorson v. Netherlands (No. 20524/92), 22 Eur. Ct. H.R. 330P ¶ 66–80 (1996); Van Mechelen v. Netherlands (No. 21363/93), 25 Eur. Ct. H.R. 647 ¶ P 46–65 (1997); Romanov v. Russia (No. 41461/02), 44 Eur. Ct. H.R. 23 ¶P 97–106 (2008)—may have had an influence on the overall thinking about the structure of the trial in Europe. *See* Weigend, *Truth*, *supra* note 193, at 406.

In the late 1980s, the Italian parliament undertook to reform its inquisitorial criminal procedure system in the direction of a more adversarial system.[258] Even the German criminal justice system has adopted many attributes of the Anglo-American adversarial system;[259] and the French have, in recent years, contemplated the idea of substituting prosecutorial for judicial investigation.[260] Defense lawyers now play a more prominent role on the continent, and suspects have more rights for those lawyers to protect.[261]

Other areas of the world have also followed suit. For example, in the 1990s, Colombia underwent a shift from an inquisitorial to a prosecutorial system of criminal procedure.[262] Though jury trials remain in disfavor

---

258 *See* William T. Pizzi & Mariangela Montagna, *The Battle to Establish an Adversarial Trial System in Italy*, 25 Mich. J. Int'l L. 429, 430 (2004). For a description of Italy's adoption of adversarial features into its previously highly inquisitorial criminal justice system, *see* Michele Caianiello, *The Italian Public Prosecutor: An Inquisitorial Figure in Adversarial Proceedings?*, *in* The Prosecutor in Transnational Perspective (Erik Luna & Marianne Wade eds., 2011). The new Italian system resembles the Anglo-American systems in significant ways. The revised code of criminal procedure treats the prosecutor as one of the parties before the court, rather than as a kind of magistrate; there is equality of representation, in which counsel for the parties (the prosecution and the defense) determine the presentation of evidence and conduct the questioning of the witnesses; the parties have the right to cross-examine each other's witnesses; and the trial court no longer has access to the prosecution's pretrial investigation dossier. *See id.*; Giulio Illuminati, *The Accusatorial Process from the Italian Point of View*, 35 N.C. J. Int'l L. & Com. Reg. 297 (2010). Except for a few small exceptions, all evidence must be presented in open court at trial in order for the court to consider it in its determination of guilt or innocence. *See* Pizzi & Montagna, *supra*, at 435. For a discussion of the Italian reforms, *see generally* Fassler, supra note 200; Jeffrey J. Miller, *Plea Bargaining and Its Analogues under the New Italian Criminal Procedure Code and in the United States: Towards a New Understanding of Comparative Criminal Procedure*, 22 N.Y.U. J. Int'l L. & Pol. 215 (1990); William T. Pizzi & Luca Marafioti, *The New Italian Code of Criminal Procedure: The Difficulties of Building an Adversarial Trial System on a Civil Law Foundation*, 17 Yale J. Int'l L. 1 (1992).

259 Germany abolished the position of investigatory judge in 1975 and replaced it with a system in which the prosecutor, recognized as a party to the litigation with an interest in conviction, conducts the pretrial investigation. *See* Merryman, *supra* note 216, at 114, 130; Corrado, *supra* note 232, at 290–91; Frase & Weigend, *supra* note 200, at 325. Now, magistrates play a similar pretrial role as those in the United States. *See* Walpin, *supra* note 221, at 182. Prosecutors can summon and interview suspects, lay witnesses, and experts. *See* Frase & Weigend, *supra* note 200, at 326. Defense counsel can also conduct an independent investigation before trial, but, unlike the prosecutor, has no right to compulsory process. *See id.* at 341. Germany has also introduced the use of pretrial party examination and cross-examination, if both parties agree. *See id.* at 357. Germany has a limited exclusionary rule, which balances the nature of the evidence against the seriousness of the crime. *See* Bradley, *Exclusionary Rule*, *supra* note 214, at 1048; Frase & Weigend, *supra* note 200, at 334.

260 *See* Jacqueline Hodgson, *Hierarchy, Bureaucracy, and Ideology in French Criminal Justice: Some Empirical Observations*, 29 J. L. Soc'y 227, 229 (2002). Since 2009, Section 257v(c) of the German Code of Criminal Procedure provides for case resolution by way of an "understanding," consisting of the court's indication of a (lenient) sentence in exchange for the defendant's admission of guilt. *See* Strafprozessordnung [StPO/Code of Criminal Procedure] § 257c, para. 3 (Ger.). Similar procedures are now available in France and Italy. *See* Code de Procedure Penale [Code of Criminal Procedure] [C. pr. p én.] Arts. 495-7–495-16 (Fr.); Codice di procedura penale [Code of Criminal Procedure] [C.c.p.] Arts. 444–8 (It.).

261 *See* Bradley, *Convergence*, *supra* note 200, at 474. On recent changes in France, *see* Stewart Field & Andrew West, *A Tale of Two Reforms: French Defense Rights and Police Powers in Transition*, 6 Crim. L.F. 473 (1995).

262 *See* Pahl, *supra* note 16, at 611. Colombia's new system replaced the investigating magistrate with a prosecutor who is responsible for the case from the investigative stage to trial. *See id.* at 615. The trial judge, who previously played an active role in the trial by interrogating the accused, is now limited to hearing evidence, ensuring fairness in the trial process, judging the culpability of the accused, and imposing punishment. *See id.* at 615–16. As such, the judge is relatively neutral in the process, except in the case of plea bargaining, in which s/he reviews the legality of the agreement. *See id.* at 616. The central prosecutor's office is responsible for investigating offenses; charging alleged offenders before the appropriate tribunal; ensuring the appearance in court of criminal suspects; determining whether there are grounds to proceed with an investigation; directing the police in their investigations; ensuring the protection of witnesses; and investigating all facts, inculpatory and exculpatory, for the accused. *See* Fiscala General de la Nacion Art. 3 *in* Fernando Carrillo Flores, Presentacion a La Revolucion Pacifica de la Justicia 99 (1991). The judicial police are now subordinate to the central prosecutor's office. *See* Pahl, *supra* note 16, at 627–8. The term "judicial police" is used broadly to include the three major Colombian police forces, the Cuerpo Tecnico, the DIJIN/SIJIN of the National Police, and the DAS (the Colombian equivalent of the FBI). *See id.* at 621 n.73.

in most of the world,[263] rights against self-incrimination at trial and involuntary confessions are now generally enforced through evidentiary suppression, and the Netherlands has adopted an exclusionary rule for evidence gained through illegal entry of the home by police.[264] Even in countries that remain primarily inquisitorial, attorney examination and argument are being given an increasingly central role.[265]

The previously American phenomenon of plea bargaining is slowly creeping into other countries' criminal justice systems. In Germany, for example, the Federal Court of Justice approved negotiated settlements in 2005,[266] and the German legislature authorized the practice under certain circumstances in 2009.[267] Negotiated case settlements have also been introduced by recent legislation in France,[268] where the number of French cases using such proceedings has grown in recent years.[269] Negotiated settlements, in the form of a defendant's voluntary submission to punishment or a prosecutor's application for conviction without a full trial, have become increasingly popular in Poland, rising from less than 8 percent of all adjudicated cases in 2002 and 2003, to a quarter of cases in 2004 and more than 40 percent of cases in 2005.[270] A substantial proportion of court cases are thereby premised upon party negotiations, which are presented for judicial approval and consented to by both parties.[271]

## Part IV: Improving the American Contribution to International Criminal Justice

### *A. The Proposal: Foreign Aid Parity and Comprehensive Criminal Justice Planning*

These trends are not inherently bad. On the contrary, the American approach to law carries many benefits, such as its capacity to vindicate rights in individual cases. The problem is that, as the adversarial system, with its dependence upon zealous defense counsel, is spreading to countries that traditionally have had primarily inquisitorial criminal justice systems,[272] foreign aid funding and training for defense attorneys is not following.

*The transition to adversarialism and the international defense crisis*

In response to this adversarial transition, a patchwork of public-defense systems has evolved across the globe, and the number of cases handled by these systems has grown, reflecting wide differences in structure and quality between and within various countries. In far too many of the countries to which the United States gives rule of law aid, representation for indigent defendants is either nonexistent or inadequate. For example, in Italy, there is no government-financed legal aid.[273] A roster of private lawyers provides legal defense, but indigent defendants usually get that for which they (do not) pay.[274] Too often, even when state-funded

---

263 *See* Bradley, *Convergence*, *supra* note 200, at 474–5. Jury trials were used in Germany between 1890 and 1920 and in the Netherlands from 1811 to 1813. *See* Nico Jorg et al., *Prosecutors, Examining Judges, and Control of Police Investigations*, *in* Criminal Justice in Europe 227, 239 (Phil Fennell et al., eds., 1995), at 229 (discussing the different rules governing police treatment of suspects as a function of the different assumptions underlying adversarial and inquisitorial criminal justice systems). Jury trials have also been abandoned in Japan and India and are used increasingly rarely in England. *See* Stephen J. Adler, The Jury xv–xvi (1994).

264 *See* Jorg et al., *Converging supra* note 202, at 48, 54.

265 *See* Bradley, *Convergence*, *supra* note 200, at 472.

266 *See* Bundesgerichtshof, 50 Entscheidungen des Bundesgerichtshofes in Strafsachen [BGHSt] 40 (Ger., Mar. 3, 2005) (approving negotiated case settlements).

267 *See* Strafprozessordnung [StPO] [Code Of Criminal Procedure], Apr. 7, 1987, Bundesgesetzblatt [BGBl] § 257c (providing statutory authorization for negotiated case settlements).

268 *See* C. pr. pen. arts. 495-7–16 (Fr.) (providing for negotiated case settlements). France adopted the "appearance before a court after prior admission of guilt" (*comparution sur reconnaissance prealable de culpabilite*) for crimes punishable by up to five years' imprisonment. *See id.*

269 *See* Luna & Wade, *supra* note 258, at 1461.

270 *See id.* at 1463.

271 *See id.*

272 *See* Bradley, *Convergence*, *supra* note 200, at 471.

273 *See* David Nelken, *Beyond Compare? Criticizing "The American Way of Law" Robert A. Kagan, Adversarial Legalism: The American Way of Law*, 28 Law & Soc. Inquiry 799, 813 n.12 (2003).

274 *See id.*

legal representation is available, insufficient resources, overwhelming workloads, and inadequate training and oversight render it ineffective. The aspirational goal of "rule of law" rings hollow to the many defendants who are provided incompetent, overworked, and undertrained attorneys who lack the skills and resources necessary to prepare a defense because the fundamental right to a lawyer that Americans assume applies to everyone accused of a crime does not exist, at least in practice, in countless countries around the globe.[275]

In many of the countries to which America provides rule of law assistance, public defenders lack the basic tools that they need to function properly. The systemic nature of the deficiencies in international defense systems means that every innocent person charged with a crime is at risk of suffering a wrongful conviction.

This crisis has only worsened during the transition from inquisitorial to adversarial systems in many of these countries, just as they need their defender systems to be on as solid footing as possible.[276] Many lawyers who trained in inquisitorial systems have never so much as made an objection. Cross-examination, in particular, often is done poorly and without meaningful testing of the accuracy or veracity of prosecution witnesses. Unfortunately, the transition to more adversarial systems of adjudication has not been accompanied by a parallel transition in the training, staffing, and funding of defense attorneys or oversight of public-counsel systems.

This is particularly concerning because defense workload is driven by the funding of police and prosecutors' offices, which determines the number and types of cases that are investigated and prosecuted. The result of these two trends—increased funds and training only for one party (the prosecution)[277] at the same time that, worldwide, systems are becoming more adversarial and more reliant on zealous defense advocacy—is that prosecutorial mistakes are less likely to be discovered and wrongful convictions become more likely.

Countries transitioning to adversarial systems are neither equipped nor generally inclined to make up for the imbalance of resources created by one-sided American contributions to law enforcement. As increased funding for investigations and prosecutions drives up the cost of indigent defense worldwide, funding shortages are likely to worsen, particularly given the international economic crisis.

At present, American foreign aid expenditures do not reflect our purported commitment to justice and due process. Diplomatic rule of law outreach should include educating other countries about the costs of underfunded, dysfunctional, and ineffective systems of indigent defense. In order to prevent the rest of the world from suffering the wrongfulconviction tragedies that have been chronicled in the United States, the American government should commit to strengthening public-defense systems abroad.

*Mo' money, fewer problems*

Public defenders cannot provide quality legal representation without adequate funding.[278] Attorneys who do not receive sufficient compensation have a disincentive to devote the necessary time and effort to provide meaningful representation.[279] Inadequate funding leads to inadequate support services. It does this by decreasing the availability of resources for training, research, and basic technology, as well as the indispensable assistance of investigators, experts, and administrative staff.[280]

This crisis cannot be adequately addressed unless the United States substantially improves its international funding for the delivery of indigent-defense services to enable the public-defense systems in countries

275 This is not to suggest that there are not jurisdictions in which indigent defendants are represented by defense lawyers with the skill, time, training, and resources to provide first-rate legal representation.

276 Unfortunately, creating a complete and accurate picture of indigent-defense systems internationally, including workloads and costs, is nearly impossible because there is no single source to provide reliable, international indigent-defense data.

277 *See supra* Section II.

278 *See* ABA Gideon's Report, *supra* note 83, at 7; *see generally* Lefstein, *infra* note 327, at 846 nn.53–4 (discussing the extensive literature on the need for adequate indigent-defense funding to ensure the provision of quality legal representation).

279 *See* ABA Gideon's Report, *supra* note 83, at 7.

280 *See id.*

with increasingly adversarial systems to support appropriate staffing levels and reasonable workloads,[281] supervision,[282] independent investigation,[283] expert assistance,[284] trial preparation,[285] plea bargaining, administrative support services,[286] and law-practice technology, such as computerized case-tracking systems.[287] America should provide support for the development of quality indigent defense that parallels the support that it provides to prosecution agencies, through direct financial aid, as well as training, mentoring, and technical assistance to the international defender community. It should also promote oversight of the private defense bar more generally, encourage comprehensive planning and reform, and encourage the adoption of guidelines and policies to promote best practices and improve legal representation for defendants abroad. Training and

---

281 Regulating attorney workload is perhaps the simplest and most direct safeguard against overloaded public-defense attorneys and deficient defense representation for low-income people facing criminal charges. *See* NLADA NY Report, *supra* note 32, at 12. An attorney with an excessive workload cannot interview clients properly, file appropriate motions, conduct necessary fact investigation, negotiate responsibly with the prosecutor, adequately prepare for hearings, or perform countless other tasks that normally would be undertaken by a lawyer with sufficient time and resources. *See* Justice Denied, *supra* note 85, at 7.

282 An absence of supervision leaves attorneys to determine on their own what constitutes competent representation, and they will often fall short of that mark. *See* NLADA NY Report, *supra* note 32, at 31.

283 Adequate investigation is one of the most basic criminal-defense requirements. Standard 4-4.1 (a) of the ABA Standards states: "Defense counsel should conduct a prompt investigation of the circumstances of the case and explore all avenues leading to facts relevant to the merits of the case and the penalty in the event of conviction. The investigation should include efforts to secure information in the possession of the prosecution and law enforcement authorities. The duty to investigate exists regardless of facts constituting guilt or the accused's stated desire to plead guilty." Guideline 4.1 of the NLADA Performance Guidelines states: "Counsel has a duty to conduct an independent investigation regardless of the accused's admissions or statements to the lawyer of facts constituting guilt. The investigation should be conducted as quickly as possible." NLADA Performance Guidelines, *supra* note 35. The outcome of a criminal case can hinge on the quality of defense investigation. *See* Kaye Commission Report, *supra* note 86, at 73: evidence and witnesses that support the defense theory must be located, photographed, interviewed, and/or subpoenaed to court. A good investigation can also give the defense leverage during plea negotiations. *See id.* at 73–4.

284 Employing an expert can be essential for an adequate defense. *See* Kaye Commission Report, *supra* note 86, at 74. In a criminal case, the prosecution has at its disposal not only public law enforcement services for investigations, but also a number of state experts, including criminalists and laboratory analysts, psychiatrists, sexual-assault interviewers and examiners, and medical examiners. *See id.* In order to confront the witnesses against him/her, including state experts, a defendant often needs an independent expert to conduct the same analysis and provide a second opinion. *See id.* In addition to confronting the prosecution's evidence, a defendant may need an expert in order to present a psychiatric defense or evaluate forensic evidence, such as DNA, fingerprints, handwriting, ballistics, or crime-scene evidence. *See id.*

285 This includes preparing a theory of defense, investigating witnesses, filing appropriate pretrial motions, and preparing for hearings and trials. *See id.* at 78.

286 National standards in the United States have long recognized that indigent-defense counsel must be provided necessary resources like office equipment, technology, legal research materials, administrative staff, paralegals, investigators, forensic services, and independent experts. *See* ABA Standards, *supra* note 35, Standard 5-1.4; NLADA, Assigned Counsel Standards, Standard 4.6; NLADA Guidelines for Negotiating and Awarding Contracts for Criminal Defense Services (1984), Guideline III-8; NSC Guidelines, Guideline 3.4; NAC Standards, Standard 13.14. For example, the ABA Standards, *supra* note 35, state: "[A jurisdiction's] legal representation plan should provide for investigatory, expert, and other services necessary to quality legal representation. These should include not only those services and facilities needed for an effective defense at trial but also those that are required for effective defense participation in every phase of the process." ABA Standards, *supra* note 35, Standard 5-1.4. The commentary to the standards describes the essential nature of ancillary services: "Quality legal representation cannot be rendered either by defenders or by assigned counsel unless lawyers have available other supporting services in addition to secretaries and investigators. Among these are access to necessary expert witnesses [and] personnel skilled in social work and related disciplines to provide assistance at pretrial release hearings and sentencing. The quality of representation at trial, for example, may be excellent and yet unhelpful to the defendant if the defense requires the assistance of a psychiatrist or handwriting expert and no such services are authorized or available."

287 The lack of quantitative data about fiscal, administrative, and practice functions can handicap strategic decision making in defender offices.

technical assistance for defenders[288] should focus on attorney qualifications and performance, advocacy skills,[289] client-centered representation, investigation,[290] trial preparation and cross-examination, forensic science, and the ethical obligation of attorneys to provide zealous and competent representation.

*Culture shift*

As international attorneys redefine their roles in newly adversarial systems, they will need to step out of the inquisitorial legal culture, which has previously defined their idea of best practices. In order to assist in the promotion of leadership and management skills for attorneys and a judicial culture that encourages competent and professional representation, America should advocate and fund certification programs to ensure that defense attorneys are familiar with criminal law and procedure in their countries and foster leadership and mentoring programs to cultivate leaders who can help change the culture of expectations regarding indigent defense.[291]

America should encourage the countries to which it gives rule of law assistance to include defense attorneys in national training and policy meetings. These efforts should focus on encouraging the judiciary, particularly in countries with inquisitorial traditions in which judge and prosecutor has until recently been a single job, to take a leadership role in ensuring that defendants are adequately represented. This includes educating judges and prosecutors (as well as American foreign-service officers) about the importance of defense counsel in an adversarial system in order to build support for defense-oriented reforms. Student engagement in criminal defense clinics abroad could encourage students to pursue careers in criminal defense, or at least have an appreciation for its importance.[292]

*Parity*

Resource parity builds on the venerable idea, with deep roots in both the historical practices and rhetoric of American criminal justice, that the defense function is as important to society as the prosecution function.[293]

---

288 Criminal law is a complex field necessitating continuous and comprehensive training for all defense attorneys. *See* ABA Gideon's Report, *supra* note 83, at 11. This training should include client interviewing and counseling, investigation, legal research and motions preparation, trial strategy, recent case developments, and ethical obligations.

289 Advocacy training should include trial skills, such as direct and cross-examination, opening statements and closing arguments, as well as other practical representation skills such as client interviewing, plea bargaining, and motions practice. In particular, defense attorneys transitioning from inquisitorial to more adversarial systems need to refine and expand their skills and update their knowledge to be able to fulfill their new advocacy roles.

290 While investigation can be essential to an adequate defense, it is often inappropriate for a defense lawyer to conduct his/her own investigation. *See* ABA Gideon's Report, *supra* note 83. For example, it is not proper for attorneys to interview witnesses whom they may later need to impeach in court. The commentary to Standard 5-1.4 of the ABA Standards, *supra* note 35, notes: "[W]hen an attorney personally interviews witnesses, the attorney may be placed in the untenable position of either taking the stand to challenge the witnesses' credibility if their testimony conflicts with statements previously given or withdrawing from the case." Professional investigators have the time and specialized experience and training to make them more effective than attorneys at critical case-preparation tasks like traveling to remote or unknown locations, finding and interviewing witnesses (particularly difficult ones), assessing crime scenes, and gathering and evaluating real and documentary evidence. *See* NLADA NY Report, *supra* note 32, at 12; Kaye Commission Report, *supra* note 86, at 74. Guideline 4.1 of the NSC guidelines directs: "Defender offices should employ investigators with criminal investigation training and experience. A minimum of one investigator should be employed for every three staff attorneys in an office."

291 *See* Jonathan A. Rapping, *Directing the Winds of Change: Using Organizational Culture to Reform Indigent Defense*, 9 Loy. J. Pub. Int. L. 177, 201 (2008). In the past 15 years, the adoption of standards and guidelines has been one of the most notable American developments in the delivery of indigent defense services. *See* Kaye Commission, *supra* note 86, at 17. Standards and guidelines pertaining to attorney performance, eligibility, workloads, conflicts of interest, and the administration of indigent-defense systems have been adopted by state and local legislatures, state supreme courts; national, state, and local public-defender organizations, indigent-defense commissions, and other entities throughout the United States. *See id.* National standards and guidelines serve a number of important purposes, including serving as a benchmark for judging the quality indigent-defense services. *See id.* at 18. An important measure of an adequately functioning indigent-defense system is whether indigent-defense counsel are able to follow performance standards in all indigent cases. *See id.* at 21.

292 *See* International Perspectives, *supra* note 45, at 48.

293 *See id.* at 225.

One reason why the Court found in *Gideon* that defense lawyers were "necessities" rather than "luxuries" was because states "quite properly spend vast sums of money" to establish a prosecution "machinery." This "machinery," which includes law enforcement agencies, government crime labs, and salaried government experts, can overwhelm a defendant unless s/he is equipped with comparable resources.[294] In his concurring opinion in *Argersinger*, Chief Justice Berger explained that "society's goal should be that the system for providing counsel and facilities for the defense should be as good as the system that society provides for the prosecution."[295] Without such resources, the defense is unable to play its appropriate roles of testing the accuracy of prosecution evidence, exposing unreliable evidence, and serving as a check against prosecutorial or police overreaching.[296]

The case of Frederick Mardlin exemplifies the dangers of asymmetry. At Mardlin's trial, three experts testified in support of the prosecution's theory that he had purposefully burned down his home to collect insurance funds.[297] Mardlin's public defender only had the funds to hire one expert to rebut the prosecution's theory.[298] As a result, Mardlin spent five years in prison for a fire that turned out to have been caused by faulty electrical wiring.[299]

The American obligation to provide counsel for indigent defendants is as much a part of its obligation to support emerging criminal justice systems as the provision of courthouses, judges, advisors, and prosecutors.[300] America should make foreign aid decisions with an eye toward impacting and strengthening entire criminal justice systems, in order to help them efficiently deliver fair outcomes, increase access to counsel and legal assistance, and improve the justice delivery systems for people who are unable to afford private attorneys.

Going forward, additional resources for prosecutors should be tied to additional defense funding, and funding, training, and continuing legal education for indigent defense abroad should be in parity with that for prosecution. This includes ensuring access to counsel at the earliest stage of criminal proceedings, providing the structure and support necessary for members of the private bar to represent indigent defendants, and encouraging equal defense access to physical tests performed in crime laboratories, even though, in most countries, the prosecution uses police forensic services.[301]

Providing parity of resources for prosecutors and defenders guarantees that increasing law enforcement resources will not disadvantage defendants, particularly innocent ones.[302] As other countries move toward more adversarial systems, the additional American resources for law enforcement necessitate additional resources for the defense, so that defenders can accommodate their increased workloads and adversarial responsibilities. If the United States were obliged to give proportional foreign aid resources to the prosecution and the defense, then the American-funded salary, personnel, and training resources in prosecutors' offices internationally would lead mechanically to a comparable increase in defense funding.

### *B. The Obstacle: American Politics and the "Law and Order" Mentality*

If American law recognizes the importance of defense counsel for a fair trial, then why is the United States so resistant to funding and training defense attorneys abroad? One answer to that question is that many Americans

294 *See* NLADA NY Report, *supra* note 32, at 28.

295 *Argersinger*, 407 U.S. at 43.

296 *See* NLADA NY Report, *supra* note 32, at 28.

297 *See* ACLU Michigan Report, *supra* note 59, at 9.

298 *See id.*

299 *See id.*

300 *See* James R. Neuhard & Scott Wallace, *The Ten Commandments of Public Defense Delivery Systems*, in 1 Compendium of Standards for Indigent Defense Systems 6, 12 (Neil Miller & Peter Ohlhausen eds., 2000) ("If one leg of the structure comprising the prosecution, the court, and the defendant is fundamentally and chronically weak, the justice system's classic three-legged stool will collapse.").

301 *See Argersinger*, 407 U.S. at 25 (Burger, C. J., concurring) ("Society's goal should be that the system for providing the counsel and facilities for the defense should be as good as the system which society provides for the prosecution." (internal quotation omitted).

302 The Louisiana Supreme Court recently recognized that the combination of low funding levels, high caseloads, and inadequate investigative support created a "rebuttable presumption" in every criminal case that public defenders were providing IAC. *See* State v. Peart, 621 So. 2d 780, 783 (La. 1993).

have deeply held attitudes about criminal justice that are a function of misconceptions about both the theory and actual workings of the criminal justice process.[303] For some years, there has been a national movement to get "tough on crime."[304] Michael Asimow recently suggested that popular American culture "glorifies heroic and dedicated prosecutors," who "protect us from predatory criminals," "unmask perjury and conspiracy in the courtroom and trounce slithery defense lawyers."[305] In contrast, the American public generally does not understand or appreciate the role of defense attorneys. Americans often harbor the perception that all accused defendants are guilty and that it is a waste of public funds to provide a zealous defense.[306] It seems like such a simple proposition that foreign aid budgets should treat prosecutors and defenders as coequal partners in a healthy, functioning criminal justice system. And yet, for many Americans, that sentence would make the same amount of sense if one replaced "defenders" with "zombies" and "criminal justice system" with "war on flesh eating."[307]

Another related answer is that politicians tend to vote in ways that ensure their reelection,[308] and, politically, conversations about unfairness to defendants go nowhere. Foreign aid parity requires legislative support, and few American legislators would vote in favor of budget increases to give accused criminals abroad a more vigorous and effective defense.[309] The constituency most directly impacted by the failure of the American government to ensure equal access to justice abroad is the least able to influence public discourse. There is no benefit to an American politician in voting for legislation that could help defendants in other countries because they are not part of his/her political constituency.[310] As Attorney General Robert Kennedy explained: "The poor man charged with crime has no lobby."[311] Forget about the poor person charged with a crime abroad.

The result of these two phenomena is an endless feedback loop, in which decades of law-and-order rhetoric from politicians and public officials have given rise to an American culture that is explicitly hostile to the rights of defendants, which in turn elects more "law-and-order" politicians.[312] The fear of crime—and, in the case of politicians, of being labeled soft on crime—has for years adversely affected the ability of Americans to discuss crime and criminal justice rationally.[313]

The equal importance of prosecutors and defenders may get recognition in judicial opinions and historical accounts of the adversarial process, but it gets neglected in practice.[314] The asymmetry in American foreign aid mirrors its domestic funding asymmetry. American indigent-defense services receive substantially less financial support than prosecution and law enforcement, and prosecutors are generally paid significantly

303 *See* Uphoff, *supra* note 37, at 811; *see generally* William J. Stuntz, *The Pathological Politics of Criminal Law*, 100 MICH. L. REV. 505 (2001).

304 *See* JUSTICE DENIED, *supra* note 85, at 70.

305 Michael Asimow, *Popular Culture and the Adversary System*, 40 LOY. L.A. L. REV. 653, 679 (2007).

306 *See* U.S. DEPARTMENT OF JUSTICE, BUREAU OF JUSTICE ASSISTANCE, PUBLIC DEFENSE REFORM SINCE GIDEON: IMPROVING THE ADMINISTRATION OF JUSTICE BY BUILDING ON OUR SUCCESSES AND LEARNING FROM OUR FAILURES (Sept. 2008), at 20 (on file with author).

307 *See* Charles Ogletree, Jr., *An Essay on the New Public Defender for the 21st Century*, 58(1) LAW & CONTEMP. PROBS., Winter, 81, 86–7 (2005) (describing the hostility of the American public toward the work of criminal-defense attorneys).

308 *See generally* JAMES M. BUCHANAN & GORDON TULLOCK, THE CALCULUS OF CONSENT (1999); David Mayhew, CONGRESS: THE ELECTORAL CONNECTION (1974).

309 *See* Wright, *infra* note 327, at 262 n.174.

310 *See generally* Donald A. Dripps, *Criminal Procedure, Footnote Four, and the Theory of Public Choice; or, Why Don't Legislatures Give a Damn About the Rights of the Accused?*, 44 SYRACUSE L. REV. 1079, 1089–90 (1993).

311 LEWIS, *supra* note 47, at 211.

312 For example, in a recent nationally televised debate, the audience cheered Rick Perry, at the time a leading American presidential candidate, for having presided over a record number of executions as the governor of Texas.

313 *See* Uphoff, *supra* note 37, at 811.

314 *See* Wright, *infra* note 327, at 230; *see, e.g.*, Adele Bernhard, *Take Courage: What the Courts Can Do to Improve the Delivery of Criminal Defense Services*, 63 U. PITT. L. REV. 293, 309 (2002) (recounting futile efforts to pass parity legislation in New York); Marcia Coyle, *Republicans Take Aim at Death Row Lawyers*, NAT'L L.J., Sept. 18, 1995, at A1 (discussing unfavorable attitudes toward funding appointed counsel in capital cases); Robert R. Rigg, *The Constitution, Compensation, and Competence: A Case Study*, 27 AM. J. CRIM. L. 1, 24–5 (1999) (recounting the failure of parity legislation in Iowa); *cf.* Mandy Welch, *Death Penalty Chaos Calls for Systemic Change*, TEX. LAW., Dec. 13, 1993, at 20.

more than their public-defense counterparts with comparable experience and workloads.[315] The American Government often subsidizes state and local prosecution but not defense functions.[316] Some federal educational loans are available only to prosecutors.[317] Procuring complementary funding for indigent defense, even domestically, has proven to be very difficult.[318] Despite decades of court rulings requiring greater funding for

---

315 *See* William Stuntz, *The Uneasy Relationship Between Criminal Procedure and Criminal Justice*, 107 YALE L.J. 1, 10–11, 70 (1997) (documenting the depressed wages and heavy caseloads of American court-appointed defense attorneys); NLADA, THE OTHER FACE OF JUSTICE 19 (1973) (pointing out that, in the United States, approximately 76 percent of full-time chief public defenders were paid less than the chief prosecutor in the same jurisdiction); JUSTICE DENIED, *supra* note 85, at 7; *see, e.g.*, *Appeals Court Rejects Bid by Deputy Public Defenders In Riverside to Replace SEIU in Pay Parity Battle*, METROPOLITAN NEWS ENTERPRISE, Mar. 18, 2003, at 1. By and large, entry-level prosecutors earn higher salaries than entry-level public defenders. *See* Wright, *infra* note 327, at 230. This salary differential persists at every level of experience, seniority, and responsibility. *See* John B. Arango, *Defense Services for the Poor*, 10 SUM. CRIM. JUST. 37 (1995); Spangenberg & Schwartz, *infra* note 327, at 14–15; *see, e.g.*, ABA STANDING COMM. ON LEGAL AID & INDIGENT DEFENDANTS, A COMPREHENSIVE REVIEW OF INDIGENT DEFENSE IN VIRGINIA 59–68 (2004), at 34–6; Rigg, *infra* note 314, at 29–35. *But see* John Flynn Rooney, *Survey: Public Defenders Earn Slightly More than Prosecutors*, CHI. DAILY L. BULL., Sept. 22, 2008, at 1 (reporting that the Cook County Public Defender's Office in Chicago made more than their prosecutor counterparts while handling fewer cases and attributing the defenders' higher salaries to the fact that they were unionized).

American prosecutors tend to fare better than public defenders when it comes to workload. *See* Richard Klein, *The Eleventh Commandment: Thou Shalt Not Be Compelled to Render the Ineffective Assistance of Counsel*, 68 IND. L.J. 363 (1993); Charles Ogletree, Jr., *An Essay on the New Public Defender for the 21st Century*, LAW & CONTEMP. PROBS., Winter 1995, at 85–6; *see, e.g.*, Ken Armstrong et al., *Attorney Profited, but His Clients Lost*, SEATTLE TIMES, Apr. 5, 2004, at A1 (profiling a defense attorney who handled 413 felony cases in one year); NLADA, IN DEFENSE OF PUBLIC ACCESS TO JUSTICE: AN ASSESSMENT OF TRIAL-LEVEL INDIGENT DEFENSE SERVICES IN LOUISIANA 40 YEARS AFTER GIDEON 34–41 (Mar. 2004) [hereinafter LOUISIANA ASSESSMENT] (profiling a defense attorney working part time in Avoyelles Parish who handled a workload equivalent to that of 6.3 full-time positions).

American prosecutors also have greater access to investigators and experts than the typical publicly funded defense attorney. *See id.* In addition to the police resources employed during the investigation phase of a criminal case, the prosecution often spends resources for follow-up investigations at the direction of prosecutors after charges have been filed. *See id.*; *see also* BUREAU OF JUSTICE STATISTICS, U.S. DEP'T OF JUSTICE, PROSECUTORS IN STATE COURTS, 2001, at 2 (May 2002) (reporting the results of a national survey that revealed that staff investigators comprised 9.4 percent of the personnel in prosecutors' offices and that large offices employed an average of 43 investigators and 151 prosecutors). Prosecutors consult with and call expert and scientific experts to testify more often than defense attorneys. *See* Darryl K. Brown, *Criminal Procedure Entitlements, Professionalism, and Lawyering Norms*, 61 OHIO ST. L.J. 801, 828–31 (2000); David A. Harris, *The Constitution and Truth Seeking: A New Theory on Expert Services for Indigent Defendants*, 83 J. CRIM. L. & CRIMINOLOGY 469, 469–72 & N.7 (1992); *see, e.g.*, INDIGENT DEFENSE IN VIRGINIA, *supra*, at 59–68. All of these components—salary, workload, and support services—combine to produce a significant overall gap in spending between the prosecution and defense functions. *See* Margaret Graham Tebo, *Promise Still Unfulfilled*, 89 A.B.A. J. 71 (2003); Wright, *infra* note 327, at 231; *see, e.g.*, LOUISIANA ASSESSMENT, *supra*, at 53–5 (reporting that the prosecution outspent the defense statewide by nearly three to one, not including police investigative resources); Alan Cooper, *Standards of Justice Needed in Virginia, Critic Says*, RICHMOND TIMES-DISPATCH, Mar. 21, 2003, at B5 (discussing a report by the Virginia Indigent Defense Coalition that gave the Commonwealth an "F" for "parity in the resources available to defense counsel and the prosecution"). *But see* HANSON ET AL., *supra* note 78, at 93–100 (describing a 1992 study of indigent defense by the NCSC that found rough parity of salary and support staff in nine American jurisdictions in 1989, but not of funding for training, legal research, and expert witnesses).

316 *See* Scott Wallace, *Parity: The Failsafe Standard*, in 1 COMPENDIUM OF STANDARDS FOR INDIGENT DEFENSE SYSTEMS 13, 16–17 (2000) (detailing training programs that the federal government funds for state and local prosecutors and judges but not for defense attorneys); Wright, *infra* note 327, at 237 n.70; *see, e.g.*, Crime Identification Technology Act of 1998, Pub. L. No. 105-251, 112 Stat. 1871, tit. I (1998) (providing $1.25 billion to fund technology for state and local agencies, including state courts prosecutors' offices, but not defender agencies). In addition, American prosecutors' offices regularly receive income from criminal asset forfeiture programs. *See* JIMMY GURULÉ & SANDRA GUERRA, THE LAW OF ASSET FORFEITURE 2-2 (1998).

317 *See* Wallace, *supra* note 316.

318 *See* Adam M. Gershowitz & Laura R. Killinger, *The State (Never Rests): How Excessive Prosecutor Caseloads Harm Criminal Defendants*, 105 NW. U.L. REV. 261, 299 (2011); *see also* HANSON ET AL., *supra* note 78, at 100 (finding that "the greatest disparities occur in the areas of investigators and expert witnesses, with the prosecutors possessing more resources"); Kim Taylor-Thompson, *Effective Assistance: Reconceiving the Role of the Chief Public Defender*, 2 J. INST. STUD. LEGAL. ETHICS 199, 202–3 (1999) (detailing budget difficulties for public defenders in the 1990s); *see, e.g.*, *A Study of Representation in Capital Cases in Texas*, 56 TEX. B.J. 333, 408 (Apr. 1993) (describing a Texas State Bar

indigent defense,[319] American legislatures have been hostile to funding increases.[320] Even when legislatures provide greater funding, the increases are sometimes rescinded shortly thereafter[321] because public defenders are an attractive target in times of budgetary austerity.[322]

It is particularly difficult to convince the public and policy makers of the need for effective criminal defense during times of austerity. In the battle for adequate funding, defenders face tough competition for resources, especially in comparison to prosecutors.[323] The fiscal crisis is already having severe adverse consequences for foreign aid funding. Like other budget priorities, there is a finite amount of foreign aid to spend on criminal justice. Money devoted to indigent defense is money not spent on police, prosecutors, prisons, or judges. At a time of budget constraints, the difficulty in convincing officials to appropriate increased funds for indigent defense abroad will continue to be a significant hurdle.

## Part V: Conclusion: A Platform for Discussion

The inquisitorial and adversarial models of criminal adjudication do not differ significantly in their aims, but they do in the way that they allocate the responsibility for reaching them.[324] For better or worse, the adversarial model of criminal justice, characterized by conviction-oriented police and prosecutors who are checked only by the aggressive assertion of rights by suspects and their attorneys, is the wave of the future.[325] To function effectively, an adversarial criminal justice system requires competitive balance to ensure the integrity of the convictions that it produces. A properly working adversarial process may offer innocent defendants better opportunities to uncover exonerating evidence, question dubious testimony and claims, and obtain post-conviction relief, but only if defense counsel adhere to the ethical duty to represent their clients zealously.[326] Put simply, bad lawyering in an adversarial system leads to wrongful convictions.

In recent decades, legal scholars have devoted enormous attention to the crisis of underfunding of indigent defense in the American criminal justice system.[327] Remarkably, however, there is virtually no scholarship

---

study that concluded: "There is a serious under-funding of essential expert services and other expenses in capital trials and appeals."); Gershowitz, *infra* note 327, at 100 (profiling one unsuccessful challenge arguing that appointed lawyers were underfunded). Massachusetts's comprehensive statewide system has had difficulty maintaining adequate compensation levels, and Indiana's 40 percent state reimbursement system has dipped to 26 percent when budget constraints reduced the program's appropriations. *See* Wallace & Carroll, *supra* note 90, at iv.

319 *See* Drinan, *infra* note 327, at 443–62 (discussing successes in "second generation" indigent-defense litigation in the United States).

320 *See* Gershowitz & Killinger, *supra* note 318, at 299; *but see* Wright, *infra* note 327, at 261 identifying a handful of state legislature and local governments that have committed themselves to salary parity for prosecutors and public defenders and a few jurisdictions that have passed statutes and ratified budgets that link overall resources, like workload and support services, for indigent defense to the resources for prosecution).

321 *See* Gershowitz, *infra* note 327, at 100–106.

322 *See* Gershowitz & Killinger, *supra* note 318, at 299; *see, e.g.*, Justice Denied, *supra* note 85, at 52–60 (2009).

323 *See* Justice Denied, *supra* note 85, at 61.

324 *See* Weigend, *Truth*, *supra* note 193, at 414.

325 *See* Bradley, *Convergence*, *supra* note 200, at 481–2.

326 *See* Luna & Wade, *supra* note 258, at 1507.

327 *See, e.g.*, David Cole, No Equal Justice: Race and Class in the American Criminal Justice System 64, 95 (1999) (identifying the lack of funding as a major obstacle to quality defense lawyering); Mary Sue Backus & Paul Marcus, *The Right to Counsel in Criminal Cases, a National Crisis*, 57 Hastings L.J. 1031 (2006); Stephen B. Bright, *Counsel for the Poor: The Death Sentence not for the Worst Crime but for the Worst Lawyer*, 103 Yale L.J. 1835, 1870 (1994) (documenting the lack of funds to "employ lawyers at wages and benefits equal to what is spent on the prosecution"); Stephen B. Bright, *Neither Equal nor Just: The Rationing and Denial of Legal Services to the Poor when Life and Liberty Are at Stake*, 1997 N.Y.U. Ann. Surv. Am. L. 783; Dennis E. Curtis & Judith Resnik, *Grieving Criminal Defense Lawyers*, 70 Fordham L. Rev. 1615 (2002); Cara H. Drinan, *The Third Generation of Indigent Defense Litigation*, 33 N.Y.U. Rev. L. & Soc. Change 427 (2009); Adam M. Gershowitz, *Raise the Proof: A Default Rule for Indigent Defense*, 40 Conn. L. Rev. 85, 87 (2007) (noting that American prosecutors' offices receive greater funding than public defenders' offices); Erica J. Hashimoto, *The Price of Misdemeanor Representation*, 49 Wm. & Mary L. Rev. 461 (2007); Richard Klein, *The Emperor Gideon Has No Clothes: The Empty Promise of the Constitutional Right to Effective Assistance of Counsel*, 13 Hastings Const. L.Q. 625, 656–63 (1986) (describing how poor funding weakens the Sixth Amendment

focusing on the way that the United States exports this defense funding disparity.[328] Not only have scholars neglected to analyze the asymmetrical nature of American foreign aid, they have also failed to consider how that asymmetry results in the potential to export our tendency to convict the innocent.[329] The asymmetrical nature of American foreign aid must be viewed within the framework of domestic discussions of the fundamental constitutional protections established to ensure fair and accurate verdicts and to prevent wrongful convictions.

Especially in light of global financial crisis, as funding for foreign aid programs has become increasingly limited and budgets for governments and nongovernmental organizations around the world have come under increasing strain, the urgency of the crisis facing criminal justice systems internationally has become more pronounced. Presumably, the United States would not support a country that held criminal trials without counsel for the accused. The asymmetrical nature of American foreign aid for criminal justice, however, risks perpetuating some of the problems that it is supposed to help eliminate by contributing to the international access-to-justice crisis in criminal justice. In some ways, it seems that defendants in these countries that are shifting to more rights-and process-based systems have won the battle but lost the war.

Admittedly, this chapter raises more questions than it answers, questions that may have no clean conceptual solution.[330] The abstract concept of parity is a simple one, but an agreement in principle that individual prosecutors and defenders deserve equivalent salary, workloads, and support services leaves many difficult questions unresolved.[331] Congress cannot mandate that prosecutors and defenders in countries to which the United States gives foreign aid employ the same number of attorneys at the same salary and workloads.

Nonetheless, the United States must be cautious not to bolster police and prosecutors' offices at the expense, or in lieu, of defenders. Instead, it should endorse general principles of fairness and respect for individual liberties in its interactions with governments that receive rule of law aid. American foreign aid for rule of law reform should provide resources to the institutional indigent-defense bar in parity with those that it provides to law enforcement entities, because disparity undermines the systemic assumption that equally matched adversaries will best ferret out the truth. Relative funding parity is hardly an impossibly revolutionary goal.

A decade ago, few observers believed that many genuinely innocent Americans were being convicted of crimes. Now, it is undeniable that it happens with some frequency. This revelation underscores the enormous importance and urgency of establishing effective systems of defense representation internationally.

---

guarantee of effective assistance); Norman Lefstein, *In Search of* Gideon*'s Promise: Lessons from England and the Need for Federal Help*, 55 HASTINGS L.J. 835 (2004); Douglas W. Vick, *Poorhouse Justice: Underfunded Indigent Defense Services and Arbitrary Death Sentences*, 43 BUFF. L. REV. 329 (1995); Robert L. Spangenberg & Tessa J. Schwartz, *The Indigent Defense Crisis is Chronic*, 9 CRIM. JUST. 13, 13–14 (1994); Ronald F. Wright, *Parity of Resources for Defense Counsel and the Reach of Public Choice Theory*, 90 IOWA L. REV. 219 (2004); Ronald F. Wright & Wayne A. Logan, *The Political Economy of Application Fees for Indigent Criminal Defense*, 47 WM. & MARY L. REV. 2045 (2006). Over the past few decades, American lawyers appointed to represent indigent defendants have raised legal challenges to excessive workloads in a variety of forms ranging from IAC claims to declaratory-judgment actions seeking structural reform. For an overview of the litigation and reform efforts, *see* Drinan, *supra.* Donald Dripps has argued that the *ex post* standards for measuring performance of defense counsel under Strickland v. Washington, 466 U.S. 668 (1984), should be supplemented by *ex ante* standards that would include attention to the resources available to the defense. *See generally* DONALD DRIPPS, ABOUT GUILT AND INNOCENCE 179 (2003); Donald A. Dripps, *Ineffective Assistance of Counsel: The Case for an Ex Ante Parity Standard*, 88 J. CRIM. L. & CRIMINOLOGY 242 (1997).

328 One reason for this paucity may be the tendency of legal scholars generally and scholars of innocence protection specifically to focus on constitutional litigation rather than the discretionary, public-policy decisions of the legislative and executive branches, *see*. Stephanos Bibas, *The Real-World Shift in Criminal Procedure*, 93 J. CRIM. L. & CRIMINOLOGY 789 (2003), but this chapter addresses a problem that litigation cannot solve.

329 *See, e.g.*, Wright, *supra* note 327, at 221–2 (concluding that increased funding, rather than constitutional standards of quality, was necessary to drive any large-scale changes for American indigent defense).

330 Perhaps the largest question is how to account for police investigation—namely whether the police should be deemed support staff or ancillary services for the prosecution, the expenditures for which must be matched by investigators or other support services for the defense. *See* Wright, *supra* note 327, at 237.

331 Comparing salary, workload, and support resources for the defense and the prosecution would require annual inquiries, and the details would necessarily shift over time. *See id.* at 252.

In the United States, the basic necessity of a functioning adversarial criminal process, one that ensured a rough equality of arms, is what prompted the creation of public defenders' offices.[332] Unfortunately, the perceived need to bring international criminals to justice that underlies much American foreign aid policy has blinded its proponents to the impact of disparity. The result is that American foreign aid for criminal justice reform exports the worst penny-wise, pound-foolish tendencies of our domestic politics.

Often, the individuals who make foreign aid decisions lack expertise in the complexity of criminal procedure or the necessity of quality legal representation for defendants. Furthermore, they tend to operate under severe time constraints, which require them to make quick and inadequately researched decisions. The agencies, lawyers, foundations, consulting firms, and governments who provide foreign aid and training do so to foster and enforce a wide array of agendas.[333] One result is that parity of resources is not currently the reality in American foreign aid for criminal justice.

While most American rule of law reform initiatives are implemented "elsewhere," we need to foster a domestic conversation about the end goal of those initiatives if we are going to respond effectively to the challenges at which our foreign aid is aimed. Blindly doing more of the same will not work.

---

332 *See* Andrew E. Taslitz, *Temporal Adversarialism, Criminal Justice, and the Rehnquist Court: The Sluggish Life of Political Factfinding*, 94 Geo. L.J. 1589, 1598 (2006) [hereinafter Taslitz, *Temporal Adversarialism*] (describing how "new constitutional rules … gave lawyers more power to conduct effective investigations, and they improved the resources with which to conduct the adversarial battle—for example, encouraging the rise of public defenders' offices").

333 *See id.*

# PART III

# Reality Bites: Problems with Investigating, Proving and Defining Innocence

# Chapter 7
# The Emerging Role of Innocence Lawyer and the Need for Role-Differentiated Standards of Professional Conduct

D. Michael Risinger and Lesley C. Risinger

## Introduction and Historical Background

There is growing awareness that a new lawyer role is emerging in American criminal litigation, separating itself from the traditional criminal defense role in ways that raise new issues of professional responsibility and ethics, both for the new role and for the traditional role of the criminal defense attorney. For want of a better term we may style this new role "innocence lawyer." This new role is, at least for now, largely limited to attempting to aid innocent persons already convicted of a crime. It differs from the normal role of a lawyer representing a criminal defendant, or even representing an ordinary convicted person post-trial. Traditionally, lawyers at the post-conviction stage, whether on appeal or in collateral proceedings, carried forward the standard assumptions of the criminal defense role that emerged in the late eighteenth century and were largely solidified by the middle of the nineteenth century. We may label two of the main elements of those assumptions the "cab rank" principle and the "I don't care if you are innocent" principle. The "cab rank" principle says that in general a criminal defense attorney is obliged, or at least encouraged and allowed, to accept as a client whoever comes to them (at least if they are not already overcommitted and the person can pay for their services).[1] The "I don't care if you are innocent" principle says that everyone, guilty or innocent,

1 British barristers (but not solicitors) have for a century or more formally embraced the "rule" version of the cab rank principle, which at least nominally requires them to accept any brief offered them in an area in which they hold themselves out as qualified to practice, as long as the fee offered is reasonable and they are not already overextended. This rule is usually traced to a short passage in Thomas Erskine's speech in defense of Thomas Payne and so has its origin in the emerging standards of the new role of criminal defense lawyer in England in the late eighteenth century (although it was later applied to all settings, civil and criminal). The cab rank image was appended to the principle sometime in the latter part of the nineteenth century (research has not revealed the originator or the date of the image, but the *OED* traces the term "cab rank" itself (meaning a line of cabs for hire) only as far back as 1878). The rule version of the cab rank principle does not seem to have had much functional reality, even in England, until formally promulgated by the General Council of the Bar (established by Parliament, 1894) in its 1908 rules. *See* R. v. Visitors to the Inns of Court [*ex parte* Calder], [1994] Q.B. 1 at 63 (opinion of Staughton, L. J.) (Eng.). There seems little evidence in nineteenth-century barrister memoirs with which we are familiar that it was a large factor in everyday practice. *See, e.g.*, Montague Williams's account of his discussion with Serjeant Ballantine in regard to returning a fee and a brief in a civil case he found distasteful, recounted in Montagu Williams, 1 Leaves of a Life: being The Reminiscences of Montagu Williams 88–9 (1890). (Ultimately the brief was kept in order to retain the fee, not because of any invocation of some moral obligation. Examples could be multiplied.) There is some debate about whether even after its formal promulgation in 1908 it has been observed mainly in the breach through various subterfuges, especially since the "rule" in practice is administered by solicitors' and barristers' clerks. *See* John A. Flood, Barrister's Clerks, The Law's Middlemen 4, 80 (1983). As Stephen Landsman put it in his review of Flood's book: "Notwithstanding the cab-rank rule, clerks pick and choose among the cases offered their barristers. By asking excessive fees or emphasizing the likelihood of long delays clerks are able to control the flow of business. According to Flood, the clerks' approach to business selection has rendered the cab-rank rule 'substantially a myth.'" Stephen Landsman, *The Servants*, 83 Mich. L. Rev. 1105, 1105 (1985) (reviewing Flood, Barrister's Clerks). But see the recent reply to John Flood's also recent observations on this point by Lucy Reed (in which Reed contends that the cab rank rule is properly administered by clerks who are properly supervised) at Lucy Reed's blog, Lucy Reed, *Bat the Rat*, Pink Tape (July 14, 2012), http://pinktape.co.uk/rants/bat-the-rat/ (last visited Mar. 16, 2013) (which contains a link to Flood's original post on his blog, John Flood's Random Academic Thoughts (RATS)). The cab rank rule has recently been formally

is entitled to put the government to its proof, and that while there are some constraints on the affirmative actions that may be taken to obtain an acquittal, the criminal defense lawyer is there to aggressively test and contest the evidence proffered by the government, and to insure that all constitutional limitations on the prosecution are respected regardless of their impact on the accuracy of the verdict of guilt, and regardless of underlying guilt or innocence. While each of the two principles may serve slightly different purposes, they are not unconnected. Together they work to create a strong "anti-signaling" ethic in which the criminal defense attorney is prevented from signaling to anyone by any means that a client is guilty, and by necessary implication, is affirmatively discouraged, and perhaps even prevented, from effectively signaling that there is real reason to believe that the client is in fact factually innocent of the crime,[2] as opposed to being formally "presumed innocent."[3]

---

loosened in England. *See* Catherine Baksi, *Bar Victory over Cab Rank rule*, LAW SOCIETY GAZETTE, (Aug. 2, 2012), *available at* http://www.lawgazette.co.uk/news/bar-victory-over-cab-rank-rule (last visited Mar. 16, 2013).

The cab rank rule has never been embraced in its strict rule form in America, but instead has been viewed as a presumptive obligation that can be overcome by individual choice in regard to individual clients that one finds repugnant. As Professor Wendel recently put it: "although the United States does not have a 'cab rank' rule, requiring lawyers to accept all representations they are competent to carry out, there is an informal norm of representing unpopular clients. In both the zealous advocacy and client selection cases, a lawyer would be subject to criticism for violating these expectations. Moreover, a lawyer viewing her role from the internal point of view—as creating justified obligations—would believe herself to be required to be a zealous advocate and to represent unpopular clients, even though there is no formal legal rule establishing these duties." W. Bradley Wendel, *Three Concepts of Roles*, 48 SAN DIEGO L. REV. 547, 555 (2011). Note that in the context of any legal setting where there is a significant number of available lawyers, rejection of a client will generally not result in signaling as the term is used in this article, since the person seeking counsel will generally find adequate representation elsewhere, and the fact that the first lawyer rejected the client will generally not become public knowledge. The best (and most entertaining) extended account of the development of the cab rank rule and the no-signaling rule in England through the 1860s, and the various American responses to it thereafter in the nineteenth and twentieth centuries remains DAVID MELLINKOFF, THE CONSCIENCE OF A LAWYER (1973).

2 It was not always so. Until the mid-nineteenth century in both England and America it was recognized as at least proper, and perhaps obligatory, for counsel to let the jury know their personal belief in the justice of their cause in at least some circumstances, though it was thought to be a practice that ought to be resorted to sparingly. The earliest explicit defense of this position was put forth by the aforementioned Thomas Erskine in a speech in the 1784 seditious libel case *R. v. Shipley, Dean of St. Asaph*, [1784] 99 E.R. 774 (Eng.), and the position was endorsed by the earliest writers on professional responsibility in America, David Hoffman and George Sharswood. *See* DAVID HOFFMAN, 2 A COURSE OF STUDY ADDRESSED TO STUDENTS AND THE PROFESSION GENERALLY, 757 (2d ed., 1836), and GEORGE SHARSWOOD, A COMPEND OF LECTURES ON THE AIMS AND DUTIES OF THE PROFESSION OF THE LAW 37–8 (1854). The rejection of this position in favor of a complete "no personal expression of belief" rule was motivated by a variety of considerations, which included the desire to make counsel free of criticism based on hostility to their clients. The absolute rule also had the effect of freeing criminal defense lawyers (and perhaps prosecutors) from the moral necessity of making personal judgments about the guilt or innocence of criminal defendants; but it also included an anti-signaling rationale, especially in criminal cases, where failure to assert personal belief in innocence would be taken as a signal of guilt. This was an explicit part of the earliest American official rule of conduct on the issue, the 1895 ALABAMA CODE OF ETHICS, §19: "If such assertions are habitually made they lose all force and subject the attorney to falsehoods, while the failure to make them in particular cases will often be esteemed a tacit admission in the belief of the client's guilt, or the weakness of his cause." Note that this phraseology does not take the position of prosecutors into account; but it seems to us that the general embrace of the absolute rule was driven by a rational fear that in the collision of personal declarations of belief by both prosecutors and defense lawyers, prosecutors would most often prevail, a fear that is even more rational today when jurors may suspect the existence of suppressed or otherwise inadmissible evidence of guilt. All this history is gone over in detail with extensive quotations and citations to the original sources in MELLINKOFF, *supra* note 1, at 237–41, 259–69. We do not disagree with the propriety of the general rule in the ordinary functions of trial lawyers.

3 Professor Mosteller has provided an extended re-examination of the traditional assumptions of the criminal defense lawyer's function in the age of innocence, and come to the conclusion that the traditional role of providing the best defense available without caring about the ultimate issue of actual guilt (or innocence) comes through the crucible of examination in light of such things as the DNA exonerations unscathed. *See* Robert P. Mosteller, *Why Defense Attorneys Cannot, But Do, Care About Innocence*, 50 SANTA CLARA L. REV. 1 (2010). We want to make it clear that we largely agree with him about both his empirical description of the role and about the virtual necessity of it being what it is, with a couple of caveats. The first significant disagreement comes from a feeling on our part, influenced by William Stuntz—*see, e.g.*, William J. Stuntz, *The Uneasy Relationship Between Criminal Procedure and Criminal Justice*, 107 YALE L.J. 1 (1997), *see* especially 37–45, procedural claims and factual claims—and by our own experience examining post-conviction innocence

The role of the innocence lawyer is significantly different. The innocence lawyer is committed to finding those who are factually innocent of the crime for which they have been convicted, and to obtaining their freedom. This entails an ethical obligation to critically investigate and examine all available information, and in general to go forward only with those cases where factual innocence is clear or highly likely. This inherently involves signaling of a well-warranted belief in actual innocence, or at least the gross unsafety of the verdict in regard to actual guilt.[4] Indeed, if the innocence lawyer is doing the right job of screening, the client is entitled to the benefit of such a signal, which is the product of the examination of many cases and the rejection of most, and countless hours of reinvestigation.

Two claims lie at the heart of the function of the innocence lawyer: the theoretic assertion that the factually innocent are more worth saving from punishment than other classes of convicted persons, and the claim that a proper review of the information available in regard to claims of factual innocence requires the rational evaluation of all available information, properly investigated and marshaled, whether formally admissible in a trial or not.

As to the first claim, there is perhaps little to be said beyond the fact that to us it seems intuitively obvious, and that at any rate it calls to us.[5] It may be that involvement in such herculean efforts is subject to a utilitarian criticism that our time could do more good if devoted to projects affecting large numbers of sufferers of various kinds, rather than being spent on rescuing one or two innocent sufferers wrongly imprisoned for a crime they did not commit. Such criticisms are sometimes registered in regard to the huge efforts that are mobilized to rescue a single child fallen down a well, when similar resources could not be mobilized to help large numbers of children in almost equally desperate but anonymous circumstances. But there is something worth respecting in the human heart when it reaches out with mighty efforts to free those down a well, whether they fell or were thrown. It is also, we believe, incumbent on a mature system of justice to be open to and facilitate the freeing of the convicted innocent, the collateral damage of the war on crime.

As for the second claim, we are happy to report that steady progress is being made in the legal recognition of such a rational "free-proof" approach to actual innocence,[6] in the recognition of actual innocence as a freestanding ground for relief from conviction,[7] and in recognition of actual innocence established by a lesser standard of proof as a means of freeing the innocent from various doctrines of waiver and time-bar

claims that criminal defense attorneys often devote too much energy to drafting procedural motions and not enough to analyzing what facts might show innocence, and then investigating them. We also believe that emphasis on not caring about innocence disadvantages the innocent because of the feeling that cases of potential actual innocence cannot be singled out for special attention in fact investigation, especially in institutional settings like public defenders' offices. Not that such fact investigation is easy, given legal, practical and budgetary restraints, just that it has become less emphasized since the procedural revolution of the 1950s and 1960s. Failure of fact analysis and investigation seems to lie behind many of the miscarriages that we believe we see. However, we do not disagree on the fundamental nature of what criminal defense must be. What we do ask is whether there is room alongside or in supplement to it for the separate function of the innocence lawyer.

4 On the distinction between claims of the affirmative establishment of factual innocence on the one hand and unsafe verdict on the other, *see* D. Michael Risinger, *Unsafe Verdicts: The Need for Reformed Standards for the Trial and Review of Factual Innocence Claims*, 41 Hous. L. Rev. 1281, 1313–21 (2004) [hereinafter Risinger, *Unsafe Verdicts*].

5 Well, perhaps a bit more can be said. See the more extended discussion, D. Michael Risinger, *Why Should We Care About Factually Wrongful Convictions, and What (If Anything) Are We Morally Obliged to Do About Them?*, section VI in *Innocents Convicted: An Empirically Justified Factual Wrongful Conviction Rate*, 97 J. Crim. L. & Criminology 761, 788–99 (2007) [hereinafter Risinger, *Innocents Convicted*]. *See also*, Risinger, *Unsafe Verdicts*, *supra* note 4 at 1298–1301. For a very different perspective, *see, e.g.*, Abbe Smith, *In Praise of the Guilty Project: A Criminal Defense Lawyer's Growing Anxiety About Innocence Projects*, 13 U. Pa. J.L. & Soc. Change 315 (2009–10).

6 It should be noted that this approach to evidence also benefits the interests of the state, since it renders available in the determination of actual innocence evidence that might have been found inadmissible against the defendant for purposes of the original trial, such as illegally seized evidence or other evidence excluded on legal grounds.

7 Six states have recognized a freestanding claim of actual innocence: three trial courts in New York (not challenged on appeal)—(*see, e.g.*, People v. Bermudez, 906 N.Y.S.2d 774 (Sup. Ct. N.Y. Cty. 2009)—and the High Courts of New Mexico, Illinois, Texas, Connecticut, and Missouri. *See* Montoya v. Ulibarri, 163 P.3d 476, 484 (N.M. 2007); People v. Washington, 171 Ill. 2d 475, 665 N.E.2d 1330, 216 Ill. Dec. 773 (1996); *ex parte* Elizondo, 947 S.W.2d 202 (Tex. Crim. App. 1996); Summerville v. Warden, 229 Conn. 397, 422 (1994); State *ex rel.* Amrine v. Roper, 102 S.W.3d 541 (Mo. 2003). Generally these states require clear and convincing evidence for the establishment of such a claim.

which sometimes bedevil the substantive consideration of their claims of "constitutional" violations and their ultimate release.[8]

While progress is being made, a majority of jurisdictions continue to have no special sensitivity to the claims of the convicted innocent in post-conviction proceedings of various kinds. As a result, in addition to representing the convicted innocent, the innocence lawyer may become intimately involved with law reform in order to create a more "innocentric" system of justice. We have begun to deal with the problems of such innocentric reform in a recent article, the introduction to which bears repeating here because it describes both the tragic irony that many current practices protect the guilty at the expense of the innocent, and also the stakeholder attitudes that may create resistance to any attempt at innocentric reform, or to the special professional practice standards that may separate the innocence lawyer from other lawyers, especially from the criminal defense lawyer:

In the project of which this paper is the first part, we will attempt an overview of what an "innocentric"[9] system would look like,[10] and what changes would be required to reform our current practices to come as close to such a system as possible. We approach this task with eyes open. In criminal procedure, most individual reforms, even the ones that should be least controversial, predictably face stiff opposition from one constituency or another that sees the reform as a lost advantage, or at least sees no advantage in the reform. Police and prosecutors may fear the loss of current practices which they perceive as useful for convicting those whom they believe to be guilty.[11] The defense bar may fear that some reforms will bring new disadvantages to the majority of their clients (the factually guilty ones) for the benefit of the innocent minority.[12] Those

---

8 The wellspring case is Schlup v. Delo, 513 U.S. 298 (1995). *Schlup* directly involved federal habeas corpus practice, and it is not entirely clear if *Schlup* itself creates a constitutional principle binding on the states; but it has been used as a model, whether such constitutional compulsion was found or not, in at least four states: New York, Virginia, Montana, and Missouri. *See* People v. Bermudez, 906 N.Y.S.2d 774 (Sup. Ct. N.Y. Cty. 2009) (due process requires that a procedural mechanism be provided for an incarcerated defendant to bring a post-conviction motion upon a claim of actual innocence, whether "freestanding" or as a means of obviating legal barriers such as prior adverse court determinations). Reedy v. Wright, 2002 WL 598434, 60 Va. Cir. 18, 26 (Va. Cir. Ct. 2002) (defendant's claim of actual innocence permits him to overcome procedural default in state court); State v. Pope, 80 P.3d 1232, 318 Mont. 383 (2003) (assuming the miscarriage of justice exception to procedural bars to be required under *Schlup*); Burton v. Dormire, Cole County No. 06AC-CC00312 (Filed Aug. 18, 2008) (new evidence of innocence and perjured trial testimony required court to address defaulted claim on the merits and grant relief, because failure to do so would constitute a manifest injustice). In addition, the principle may find expression in court rules: *see, e.g.*, Delaware, Del. Super. Ct. Crim. R. 61(i)(5), under which otherwise applicable procedural bars do not apply if the petitioner makes a "colorable claim that there was a miscarriage of justice because of a constitutional violation that undermined the fundamental legality, reliability, integrity or fairness of the proceedings leading to the judgment of conviction"; and Michigan, Mich. Ct. R. 6.508(d) (under which a procedural default may be excused if the court finds a "significant possibility that the defendant is innocent of the crime").

9 "Innocentric" is the adjective form of the term "innocentrism," which was coined by Daniel Medwed to connote an approach to criminal procedure that explicitly foregrounds exoneration of the factually innocent as a criminal justice value, and privileges, at least to some degree, the exoneration of the factually innocent over other competing values. *See* Daniel S. Medwed, *Innocentrism*, 2008 U. Ill. L. Rev. 1549.

10 A particularly useful work manifesting a similar concern for systemic reform, but differing significantly in some important respects, is George C. Thomas III, The Supreme Court on Trial: How the American Justice System Sacrifices Innocent Defendants (2008).

11 Stephen Saloom offers a sympathetic view of various actors' resistance to change, borrowing from comments made by Manhattan District Attorney Cyrus Vance at a recent symposium:

[T]he crushing demands of peoples' respective roles within the system do not encourage—and rarely allow—them as individuals to seek to alter the system. Prosecutors, defense lawyers, police and judges know what they know, and have to work their tails off to simply establish their version of the story and otherwise keep their end of the system working. So it's hard to break out of the daily onslaught and say "I'm going to do it differently today. I'm going to tell the judge I'm not going to proceed with my cases because I haven't taken the necessary time." Or for the judge to say "From now on I'm going to take the time necessary to really appreciate what's going on in each of these cases." Or for the police officer to say "I don't care if this is how we've always done things, I'm going to research and apply best practices in my own work."

Stephen Saloom, *Adversaries as Allies: Joining Together to Prevent Criminal Injustice*, 73 Alb. L. Rev. 1235, 1237 (2010).

12 The tension between "innocence people" and criminal defense attorneys has become the subject of explicit discussion. The general outline of the multi-centric tensions set out in the text was developed by one of us (Michael) during discussions with George Thomas and later Bob Mosteller, and was at least one impetus for Professor Mosteller's recent published reflections on that tension. *See* Robert P. Mosteller, *Why Defense Attorneys Cannot, But Do, Care About*

whose main interest is in the root-and-branch abolition of capital punishment may fear that some reforms will derail such abolition efforts, as concerns about the execution of the factually innocent are reduced.[13] Others may believe that emphasis on factual innocence diverts attention from the normative miscarriages of harsh sentencing imposed upon defendants guilty of something less than would justify their sentence.[14] Still others may feel that emphasis on factual innocence demeans the value of procedures meant to protect all of society, including the guilty, from tyrannical use of power or from fundamental dignitary abuse.[15] Those whose main focus is giving crime victims "closure" may fear that some of the reforms may banish public fury from the trial of guilt in ways that disappoint the desires of victims.[16] Judges, who by definition have been successful players under the current system, may indulge the well-known human tendency to believe that the system in which they have been personally successful has virtues beyond those it appears to have when subjected to critical analysis.[17] Lawyers in general may indulge the quite common romantic notion that "our adversary system" is already the best of all possible worlds,[18] reinforced by the Burkean notion that the unintended consequences of changing institutions hallowed by long practice are likely to be worse than simply pursuing business as usual.

---

*Innocence*, 50 SANTA CLARA L. REV. 1, 32 n.44 (2010) (documenting discussions with D. Michael Risinger); *see also, e.g.*, Medwed, *supra* note 9_ (attempting a reconciliation of the conflicting views). The main objection of the criminal defense bar seems to be a signaling objection. If actual innocence is signaled in any way, failure to signal in other cases will in fact signal at least factual guilt. Again, the innocent are held hostage for the benefit of the guilty. For a discussion of such a signaling problem in the context of plea bargaining practice, see Russell D. Covey, *Signaling and Plea Bargaining's Innocence Problem*, 66 WASH. & LEE L. REV. 73 (2009).

13 The tension between "innocence people" and "anti-death penalty people" has been apparent for a while. *See, e.g.*, D. Michael Risinger, *Innocents Convicted: An Empirically Justified Factual Wrongful Conviction Rate*, 97 J. CRIM. L. & CRIMINOLOGY 761, 781–82 (2007) (hereinafter *Innocents Convicted*); Carol. S. Steiker & Jordan M. Steiker, *The Seduction of Innocence: The Attraction and Limitations of the Focus on Innocence in Capital Punishment Law and Advocacy*, 95 J. CRIM. L. & CRIMINOLOGY 587 (2005).

14 *See generally* DOUGLAS HUSAK OVERCRIMINALIZATION: THE LIMITS OF THE CRIMINAL LAW 3 (2008); HARVEY A. SILVERGLATE, THREE FELONIES A DAY: HOW THE FEDS TARGET THE INNOCENT (2009) (setting out an analysis of the prevalence of over-criminalization and over-punishment).

15 *See, e.g.*, Emily Hughes, *Innocence Unmodified*, 89 N.C. L. REV. 1083, 1083–84 (2011) (analyzing "the degree to which the Court has reduced innocence to a binary—prioritizing actual innocence over fundamental protections for all people, including people who might be wrongly convicted if the courts do not safeguard their constitutional rights." Professor Hughes counts as "innocent" those who are factually (and normatively) guilty as charged but who have been convicted in derogation of their procedural rights. *See id.* at 1089; *see also* Susan A. Bandes, *Protecting the Innocent as the Primary Value of the Criminal Justice System* (reviewing Thomas, *supra* note 10); Susan A. Bandes, *Framing Wrongful Convictions*, 2008 UTAH L. REV. 5; Mosteller, *supra* note 3_, at 2; Margaret Raymond, *The Problem with Innocence*, 49 CLEV. ST. L. REV. 449 (2001).

16 For a treatment of many criminal justice issues from a victims' rights perspective, see DOUGLAS E. BELOOF, PAUL G. CASSELL & STEVEN J. TWIST, VICTIMS IN CRIMINAL PROCEDURE (3d ed. 2010).

17 See the discussion of this phenomenon in the context of judicial abdication in the control of weak prosecution-proffered expertise in D. Michael Risinger, *Goodbye to All That or A Fool's Errand, by One of the Fools: How I Stopped Worrying About Court Responses to Handwriting Identification (and "Forensic Science" in General) and Learned to Love Misinterpretations of* Kumho Tire v. Carmichael, 43 TULSA L. REV. 447, 473–74 (2007).

18 The tendency to thoughtlessly and uncritically invoke the virtues of "our adversary system" in response to calls for reform is well illustrated by the fact that as of February 11, 2011, this buzz phrase occurs in 2997 cases in the Westlaw ALLCASES (all federal and state cases) database (1945 to the present) and in 1654 articles in the Westlaw JLR (journals and law reviews) database (generally 1980 to the present). Professor Sklansky has recently skewered this attitude. *See* David Alan Sklansky, *Anti-Inquisitorialism*, 122 HARV. L. REV. 1634 (2009). Professor Langbein has long argued that the adversary system, in his words, "had the effect of perpetuating the central blunder of the inherited system: the failure to develop institutions and procedures of criminal investigation and trial that would be responsible for and capable of seeking the truth." JOHN H. LANGBEIN, THE ORIGINS OF ADVERSARY CRIMINAL TRIAL 343 (2003). For international perspectives on the weaknesses of the adversary system, see, for example, COSMAS MOISIDIS, CRIMINAL DISCOVERY: FROM TRUTH TO PROOF AND BACK AGAIN 126–45 (2008); Marvin Zalman, *The Adversary System and Wrongful Conviction*, in WRONGFUL CONVICTION: INTERNATIONAL PERSPECTIVES ON MISCARRIAGES OF JUSTICE 71 (C. Ronald Huff & Martin Killias eds., 2008).

We will deal with such concerns as we judge they may arise in regard to any given change espoused below. But in general, we think it appropriate at the outset to call on the members of all these "stakeholder" groups (as they appear to be called today) to recognize the special claims of another stakeholder group, that is, the convicted innocent (including the innocent who will be convicted if the proposed reforms are not undertaken). We call upon all constituencies to realize consciously and explicitly that, whatever other concerns are at stake, "innocence is different." [19]

As we previously suggested, what has been said here regarding system reform is also directly applicable to any assertion of a special "innocence lawyer" role or function in the world of post-conviction review. These issues start to arise the minute it becomes known that, individually or as part of an organization, you hold yourself out to be an innocence lawyer. In that role, you will receive communications from convicted persons claiming factual innocence. From that point on (and in one important aspect, from even before that point), one must consider what, if any, are the special criteria and the special constraints from which to judge one's professional responsibilities. It is our main thesis that the role of innocence lawyer necessitates different criteria of professional responsibility from those of other lawyer roles.[20]

Certainly since the eighteenth century, and perhaps since the beginning of time, social critics and commentators have criticized lawyers for advancing interests that are, by some or most standards of common morality, immoral or anti-social. It is not surprising that such critiques became more pointed with the rise of the criminal defense function in the late 1700s, and these "how can you morally represent such people and do such things" attacks grew to a crescendo by the 1840s as a result of the conduct of the leader of the English criminal bar at the time, Charles Phillips, in his defense of William Courvoisier, a valet, for the murder of his master, Lord Russell.[21] As was commonly the case, no one could top Macaulay in encapsulating the general issue in a rhetorical question thus: "...whether it be right that a man should, with a wig on his head and a band

---

19 D. Michael Risinger & Lesley C. Risinger, *Innocence Is Different: Taking Innocence into Account in Reforming Criminal Procedure*, 56 N.Y L.S. L. Rev. 869, 870–73 (2012) (footnotes in original renumbered to conform to numbering in this chapter).

20 We believe that, whatever adjustments should be made to current rules to take account of the special role of the innocence lawyer, because of our extensive explanations concerning the conditions and limitations we put on our post-conviction role, both in our application and otherwise, we are in full compliance with existing American professional responsibility rules, including those in the jurisdiction in which we now work, New Jersey. Both the American Bar Association Model Rules of Professional Conduct and the New Jersey Rules of Professional Conduct contain the same applicable language. Rule 1:2(c) of both provides: "A lawyer may limit the scope of the representation if the limitation is reasonable under the circumstances and the client gives informed consent." *See* ABA Model Rules of Prof'l Conduct R 1.2(c), N.J. Rules of Prof'l Conduct R 1.2(c). Certainly both our written application and our communications with applicants stress those limitations we place on our role that are, shall we say, unusual, as far as the normal lawyer role is concerned. Consequently, informed consent to these limitations is obtained before we undertake even initial screening, conduct any investigation, or agree to any representation at all. As for these limitations being reasonable under the circumstances, we think that since we could not credibly conduct ourselves in the role we undertake to perform without those limitations, they are clearly reasonable under the circumstances, even though we must admit that they induce a cringe response in many criminal defense attorneys. For an analysis of the application of the Model Rules to the demands of innocence organizations' work, *see* Ellen Suni, *Ethical Issues for Innocence Projects: An Initial Primer*, 70 U.M.K.C. L. Rev. 921 (2002).

21 *See, e.g.*, *The Defence of Courvoisier, and the Plea for It*, 12 Law Mag. Quart. Rev. Juris. n.s. 26 (1850). There were a number of strains to the storm of public criticism of Phillips after Courvoisier's confession became publicly known. They ranged from criticism of Phillips's continuing to act for Courvoisier after the confession, to criticism of the manner in which Phillips attacked the credibility of both Courvoisier's fellow servant, the housemaid, and also his similar attack on the final surprise witness against Courvoisier, the former employer with which Courvoisier had left the silver that had disappeared from the Lord Russell's house, the disappearance of which was the main support of the claim that an intruder had committed the murder (indeed, it was the appearance of this witness that precipitated Courvoisier's confession to Phillips). It was commonly believed that Phillips had implied in his closing speech that the housemaid was in fact guilty of the murder, knowing that to be untrue. The explicit eschewing of any such intent in the speech was taken as sly insinuation of the opposite. This attribution of third-party guilt to a defenseless and guiltless person, knowing it to be false, was perhaps the main target of the critics, or the one that gained the most traction. Phillips denied that his speech could be fairly construed in that way. For good short accounts of the Courvoisier affair and its aftermath, *see* Allyson N. May, The Bar and the Old Bailey, 1750–1850, 212–19 (2003); David J. A. Cairns, Advocacy and the Making of the Adversarial Criminal Trial 1800–1865, 126–36 (1998). For a much more extended treatment, *see generally* Mellinkoff, *supra* note 1 (reproducing much of the extant record of the trial and the controversy). It is unclear who leaked Courvoisier's confession

around his neck, do for a guinea what, without those appendages, he would think it wicked and infamous to do for an empire."[22]

This lays out pretty well the debate that has come to be known as the "general ethics" vs. "role-differentiated ethics" debate, which is as alive and well today as ever.[23]

For our part, we think the proponents of "role-differentiated ethics" generally have the better part of the argument on the most general level. It is not just lawyers whose role is taken to justify actions which would be wicked and infamous otherwise. Diplomats, soldiers, spies, parents, the list is endless. On the other hand, there must be limits to such role-differentiated excuses, as the Nuremburg trials established in response to claims that some war crimes were merely an exercise in a soldier carrying out orders.

It struck us, as we came to contemplate the role-differentiation claims reflected in such authorities as the ABA Rules of Professional Conduct, that the assumptions about lawyers' roles implied they were in fact not differentiated enough. The model seems in general to be a one-size-fits-all set of standards for a presumed unitary lawyer role. We have serious doubts about the efficacy of this approach. And indeed, there is an increasing awareness that the proper role-differentiated ethics of prosecutors must be different from those of criminal defense attorneys.[24] How far one should go in promulgating specialized codes for other specialized

---

to the press, as the fact was known to at least four people: Courvoisier, Phillips, Phillips's junior, Mr. Clarkson, and the judge from whom Phillips sought guidance, Baron Parke.

The English debate over the limits of advocacy spawned by the Courvoisier case received much public attention in the English press in the 1840s and 1850s as the result of a number of high-profile criminal cases that brought such issues to the fore, perhaps most dramatically in the 1848 case of Reid and M'Cabe, described not long after the trial took place in *Licence of Counsel*, 8 Law Mag. Quart. Rev. Juris. n.s. 52, 56–61 (1848). The case was a murder prosecution in which each co-defendant put exclusive blame on the other. Both were convicted and sentenced to hang, but Reid then confessed his sole guilt (convincingly), and M'Cabe was pardoned. The criticism fastened on Reid's counsel, Digby Seymour, who was alleged to have argued M'Cabe's sole guilt after Reid had confessed to him. Seymour denied that Reid's confession was either coherent or entirely exculpatory of M'Cabe, but said that even if it had been, he would still have proceeded as he did. It is unclear whether, if M'Cabe had been convicted and Reid had not voluntarily confessed (whether convicted or acquitted), Seymour would have stepped forward to save M'Cabe. *See* Cairns, *supra*, at 135, and Mellinkoff, *supra* note 1, at 194–8.

The English debate was echoed in America in two of the first extended essays on professional responsibility in America: Sharswood, *supra* note 2, and David Paul Brown, 2 The Forum: Forty Years Full Practice at the Philadelphia Bar 25–75 (1856). Brown, the leading Pennsylvania criminal defense lawyer of his day, is especially hard on what he considers to be the excesses of Lord Brougham's absolute position on loyalty to clients. *See, e.g., id.* at 44, calling it "erroneous and flagitious." This is perhaps somewhat surprising, since most American states had early adopted the full adversary model for ordinary criminal trials in the eighteenth century—*see* Randolph N. Jonakait, *The Rise of the American Adversary System: America Before England*, 14 Wid. L. Rev. 323 (2009)—a process that, as noted above, was only being completed in England in the 1840s and 1850s following the passage of the Prisoner's Counsel Act in 1836. *See generally* Cairns, *supra*, at 67–180. For a recent exposition and defense of Brougham's position *see* Monroe H. Freedman, *Henry Lord Brougham: Advocating at the Edge for Human Rights*, 36 Hofstra L. Rev. 311 (2007).

22 Thomas Babington Macaulay, *Lord Bacon*, reprinted from the Edinburgh Review of July 1837 in Thomas Babington Macaulay, Lord Macaulay, 3 Critical, Historical and Miscellaneous Essays 336, 376 (1886). The actual passage is in the form of an ironic declaration—"We will not at present inquire whether …"—because his charge against Bacon was that he acted in prosecuting Essex against all standards of the English bar that had ever existed. That was probably not totally accurate, as similar performances by Lord Coke and others during the period attest.

23 *See, e.g.*, William H. Simon, *Role Differentiation and Lawyers' Ethics: A Critique of Some Academic Perspectives*, 23 Geo. J. Legal Ethics, 987 (2010) (criticizing too much role differentiation); Monroe H. Freedman, *A Critique of Philosophizing about Lawyers' Ethics*, 25 Geo. J. Legal Ethics 91 (2012) (responding).

24 *See e.g.*, Model Rules of Prof'l Conduct R. 3.8, and Model Rules of Prof'l Conduct R. 3.8 cmt. *available at* http://www.americanbar.org/groups/professional_responsibility/publications/model_rules_of_professional_conduct/rule_3_8_special_responsibilities_of_a_prosecutor/comment_on_rule_3_8.html; and the separate ABA standards on the prosecution and defense function, *available at* http://www.americanbar.org/groups/criminal_justice/policy/standards.html. This is not a new development, exactly. For instance, in England, prior to defense counsel obtaining the right to address the jury in felony cases, the prosecution's lawyer was expected to show restraint in his speech. *See* Cairns, *supra* note 21, at 38–46. However, with the coming of full adversarialism, such special restrictions on prosecutors conceived of as "having no client but justice" have often tended to become mostly rhetoric. Hopefully the new proposed ABA standards, if adopted, will give such role-differentiated obligations more real bite. This raises the general question of whether, at least in the post-

lawyer functions is beyond the scope of this chapter.[25] But it seems clear that the example of prosecutors and defenders opens the way for a realization that different roles may require different ethical standards, which brings us again to the emerging role of the innocence lawyer.

In his recent book *Counsel of Rogues?*, the philosopher Tim Dare sets out what he sees as the three foundational principles undergirding lawyers' claims to a special role-based and role-necessitated set of precepts that can trump what most would agree should be the obligations of common morality in the same situations. In his view, these precepts are apparently claimed to apply to all lawyers in all settings. He labels them the principle of partisanship, the principle of neutrality, and the principle of non-accountability. Under the principle of partisanship, a lawyer is obliged to use best efforts (zealous advocacy) in advancing the client's interests "within the law."[26] Under the principle of neutrality, the lawyer is to take no personal position on the moral merits of a client's case after forming a lawyer/client relationship, and perhaps in making the decision to form that relationship; and, finally, under the principle of non-accountability the lawyer cannot and should not be held accountable for the moral positions or vices of his client or his client's case. These principles are conceived of as having general application, but they were only put forth in explicit forms (as previously noted) after the role of criminal defense lawyer emerged in the late eighteenth and early nineteenth centuries (although this standard conception was later generalized to all or most settings).[27] As should be clear from what we have already set out, we claim that the role of innocence lawyer has a set of precepts different from and sometimes in conflict with those given in the standard conception. Because we believe signaling is a requirement of the innocence lawyer function, we reject the principle of neutrality. A fortiori, we believe we are therefore responsible for the fundamental tenability of any claim brought in the name of innocence, which in turn causes us to reject the principle of non-accountability and through waivers to constrain significantly the principle of partisanship. We understand why the principles of the standard model must be embraced by criminal defense lawyers, but we believe there is both room for, and substantial need for, the innocence lawyer function as we have conceived it.

It is clear that at Seton Hall's Last Resort Exoneration Project we go significantly further in these regards than other innocence organizations. For instance, we have not yet joined the Innocence Network, at least in part because that organization has a set of ethical best practices which we think do not go far enough in separating the innocence function from the criminal defense function.[28] This is perhaps entirely understandable, since most lawyers involved in innocence work have come to it from the criminal defense function, and as long as DNA was the main driver of exoneration, perhaps the differences we believe are appropriate did not make as much practical difference either in how cases were handled or in outcomes. But now that the DNA era is inevitably drawing mostly to a close, and most exoneration efforts will involve the much more complex and

---

conviction setting, there is a special role for the "innocence prosecutor." *See generally*, David Luban, *The Conscience of a Prosecutor*, 45 VALP. U. L. REV 1 (2010).

25 In line with our instinct that the standard model of professional responsibility is not role-differentiated enough, we somewhat fortuitously happened on an article examining this issue in substantial detail. The article is Alexander A. Guerrero, *Lawyers, Context and Legitimacy: A New Theory of Legal Ethics*, 25 GEO. J. LEGAL ETHICS 107 (2012). Guerrero's taxonomy of lawyer roles does not bear directly on our claim here, and we have some reservations about it in places, but it clearly shows that "the lawyer role" can be subdivided into a variety of roles, each with somewhat different "role-differentiated" ethical considerations and components.

26 TIM DARE, THE COUNSEL OF ROGUES? A DEFENCE OF THE STANDARD CONCEPTION OF THE LAWYER'S ROLE (2009). There is disagreement, however, about what specific limits may be implied by the requirement to act only within the law, and Dare identifies two competing versions of this principle, the "zealous" and the "hyper-zealous" versions, the latter of which he rejects. Again, it is not always easy to tell the difference between the two in practical situations.

27 Interestingly, non-lawyer Samuel Johnson gave voice in 1768 to the assertion that a lawyer could not be judged by the positions he put forth to a court on behalf of a client. *See* MAY, *supra* note 21, at 205–6. But Johnson was speaking only of lawyers arguing points of law.

28 For instance, one of the Innocence Network's guidelines suggests that when information derived from one applicant would be useful to another applicant whose case for innocence is clearer (a co-defendant, say), such a situation may end up requiring withdrawal from consideration of both cases, and therefore not coming to the aid of either, even the more clearly innocent person. The Innocence Network, *Guide to Ethics & Best Practices for Innocence Project Practitioners*, at 9, *available at* http://law.umkc.edu/innocence/Conference%20materials/innocence-101-best-practices-practitioners.pdf. We believe our required waivers allow us to avoid this result, and it would be ironic if, once again, rules whose main beneficiaries are the less clearly innocent are deployed to disadvantage the clearly innocent.

difficult task of building a case for innocence out of less god-like materials, we believe the differences in approach are likely to make a substantial impact in how cases are selected, how they are investigated, how they are presented, their outcomes, and how those outcomes are viewed.

With all this as background, we will take up in somewhat more detail what we see as the main issues of the role of the innocence lawyer in the context of a series of individual topics.

## What Kind of Innocence?

When we speak of innocence, we mean what is sometimes called "factual innocence." One must be clear in one's definition of innocence, because otherwise one can be easily led to conflate three importantly different problems of justice. The first is the problem of convicting those who are factually innocent, either because no crime was committed or, more commonly, because a crime was in fact committed, but by someone else (wrongful conviction in the factual sense). The second is the problem of convicting a person who has undoubtedly performed the *actus reus* of a crime for which they are not culpable, either because of insanity or the absence of some other required indicium of culpability, usually a particular required mental state (wrongful conviction in the culpability sense). This is a serious problem because it is tied up with the notions of overcharging, oversentencing, and improper conviction of offenses more serious than the facts would warrant, but we exclude such considerations from the general notion of factual innocence. The third is the conviction of persons who may very well be both factually guilty and culpable, but who were convicted in trials containing procedural errors not easily dismissed as harmless error (wrongful conviction in the procedural sense). When we speak of "innocence," we are referring to factual innocence rather than innocence by virtue of a mischaracterization of culpability or a conviction rendered wrongful by procedural irregularities.[29] As Daniel Givelber has pointed out, adopting this definition of innocence excludes wrongful convictions based on jury misjudgments concerning *mens rea*, or other normatively charged determinations of the appropriate level of responsibility, including many affirmative defenses.[30]

Adopting this general approach does not answer all questions. For instance, how is one to deal with convincing evidence that the defendant was convicted as playing a role in the case he did not play (actual shooter, for instance), but where it is relatively clear he played some other role (driver, lookout). A step from that: what does one do in cases where the defendant played no role in the specific criminal episode (he wasn't present when the murder occurred) but he appears to bear some accessory liability, ranging from ordering the murder (a clear case) to being a member of a conspiracy, to being a person with foreknowledge but not a conspirator (depending on your definition of conspirator in gang situations, for instance), to being someone who knew who the actual perpetrator was but kept silent during his own trial (sometimes called "doing someone else's time"). These variables raise both theoretical issues (what is the innocence lawyer signaling) and practical issues (which kinds of cases justify the resources that are being put into such a case). None of these issues are live issues for criminal defense lawyers, but they are for innocence lawyers. We will return to how money (and resources of all kinds) impacts these questions below.

## How Clearly Innocent?

This question raises many difficult issues which can only be touched upon here.[31] Putting aside issues of uncharged and untried accomplice liability, which arise only in the minority of cases, from a god's-eye

---

29 *See* Risinger, *Unsafe Verdicts*, *supra* note 4, at 1295–1302.

30 Daniel Givelber, *Meaningless Acquittals, Meaningful Convictions: Do We Reliably Acquit the Innocent*? 49 RUTGERS L. REV. 1327–8 (1997).

31 An excellent discussion of the complex of issues involved can be found in Keith A. Findley, *Defining Innocence*, 74 ALB. L. REV. 1157 (2011). Because we believe in the appropriateness of classifying some cases not as affirmative exonerations but as radically unsafe verdicts, our criteria for the label "exoneration" are somewhat more stringent than Professor Findley's, or Professor Gross's, for that matter—see discussion in fn. 35 *infra*. On a related issue, *see* DANIEL GIVELBER & AMY FARRELL, NOT GUILTY—ARE THE ACQUITTED INNOCENT? (2012).

perspective the question of factual innocence is generally binary—either the person convicted did the crime or they didn't. However, a god's-eye perspective can rarely be approached in many claims of actual innocence. The innocence movement was in a sense spoiled by the DNA era, when in most cases the power of DNA to establish that ground-truth about innocence in a very high percentage of cases where it could be used at all has led to perhaps unrealistic hope in regard to what can be accomplished in non-DNA cases. That is not to say that there are not non-DNA cases where the conclusion of innocence is as well warranted as it is in the average DNA exoneration. But the average non-DNA case (if such radically individualized human circumstances can ever be so characterized) presents an epistemically much more complicated situation, being almost inevitably constructed out of a huge amount of interconnecting circumstantial evidence. The result will almost inevitably be more subject to at least semi-tenable counter-interpretations at a variety of points. In these circumstances, the judge as factfinder will have to decide whether actual innocence is established sufficiently clearly. The emerging consensus seems to be that the standard of proof for this exercise will be "clear and convincing" evidence of actual innocence if actual innocence is being used as a freestanding claim for relief, and "by a preponderance" if it is being used as a gateway to avoid waivers and time bars for consideration of various "constitutional" claims. In the former situation the prisoner would be entitled to release more or less by definition, but in the latter would formally be entitled only to a new trial, although such a trial will often not be pursued.[32] How is one to characterize the status of such results? The first is a clear exoneration.[33] The latter is less clear, but the finding of innocence by a preponderance certainly suggests that such a case is properly classed as an actual exoneration.[34]

Cases of the former type are fairly rare in today's world, given the fact that most jurisdictions have not yet adopted a specific innocence jurisprudence. Even in those jurisdictions that recognize actual innocence as either a freestanding claim or a gateway, the most common kind of case where release occurs appears to be one where a claim of innocence is made but not adjudicated, the case is reversed on some other ground, and the decision is made not to retry, often because the passage of time since the crime has made a retrial too difficult to justify the expense, given how long the person has already served. Exoneration? We believe that the preeminent cataloguer of cases of exoneration, Professor Samuel Gross, counts such cases.[35] We would not do so without more detailed analysis of the state of the actual evidence of innocence. And it is here that we would raise a caveat for the innocence movement, if we may. We see a future risk in having too expansive a definition of exoneration. It threatens to precipitate a backlash from those who think that the phenomenon of actual innocence among convicted persons is so rare as to not justify the expenditure of any significant resources trying to discover who they might be. Rather than go there, in the absence of a full-scale

32 For an examination of the implications of retrying a defendant when a court, in ordering a retrial under the *Schlup* standard, has already functionally made a finding of innocence by a preponderance of the evidence, *see* Jordan M. Barry, *Prosecuting the Exonerated: Actual Innocence and the Double Jeopardy Clause*, 64 Stan. L. Rev. 535 (2012).

33 Of course there is smaller or larger residual possibility of guilt which it is only honest to acknowledge when making statistical collations and such, but for the individual, this must count as exoneration if anything can.

34 The same thing can be said when the former prisoner sues for and is awarded compensation based on actual innocence.

35 In his first major collection of such cases, Samuel R. Gross et al., *Exonerations in the United States, 1989 Through 2003*, 95 J. Crim. L. & Criminology 523 (2005), Professor Gross sets out four criteria for determining what he will count as exonerations: (1) whether "governors (or other appropriate executive officers) issued pardons based on evidence of the defendants' innocence"; (2) whether "criminal charges were dismissed by courts after new evidence of innocence emerged, such as DNA"; (3) whether "defendants were acquitted at a retrial on the basis of evidence that they had no role in the crimes for which they were originally convicted"; and (4) whether a state "posthumously acknowledged the innocence of defendants who had already died in prison." *Id.* at 524. (In 2012, Professor Gross co-authored an updated report, which explains again how decisions are made to count exonerations in the newly created National Registry of Exonerations. *See* Samuel R. Gross et al., Exonerations in the United States, 1989–2012, *available at* http://www.law.umich.edu/special/exoneration/Documents/exonerations_us_1989_2012_full_report.pdf.)

It is the second criterion that presents problems, since it can be applied to cases where reversals were explicitly based on non-innocence grounds with a judicial declaration that the reversal was not an endorsement of innocence, and the subsequent failure to retry was explicitly based on the passage of time and loss of witnesses making the retrial impossible independent of innocence. We believe such cases require much more examination of the underlying case before they are declared "exonerations," although we concede that Professor Gross's approach has the virtue of not requiring contentious judgments.

examination of the case for innocence by anyone doing the classification, we would prefer such cases be referred to by the British term, "unsafe verdicts."

Finally, there is a fourth kind of case that might actually be generally more proper for the label "exoneration" than the category just discussed. It occurs when someone is convicted on the evidence of a witness or witnesses who are clearly shown to have given testimony that was false, either because it radically conflicts with subsequent scientific analysis of the physical evidence or because it is shown to have been the result of improper police creation, or both. In such cases, it is true that no affirmative evidence of actual innocence may be available. However, by definition, the defendant had no evidence left against him at the end of the day, and so is no more likely to be guilty than any number of others with the same general relationship to the time and place of the crime. We may call such cases "radically unsafe verdicts," and we think that the label of "exoneration" might be put on them without too many worries of the backlash effects we outlined above.

## What Should Those Claiming Innocence Expect When Dealing with an Innocence Lawyer Rather Than a Criminal Defense Lawyer Post-conviction?

First: As Professor Mosteller observes, at some fundamental level criminal defense lawyers can't, and usually don't, care if their clients are factually innocent—that is in some ways their privilege and the essence of their role. Innocence lawyers must and do care deeply about whether their clients are factually innocent—that is the essence of *their* role.

How does this change things? First, it eliminates any version of the cab rank principle. An innocence lawyer cannot represent someone simply because they claim innocence, or because they contact them, or even because they can pay a lot of money (not usually a consideration even if the convicted person has money, but we will return to money issues below), but must devote substantial investigatory resources to a case before even deciding to take it. The result of this obligation will be that most cases will be turned down after an expenditure of some significant amount of time and effort.

Second, it changes both what can be expected and what can be given the individual convicted person reaching out to the innocence lawyer (we hesitate to use the word "client" at this point for reasons that will become obvious). In the Last Resort Exoneration Project (which Lesley C. Risinger directs and of which D. Michael Risinger is the associate director), inquiries from prisoners[36] are generally responded to by sending them an application for case review. Our application is 23 pages long and contains some provisions that not all such prisoners like, including various waivers in regard to aspects of the attorney–client privilege and potential conflicts of interest. In this we echo Professor Mosteller's favorite line: we don't care. Under our view of the role of the innocence lawyer we have no obligation to any of them unless and until certain criteria are met, and they agree to accept certain conditions, which are fully outlined in the application.[37] For one thing, as we just indicated, they must waive all attorney–client privilege as it applies to former lawyers. We have no time for prisoners who try to insulate their former lawyers' knowledge of the case and their previous communications with those lawyers from our scrutiny. In addition, they must understand that we retain the right to use any information they provide, or that our investigation subsequently uncovers, in aid of any other person that this information shows is likely to be innocent; and we will not spend resources investigating a case where a person asserting their own innocence is not willing to accept that proviso. In addition, we retain the right to communicate our evaluation of their claim of innocence, upon inquiry, to any other innocence organization to which they may apply if we decide not to go forward with their case. The limited resources of such organizations cannot reasonably be asked to bear the burden of such serial applications and duplicative reviews. Finally, we make it clear in the application that we expect truth and candor, and that if we conclude

36 We do recognize the possibility of representing persons whose sentence has been completed but who can be shown to have been factually innocent, but they are rare enough to use the word "prisoner" in this context.

37 No obligation beyond a general obligation of confidentiality, that is. But we have no affirmative obligation to act for any persons seeking our aid until they voluntarily agree to the conditions of our representation, and even then (as the application makes clear) until we make a decision to offer them our aid after full investigation, and even then, only on the conditions that we set out when we offer such aid.

during our dealings with them that they have been substantially untruthful in their dealings with us, we retain the right to terminate consideration of their case on that basis. Further, they must understand that we will not agree to represent them until our initial screening and investigation is concluded, and as a result we conclude that they are very likely factually innocent, and that further investigation is likely to aid in establishing this in court. They also must understand that we will drop them immediately if substantial new evidence of their actual guilt emerges. Only if they are willing to accept this kind of relationship at the outset will we proceed to evaluate their application and go forward with preliminary screening investigation and evaluation.

It is of some interest that in the first year or so of this approach in New Jersey we received about 225 inquiries and we sent out about 175 applications, of which only about 125 have been returned completed. Of these, we have so far identified only three or four which we believe are appropriate for our involvement. We are hard screeners because once we start on a case we face many years and thousands of hours of litigation. Our decision thresholds are hardly set to undertake such an awe-inspiring burden lightly. It is this circumstance which, if we stick to it, lays the foundation over time for courts to learn that they should take the cases we bring seriously, and evaluate them with an open mind.

## The Innocence Lawyer and Money (and Other Resources)

### *The Costs of Individual Cases*

There are a number of considerations that together lead to the conclusion that no one can consider a career as an innocence lawyer and have the ambition to make a substantial amount of money doing it. However, these same considerations mean that the criminal justice system in general need not fear any flood of either substantial claims or successful claims by innocence lawyers, and also that the system in general (meaning judges) should take the signal behind an innocence lawyer's assertion of innocence for a client seriously.

First, the age of post-conviction DNA exonerations is passing, even as the tail-end of such cases continues to produce exonerations. Cases involving the potential for DNA exoneration are by no means easily carried out, but they are substantially less expensive and less onerous than non-DNA exonerations, which require on the average much more investigation and litigation, especially now that the right of defendants who might be exonerated by DNA to obtain testing is more or less accepted. DNA cases are now in a sense capable of being viewed as off-the-rack litigation, while non-DNA cases are cases requiring elaborate hand-tailoring. The best estimate for what the average non-DNA exoneration costs in lawyer and other time and direct expenditure of money is probably that given by the organization most experienced with such cases, Centurion Ministries. Their estimate is around $350,000 per case.[38] In addition, the Northern California Innocence Project estimates that the exonerations of Obie Anthony, Maurice Caldwell, and Franky Carillo, Jr. averaged over 5,300 attorney hours each, which, even at modest billing rates, would total more than $500,000 per case.[39] This accords with our own experience in two non-DNA exonerations, each of which consumed many thousands of hours in lawyer and support staff time. There are two implications of such numbers: First, given the amount of prescreening and the other burdens of bringing and persevering in non-DNA exoneration cases, there is, as we said, unlikely to be such a volume of them as to create a serious problem for the legal system. There will be no haystack problem created by seriously supported non-DNA actual innocence cases (and so the legal system, meaning judges, ought to be more open to such cases than they sometimes appear to be at present). Second, there must be some source of funding for these resources to make such cases work at all.

---

38 *Investment in 8 Pressing Cases*, document sent to contributors by Centurion Ministries, 2010 (copy on file with authors). The average for the eight cases, including estimated costs of completion, was $347,625. Centurion is the oldest operating innocence organization in America. Centurion is not an organization of lawyers, but often actually pays outside lawyers in the cases it has investigated and determined to support. We think it likely that they often get discounted rates, but we are not privy to the details of their cost estimates beyond what we have described here.

39 *See The Impact of Your Gift: The Costs*, Northern Cal. Innocence Proj. Newsl. (Northern California Innocence Project) (Spring, 2012), at 8 (copy on file with authors).

**Combining the Innocence Lawyer Role with Other Lawyer Roles in General: Criminal Defense**

Can a lawyer combine the role of innocence lawyer in some cases with the role of criminal defense lawyer in others? The answer to that requires a careful contrast between the roles and their conflicting demands, and some reflection on the implications of those conflicting demands across cases. The provisional answer we will give is that the same person can do both, under some circumstances, as long as the role being played is clearly enough signaled. However, many criminal defense lawyers might not be comfortable with such an arrangement, because of the potential negative signaling impact on his or her largely guilty criminal defense clients.

*Innocence Lawyers and Post-Exoneration Compensation*

What about the time-honored practice of obtaining relief for a client criminally charged, and then suing for compensation, should there be good ground to do so? One of us has certainly been involved in somewhat analogous cases in his career, defending persons shot by the police from charges thereafter lodged against them, and, upon securing a positive outcome, suing for compensation for the wrongful shooting. But it seems to us that when one is acting as an innocence lawyer, one's signaling integrity is a large part of what one has to offer the convicted innocent, and the prospect of large monetary recovery may distort one's view of what constitutes what can credibly be claimed as exoneration. This can lead in the direction of undermining the credibility of one's evaluations of innocence. If such became general practice, it could undermine the credibility of the innocence lawyer role and the innocence movement in general in the long run. So, in most situations, at least unless there is an official indication of actual innocence, such an inviting prospect of substantial monetary reward is perhaps best left alone. Therefore, we think that anyone who aspires to anything like a career role as an innocence lawyer in the post-DNA era should probably resign themselves to relatively modest compensation for such work (if any).

**The Present and Future of the Innocence Lawyer**

People who act or have acted as innocence lawyers in the last couple of decades in America have come to that role in a number of ways. For some, it was the call of an individual case that they otherwise had become involved in[40] or had become aware of from the press,[41] such *pro bono* service sometimes leading to near career-threatening commitment. For others, the involvement has been through organizations committed to

40 This was the case for Mark Rabil, who was assigned to be Darryl Hunt's defense lawyer for his trial, and found himself compelled by his belief in Hunt's innocence to pursue (and ultimately secure) Hunt's exoneration as an innocence lawyer over decades, in the face of huge obstacles. *See* Mark Rabil, *My Three Decades With Darryl Hunt*, 75 Albany L. Rev. 1535 (2012).

41 This was the case for both of us in the Fernando Bermudez case (which resulted in a finding of actual innocence by a Manhattan judge), and for Lesley C. Risinger even before she became a lawyer. She and her mother, Priscilla Read Chenoweth (who was and is a lawyer), in 1993 read a story in a local newspaper in Hudson County, New Jersey, concerning a young local man, Kevin Luis Rojas, who had been convicted of a shooting death in Manhattan and sentenced to 15 years to life for the crime, and through their persistent efforts they ultimately managed to obtain his exoneration. Mr. Rojas was subsequently compensated for his wrongful conviction under New York's wrongful conviction compensation statute, Ct. Cl. Act. §8-b, which requires a clear and convincing showing of actual innocence. This case settled after the Court of Claims found that he was likely to prevail on this claim at trial. Rojas v. New York, 2000 N.Y. Ct. Cl. 100601, Mot. No. M-614461, (#2000-014-515), *available at* http://vertumnus.courts.state.ny.us/claims/search/display.html?terms=&url=/claims/html/2000-014-515.html. A substantial settlement thereafter ensued. Some of the facts of this case are recited in that Court of Claims opinion, as well as in a court opinion issued in Mr. Rojas's suit against the city and police for violation of constitutional rights in conducting suggestive identification procedures, Rojas v. Iannatto, 2003 U.S. Dist. LEXIS 938 (S.D.N.Y. Jan. 23, 2003). For some of the press coverage in this case, *see, e.g.*, Kevin Flynn, *Persevering Woman Helps Free Stranger in '90 Murder Case,* N.Y. Times, Oct. 23, 1998, http://www.nytimes.com/1998/10/23/nyregion/persevering-woman-helps-free-stranger-in-90-murder-case.html?pagewanted=all&src=pm. The Bermudez case is discussed in, *e.g.*, John Eligon, *Man Jailed for '91 Murder Is Cleared by Judge,* N.Y. Times, Nov. 12, 2009, at A23.

freeing the convicted innocent, whether free-standing or connected to an academic institution, often a law school. For yet others, it has been through the *pro bono* efforts of a large and prosperous law firm whose main practice otherwise was largely unrelated to the convicted innocent,[42] or even to criminal law. Each of these has its strengths and weaknesses as a way to take up and discharge the special role of innocence lawyer. All will be needed for the foreseeable future, but we believe the most necessary component for the innocence lawyer and the innocence effort in America is the creation of state innocence commissions in each of the several states. In this particular regard, as in others in the area of the protection of the convicted innocent, the UK is well in advance of America, since England, Wales, and Northern Ireland combined[43]—and also Scotland independently[44]—have functioning innocence commissions within our intended meaning.[45] The reason government innocence commissions are so important can be easily summed up: resources, subpoena power, and weight.

"Resources" is self-explanatory. While one or two innocence organizations in America may be relatively handsomely funded by their institutions or by donors, most (like ours) operate on shoestrings, certainly by comparison to the screening and investigation demands that the applications entail.[46] While one can never guarantee that a government agency will be adequately funded, either at the outset or in later years, it seems generally appropriate that the function of providing adequate resources be a public one.

Subpoena power, along with other attendant discovery and investigatory devices, is perhaps the most important advantage of a state innocence commission. Post-conviction innocence work, which is ideally a thorough exercise in truth-finding, is constrained by the assumptions of both adversarialism and the finality of criminal judgments. Prosecutors often do not cooperate in providing needed discovery or investigative resources, even when presented with good reason to do so. And many years of experience attempting to investigate innocence claims among the poor of New York and New Jersey (particularly Camden) show that many people refuse to talk to you, and those who will talk are very reluctant to sign anything. Since many legal systems place unrealistically high value on such willingness to sign a document as a precondition to the person's information being even preliminarily considered, the difficulties for a non-governmental organization are obvious. Governmental innocence commissions, however, can be given the power to require (for example) that the government's entire file be turned over and to take depositions upon subpoena, powers that can make all the difference in gathering the information needed to make a rational evaluation of a claim of innocence.[47]

---

42 This was the case for Barry Pollack, originally of Kelley Drye & Warren, in the Bermudez case, *supra* note 41. Two other well-publicized cases are the Palladium case in Manhattan, in which the well-heeled Cooley Godward Kronish firm took up the very difficult cause of exonerating two innocent men convicted of murder in a gang case, Luban, *supra* note 25, and the case of Jose Garcia, which was taken up by Willkie Farr & Gallagher; *see* Matthew Bosher, *The "Exceptionally Troubling" Murder Conviction of Jose Garcia*, CRIMINAL LAW BRIEF Vol. 2, issue 2, p. 16 (Spring, 2007), *available at* http://www.wcl.american.edu/journal/clb/documents/Spring2007Issue.pdf. This is an online student-edited journal produced at American University's Washington College of Law, and it does not yet seem to have a standardized bluebook citation form.

43 The story of the creation of the Criminal Cases Review Commission (CCRC), which began operation in 1997, and its operational structure is well told in David Wolitz, *Innocence Commissions and the Future of Post-Conviction Review*, 52 ARIZ. L. REV. 1027, 1041–5 (2010). *See also* the official CCRC website, *available at* http://www.justice.gov.uk/about/criminal-cases-review-commission.

44 The Scottish Criminal Cases Review Commission was established in 1999. *See* SCOTTISH CRIMINAL CASE REVIEW COMMISSION, http://www.sccrc.org.uk/aboutthecommission.aspx (last visited Mar. 20, 2013).

45 The label "innocence commission" is given to a surprisingly broad array of institutions. In many places in America the term is used for "study" commissions, usually public but in at least one instance private, whose role is to study the causes of the conviction of the innocent in a particular state and make recommendations for corrective action to state legislatures or other authorities. *See* Wolitz, *supra* note 43, at 1045–7. Needless to say, this is not the definition used in this chapter. Rather, the term "innocence commission" is used only for an official government body with the role of re-examining claims of actual innocence in regard to final convictions.

46 *See generally* Steven A. Krieger, *Why Our Justice System Convicts Innocent People and the Challenges Faced by Innocence Projects Trying to Exonerate Them*, 14 NEW CRIM. L. REV. 333, 371–6 (2011).

47 For instance, the sole current American innocence commission, the North Carolina Innocence Inquiry Commission, has the power to compel testimony and give limited immunity for such testimony. *See* N.C. GEN. STAT. §15A-1468(a1) (2010). Our colleague at Seton Hall, Erik Lillquist, is skeptical of the innocence commission mechanism, largely because he fears an impact on the operational standard of reasonable doubt that juries will use at trial when they know there is an innocence commission as a backstop, and also because such commissions are so expensive per exoneration that he fears

Finally, by "weight" we mean the presumptive deference that courts may give to the conclusions of an innocence commission bringing forth a case as a serious claim of actual innocence after investigation. This has to do not only with the clarity of the right to signal, but also with the weight that will be accorded to that signal. We believe that judges should give substantial weight to the signal of innocence we communicate when we bring any case as a case of actual innocence after our review process. However, we know that a great many judges will resist this, a resistance that will be reduced or overcome by the case coming from an official effort of the state itself.

As of now, only one American state has an innocence commission as we use the term: North Carolina.[48] American states seem to have much more stomach for study commissions to redundantly consider the factors that lead to the conviction of the innocent than they do for doing anything about them, either by significant changes in legal arrangements for investigation and trial, or by reform of standards of review and post-conviction relief. Or, for that matter, by instituting true innocence commissions.[49]

It is probably worth noting that state innocence commissions are not being recommended as a panacea, or a solution to all problems. In many ways, upstream reforms in investigation and trial procedures, and in review standards after conviction, are more important, since they will hopefully ameliorate the problems that create the preconditions of miscarriages of justice, and reduce the number of convicted innocent. And even when an innocence commission is established, there is always the danger that it will be underfunded or that it will, over time, become too bureaucratized and insensitive to the task of separating the few innocent applicants among the many guilty ones to continue doing its job well. For that reason, it is important that private innocence efforts continue in order to provide a watchdog evaluating the job of the official innocence commission, and to keep it on its toes through "rivalrous redundancy" by providing an alternative forum for claims of innocence.[50] But first we must institute the innocence commissions and worry about reforming their then-discovered imperfections later.

---

that public resources for other parts of the criminal justice system will be cut, with unintended consequences that may in fact reduce the net accuracy of outcomes. *See* Erik Lillquist, *Improving Accuracy in Criminal Cases*, 41 U. Richmond L. Rev. 897, 908–11 (2007). We do not believe his first fear is a likely outcome of the social process of jury decision. We suspect that jurors already assume (wrongly, more's the pity) that such review is one of the functions of the appeal/post-conviction review process generally. We know of no complaints of such an effect in the British experience over a decade and a half. As for the second point, how reallocation of resources might affect accuracy is a pure guess, and we believe that society should be willing to run the risk of the experiment on moral grounds, and devote additional resources to the system if necessary. At any rate, if an innocence commission is not the answer to the problem of the convicted innocent, at least private innocence organizations should be allowed easy access to some sort of compulsory process and discovery mechanism for the investigation of significant claims of innocence.

48 The workings of the North Carolina Innocence Inquiry Commission, which began operating in 2007, are detailed in Wolitz, *supra* note 44, at 1049–54. *See also*, the Commission website, North Carolina Innocence Inquiry Commission, http://www.innocencecommission-nc.gov/ (last visited Mar. 20, 2013). The NCIIC has done full-scale review on five cases involving six defendants to date (Mar. 20, 2013). In one, State v. Reeves, it referred the case to the appropriate court, but the court failed to find factual innocence by clear and convincing evidence. In another, State v. McNeil, the Commission itself decided against court referral. However, in State v. Taylor, State v. Kagonyera and Wilcoxson, and State v. Grimes, the Commission referred the cases to the appropriate courts, which found innocence by clear and convincing evidence and discharged the prisoners. Thus, to date, the work of the NCIIC has led to the overturning of three cases and the exoneration of four defendants. *See Case Statistics*, NC Innocence Commission, http://www.innocencecommission-nc.gov/stats.html (last visited July 28, 2013).

49 Various objections, from both the right and the left, to the establishment of innocence commissions (including those of Professor Lillquist, *supra* note 47) are carefully catalogued and discussed in Wolitz, *supra* note 43, at 1053–72. For an extended comparison of American and Finnish post-conviction review processes, including specifically post-conviction review of innocence claims, *see* Christopher M. Johnson, *Post-Trial Judicial Review of Criminal Convictions: A Comparative Study of the United States and Finland*, 64 Me. L. Rev. 425 (2012).

50 The term "rivalrous redundancy" was coined by the economist Roger Koppl in the context of a proposal to obtain "competitive self regulation" of forensic laboratories by virtue of the existence of competing laboratories available to perform the same tests. Roger Koppl, *How to Improve Forensic Science,* 20 Eur. J. L. & Econs. 255, 257 (2005).

## Conclusion

If you accept that in an important sense, "innocence is different," we hope to have persuaded you that the role of the innocence lawyer must be, in important respects, different too. It is a role that cannot be a career path for many, and those few must almost certainly harbor only modest material goals; but it is an honorable role that ought to be supported by any mature legal system calling itself a system of individual justice.

# Chapter 8
# When Finality and Innocence Collide

Carrie Sperling

## Introduction

After hearing the compelling stories of innocent inmates finally exonerated after years in prison, many in the United States may believe that the American criminal justice system, although fallible and slow moving, has adequate post-conviction safeguards to protect the innocent. They would be wrong. Instead, a prisoner claiming factual innocence will find a shockingly confusing web of procedures that make exoneration based on innocence a near impossible feat.[1] Exonerations of innocent inmates too frequently result from pure luck or happenstance rather than through procedures designed to ensure the accuracy of the conviction.[2]

Why is it so hard to free an innocent inmate? Sometimes the fault lies in the nature of the evidence. Powerful circumstantial evidence of guilt is hard to overcome, and inmates often cannot access evidence that would clearly demonstrate their innocence. For example, if several eyewitnesses identified the inmate as the armed gunman who robbed the convenience store, without video evidence or a rock-solid alibi, the inmate cannot muster the evidence to overcome the witnesses' mistaken identifications. Likewise, a defendant who, after a coercive interrogation, falsely confesses to a robbery will find it difficult to overcome the confession without the same kind of definitive video or alibi evidence.[3] However, often the fault lies in the procedures in place that prevent inmates from asserting their innocence. For instance, even when inmates do find highly reliable evidence that undermines the conviction, they have few avenues available to them to investigate,

---

1 Barry Friedman, *A Tale of Two Habeas*, 73 Minn. L. Rev. 247, 253 (1988) ("[T]he rules governing access to habeas review have become hopelessly confusing and confused."); Stephanie Hartung Roberts, *Missing the Forest for the Trees: Federal Habeas Corpus and the Piecemeal Problem in Actual Innocence Cases,* 10 Stan. J. Civ. Rts. & Civ. Liberties 101 (discussing the confusing procedures an innocent inmate faces when asserting a post-conviction challenge and suggesting reforms).

2 Larry Youngblood's case offers an example of how dumb luck led to exoneration. Prosecutors in Arizona convicted Youngblood of child molestation, sexual assault, and kidnapping in 1985, a horrific crime in which the perpetrator sodomized a young boy over an extended period. Youngblood fit the description of the perpetrator that the victim had given police. The child victim also picked Youngblood out of a photo line-up. Youngblood's car met the description of the car the perpetrator drove. Although serology testing of the perpetrator's semen may have excluded Youngblood as a suspect at the time, the police mishandled the samples, rendering them untestable. After the jury convicted Youngblood, he appealed all the way to the United States Supreme Court, claiming that the prosecution's failure to properly handle the biological evidence in the case violated his constitutional rights. The Supreme Court rejected that argument, holding that only intentional destruction of evidence would implicate Youngblood's due process rights, and here the police department was simply negligent. In 2000, Youngblood renewed his attempts to prove his innocence. Surprisingly, the hospital that conducted the exam of the victim had retained the victim's clothing, and because the clothing contained small amounts of semen, Youngblood was able to use new, more sophisticated DNA tests to analyze the semen. Those tests demonstrated that it was not Youngblood's semen on the victim's clothing, but the semen of a man who also fit the victim's description. If the hospital had not retained the clothing long after the conviction, and if the semen on the clothing was too degraded to test, and if Youngblood did not have access to newer, more sophisticated testing, he would never have been exonerated. For an excellent journalistic treatment of this case, *see DNA and Fair Trials*, Religion & Ethics Newsweekly (June 9, 2006), http://www.pbs.org/wnet/religionandethics/2006/06/09/june-9-2006-dna-and-fair-trials/15673/.

3 Daniel S. Medwed, *Up the River without a Procedure: Innocent Prisoners and Newly Discovered Non-DNA Evidence in State Courts*, 47 Ariz. L. Rev. 655, 658 (2005) ("Without a doubt, non-DNA cases are difficult for defendants to overturn through state court proceedings given the subjectivity involved in assessing most forms of new evidence and the absence of a method to prove innocence to a scientific certainty.").

collect, test, and present that evidence after the conviction is final.[4] Therefore, even in cases where DNA could almost certainly prove an inmate's innocence, the inmate often spends years or decades navigating outmoded procedures in a quest for exoneration and release.[5]

Innocent prisoners face numerous procedural hurdles that often prevent them from successfully presenting their claims after their conviction. There are many reasons for this. Although our criminal justice system presumes innocence before conviction, that presumption is turned on its head after conviction. The defendant is now legally guilty of a crime. In our system, great deference is given to a jury determination of guilt. Many claim that the jury's verdict should only be overturned in the rarest of circumstances—where the judge made an error at trial that probably led to a guilty verdict; where the trial failed to give the defendant the protections guaranteed by the constitution; or where the trial was fundamentally unfair.[6]

These post-conviction procedures grow out of a strong tradition that values the finality of criminal convictions. Finality in the criminal law context means that the case is over, with no avenues remaining to challenge the conviction. Finality assigns guilt, puts the case to rest, and assures all parties that it will not be re-opened. Assuming that the criminal process is error-free, finality serves the ends of justice. Theoretically, once the system convicts the right person and assesses the right punishment, society is better off when prosecutors, law enforcement professionals, defense attorneys, and judges move on to other concerns.[7]

Of course, the criminal process is not completely error-free, so the point at which to end inmates' opportunities to challenge their convictions becomes difficult to define. Some advocates, judges, and scholars have argued for expansive avenues to challenge convictions after trial and appeals.[8] Others have called for narrowing the avenues and bringing finality to most convictions much sooner.[9] Most, however, recognize that special exceptions should be made for those who are factually innocent of the crimes for which they were convicted.[10] In other words, innocent inmates should be privileged above others in the system when it comes to challenging their convictions. However, the current system continues to value finality over accuracy. The system has not yet provided sufficient procedures to test the accuracy of convictions that have become suspect due to our advanced understanding of the myriad ways in which inmates are wrongly convicted. The problem is that we're stuck with an antiquated system of justice, which has not sufficiently incorporated new knowledge. The American criminal justice system still embraces the notion of finality even when the rationale for finality no longer exists.

This chapter describes what finality is, where it comes from, why it led to current post-conviction procedures, and why those procedures are outdated and unjust. Part I explains the finality doctrine and the arguments that support it. Part II addresses some of the common misconceptions about the processes available

---

4 *See* Brandon L. Garrett, *Judging Innocence*, 108 Colum. L. Rev. 55, 126 (2008) ("Our system of criminal review certainly does not privilege factual claims. Locating an alibi witness, obtaining experts to challenge forensic evidence or undermine eyewitness identifications, or presenting evidence of defendants' lack of capacity requires substantial resources and time.").

5 For example, Daryl Hunt's attorneys successfully sought testing of semen samples from the victim of a sexual assault and murder to prove that Hunt did not commit the crime. In 1994, the DNA tests excluded Hunt, but despite the exclusion, the prosecutors continued to oppose Hunt's release. Hunt was finally exonerated in 2004, 10 years after DNA tests provided the exonerating results. *See Know the Cases*, Innocence Project, http://www.innocenceproject.org/Content/Darryl_Hunt.php (last visited July 12, 2013).

6 Keith Findley, *Innocence Protection in the Appellate Process*, 93 Marq. L. Rev. 591, 602 (2009).

7 *See generally* Paul M. Bator, *Finality in Criminal Law and Federal Habeas Corpus for State Prisoners*, 76 Harv. L. Rev. 441 (1963).

8 *See, e.g.*, Louis H. Pollak, *Proposals to Curtail Habeas Corpus for State Prisoners: Collateral Attack on the Great Writ*, 66 Yale L.J. 50, 65 (1956) (arguing that "where liberty is involved, a democratic society employs a different arithmetic and insists that it is less important to reach an unshakable decision than to do justice").

9 *See, e.g.*, Henry J. Friendly, *Is Innocence Irrelevant? Collateral Attack on Criminal Judgments*, 38 U. Chi. L. Rev. 142, 142 (1970) (arguing for greater finality in post-conviction, but advocating a privileged position for innocence claims).

10 *See id.* at 142 (arguing that "with a few important exceptions, convictions should be subject to collateral attack only when the prisoner supplements his constitutional plea with a colorable claim of innocence"). Note, *Federal Habeas Corpus Review of State Convictions: An Interplay of Appellate Ambiguity and District Court Discretion*, 68 Yale L.J. 98, 101 n.13 (1958) (stating that the "policy against incarcerating or executing an innocent man ... should far outweigh the desired termination of litigation").

to free the innocent, and explains how post-conviction procedures clash with notions of justice and fairness because they operate to prevent courts from reassessing the accuracy of a conviction once the trial is over. Part III provides a hypothetical case to explain how the current post-conviction procedures clash with an inmate's claims of innocence. Part IV suggests a new approach to post-conviction procedures—one that accounts for a new understanding of the accuracy of most traditional forms of criminal evidence.

## Part I: The Focus on Finality in the American Criminal Justice System

The American criminal justice system must balance competing interests. The primary goal is justice, and justice requires accuracy; therefore, the criminal justice system functions properly when it convicts the guilty and frees the innocent. No one benefits when the state punishes the wrong person for a crime.[11] Many would argue that justice also requires a sense of completion or finality.[12] And, often, this need for finality collides with the desire for accuracy.

A system that places the highest value on accuracy might continually reassess convictions as new evidence arises that weakens the case against the convicted person.[13] For example, if a rape occurred before DNA testing was available, so that the defendant was convicted without the benefit of subjecting the semen sample to DNA analysis, upon the inmate's request, the state would test any preserved samples when testing becomes available.[14] Subjecting the older evidence to newer, more reliable testing would ensure that the conviction remains sound. The state would also reassess whole classes of cases where the evidence used at the time of conviction becomes scientifically unreliable. For example, when the methods of determining arson fires were scientifically undermined, a system that valued accuracy would review all arson cases where the state used unreliable methods in obtaining a conviction.[15] In this type of system, the conviction is only as reliable as the evidence today would suggest. If a jury determined guilt based on unreliable testimony, the inmate should, theoretically, have another opportunity to challenge the evidence either by new trial or through an evidentiary hearing.[16]

However, finality has also been a compelling goal in the American criminal justice system.[17] Revisiting the facts of a case after a final decision would, as some contend, foster a lack of confidence in the justice system

---

11 David P. Kennedy, *The End of Finality*, 37 Md. B.J., Nov.–Dec. 2004, at 24, 27 ("incarcerating innocent and presumably productive members of society while dangerous criminals remain free is economically irrational").

12 Even in cases where the death penalty has been imposed, some argue that it would "paralyze society" to become too concerned about the "unavoidable risk of error in the administration of capital punishment." Stephen J. Markman & Paul G. Cassell, *Protecting the Innocent: A Response to the Bedau-Radelet Study*, 41 Stan. L. Rev. 121, 159–60 (1988).

13 *See DNA and Fair Trials*, *supra* note 2. When interviewed for the story about Larry Youngblood's exoneration, Larry Hammond (former President, American Judicature Society) said, "We must have a system that preserves evidence and that makes it available for inspection and that opens the courthouse door to the consideration of that evidence … . At any time. No scientist would disagree with that. No one who cares about getting it right would disagree with that." *Id.*

14 Instead of seeking accuracy through DNA testing, states have opposed post-conviction testing, arguing that inmates have no right to post-conviction testing. For example, Alaska denied William Osborne DNA testing even though it admitted that DNA exclusion would definitively prove his innocence. The United States Supreme Court agreed, ending Osborne's long battle to test the semen retained from his conviction. *See* Dist. Attorney's Office for the Third Judicial Dist. v. Osborne, 557 U.S. 52 (2009).

15 For a fascinating look at how state officials go out of their way to prevent review of convictions based on invalidated forensic science, see the ongoing controversy surrounding the Cameron Todd Willingham case in Texas. Governor Perry refused to review scientifically undermined arson evidence in a capital case in the days before Cameron Todd Willingham's execution. After his execution, the Texas Forensic Science Commission agreed to review the case, but the Governor attempted to block its review. The twists and turns of the attempts to review the evidence in the Willingham case is set forth at *Cameron Todd Willingham: Wrongly Convicted and Executed in Texas*, Innocence Project, http://www.innocenceproject.org/Content/Cameron_Todd_Willingham_Wrongfully_Convicted_and_Executed_in_Texas.php (last visited July 15, 2013).

16 Garrett, *supra* note 4, at 131 ("Our criminal system need not remain structurally averse to the correction of factual errors.").

17 Kennedy, *supra* note 11, at 27 ("Only the risk of inaccurate results makes finality problematic.").

and a lack of respect for the jury's verdict.[18] Providing inmates with ways to challenge their convictions after the fact would allow the guilty to clog the system with endless frivolous appeals,[19] and it would continually and cruelly force the victims and their families to revisit the injustices that they experienced at the hands of the guilty inmate.[20] Furthermore, when convictions remain open to challenge, the rehabilitation process is delayed because an inmate has no incentive to accept responsibility for the crime. Finally, victims receive no satisfaction when society cannot effectively punish wrongdoers because it is continually conceding the theoretical possibility that every trial contains error and every incarceration is unfounded.[21]

When these competing interests conflict, policy dictates whether the system errs on the side of accuracy or finality.[22] Throughout history, the American criminal justice has erred on the side of finality.

*The Cornerstone of the Finality Argument is the Historical Belief that the American Criminal Justice System Rarely Makes Serious, Uncorrected Errors*

The arguments favoring finality focus on different values and functions of the criminal justice system, but they all start with the assumption that wrongful convictions are a rarity.[23] When one starts from this assumption, post-conviction claims of innocence are almost certainly meritless, and re-litigating criminal cases to find the rare case of wrongful conviction[24] would waste scarce resources, delay appropriate punishment and rehabilitation, and undermine confidence in the integrity of the system, all while leaving the victims and their families in a "cruel state of limbo."[25]

Those who have historically argued for stricter adherence to the finality doctrine seem so steadfastly certain that the American criminal justice system is unlikely to make serious mistakes, or leave serious mistakes uncorrected, that they have proclaimed it even without any supporting evidence. In 1923, Judge Learned Hand declared, "Our procedure has been always haunted by the ghost of the innocent man convicted. It is an unreal dream."[26]

18 *See id.* (stating that "finality is a choice society makes to express its collective faith in the criminal justice system").

19 Bator, *supra* note 7, at 508.

20 Kennedy, *supra* note 11, at 28–9.

21 Professor Paul Bator eloquently set forth the case for finality in his frequently cited law review article as such: "Repose is a psychological necessity in a secure and active society, and it should be one of the aims—though, let me make explicit, not the sole aim—of a procedural system to devise doctrines which, in the end, do give us repose, do embody the judgment that we have tried hard enough and thus may take it that justice has been done. There comes a point where a procedural system which leaves matters perpetually open no longer reflects humane concern but merely anxiety and a desire for immobility. Somehow, somewhere, we must accept the fact that human institutions are short of infallible; there is reason for a policy which leaves well enough alone and which channels our limited resources of concern toward more productive ends. I want to be careful to stress that I do not counsel a smug acceptance of injustice merely because it is disturbing to worry whether injustice has been done. What I do seek is a general procedural system which does not cater to a perpetual and unreasoned anxiety that there is a possibility that error has been made in every criminal case in the legal system." Bator, *supra* note 7, at 452–3.

22 *See* Kennedy, *supra* note 11, at 27.

23 *See, e.g.*, Friendly, *supra* note 9, at 142–3; Daniel Givelber, *Punishing Protestations of Innocence: Denying Responsibility and Its Consequences*, 37 Am. Crim. L. Rev. 1363, 1394 (2000) (addressing guilty pleas and noting that the "inherent inaccuracy of trials may very occasionally result in an innocent person being convicted and this person will then be punished both for a crime he did not commit (the underlying offense) and for insisting upon a trial" and noting that "this is a small price to pay for a system that otherwise furthers accuracy and efficiency"); Kennedy, *supra* note 11, at 28.

24 The term "wrongful conviction" can have different meanings. Some use the term narrowly to mean only cases in which DNA provided definitive evidence that the wrong person was convicted for the crime. The Center on Wrongful Convictions uses the term "wrongful conviction" more broadly to describe "any case in which a defendant was convicted of a crime and later restored to the status of legal innocence based on evidence not presented at the defendant's trial." I often use the term "wrongful conviction" in an even broader sense to describe cases in which an inmate can demonstrate in post-conviction, through substantial evidence, that a jury, hearing the new evidence, likely would have found the inmate not guilty. I use this definition in this chapter because it reflects the reality that many, if not most, innocent inmates cannot obtain DNA testing or work their way through the procedural hurdles required to obtain a legal finding akin to actual innocence.

25 Kennedy, *supra* note 11, at 27.

26 United States v. Garsson, 291 F. 646, 648 (S.D.N.Y. 1923).

In 1986, former United States Attorney General Edwin Meese was confident that innocent people were not, in large number, lingering in our prisons because, with near certainty, investigators target the right man. The Attorney General espoused this belief when he commented, "The thing is you don't have many suspects who are innocent of a crime. That's contradictory. If a person is innocent of crime, then he is not a suspect."[27] Of course, if one holds this belief, then juries who convict are nearly always right, and post-conviction review is unnecessary.

At the time the Attorney General made these statements, DNA had not yet entered the criminal arena, and there was only scant proof that wrongful convictions or executions occurred. Jurists, academics, and prosecutors could proclaim the conviction of an innocent person a rarity. However, by 2006, when the United States Supreme Court, in *Kansas v. Marsh*,[28] addressed the constitutionality of Kansas's death penalty statute, DNA exonerations numbered 190.[29] It was in this new DNA era that the debate over the frequency of wrongful convictions flared in the United States Supreme Court's opinions.

Justice Souter questioned the constitutionality and morality of Kansas's capital sentencing scheme when our recent history "has seen repeated exonerations of convicts under death sentences, in numbers never imagined before the development of DNA tests."[30] Souter's dissent cited several prominent studies estimating the number of innocent inmates released from death row on account of their innocence, with numbers ranging from 74 to 110 inmates since 1973. To Justice Souter and the dissenters, these exonerations caused them to question the appropriateness of finality—especially in death penalty cases. Because "these false verdicts defy correction after the fatal moment, … maintaining a sentencing system mandating death when the sentencer finds the evidence pro and con to be in equipoise is obtuse by any moral or social measure."[31]

Justice Scalia's concurrence, however, voiced the views of the finality proponents. The recent onslaught of DNA exonerations, many from death rows, fails to prove that an innocent person has been executed, he argued. "It should be noted at the outset," he wrote, "that the dissent does not discuss a single case—not one—in which it is clear that a person was executed for a crime he did not commit. If such an event had occurred in recent years, we would not have to hunt for it; the innocent's name would be shouted from the rooftops by the abolition lobby."[32] Furthermore, according to Justice Scalia, exonerations prove that the system is working properly. After criticizing the dissent's focus "on the large numbers of *non*-executed 'exonerees' paraded by various professors" to support the notion that we have likely executed an innocent person, Justice Scalia argued that the growing number of exonerees is not an indication that our criminal justice system is error prone, but instead, they are "a consequence of the functioning of our legal system."[33] According to Justice Scalia, "Reversal of an erroneous conviction on appeal or on habeas, or the pardoning of an innocent condemnee through executive clemency, demonstrates not the failure of the system but its success."[34] Using Justice Scalia's logic, with every new exoneration, we should grow more confident in the ability of our criminal justice system to identify and release innocent inmates and more comfortable with the notion of finality.[35]

Justice Scalia's confidence in the ability of our criminal justice system to get it right and to correct the wrongs suggests that relaxing procedures so that inmates can continually revisit their convictions is an unnecessary waste of resources, at best.

---

27 Jim Dwyer et al., Actual Innocence: Five Days to Execution and Other Dispatches from the Wrongly Convicted xi (2000).

28 548 U.S. 163 (2006).

29 By the end of 2012, the number of DNA exonerations grew to 352, and all exonerations, including DNA and non-DNA, totaled 873. Samuel R. Gross & Michael Shaffer, Exonerations in the United States, 1989—2012: Report by the National Registry of Exonerations, (June 2012), http://www.law.umich.edu/special/exoneration/Documents/exonerations_us_1989_2012_full_report.pdf.

30 Kansas v. Marsh, 548 U.S. at 203 (Souter, J., concurring).

31 *Id.* at 211.

32 *Id.* at 188 (Scalia, J., concurring).

33 *Id.* at 193.

34 *Id.*

35 Justice Scalia's logic has been challenged by scholars who study wrongful convictions. *See, e.g.*, Brandon L. Garrett, Convicting the Innocent: Where Criminal Prosecutions Go Wrong 263 (2011).

*If Wrongful Convictions Are Rare, Re-litigating Cases after Conviction Would Thwart the Interests of Justice*

Over the years, scholars, courts, and prosecutors have voiced the same concerns that Justice Scalia has—that endless inmate attacks on their convictions would thwart justice. "No one, not criminal defendants, not the judicial system, not society as a whole is benefited by a judgment providing a man shall tentatively go to jail today, but tomorrow and every day thereafter his continued incarceration shall be subject to fresh litigation."[36] Justice Harlan's oft-quoted defense of finality was almost certainly based upon the common belief that wrongful convictions were extremely rare. The same is true for the oft-cited law review article in which Paul Bator expressed the argument for finality thus:

> There comes a point where a procedural system which leaves matters perpetually open no longer reflects humane concern but merely anxiety and a desire for immobility. Somehow, somewhere, we must accept the fact that human institutions are short of infallible; there is reason for a policy which leaves well enough alone and which channels our limited resources of concern toward more productive ends.[37]

Today, the American criminal justice system's resources are stretched thinner than ever before.[38] Therefore, not surprisingly, the most-cited reason for limiting inmates' post-conviction claims is conservation of resources.[39] When courts review successive claims of innocence after conviction, it taxes judicial resources, spreading them too thin to adequately provide justice to litigants facing trial or pursuing their first appeal. Re-litigating fair trials that took place long ago robs first-time litigants in the criminal justice system of precious judicial resources.[40] Post-conviction litigation drains economic resources as well. Some argue that the accuracy of the system overall would benefit from curbing post-conviction review because the funds saved on reviewing challenges to old convictions could be used to provide better investigations and more protections to defendants prior to trial—i.e., providing better lawyers, investigators, experts, and forensic testing.[41] Proponents of finality often remind us that an endless supply of resources does not exist; and while it is noble to say that we must dedicate time, money, and resources to both post-conviction claims and first-time litigants, this sentiment ignores the fact that our resources are in short supply and our judicial system clogged with cases.[42]

Without finality, criminal law becomes impotent—or so the argument goes.[43] If the traditional aims of the criminal law are retribution, deterrence, and rehabilitation, lack of finality robs the law of its very purpose. Retributive punishment requires certainty and immediacy. Victims receive no satisfaction when they must carry on without knowing if a moral judgment will finally attach to the crime.[44] Furthermore, classic criminal law theory tells us that the most effective method of deterrence is immediate and certain punishment. We must be able to firmly say to those who violate the law that they will be subject to a just and swift punishment.

Most members of the public would probably agree with these reasons for limiting inmates' access to courts after conviction if, as Justice Scalia continues to claim, wrongful convictions are rare events. But the

36 Mackey v. United States, 401 U.S. 667, 691 (1971) (Harlan, J., concurring in part and dissenting in part).

37 Bator, *supra* note 7, at 452–3.

38 Nancy J. King & Joseph L. Hoffmann, Habeas for the Twenty-First Century: Uses, Abuses, and the Future of the Great Writ 793 (2011).

39 Bator, *supra* note 7, at 451.

40 Schneckloth v. Bustamonte, 412 U.S. 218, 260–61 (1973) (Powell, J., concurring) ("To the extent the federal courts are required to re-examine claims on collateral attack, they deprive primary litigants of their prompt availability and mature reflection. After all, the resources of our system are finite: their overextension jeopardizes the care and quality essential to fair adjudication.").

41 *See* King & Hoffman, *supra* note 38, at 100–101.

42 Friendly, *supra* note 9, at 148–9.

43 Bator, *supra* note 7, at 452.

44 Calderon v. Thompson, 523 U.S. 538, 555 (1998) ("Only with real finality can the victims of crime move forward knowing the moral judgment will be carried out.").

flood of DNA exonerations has dampened the public's confidence in the system's to get it right.[45] The public is growing savvier about the causes of wrongful convictions, and most, unlike Justice Scalia, believe that we have executed an innocent person in recent years.[46] One is left to wonder whether the public would be comfortable with our system's emphasis on finality, knowing how likely it is that thousands of wrongly convicted people remain in prison. And if the public has been tolerant of our system's tendency to overvalue finality, perhaps it is because the procedures that thwart innocent inmates' attempts to overturn their convictions remain mostly hidden from the public's view. What the public sees is the innocent person walking out of prison. What it doesn't see is the long and labored fight to challenge the conviction under procedures designed to silence their claims. What it doesn't see are the innocent inmates who are condemned to serve out lengthy sentences because they have no way to adequately present their evidence of innocence to the courts.

## Part II: Finality Concerns Breed Incoherent Procedures That Are Ineffective at Bringing Justice to the Wrongly Convicted

After a jury has determined guilt beyond a reasonable doubt and the defendant has been convicted and sentenced, the legal presumption of guilt attaches. It is at this juncture that the safeguards within the system shift from protecting the innocent to protecting the conviction.

This chapter does not attempt to set forth the vast and confusing web of procedures that govern the post-conviction claims available to inmates in every state and within the federal system.[47] The procedures differ from state to state and from state courts to federal courts. The chapter includes an overview of the post-conviction procedural process. However, it is an overly simplified view meant only to give a rudimentary understanding of the way that post-conviction procedures generally work.

With the shock of conviction setting in, and while adjusting to a new life in prison, the inmate must now make immediate decisions about challenging the conviction. The most obvious challenge to a conviction is the motion for new trial. However, the deadlines to file such motions are usually very short, some as short as 30 days after the conviction.[48]

Every convicted inmate also has a right to appeal the conviction and to have the assistance of a lawyer for the appeal,[49] but in most states the appeal is not the place to lodge an innocence challenge. The appellate procedures developed long ago, when certainty regarding the rarity of wrongful convictions was strong. Therefore, courts were much more willing to defer to the jury's findings and the appeal process was simply a way to ensure that the defendant had a fair shot at challenging the evidence against him.[50] The appellate system was not intended to review the substantive evidence presented at trial to determine its accuracy, and if it ever was, it has not fulfilled that purpose.[51] That's because appeals are limited to the trial record, i.e.,

---

45 As of the writing of this chapter, there have been over 312 DNA exonerations in the United States. *See Know the Cases*, INNOCENCE PROJECT, http://www.innocenceproject.org/know/ (last visited Jan. 20, 2014).

46 In a December 2000 National Law Journal poll, 31 percent of respondents claimed that concerns about wrongful convictions made them less likely to impose the death penalty. By July 2001, a Harris Poll showed that 94 percent of respondents believed innocent people are sometimes convicted of murder. By 2007, polls showed that 87 percent of respondents believed an innocent person had been executed in recent years. Michael L. Radelet, *The Role of the Innocence Argument in Contemporary Death Penalty Debates*, 41 TEX. TECH L. REV. 199, 216 (2008).

47 *See* GARRETT, *supra* note 35, at 195 (noting that "the rules for filing post-conviction petitions can be byzantine in their complexity").

48 *See* Brandon L. Garrett, *Claiming Innocence*, 92 MINN. L. REV. 1629, 1671–2 (2008); George C. Thomas III et al., *Is It Ever Too Late for Innocence? Finality, Efficiency, and Claims of Innocence*, 64 U. PITT. L. REV. 263, 277–9 (2003).

49 Evitts v. Lucey, 470 U.S. 1065 (1985) (establishing the constitutional right to effective assistance of counsel for criminal defendants on their first appeal as of right).

50 *See* Findley, *supra* note 6, at 593.

51 *See* Keith Findley, *Adversarial Inquisitions: Rethinking the Search for the Truth*, 56 N.Y.L. SCH. L. REV. 911, 917 (2012) ("Appeals instead focus almost entirely on *process* questions—was the trial conducted in accordance with the rules?—rather than truth questions. Truth is simply not a central or often even significant concern on appeal."); Findley, *supra* note 6, at 592 (stating that "the appellate process in criminal cases is largely a failure" when it comes to protecting against mistaken convictions of innocent defendants); GARRETT, *supra* note 35, at 184–5 (finding that in the first 250 DNA

the evidence that was admitted at trial.[52] Did the judge correctly sustain the objection? Did the prosecutor make an inappropriate closing argument? Were the jury instructions properly written? Because most claims of innocence rely on evidence gathered after trial or not presented at trial, they cannot be part of the appeal.

Limited to the cold record compiled at trial, attorneys representing innocent inmates on appeal usually resort to culling the record for serious error that occurred in the trial and that affected the outcome of the trial. If they can find such error, the appeals court may grant a new trial, and the inmate could launch a new challenge to the evidence against him in the first trial. But this strategy focuses on the trial process rather than the evidence used to convict the inmate and any evidence that might exonerate him.[53]

In addition to the appeal, the inmate may bring a post-conviction claim challenging the conviction. However, although every state provides inmates with some right to what is commonly called post-conviction review or "state habeas," inmates have no constitutional right to counsel in this post-conviction stage.[54] While some states do provide indigent inmates with lawyers, others do not. In most states that do provide lawyers, they are often poorly paid and inexperienced.[55]

It is at this post-conviction stage—this under-resourced stage—that the inmate has the opportunity to challenge the evidence from trial, present new evidence that isn't in the record, and challenge unfair or unconstitutional procedures that led to the conviction. These post-conviction proceedings are called collateral proceedings because they occur outside the direct appeal timeline and the inmate is not limited to the evidence directly culled from the record.[56] Instead, the inmate can bring forth evidence outside the record to challenge the conviction.[57] For example, an inmate may conduct further investigation, find that the prosecutor withheld information favorable to the inmate, and may present that favorable evidence and the prosecutor's misconduct in a post-conviction petition. If the evidence probably would have changed the verdict, the court would grant the inmate a new trial.[58] This post-conviction stage is where most claims of innocence hinge. However, the inmates generally have very little time to investigate and present their claims, and they are often left to make these challenges alone, without the assistance of an attorney or investigator.[59] Furthermore, inmates must file their post-conviction petitions in the court of conviction.[60] That means that the judge who presided over the trial and recently sentenced the inmate to prison decides whether the trial itself was so flawed that the inmate is entitled to a new trial. If the trial judge denies the inmate's petition, the inmate may appeal that denial in the state appellate courts. But the inmate's burden of proof is extremely high, and the courts of appeal must give extreme deference to the trial judge.[61] Finally, this stage of the process involves high-stakes litigation because if an inmate fails to raise a claim that could have been raised or fails to uncover a crucial fact that could have been uncovered with due diligence, the inmate is barred from bringing that claim in the future.[62]

---

exonerations, the exonerees obtained favorable results on appeal at the same rate as a control group and that all claims based on innocence were rejected).

52 Eve Brensike Primus, *Structural Reform in Criminal Defense: Relocating Ineffective Assistance of Counsel Claims*, 92 Cornell L. Rev. 679, 681 (2007).

53 This strategy is also ineffective at obtaining relief for innocent defendants. As Brandon Garrett's research reveals, innocent defendants receive relief on appeal at the same rate as inmates in a control group, and not one DNA exoneree was granted relief on a claim of actual innocence. *See* Garrett, *supra* note 35, at 184–5.

54 The right to post-conviction review is found either in state statutes or the state's constitution. *See id.*, at 195.

55 For examples of inadequate post-conviction counsel in the death penalty context, see Stephen B. Bright, *Elected Judges and the Death Penalty in Texas: Why Full Habeas Corpus Review by Independent Federal Judges Is Indispensable to Protecting Constitutional Rights*, 78 Tex. L. Rev. 1805, 1819 (2000).

56 Garrett, *supra* note 35, at 195.

57 *Id.*

58 For a good summary of how "*Brady*" claims are handled in post-conviction proceedings, *see* Bennett L. Gershman, *Litigating Brady v. Maryland: Games Prosecutors Play*, 57 Case W. Res. L. Rev. 531 (2007).

59 Garrett, *supra* note 35, at 195; Sarah L. Thomas, *A Legislative Challenge: A Proposed Model Statute to Provide for the Appointment of Counsel in State Habeas Corpus Proceedings for Indigent Petitioners*, 54 Emory L.J. 1139, 1144 (2005).

60 *See* Medwed, *supra* note 3, at 659 (pointing out that the original trial judge may have a vested interest in the outcome of the post-conviction proceeding).

61 There is no deference to the trial court on pure matters of law, but most innocence cases are fact-based rather than law-based claims. *See id.* at 680.

62 Brent E. Newton, *A Primer on Post-Conviction Habeas Review*, Champion, June 2005, at 16, 19–20 ("In order to exhaust state remedies, a state prisoner must have 'fairly presented' both the *legal* and *factual* bases of all claims to the state

After the state post-conviction stage is over, inmates may file a federal habeas petition in the federal district court.[63] Federal habeas review gives innocent inmates a sliver of hope for a new trial, but only a sliver.[64] Habeas review is also collateral, so the inmate may attack the evidence at trial by presenting the new evidence found in the state post-conviction proceedings. But Congress and the federal courts have so limited habeas review that scholars and lawyers have questioned whether it remains a realistic avenue for innocent inmates to challenge their convictions.[65]

Federal courts sing the praises of finality, and, in addition, they are bound by federalism concerns. The federal court will only overturn state court rulings that misapply federal constitutional law because states retain a certain amount of autonomy over their own criminal justice systems.[66] Therefore, inmates cannot challenge state court decisions that are based on state law in the federal courts. Nor can they successfully challenge state court decisions that misapplied federal constitutional law, unless the state court *unreasonably* applied the federal law.[67] Claims that weren't raised in the state court, under the state's strict time constraints, are also barred from federal court review.[68] Finally, federal habeas rules also impose a strict deadline of one year after the state post-conviction process is final.[69] If an inmate misses that strict deadline, the inmate loses the right to federal court review.[70] In response to recent restrictions to federal habeas review, one scholar has said that "state prisoners now face unique procedural barriers and one of the most uncharitable standards of review known to law."[71]

In addition to these traditional avenues of post-conviction relief, the rise of DNA exonerations led states to provide inmates yet another procedural mechanism to challenge their convictions. Because the traditional avenues of review had so often proven fruitless for inmates with post-conviction DNA challenges, states were forced to enact new statutory schemes so that inmates could access and present this new and powerful evidence of innocence to the state courts.[72] These newly created inlets into post-conviction review differ from state to state, but they provide innocent inmates new hope. Of course, these DNA statutes provide relief only to inmates lucky enough to have biological evidence in their case that was properly collected and preserved, and that could prove their innocence. Most inmates are not so lucky.[73]

These are the basic steps of post-conviction review.[74] Although it may seem to the public that inmates, especially those on death row, have many more bites at the apple than are mentioned here, endless bites at the apple are really just illusory. It's true that many inmates—especially those under a sentence of death—make

---

courts that the petitioner later raises on federal *habeas corpus* review.").

63 28 U.S.C. § 2254 (2006).

64 King & Hoffman, *supra* note 38, at 81–4 (stating that "federal habeas review of state convictions has become futile, illusory, and so improbable as to be 'microscopic'").

65 *See, e.g.*, Garrett, *supra* note 35, at 196; Justin F. Marceau, *Challenging the Habeas Process Rather Than the Result*, 69 Wash. & Lee L. Rev. 85, 89 (2012); Roberts, *supra* note 1, at 121-26; Kenneth Williams, *The Antiterrorism and Effective Death Penalty Act: What's Wrong with It and How to Fix It*, 33 Conn. L. Rev. 919, 942 (2000).

66 *See* Marceau, *supra*, at 112.

67 Congress has precluded federal habeas corpus relief with respect to any "claim that was adjudicated on the merits in State court proceedings" unless the state court's adjudication (1) "resulted in a decision that was contrary to, or involved an unreasonable application of, clearly established Federal law, as determined by the Supreme Court of the United States"; or (2) "resulted in a decision that was based on an unreasonable determination of the facts in light of the evidence presented in the state court proceeding." 28 U.S.C. § 2254(d)(1)&(2).

68 *See* Newton, *supra* note 62, at 17–18.

69 *See id.* at 19; Roberts, *supra* note 1, at 126-27.

70 *See* Limin Zheng, *Actual Innocence as a Gateway Through the Statute-of-Limitations Bar on the Filing of Federal Habeas Corpus Petitions*, 90 Cal. L. Rev. 2101, 2131 (2002) (criticizing the one-year limitation requirement because it makes no sense in innocence cases where the inmate has nothing to gain by waiting longer to file a federal habeas, and everything to lose).

71 Marceau, *supra* note 65, at 97.

72 *See* Heidi C. Schmitt, Note, *Post-Conviction Remedies Involving the Use of DNA Evidence to Exonerate Wrongfully Convicted Prisoners: Various Approaches Under Federal and State Law*, 70 UMKC L. Rev. 1001, 1007 (2002).

73 Garrett, *supra* note 35, at 12 (stating that "for most crimes, there is no useful evidence collected at a crime scene that can be tested using DNA" and "[i]f DNA is a 'truth machine,' it tells us only about a sliver of very serious convictions").

74 This chapter does not discuss clemency and commutation, avenues of post-conviction relief that take place outside the courts. For a discussion of extra-judicial avenues of exoneration, *see generally* Ryan Dietrich, Comment, *A*

seemingly endless filings in various courts, but their filings are usually procedural in nature. The inmates spend much of their time arguing that the court *should* hear the inmate's case rather than arguing the merits of the case itself. And usually, the courts deny the inmates' pleas to hear the case and side with finality concerns instead.[75]

## Part III: An Innocent Inmate Confronts a Procedural Quagmire

To explain how innocent inmates wind their way through post-conviction procedures, consider a hypothetical inmate, Michael, in a hypothetical jurisdiction. Michael was convicted of murder for stabbing a woman to death in her home. The case went unsolved for several years until Michael's former girlfriend, Lisa, told police and prosecutors that Michael had confessed to killing the woman. Along with Lisa's testimony, the state presented evidence at trial that police found Michael's fingerprint on a bloody pillowcase near the victim's body. The state also introduced a shoeprint found at the crime scene. The state's expert testified that the shoeprint "perfectly matched" a pair of size-10 Converse tennis shoes found in Michael's closet. Prosecutors presented other circumstantial evidence. A witness said she saw a tall white man leave the victim's house in a black car the day of the murder, but he was too far away to identify. Michael is a white male, 6 feet tall, and drove a black Toyota at the time.

On the advice of his attorney, Michael chose not to testify at trial because he had a previous conviction for attempted assault on his girlfriend and the prosecution intended to use this crime to impeach Michael's credibility. Michael's defense consisted solely of the attorney's cross-examination of the state's witnesses. First, Michael's attorney focused on the fact that Lisa, Michael's girlfriend at the time, continued living with Michael for six months after his alleged confession. She disclosed Michael's alleged confession only when she was being questioned about a drug possession charge. Second, the attorney questioned the bloody fingerprint testimony, pointing out that at the time of the crime no officer was able to compare it to a suspect print because of its poor quality. Instead, the state flew an expert in from out of state to testify that the fingerprint on the pillowcase "matched" Michael's fingerprint. Finally, Michael's attorney countered the state's testimony about the shoeprint solely through cross-examination, prodding the investigating officer to agree that just about anyone could have left the Converse shoeprint considering the popularity of that brand of shoe at the time.

### *A. Motion for New Trial*

Once convicted, Michael's first option to challenge the conviction is a motion for new trial. A motion for new trial allows Michael to introduce new evidence of his innocence, but motions for new trial usually have strict deadlines, some as little as 30 days after the trial.[76] Unfortunately, at this point, so soon after trial, Michael is still represented by the same lawyer and there's no new evidence to present. Therefore, Michael misses the opportunity to challenge his conviction with a motion for new trial.

### *B. The Appeal*

Michael's next step is to appeal the conviction. Appeals generally take place almost immediately after the conviction and sentencing. For his appeal, Michael is entitled to a lawyer, usually a different lawyer than his trial attorney.[77] That lawyer will, often without even meeting Michael, read the trial transcripts, research the

---

*Unilateral Hope: Reliance on the Clemency Process As a Trigger for a Right of Access to State-Held DNA Evidence*, 62 Md. L. Rev. 1028 (2003).

75 *See* Garrett, *supra* note 48, at 1685–6.

76 *See* Medwed, *supra* note 3, at 676 (observing that "many time limits governing motions for a new trial on the grounds of newly discovered evidence are remarkably brief").

77 Primus, *supra* note 52, at 681.

law, and file his direct appeal in the state court of appeals. Remember, at this stage the lawyer is limited to claims that are considered record-based claims.[78]

During the appeal, Michael finds some evidence that calls into question the strength of the state's case against him. While in prison, Michael is contacted by one of Lisa's friends. She tells him that Lisa admitted she lied to prosecutors about Michael's alleged confession. Lisa told her that Michael never said he killed the woman. Lisa knew that if she lied to police about Michael, providing them with a suspect in an unsolved murder, she probably wouldn't go to jail on the drug charges. Lisa said she had no idea that Michael would eventually be charged with and convicted of murder. Michael contacts his lawyer, giving her this compelling new evidence. Although the lawyer sees this as powerful evidence that undermines Michael's conviction, she can't present the evidence to the appellate court. That's because the evidence was not part of the trial record. Instead, it is new evidence that should have been presented in a motion for new trial, but the time has passed to file such a motion.

The appellate lawyer searches for other ways to attack the trial evidence. She notes that the trial lawyer never hired his own fingerprint and shoeprint experts to determine the quality of the only evidence directly linking Michael to the murder scene. Were the prints really a match? Would others in the field of forensic science agree? But again, the lawyer would be barred from making the claim that Michael's lawyer should have hired an expert because that claim—a claim of ineffective assistance of counsel—cannot be made on appeal in many states.[79] Such a claim would require evidence from outside the record, like what an expert would have said about the prints and what the lawyer would have done with the experts' findings. Michael's appellate lawyer settles with raising some technical sentencing errors on appeal because there's no avenue to directly challenge the credibility of the evidence presented at trial.

Once filed, the appeal might take years to resolve because, generally, the appellate review goes through three stages—review by an intermediate state appellate court and then by the state's highest appellate court, and finally, when that review is complete, a petition for certiorari in the United States Supreme Court.[80] Although the United States Supreme Court will not likely hear the appeal, time goes by waiting for its decision, and Michael has now been incarcerated for more than two years.

### *C. State Post-Conviction Review*

State post-conviction proceedings give Michael hope that he can find new evidence that counters the credibility and accuracy of the prosecutor's evidence at trial. Unfortunately, he will have very little time and fewer resources available to investigate. In some states, he would either have to hire an attorney, investigator, and experts, or conduct the investigation and litigation from his prison cell on his own.[81] In addition, he must be thorough in his attack on the conviction because if he fails to raise a claim he could have raised at this crucial stage, he will not be allowed to raise the claim in future litigation.[82] This time, Michael is lucky. He is incarcerated in a state that provides an attorney for indigent inmates raising post-conviction claims.

Michael's post-conviction attorney first notes the short deadline for filing Michael's petition—90 days. Immediately, Michael's new attorney contacts the trial and appellate attorneys. She needs the trial and appellate transcripts, and she wants to know more about the case. Why did they make the choices they did? Was there anything that made them think twice about the case? Was there evidence they wish they could have found or presented? At this point, the attorney must investigate everything anew, including whether the lawyers at trial and on appeal were effective in presenting Michael's case and whether they and the prosecutors acted

78 *See id.* at 681–2 (noting that "the issues that the defendant may raise on direct appeal are limited only to those matters that appear on the face of the trial court record"; therefore, "if an attorney fails to preserve issues at trial, appellate counsel is generally left without grounds for appeal").

79 *Id.* at 680.

80 See *id.*

81 *See* Donald A. Dripps, *Ineffective Litigation of Ineffective Assistance Claims: Some Uncomfortable Reflections on Massaro v. United States*, 42 Brandeis L.J. 793, 799 (2004) ("Would the typical prisoner be able to interview trial counsel with an eye to developing Strickland claims, or to interview and take testimony from witnesses trial counsel did not call, or to support a defense that counsel did not raise?").

82 *See* Newton, *supra* note 62, at 17–18.

ethically. The appellate lawyer tells Michael's new lawyer about Lisa's friend and gives her the friend's contact information. The post-conviction lawyer follows up. She calls the friend. The friend tells the lawyer the same story she told Michael, and she agrees to sign an affidavit. The lawyer prepares the affidavit and sends someone to meet the friend. Everything goes as planned, and the lawyer now has an affidavit saying that the state's key witness lied under oath.

The fingerprint evidence still bothers Michael's new lawyer, so she calls the trial attorney. Why didn't he hire a fingerprint expert? He tells her that the photos of the print show a smeared mess that hardly looks like a fingerprint at all. He didn't think a jury would take the state's expert seriously, especially when no one on the investigation team thought the print was worthy of comparing to the suspect's prints. To the trial attorney's surprise, the expert didn't show a photo of the print to the jury. The expert said he forgot the photo. Without the photographic evidence to contradict him, the expert confidently told the jury that he was able to match at least 14 points of comparison between the print on the pillowcase and Michael's print—more than enough to satisfy the FBI standards. Michael's attorney wasn't prepared for the expert's sly testimony, and he didn't bring any photographs of his own into the courtroom to show the jury. He also couldn't think of any objections to the expert's testimony, so he didn't make any. Michael's trial attorney thought he did a good job attacking the expert's credibility on cross-examination; nevertheless, his new post-conviction attorney disagrees that the trial attorney's cross-examination caused the jury to lose confidence in the fingerprint evidence.

Armed with the friend's affidavit, the post-conviction lawyer drafts Michael's petition. Under the state's fairly generous post-conviction statute, she has one fairly good claim of newly discovered evidence. To obtain a new trial on this claim, she'll have to show that the new evidence is factual evidence, not discoverable before trial, and is not cumulative of other evidence presented at trial.[83] In addition, she must convince the trial judge, because that's where the petition will be filed, that the new evidence probably would have changed the verdict.[84] Despite this high standard, Michael's attorney is hopeful she'll get a hearing.

To be safe—remember, all claims must be raised in this petition or the inmate will not be able to raise them later—Michael's attorney also lodges an ineffective assistance of counsel claim. Thc claim relates to the bloody fingerprint. She argues that Michael's trial lawyer was ineffective for failing to hire his own expert to compare the prints, and she says that the trial lawyer should have objected to the state's expert testimony because the expert had no foundation for his opinion; that is, he had no documentary evidence to demonstrate that he had actually compared the print from the crime scene to Michael's print.

As expected, the trial judge denies Michael's ineffective assistance of counsel claims. The judge says that the trial lawyer had strategic reasons for not hiring an expert—that the fingerprints were so smudged a jury would not find the state's expert credible. As for failing to object to the expert's lack of foundation for his testimony, the court says that experts have never had any duty to supply photographic evidence of their work. If Michael's attorney had wanted to present his own photos of the bloody print, he should have asked for a trial recess so that he could retrieve his own photos from his office to use in his cross-examination. Because he failed to make the request, the trial error was not preserved, and Michael could not raise it now.[85] As for the friend's affidavit, the court says that an affidavit secured after trial could not outweigh the testimony, under oath, of a crucial trial witness. After all, Lisa told the jury her story under penalty of perjury and subject to the defense's cross-examination. An affidavit based on hearsay long after the trial could not outweigh Lisa's testimony, especially considering that the testimony was consistent with the physical evidence—the bloody fingerprint and shoeprint—that placed Michael at the scene. Despite the adverse ruling from the trial judge, Michael's lawyer appeals the decision to the intermediate court of appeals and the state's Supreme Court. Both courts, however, side with the trial judge. Michael is out of state post-conviction options.

83 *See, e.g.*, Ariz. R. Crim. P. 32.1.

84 *See* Medwed, *supra* note 3, at 684–5.

85 *See* Newton, *supra* note 62, at 17 ("If the defense failed to object to a violation of the defendant's rights in the trial court or failed to raise a claim on direct appeal (even if it was raised in the trial court), ordinarily the defendant's claim will be 'procedurally defaulted' or 'procedurally barred' on federal *habeas corpus* review.").

*D. Federal Habeas Review*

Michael's lawyer tells him he may file a federal habeas petition challenging his conviction in the federal courts. She, however, will not be able to represent him. In fact, he is not entitled to an attorney at this stage of the process unless he can afford to hire one at his own expense. Michael has heard that the law surrounding federal habeas is complicated, that he only has one year to investigate and file the petition, and that missing the deadline by even a day means that his federal habeas would be barred. Michael was lucky to have representation in his state post-conviction proceedings, but he cannot afford a lawyer to assist him at this stage. Remember, most inmates must navigate through federal court on their own.[86]

Although he doesn't have a lawyer, Michael does have family members who believe in his innocence. They are willing to help him investigate and prepare his petition. Michael's sister meets with Michael's former girlfriend. Lisa becomes remorseful and admits that she lied to keep herself out of prison. She didn't think that Michael would actually be charged or convicted. She says she's willing to testify that she fabricated the story. Amazed that she was able to uncover such an important confession, Michael's sister persuades Lisa to write out a statement and sign it in front of a notary before Lisa changes her mind about testifying.

Feeling good about discrediting the state's main witness, Michael turns to the fingerprint and shoe evidence. Michael knows he must discredit the state's pattern evidence, especially because the state's experts gave such unwavering testimony concerning the pattern evidence—that the fingerprint "matched" Michael's print and that the shoeprint was a "perfect match" for the Converse shoes in Michael's closet.[87] Michael wonders whether there is a way to attack the state's expert evidence now, in a federal habeas proceeding. Michael's brother knows a police officer who often works crime scenes. He agrees to look at the print for Michael. Based on this police officer's review of the prints, he says that "no credible expert in the field would have testified that the fingerprint on the pillowcase 'matched' Michael's." He says that the print on the pillowcase was of such poor quality that the police department would not use it for comparison purposes. The expert agrees to provide Michael with a signed statement.

Finally, Michael turns to the shoeprint. He had always been bothered by the claim that his shoes perfectly matched the print at the crime scene because he knew he had purchased those shoes after the murdered occurred. Without a receipt, is there a way to tell when shoes were purchased? Michael's mother looks carefully at the photographs of the shoes. She calls the store where Michael purchased the shoes. A person who works there gives her a phone number at the company's headquarters. After several calls, Michael's mother contacts the manufacturer. She tracks down information about when the shoes were distributed to local retailers. It turns out that the pair of Converse shoes in Michael's closet were made and distributed two years after the murder. She asks the person at Converse to send her a letter confirming the information. He agrees.

After several months of investigation, Michael believes he has collected compelling evidence of innocence. He has a statement from his former girlfriend, Lisa. She admits that she lied on the stand, that Michael never confessed to the murder, and that she made the story up to keep herself out of prison on an unrelated drug charge. He also has the affidavit from Lisa's friend. In it she says that after Michael's trial, Lisa confided in her. Lisa says Michael didn't confess to the murder; she made it up to protect herself. He believes that these two statements must certainly discredit Lisa's testimony at trial.

Michael also has the statement from the crime scene investigator stating that the fingerprint should not have been used as a comparison print because it was too degraded, and that the state's expert testimony was completely unfounded. Finally, Michael has the statement from the Converse shoe company. It says that the shoes collected from Michael's closet and introduced as evidence in his trial were not manufactured or

---

86 For a good discussion of the difference a lawyer makes post-conviction, see Marceau's discussion of study results that show that inmates sentenced to death, who often have attorneys, have a 12 percent chance of success in federal habeas compared to a less than 1 percent chance of success for inmates not facing the death penalty and navigating the federal habeas procedures pro se. Marceau, *supra* note 65, at 131–2.

87 In the last several years, pattern evidence, like fingerprints and shoeprints, has come under attack from a highly credentialed committee of scientists. For a good discussion of the committee's findings, *see* Sarah Lucy Cooper, *The Collision of Law and Science: American Court Responses to Developments in Forensic Science*, 33 PACE L. REV. 234 (2013).

distributed until at least two years after the murder. Michael's next step is to figure out how to present these new claims, based on new evidence, in a federal habeas corpus proceeding.

Seeking help from a fellow inmate, Michael presents three claims. First, as he did in his state post-conviction petition, he claims that his trial lawyer was ineffective for failing to hire a fingerprint expert. Armed with the crime scene investigator's statement, he believes this claim is even stronger now than when it was presented in the state courts. Next, he claims that his trial lawyer was ineffective for failing to investigate the Converse shoe issue. He argues that if the jury had heard this new evidence about the shoes and the fingerprint, it would not have convicted him. Finally, he claims that his girlfriend's recantation, bolstered by her friend's affidavit, shows that his trial was fundamentally unfair. He was convicted on testimony now known to be false, and he is entitled to a new trial because he is innocent.

More than a year passes before the federal district court finally rules on Michael's claims. In a short, curt opinion, the court draws the curtain on Michael's efforts at exoneration. The court starts by reciting its limited jurisdiction. It may only consider claims that have been raised and decided on the merits in the state courts, and those claims must allege a violation of the Constitution or laws of the United States.[88] Furthermore, if a petitioner failed to raise facts supporting a claim in the state courts, he must show that the facts could not have been discovered earlier through the exercise of due diligence.[89]

Turning to Michael's claims, the court picks them off one by one. The court denies Michael's first ineffective assistance of counsel claim because the state court's ruling denying relief on that claim was not an unreasonable application of federal law.[90] As for the additional evidence that Michael presented—the expert's affidavit regarding the fingerprint evidence—the court refuses to consider it. That's because the Supreme Court recently held that new evidence that was not part of the state court record could "have no bearing" on the federal court's review of state court decisions.[91] Because Michael's attorney did not present the expert's opinions in the state post-conviction proceeding, the federal court cannot consider it now.

Moving on to the recantation, the court quickly dispenses with it on procedural grounds as well. Again, the claim that Michael's girlfriend testified falsely is a state law claim. The state has ruled on that claim, and the federal court is not able to override that decision even though new evidence might bolster the claim. The state courts get final say on claims that arise under state law.

Finally, the court will not consider Michael's claim about the shoeprint because he did not present the claim to the state court when he had the opportunity.[92] As the court explains, the evidence was easily discoverable in Michael's state court proceedings; therefore, his failure to raise the claim in the state court means it is forever lost.

Although not specifically raised, the district court reads Michael's pleadings liberally and considers Michael's claim of innocence as both a "bare" or "free-standing" innocence claim and a "gateway" innocence claim. A "bare" innocence claim asserts that imprisoning an innocent person violates the Constitution, and the inmate seeks relief from the conviction based on actual innocence without asserting a constitutional defect in the trial or appeal.[93] The United States Supreme Court has rejected bare innocence claims in non-death penalty cases, and it has danced around the issue in death penalty cases, leaving the question of whether it's

88 *See* Marceau, *supra* note 65, at 93–4.

89 *See id.*, at 118.

90 *Id.* at 94.

91 Cullen v. Pinholster, 131 S. Ct. 1388, 1400 (2011) ("Today, we reject that assumption and hold that evidence introduced in federal court has no bearing on § 2254(d)(1) review. If a claim has been adjudicated on the merits by a state court, a federal habeas petitioner must overcome the limitation of § 2254(d)(1) on the record that was before that state court.").

92 Hugh Mundy, *Rid of Habeas Corpus? How Ineffective Assistance of Counsel Has Endangered Access to the Writ of Habeas Corpus and What the Supreme Court Can Do in Maples and Martinez to Restore It*, 45 Creighton L. Rev. 185, 186 (2011) ("Despite the broad promise of access to habeas corpus relief, restrictive state procedural rules often rob habeas petitioners of the right to federal review of valid constitutional claims. Indeed, in order to advance a constitutional claim in a federal habeas petition, the same claim must be timely raised and fully litigated during state trial, appellate, or post-conviction proceedings. The consequences of failing to comply with state procedural rules are severe. With rare exception, a claim raised for the first time in a federal habeas petition is rejected without review on the merits.").

93 Nicholas Berg, Note, *Turning A Blind Eye to Innocence: The Legacy of Herrera v. Collins*, 42 Am. Crim. L. Rev. 121, 122 (2005).

unconstitutional to execute an innocent person unanswered.[94] The precedent seems clear, however, that if a non-capital defendant had a fair trial, he cannot receive federal review of his claim simply because he is actually innocent and imprisoned.[95] Therefore, to the extent that Michael's petition alleged his imprisonment violated the Constitution because he is actually innocent of the crime, the claim could not succeed.

The court notes, however, that Michael could have been making a "gateway" innocence claim. The United States Supreme Court has left an opening for inmates who can make a truly persuasive showing of innocence. These inmates may raise constitutional claims that would otherwise be barred. A truly persuasive showing of innocence means the prisoner "must show that it is more likely than not that no reasonable juror would have convicted him" in light of new evidence that was not presented at trial.[96] That showing of innocence does not alone entitle one to relief; instead, it merely "opens the gate" so the federal habeas court can consider other constitutional claims that are otherwise procedurally barred. The district court finds that Michael's new evidence does not meet this very high threshold. First, it notes that the fingerprint evidence only showed that experts disagreed about the quality of the print, something the trial attorney brought out in cross-examination. Second, the court notes that recantations have been disfavored in post-conviction review.[97] That's because the witnesses may feel pressed to make statements after the trial, especially if they have a close relationship with the inmate. The most credible evidence, the court says, was the testimony given under oath and under penalty of perjury at trial. Finally, with a fingerprint at the scene and a confession to a girlfriend, the court believed that a reasonable juror could convict Michael—even if the shoes from the closet could not have been the source of the shoeprint at the crime scene. Therefore, even Michael's gateway innocence claim fails because he failed to make a "truly persuasive" showing of innocence.

Without a hearing, the court dismisses Michael's federal habeas claims. Michael thinks about appealing the decision, but when he learns he must first get permission to appeal from the same judge that just denied his petition,[98] he decides to give up on his claims. He has been in prison now for six years. His parents are growing old. His nieces and nephews are growing up. His family doesn't need to be burdened by his case any longer.

### *E. Out of Procedures and Out of Luck?*

Stories like Michael's populate courts throughout the country in numbers probably much greater than we've ever approximated. Of course, Michael's story could change dramatically if he persisted with his case, sought assistance from an innocence project, and was able to pursue DNA testing. Most states now allow inmates access to DNA testing even after their post-conviction claims have failed.[99] Of course, in his case, the presence of DNA that could exonerate him would be a complete fluke. There was no real indication that biological evidence that could identify the killer was collected from the crime scene and preserved. But fluky justice seems to be the norm in this post-conviction world.[100]

---

94 Perceiving the Court's order as contrary to the Court's pronouncements on bare-innocence claims, Justice Scalia wrote, "This Court has *never* held that the Constitution forbids the execution of a convicted defendant who has had a full and fair trial but is later able to convince a habeas court that he is 'actually' innocent. Quite to the contrary, we have repeatedly left that question unresolved, while expressing considerable doubt that any claim based on alleged 'actual innocence' is constitutionally cognizable." *In re Davis*, 130 S. Ct. 1, 3 (2009) (Scalia, J., dissenting).

95 *See* Garrett, *supra* note 48, at 1635.

96 Schlup v. Delo, 513 U.S. 298, 327 (1995).

97 *See* Michael McDonnell Hill, *Seen but Not Heard: An Argument for Granting Evidentiary Hearings to Weigh the Credibility of Recanted Testimony*, 46 GA. L. REV. 213, 227 (2011) (stating that "[a]s a general rule, courts are wary of witness recantations and have been so throughout much of our jurisprudence").

98 *See* 28 U.S.C. § 2253(c)(1) (providing that the district judge, who just denied petitioner relief on habeas, also decides whether the petitioner may appeal to the Court of Appeals).

99 *See* Garrett, *supra* note 48, at 1673 (noting that a vast majority of states have enacted post-conviction DNA testing statutes because there was no real avenue for relief in the courts).

100 *See* Deborah Tuerkheimer, *Science-Dependent Prosecution and the Problem of Epistemic Contingency: A Study of Shaken Baby Syndrome*, 62 ALA. L. REV. 513, 523 (2011) (using the term "fluky justice" to describe the inconsistent results in prosecutions based on so-called shaken baby syndrome).

Imagine that Michael could use the state DNA post-conviction testing statutes to test the bloody fingerprint on the pillowcase. Perhaps the pillowcase has been sufficiently preserved over the years. Perhaps enough skin cells from the person whose print remains on the pillowcase rubbed off on the pillowcase. Perhaps enough to perform DNA testing. Perhaps the testing excludes Michael. Perhaps the testing, when uploaded into the state's DNA database, is consistent with a man who had once been involved with the victim. All of these "what ifs" are long shots, but they represent the kind of luck an inmate must have to secure exoneration from a wrongful conviction. That's because instead of altering our post-conviction procedures for all inmates, we have provided an avenue only for those with this kind of luck. This favoring of DNA claims above all others creates a haphazard system of justice.

When post-conviction procedures produce haphazard results, people are bound to lose faith that the criminal justice system's goal is justice. To prevent the corrosive effects of our "byzantine" post-conviction procedures, we must refocus. Finality should give way to accuracy.

## Part IV: The Current Post-Conviction Procedures Are Inadequate for the New Era of Innocence

Two decades ago, most Americans probably would have agreed with United States Supreme Court Justice Sandra Day O'Connor when she said, "our society has a high degree of confidence in its criminal trials, in no small part because the Constitution offers unparalleled protections against convicting the innocent."[101] In the past, we assumed that conviction accuracy flowed from fair processes. But modern science has challenged those assumptions. Because of highly publicized DNA exonerations, we know that prophylactic measures emanating from the Constitution often fail to prevent wrongful convictions. Simply evaluating a trial to determine whether the defendant was afforded the protections guaranteed by the Constitution does not guarantee an accurate result. Therefore, our post-conviction review should do more than simply assess the fairness of trial and pre-trial procedures. In addition, post-conviction procedures should create an avenue to assess the accuracy of the trial's result.

Unfortunately, the trend has been moving in the other direction. The Anti-Terrorism and Effective Death Penalty Act (AEDPA) has codified draconian post-conviction procedures that create additional hurdles for innocent inmates to obtain relief from their convictions. The passage of AEDPA in 1996, curtailing federal habeas review of inmates' convictions, moved the federal courts further away from reliability assessments.[102] Despite its name, the Anti-Terrorism and Effective Death Penalty Act placed procedural hurdles in front of all inmates making post-conviction claims, not just those on death row. AEDPA imposed a strict one-year time limit for filing, limits on the number of petitions a prisoner could file, severe rules excluding defaulted claims, and a requirement that federal judges defer to state court rulings even when their decisions are simply wrong, as opposed to unreasonably wrong.[103] AEDPA narrowed the already small passage through which innocent inmates could pass in order to claim relief.

In addition to AEDPA, numerous high-profile DNA exonerations may have unintentionally moved the bar higher for innocent inmates' claims for relief. One way this may have happened is through the passage of DNA statutes in almost every state. Frustrated and embarrassed by the inability to find post-conviction procedures adequate for exonerating inmates who were clearly shown to be innocent through DNA testing, those interested in the plight of the wrongly convicted were able to secure an entirely different set of procedures for accessing and testing biological evidence and challenging a conviction once DNA gave exonerating results.[104] Creating this new avenue was crucial for the release of those inmates lucky enough to find relevant DNA evidence in their cases. But it probably harmed vast numbers of innocent inmates who have no such luck. While states have put substantial resources into new avenues for DNA testing, preservation, and litigation, they have all but ignored the procedures that deny the rest of innocent inmates the resources to investigate their claims and a forum in which to present them.

---

101 Herrera v. Collins, 506 U.S. 390, 420 (1993) (O'Connor, J., concurring).

102 *See* Marceau, *supra* note 65, at 88–9.

103 *See* Garrett, *supra* note 35, at 205.

104 *See* Garrett, *supra* note 48, at 1671–4.

Furthermore, DNA exonerations may have created an expectation that all "criminal defendants can and, perhaps, should offer substantial, convincing, and irrefutable proof of their own innocence, ideally, evidence that is as substantial, convincing, and irrefutable as DNA evidence."[105] However, "[m]ost defendants—indeed, most innocent defendants—can offer no such thing."[106] This DNA bias has led some courts to apply a higher burden to innocence cases than the state's statute intends. For example, the Texas legislature passed a DNA testing statute that would provide inmates an avenue to challenge their convictions. To receive testing under the statute, the applicant was required to "establish by a preponderance of evidence that a reasonable probability exists that *he would not have been prosecuted or convicted* if exculpatory results had been obtained through DNA testing."[107] The Texas Court of Criminal Appeals, however, simply changed the test and shifted the burden, requiring an applicant to demonstrate "a reasonable probability exists that exculpatory DNA tests *will prove [his] innocence*."[108]

The Court of Criminal Appeals ignored the presumption of innocence that exists in the American criminal justice system. A defendant cannot be convicted of a crime unless the state convinces the jury of the defendant's guilt beyond a reasonable doubt. The burden never shifts to the defendant to prove innocence.[109] However, in the post-DNA criminal justice system, some courts have come to expect proof of innocence.[110]

This heightened standard of proof has developed over the last few decades. However, not long ago proponents of finality urged the adoption of stricter post-conviction procedures that, ironically, would have afforded more relief to many of the innocent inmates now lingering in prison. For example, Paul Bator suggested, in his frequently cited article on finality, that the ultimate question in post-conviction should not be "whether the fact [of innocence] exists in any absolute sense but whether the evidence is adequate to justify the exercise of power: ultimately, whether the evidence is a sufficient moral predicate in the sense that society will accept it as sufficient for the exercise of the power in question."[111] In other words, when assessing a criminal conviction, would society see the evidence as sufficient to warrant continued imprisonment? Likewise, Judge Friendly's well-known article on finality sought to remedy inmates' abuse of post-conviction procedures by requiring that an inmate show "a fair probability that, in light of all the evidence, including that alleged to have been illegally admitted (but with any due regard to any unreliability of it) and evidence tenably claimed to have been wrongly excluded or to have become available only after trial, the trier of facts would have entertained a reasonable doubt of his guilt."[112]

Professor Bator and Judge Friendly's tests would be far more favorable to innocent inmates today than the current post-conviction rules inmates currently confront. Their tests assumed that an inmate would have an opportunity to present new evidence after their convictions were final. These tests also assumed that courts would weigh the evidence presented with "due regard" to its reliability. Few inmates today have the opportunity to present new evidence to a court and have that evidence weighed against the evidence presented at trial to determine the reliability of the conviction. Furthermore, to obtain relief based on innocence, most jurisdictions require more than a simple showing that the new evidence probably would have raised reasonable doubt in the trier of facts.

---

105 Margaret Raymond, *The Problem with Innocence*, 49 Clev. St. L. Rev. 449, 455 (2001).

106 *Id.*; *see also* Keith A. Findley, *Defining Innocence*, 74 Alb. L. Rev. 1157, 1188–9 (2011) (stating that "DNA also threatens to mislead courts and litigants into thinking that only conclusive evidence of innocence, analogous to that in the cleanest DNA cases, counts as a legitimate claim of innocence, and [t]hat misconception, in turn, threatens to undermine the established legal bases for granting relief from unjust convictions").

107 Kutzner v. State, 75 S.W.3d 427, 438 (Tex. Crim. App. 2002).

108 *Id.* Because of the Court of Criminal Appeals' reinvention of the statutory standard, the Texas legislature amended the statute to make clear that its intent was not to require a defendant to prove actual innocence but instead to show that if DNA had been available at trial, there is a 51 percent chance the defendant would not have been convicted. Smith v. State, 165 S.W.3d 361, 364 (Tex. Crim. App. 2005).

109 *See* Findley, *supra* note 106, at 1191.

110 *See also id.* at 1189 (noting that courts sometimes reject petitions "based on claims of innocence by comparing the new evidence to DNA and finding it lacking" and arguing that "assessing guilt and innocence" according to the simplistic DNA paradigm "threatens to undermine fundamental principles of our justice system—such as the presumption of innocence").

111 Bator, *supra* note 7, at 448.

112 Friendly, *supra* note 9, at 160.

To curb the bias created by DNA exonerations, the system must refocus. The new knowledge gained from DNA exonerations should force us to shift the balance in post-conviction from finality toward accuracy. After all, it is because DNA is such a reliable method of identification—the gold standard of the forensic sciences—that we have become aware that the criminal justice system often convicts innocent people.[113]

Two changes to state post-conviction procedures would give more innocent inmates a fairer opportunity to challenge their convictions. First, states should remove time limits on motions for new trial, allowing inmates to file a motion for new trial on a claim of innocence at any time. Second, states should adopt the test contemplated in the 1970s by Judge Friendly and Paul Bator to determine whether an inmate's claims of innocence would succeed.

Although scholars have offered different ways to tweak current procedures to allow courts to evaluate more post-conviction innocence claims, the procedure best suited for challenging the evidence at trial and presenting new evidence is the motion for new trial.[114] The problem with the motion for new trial is that in most jurisdictions strict deadlines make them meaningless for innocence claims. That's because the facts that produce exonerations generally evolve over time. They are not usually evident, if they exist at all, immediately after trial.

Funneling all innocence claims through the motion for new trial makes sense especially if the time limits are removed. Inmates could proceed immediately with their appeals process, challenging errors in the trial, perhaps even getting relief. If their appeals failed, they would also be entitled to lodge collateral claims raising constitutional violations—such as ineffective assistance of counsel claims or *Brady* claims—without worrying that a strong claim of innocence would be precluded by not making the claim in this first collateral attack. Instead, the inmate would have an assurance that if a thorough investigation raised a strong case of innocence, that claim would be heard in a motion for new trial no matter what other procedures had preceded it.

In assessing the motion for new trial, courts should be guided by a test that never shifts the burden back to the inmate to prove innocence by clear and convincing evidence or some other heightened standard. Proving innocence becomes a fool's errand. As Keith Findley has pointed out, "The demand for clear proof of innocence is a misfit in our system of justice."[115] For one thing, in the American system of justice, a criminal defendant is presumed innocent until proven guilty beyond a reasonable doubt. The state carries a heavy burden to remove this presumption of innocence and imprison a defendant. Although a conviction means the state once met this high burden at trial, the defendant should not bear the entire risk of erroneous conviction.[116] In other words, convicted defendants should not be thrust into the role of the state, proving that another person committed the crime or that a crime never occurred—a nearly impossible feat. Instead, defendants' relief in post-conviction should be based on whether they can undermine the state's evidence against them with more reliable evidence. As Judge Friendly proposed in 1970, courts should assess the evidence with due regard to its reliability, and an inmate should be entitled to a new trial if the inmate demonstrates a fair probability that the trier of facts would have entertained a reasonable doubt about the defendant's guilt. In addition, courts should apply the best current understanding of science to the evidence when determining its reliability.

One of the most significant benefits of this approach is that it would likely produce more reliable evidence early in the case—from the investigation to the prosecutor's case at trial. Investigators would have to assess their methods and choose the most reliable, lest a hard-won conviction is overturned because the investigators failed to record a confession, conducted a questionable photo line-up, or failed to conduct DNA testing on crucial pieces of evidence. Likewise, if prosecutors chose to use discredited experts or questionable science or failed to provide the defense with evidence that might exculpate the defendant, they would face a difficult post-conviction battle. The only way to ensure that reliable measures are used in the investigation and trial of a defendant is to create a system of review and accountability. Post-conviction reliability testing would serve that purpose.

---

113 *See* The Comm. on Identifying the Needs of the Forensic Sci. Cmty., Nat'l Research Council of the Nat'l Acads., *Strengthening the Forensic Sciences in the United States: A Path Forward* 7, 8 (2009) (referring to DNA as the "gold-standard" of the forensic sciences).

114 *See* Medwed, *supra* note 3, at 666.

115 Findley, *supra* note 106.

116 *See id.* at 1201.

How would this system work in Michael's hypothetical case? When Michael learned that his girlfriend confessed to lying on the stand, he would have to assess whether this new evidence sufficiently undermined his girlfriend's credibility and whether the new evidence was enough to overcome the other evidence in his trial—mainly the fingerprint and shoeprint. Knowing that courts do not look favorably on recantations—especially those supported only by hearsay—he may wait to gather more evidence before filing a motion for new trial. Once he found evidence that his shoes were manufactured after the murder took place, he may consider filing a motion at that time. But he may want to wait. Almost certainly, the prosecutor would argue that Michael could have owned a similar pair of Converse shoes when the murder occurred. Michael may decide to investigate the fingerprint expert's testimony. Armed with more knowledge about the unreliability of fingerprint comparisons, especially since the National Academy of Sciences (NAS) released its report on the forensic sciences, he may seek his own expert. The expert may conduct further testing, perhaps submitting the print to other experts in the field and measuring their ability to accurately "match" the print to Michael's prints. He may also research the ability to evaluate the print for testable DNA.

Once Michael fully investigated his attack on the reliability of the trial evidence and believed he could successfully challenge it, he would submit his motion for new trial. The court would then decide whether the recantation from his girlfriend, backed up by her friend's affidavit, made her testimony at trial less reliable. The court would consider all the evidence surrounding that testimony: that the girlfriend continued to live with Michael after the alleged confession; that she only disclosed the confession when she was charged with drug possession; that the charges were dropped after she provided the information; and that the prosecution never had a convincing motive for Michael to commit the murder. Moving on to the fingerprint evidence, the court would note that, recently, the reliability of fingerprint identification has been hotly contested. The NAS recently proclaimed that the field has never been subjected to reliability testing. Add to that the fact that the print seemed so smudged that no investigator on the crime scene thought it was of value; that the prosecutor hired an out-of-state expert; that the expert did not disclose his methods at trial; and that Michael's new expert has demonstrated that five out of five fingerprint experts were unable to match the bloody print to Michael's. Finally, the new evidence about the shoes certainly undermines the testimony at trial that the print must have come from the shoes found in Michael's closet. With this new evidence, that powerful trial testimony could not have been true. Taking all of the evidence into consideration, the court must decide whether the trier of facts would have entertained a reasonable doubt. With this holistic approach to claims of innocence, inmates with strong challenges to the reliability of the evidence that convicted them should stand a better chance at obtaining relief.

## Part V: Conclusion

A growing tension exists in the American criminal justice system, where the respect for the finality of criminal judgments collides with the realization that the system also makes mistakes, convicting the wrong person frequently enough to discomfort most of us. As the number of DNA exonerations rises, concerns about flaws in the system have turned to a realization that evidence we once thought to be hard proof of guilt—confessions, eyewitness identifications, bite marks, ballistics—lack reliability. DNA exonerations have also exposed flaws in the very structure of the criminal justice system, calling into question its ability to sort the innocent from the guilty. Despite these new realizations, our procedures lag behind. It is time to enter a new era of reliability and accuracy in the American criminal justice system. To usher in the new era, the system needs new procedures for post-conviction review. By reaching back to the days before DNA, we may be able to push valuable reforms forward.

# Chapter 9
# Narrowing the Construction of "Innocence": Societal and Constitutional Consequences

Francine Banner

## Introduction

The first task faced by the criminal law professor is to disabuse students of the myth of innocence. At trial, criminal defendants face two potential verdicts. Those verdicts are not "guilty" and "innocent," but guilty and not guilty. This is highlighted in occasionaal high-profile cases, such as that of O.J. Simpson and, more recently, Casey Anthony or George Zimmerman, where individuals are freed but go on to face civil liability or harsh outcomes in the court of public opinion. For law students, it can be a difficult reckoning that the commonsense, factual truth and the legal truth are not synonymous. Those freed are not always 100 percent innocent; they may have been released based on a "technicality," such as an un-credible government witness, a lack of physical evidence or poor witness identification, or there may have been a failure by the prosecution to prove its case.[1] Conversely, we do not require certainty that those convicted are 100 percent guilty, simply that the prosecution establishes guilt "beyond a reasonable doubt."[2]

Upon conviction, the constitutional burden of proof shifts dramatically and decisively onto the defendant. On habeas, "[t]he presumptions and burdens are the reverse of those in the investigative and trial phases of a case."[3] "[I]n the eyes of the law, [the] petitioner does not come before the Court as one who is 'innocent,' but, on the contrary, as one who has been convicted by due process of law ... ."[4] The drastic shifting of burdens of proof after conviction is apparent in recent discussions in Georgia, where the state is arguing that, in proving mental retardation, the post-conviction standard borne by the defendant should be as onerous as that borne by the prosecution at trial.[5] Georgia's mandate that appellants prove mental incompetence beyond a reasonable doubt highlights that the standard post-trial is much greater than simply "non-guilt." The standard is innocence, a term that remains elusive, undefined, and increasingly difficult for many petitioners to meet.

This chapter critically examines the contemporary post-conviction innocence standard in light of the rise in the use and availability of DNA evidence. The first part discusses the Byzantine legal standard for proving post-conviction innocence, using the case of Troy Davis to exemplify the challenges inherent in proving innocence in the contemporary context. Part II focuses on the "DNA revolution," highlighting recent discussions regarding the constitutional consequences of DNA testing on criminal suspects and defendants. Here, I provide an overview of current debates about DNA testing pre- and post-conviction, the impact scientific evidence has on American criminal procedure in recent years, and the import of privileging

---

1 Margaret Raymond, *The Problem with Innocence,* 49 Clev. St. L. Rev. 449, 456 (2001).

2 *In re* Winship, 397 U.S. 358 (1970); Coffin v. United States, 156 U.S. 432 (1895).

3 Judith A. Goldberg & David M. Siegel, *The Ethical Obligations of Prosecutors* in *Cases Involving Postconviction Claims of Innocence*, 38 Cal. W. L. Rev. 389, 410 (2002).

4 Herrera v. Collins, 506 U.S. 390, 398–400 (1993).

5 In July 2012, the Georgia Supreme Court stayed the execution of Warren Lee Hill, scheduled to face lethal injection after stabbing another inmate. *Georgia Halts Execution of Death-Row Inmate Warren Lee Hill*, NBC News (23 July, 2012, 7:00 PM), http://usnews.nbcnews.com/_news/2012/07/23/12910830-georgia-halts-execution-of-death-row-inmate-warren-lee-hill?lite. Although Hill's attorneys argued he was mentally disabled, thus his execution would violate Atkins v Virginia, 536 U.S. 304 (2002), Hill was unable to prove his retardation beyond a reasonable doubt. Ironically, the fact that Hill had participated in military service was a factor against his ability to prove to this standard that he was of sub-average intelligence. *See* Laura Kagel, *'Meaningful' Prohibition: Mental Disability in Georgia Capital Cases*, JURIST Forum (Aug. 2, 2012), http://jurist.org/forum/2012/08/laura-kagel-hill-execution.php.

scientific discovery over other types of errors in the post-conviction process. Last, I outline a few potential consequences of this shift in reliance on DNA evidence for constitutional claims. I suggest that there may be "truths" in the trial process beyond the simple fact of who perpetrated the crime.

This chapter is meant to be an exploration to highlight the accomplishments of the contemporary Innocence Movement while offering a word of caution for potential constitutional consequences going forward.

## Part I: Innocence, Undefined

In 2011, Georgia inmate Troy Anthony Davis was executed after the United States Supreme Court unanimously declined to provide an eleventh-hour stay.[6] Davis' case drew outrage among the American public, as seven of the nine witnesses who testified against Davis at trial had recanted their testimony, and jurors expressed reservation about the sufficiency of evidence for conviction.[7] As Metze observes, the Davis case raised the vital questions: "When is an accused person innocent of a crime? When does the accused lose that innocence, and if lost, is it possible to regain one's innocence?"[8]

Davis' case highlights that, although exonerations of innocent persons make a splash in the media today, in the legal context the term "innocence" lacks a precise definition. "The public connotation of the term invokes the image of a blameless individual," perhaps an infant or young child.[9] Legally speaking, however, the parameters are quite different. In the courtroom today, issues of innocence arise in basically three different ways: factual innocence; innocence in regard to the burden of proof; and legal—or procedural—innocence, where the petitioner seeks a new trial based on a constitutional defect during her trial, such as an issue with jury composition,[10] failure of the prosecution to deliver exculpatory evidence,[11] or ineffective assistance of counsel.[12] Unquestionably, the primary focus of the Innocence Movement and of public opinion today is on those parties claiming factual innocence. These claims primarily hinge on presentation of DNA evidence and constitute nearly half of exonerations.[13]

Contemporary legal notions of innocence are shaped by two key United States Supreme Court cases, *Herrera v. Collins*,[14] in which the Court assumed without deciding that a "truly persuasive demonstration" of actual innocence would give rise to a constitutional claim; and *Schlup v. Delo*,[15] where the Court held that actual innocence claims alone will not suffice to overturn a conviction. The former decision is particularly notorious, as Justice Rehnquist, writing for the majority, disregarded Herrera's argument that the discovery of new evidence demonstrating his innocence meant that his execution would violate the Eighth Amendment. In upholding Herrera's death sentence, Justice Rehnquist noted that "[f]ew rulings would be more disruptive of our federal system than to provide for federal *habeas* review of freestanding claims of actual innocence."[16]

---

6 K. Severson, *Davis is Executed in Georgia*, N.Y. TIMES, Sept. 21, 2011, http://www.nytimes.com/2011/09/22/us/final-pleas-and-vigils-in-troy-davis-execution.html.

7 Patrick S. Metze, *Troy Davis, Lawrence Brewer and Timothy McVeigh Should Still Be Alive: Certainty, Innocence and the High Cost of Death and Immorality*, 6 CHARLESTON L. REV. 333, 338 (2011–12).

8 *Id.*; *see also* Keith A. Findley, *Defining Innocence*, 74 ALBANY L. REV. 1157, 1158 (2010/11).

9 Cathleen Burnett, *Constructions of Innocence*, 70 UMKC L. REV. 971, 973 (2002).

10 Batson v. Kentucky, 476 U.S. 79 (1986).

11 Brady v. Maryland, 373 U.S. 83 (1963).

12 *See* Findley, *supra* note 8, at 1159; and *see generally*, Burnett, *supra* note 9; Raymond, *supra* note 1; William S. Laufer, *The Rhetoric of Innocence*, 70 Wash. L. Rev. 329 (1995).

13 S.R. Gross et al., *Exonerations in the United States 1987 Through 2003*. 95 J. CRIM. L. & CRIMINOLOGY (2003). I utilize herein the definition of exoneration provided by Gross et al., who provide that exoneration is "an official act of declaring a defendant not guilty of a crime for which her or she previously had been convicted." *Id.*, at 524. This definition should not be confused or conflated with the idea of "wrongful conviction" or "miscarriage of justice," which encompass release of inmates with and without official statement that they are not guilty.

14 506 U.S. 390 (1993).

15 513 U.S. 298, 327 (1995).

16 506 U.S. at 401.

In dissent, Justice Blackmun opined that "[n]othing could be more contrary to contemporary standards of decency or more shocking to the conscience than to execute a person who is actually innocent."[17]

Although debate continues as to whether or not it is constitutional to execute a convicted defendant who is actually innocent, the pragmatic import of *Schlup* and *Herrera* is that, in the post-conviction context, any actual innocence argument is merely a "gateway" claim; a petitioner must also demonstrate that a "constitutional violation has probably resulted in the conviction of one who is actually innocent."[18] In other words, in order to gain entry to consider legal innocence claims, the court must be presented with a door of actual innocence.[19] In order to succeed in a post-conviction proceeding, a petitioner must not only allege a constitutional error, but must also support that claim with new and reliable evidence, such as exculpatory physical or scientific evidence, that was not presented at trial.[20] For a petitioner to show that he or she has been wrongfully convicted, it must be "more likely than not that no reasonable juror would have found [the] petitioner guilty beyond a reasonable doubt."[21]

The types of constitutional claims that are likely to enable a petitioner to be heard are limited. For example, the Sixth Amendment standard for ineffective assistance of counsel (IAC) under *Strickland v. Washington*[22] and United States v. Cronic[23] recently has been interpreted by the Sixth Circuit Court of Appeals to permit defense counsel to sleep during the trial, as long as "substantial portions" are not missed.[24] Although the United States Supreme Court has upheld or expanded the right to counsel in a couple of recent cases,[25] between 1976 and 2002, the Court reversed only one case based on IAC.[26] As Garrett observes, even where viable constitutional claims are brought by petitioners proclaiming innocence, courts are unlikely to grant relief, most often finding constitutional errors to be harmless.[27]

In addition, although the ability to challenge convictions via habeas corpus is borne textually from the United States Constitution,[28] the availability of the writ has been severely circumscribed over the past 30 years.[29] Numerous scholars have attempted to provide a roadmap to federal habeas corpus procedures, characterizing access to the courts post-conviction as "incoherent,"[30] "hopelessly confusing,"[31] and "a blot on the adversary system."[32] The profound lack of clarification by the United States Supreme Court is highlighted by the fact

17 506 U.S. at 430.

18 513 U.S. at 327. In House v. Bell, 547 U.S. 518 (2006), the Supreme Court held that newly discovered DNA evidence met the Schlup v. Delo standard.

19 Emily Hughes, *Innocence Unmodified*, 89 N.C. L. Rev. 1083, 1106–7 (2011).

20 Myrna S. Raeder, *Postconviction Claims of Innocence*, 24 Crim. Just. 14, 15 (2009).

21 513 U.S. at 327.

22 466 U.S. 668 (1984).

23 *Id.*

24 Muniz v. Smith, 647 F.3d 619, 623 (6th Cir. 2011).

25 Missouri v. Frye, 132 S. Ct. 1399 (2012) (holding that the Sixth Amendment right to effective assistance of counsel extends to consideration of plea offers that lapse or are rejected); Martinez v. Ryan, 132 S. Ct. 1309 (2012) (recognizing a remedy for state criminal defendants who claim that counsel in their collateral state post-conviction proceeding failed adequately to challenge the effectiveness of trial counsel).

26 Ira Mickenberg, *Drunk, Sleeping, and Incompetent Lawyers: Is it Possible to Keep Innocent People off Death Row*, 29 U. Dayton L. Rev. 319, 322 (2003–04), *citing* Williams v. Taylor, 529 U.S. 362 (2000).

27 Brandon Garrett, *Innocence, Harmless Error and Federal Wrongful Conviction Law*, 2005 Wisc. L. Rev. 35, 55 (2005); *see also* Raeder, *supra* note 20, at 15.

28 U.S. Const., art. 1, sec. 9, cl. 2.

29 A significant narrowing of access to habeas corpus relief took place during the tenure of Chief Justices Burger and Rehnquist, who shifted the view of habeas from being "a mechanism for vindicating federal constitutional rights" to "an improper federal intrusion into state criminal justice systems and as a tool by which criminals could prevent their punishment from becoming final." *See* Lynn Adelman, *Federal Habeas Review of State Court Convictions: Incoherent Law but an Essential Right*, 64 Maine L. Rev. 380, 381 (2012). Another narrowing of rights occurred in the mid-1990s, with passage of the Anti-Terrorism and Effective Death Penalty Act and Prison Litigation Reform Act, which created a new limitations period for petitions for writ of habeas corpus brought by state prisoners. *See* Raeder, *supra* note 20, at 21; Jordan Steiker, *Innocence and Federal Habeas*, 41 UCLA L. Rev. 304, 305 (1993–94).

30 Adelman, *supra*, at 385.

31 Barry Friedman, *A Tale of Two Habeas*, 73 Minnesota L. Rev. 247 (1988).

32 Graham Hughes, *Sandbagging Constitutional Rights: Federal Habeas Corpus and the Procedural Default Principle*, 16 N.Y.U. Rev. L. & Soc. Change 321 (1987–88).

that the Troy Davis case marked the first time in 50 years that the United States Supreme Court had exercised its original habeas jurisdiction.[33]

Punctuating the extent of confusion in the federal habeas arena is the fact that there is no constitutional provision prohibiting executing innocent persons.[34] Although five justices in *Herrera v. Collins* agreed that "executing the innocent" was "a constitutionally intolerable event,"[35] in dissenting from the Court's decision in Troy Davis' case, Justices Scalia and Thomas appear to believe that the law provides that an innocent person may be executed as long as that person was tried fairly.[36]

As Raymond observes, the standard for post-conviction relief today requires "overwhelming proof," the "most visible type" of which is DNA evidence.[37] The claims the Court finds most favorable are those in which the defendant has solid evidence she did not do the crime.[38] Today, there is a pervasive "myth" that all types of innocence are treated the same; however, the system in reality is "not indifferent to these categories."[39] There is a great temptation for courts and citizens alike to revere scientific evidence over other evidence of innocence, as:

> Non-DNA exposed criminal justice errors lack a certain rhetorical sharpness, in that, even when the justice system essentially admits error by exonerating the defendant, a certain epistemological "haze" remains around the case. "The truth" is not unambiguously known, at least not to all actors' satisfaction, and determined advocates can still make plausible arguments for guilt, even in exoneration cases.[40]

As I discuss below, even in today's scientifically articulate society, however, DNA evidence is not readily available for all, or even most, criminal defendants.[41]

Despite the exceptionally challenging criteria for demonstrating post-conviction innocence and, perhaps, even judicial resistance to exonerating actually innocent persons, as of this writing, there have been more than 300 individuals freed in America based on DNA evidence.[42] At present, nearly 80 innocence projects nationwide work toward this vital end.[43] The claims of these individuals increasingly are aided by the development of more "forensic bio-banks," DNA databases created by law enforcement that enable convicted persons to access proof that they did not commit the felonies of which they were convicted. As Tuerkheimer observes, DNA evidence has become the "benchmark," the "touchstone for post-conviction relief."[44]

---

33 In his dissent from the Court's consideration of Troy Davis' claim, Justice Scalia observed that the Court made an "extraordinary step not taken in nearly 50 years" when it instructed the district court to adjudicate a claim of innocence. *In re* Davis, 2009 WL 2486475 (Aug. 17, 2009). *See* Robert Smith, *Recalibrating Constitutional Innocence Protection*, 87 Wash. U. L. Rev. 139, 175 (2012).

34 Smith, *supra*, at 140, 146; Raeder, *supra* note 20.

35 Herrera v. Collins, 506 U.S. 390, at 418.

36 Raeder, *supra* note 20, at 21.

37 Raymond, *supra* note 1, at 452.

38 Steiker, *supra* note 29, at 304–5. The current Court under Chief Justice Roberts has continued to impose new procedural restrictions on habeas, most notably in Cullen v. Pinholster, 131 S. Ct. 1388 (2011) (limiting review under federal habeas law to the record that was before the state court which ruled on the claim on the merits). However, the Court has also shown itself concerned with wrongful convictions, as illustrated in its willingness to consider the case of Troy Davis. *In re* Davis, 2009 WL 2486475 (Aug. 17, 2009).

39 Raymond, *supra* note 1, at 457.

40 Simon A. Cole, *How Much Justice Can Technology Afford? The Impact of DNA Technology on Equal Criminal Justice*, 34 Sci. & Pub. Pol'y 95, 98 (2007).

41 Raymond, *supra* note 1, at 452.

42 *Facts on Post-Conviction DNA Exonerations (2012)*, Innocence Project, http://www.innocenceproject.org/Content/Facts_on_PostConviction_DNA_Exonerations.php (last visited Oct. 1, 2012) [hereinafter Innocence Project].

43 William Tucker Carrington, *A House Divided: A Response to Professor Abbe Smith's In Praise of the Guilty Project: A Criminal Defense Lawyer's Growing Anxiety about Innocence Projects*, 15 U. Penn. J. L. & Soc. Change 1 (2012).

44 Deborah Tuerkheimer, *The Next Innocence Project: Shaken Baby Syndrome and the Criminal Courts*, 87 Wash. U. L. Rev. 1, 54–5 (2009).

I discuss just some of the impact of this DNA revolution on the process of law enforcement and trial in Part II below.

**Part II: DNA Evidence: New Directions, New Challenges**

The film *Minority Report* introduces the idea of "pre-crime," presenting a fictional, future world in which law enforcement has the capacity to identify would-be criminals prior to their commission of any wrongdoing.[45] Since the film was released, we have moved exponentially closer to that world. With the passage of the DNA Identification Act in 1994,[46] the Federal Bureau of Investigation (FBI) explicitly was granted authority to create the Combined DNA Index System (CODIS) database, which houses over 250,000 DNA profiles. In 2004, the passage of the Innocence Protection Act (IPA)[47] granted federal inmates access to DNA testing to prove factual innocence.[48]

After the revelation of the Tuskegee syphilis experiments and other non-consensual research projects came to light in the 1960s and 1970s, there was a public resistance to genetic testing, particularly as performed on women and minorities. However, since President Nixon's and Reagan's wars on crime in the 1970s and 1980s and America's entrance into the seemingly permanent war on terror in 2001, the need to protect politically disenfranchised groups against scientific incursions on privacy has been balanced against a profound need for national and personal security. The significant interest of the lab and educational lobby and the privatized prison industry fuels a system in which we are encouraged or mandated to contribute biological material on a regular basis.[49] The extent to which anxieties about and fear of criminal activity shape political decision-making and everyday life in America has prompted some commentators to categorize ours as an age in which politicians "govern through crime."[50]

Despite the fears of racism, eugenics, and exploitation which emerged during the Civil Rights era, interest in searching for genetic and biological predispositions to crime has been reinvigorated among contemporary scientists.[51] Some of this interest likely stems from increased capacities of science—scientists research these issues because they can. As I discuss in the subpart below, this shift to reliance on scientific evidence of guilt and innocence also has occurred consonant with emerging failures in the trial process and erosion of public trust in the criminal justice system.

---

45 MINORITY REPORT, Dir. Steven Spielberg (Amblin Entertainment, 2002).

46 42 U.S.C. §14132.

47 18 U.S.C. § 3600.

48 As Raeder explains, the IPA requires incarcerated individuals to meet a number of relatively complex criteria to gain access to DNA testing: for example, the petitioner must show that current methods of testing are "substantially more probative" than methods previously available, and that "the proposed testing would provide new material evidence that would raise a reasonable probability that the applicant did not commit the offense." Raeder, *supra* note 20, at 15. Forty-seven states currently have adopted such statutes. *See id.*

49 The United States Supreme Court held in Schmerber v. California, 384 U.S. 757 (1966) that blood tests to not implicate the Fifth Amendment privilege against self-incrimination. Further, the Fourth Amendment has been deemed not to require law enforcement to obtain a search warrant prior to obtaining saliva, semen, urine, or other bodily fluids or tissue from criminal suspects. *See, e.g.*, United States v. Nobel, 433 F. Supp. 2d 129 (D. MD 2006); United States v. EDMO, No. 96-30215 (9th Cir., 1998). Recent data show, in addition, that the majority of US workplaces require drug testing of potential employees. *See* A. Delaney, *Obama Administration Pushes Drug Testing in Workplace, But Not for Everybody*, THE HUFFINGTON POST (Apr. 18, 2012), http://www.huffingtonpost.com/2012/04/18/obama-administration-drug-testing_n_1434624.html.

50 Cole, *supra* note 40, at 96; *see generally* DAVID GARLAND, THE CULTURE OF CONTROL: CRIME AND SOCIAL ORDER IN CONTEMPORARY SOCIETY (2001).

51 *Genetics and Criminal Behavior*, THE DIANE REHM SHOW (June 23, 2011), http://thedianerehmshow.org/shows/2011-06-23/genetics-and-criminal-behavior/transcript [hereinafter REHM].

*False Witness: Profound Failures in the American Criminal Trial Process*

In case after highly publicized case, the American public increasingly is made aware of the failings of the contemporary criminal trial process. The issues cannot be traced to a specific source but, seemingly, underlie numerous aspects of the endeavor. A striking example is that of false confessions.[52] Perhaps surprisingly, of the over 300 individuals freed based on DNA evidence, a quarter actually had confessed to their crimes.[53] Similar issues have surfaced in the case of five youths who falsely confessed to rape in the Central Park Jogger case in 1989,[54] and in the case of abducted child Etan Patz.[55] Scholars such as Saul Kassin identify several risk factors for false confessions commonly found in the American criminal justice system, some relating to "dispositional vulnerabilities" of criminal suspects, such a youth or mental illness, and others connected to "situational pressures inherent in the conditions of custody and interrogation, such as excessive time, the presentation of false incriminating evidence, and the [police] use of minimization themes that imply leniency."[56] As Davis et al. discuss in Chapter 4, although both American law enforcement and the public tend to underestimate the pervasiveness of false confessions, they occur more frequently than lay persons would assume.[57] Further, the assumption that false confessions are rare has impeded adoption of even the simplest of fixes to interrogation procedures.[58]

Another example of the profound failures endemic in the trial process is eyewitness testimony. Once thought to be irrefutable, eyewitness evidence now has been demonstrated by researchers to be inaccurate a substantial percentage of the time.[59] The problem is particularly prevalent in the case of rape, where "crossracial misidentification in particular … accounts for the extraordinary number of false rape convictions with black defendants and white victims."[60] According to the Innocence Project, faulty eyewitness testimony has been the largest factor in convicting the innocent, playing a role in more than 70 percent of DNA exonerations.[61]

An overarching concern that relates to each of these issues is a generalized distrust in the jury system among members of the American public. After the releases of Casey Anthony and George Zimmerman after not-guilty verdicts, jurors reported receiving hate mail and even death threats from observers who believed they did not accurately evaluate the evidence and apply the law in the case.[62] Jurors in the O.J. Simpson case

---

52 Richard J. Ofshe & Richard A. Leo, *The Decision to Confess Falsely: Rational Choice and Irrational Action*, 74 U. Denver L. Rev.74, 983 (1997); Garrett, *supra* note 27, at 55; Melissa B. Russano et al., *Investigating True and False Confessions Within a Novel Experimental Paradigm*, 16 Psychol. Sci. 481 (2005).

53 Innocence Project, *supra* note 42.

54 In the high-profile case of the "Central Park Jogger," five black and Hispanic youths confessed, were convicted, and served one- to three-year sentences for rape. Subsequently, another man, Matias Reyes, confessed to the crime and was identified as the true perpetrator. R. Stodghill, *True Confession of the Central Park Rapist*, Time Magazine, Dec. 9, 2002, *available at* http://www.time.com/time/magazine/article/0,9171,397521,00.html.

55 Experts are currently debating the validity of the confession of Pedro Hernandez, who confessed to kidnapping and killing six-year-old Etan Patz more than 30 years ago, suspecting that mental illness may have prompted Hernandez to falsely admit to the crime (ABC News 2012). Stodghill, *supra*; Dan Childs & Anthony Castellano, *Etan Patz Case: Pedro Hernandez's Mental Health, Confession Questioned*, ABC News (May 30, 2012), http://abcnews.go.com/Health/etan-patz-case-pedro-hernandezs-mental-health-confession/story?id=16456499#.UGxgUVGWgul.

56 Jennifer T. Perillo & Saul M. Kassin, *Inside Interrogation: The Lie, the Bluff, and False Confessions*, 35 L. & Hum. Behav. 327 (2011).

57 Deborah Davis, Richard A. Leo & Michael J. Williams, Chapter 4, this volume.

58 *Id.*

59 Sandra G. Thompson, *Beyond a Reasonable Doubt? Reconsidering Uncorroborated Eyewitness Identification Testimony*, 4 U.C. Davis L. Rev. 1487 (2008); K.J. Nelson et al., *Eyewitness Testimony*, Wiley Encyclopedia of Forensic Science (2009).

60 Gross et al., *supra* note 13, at 26.

61 Innocence Project, *supra* note 42.

62 *Casey Anthony Juror, 60, Quits Work and Flees Town in Fear of Her Life*, Daily Mail (July 12, 2011), http://www.dailymail.co.uk/news/article-2013371/Casey-Anthony-juror-60-quits-work-flees-town-fear-life.html; Oren Dorrell, *Casey Anthony Verdict Could Haunt Jurors*, USA Today (July 11, 2011), *available at* http://usatoday30.usatoday.com/news/nation/2011-07-07-casey-anthony-juror-oj-simpson_n.htm?csp; Joe Newby, *'Twitter Lynch Mob' Targets Zimmerman Jury with Death Threats*, Examiner.com (July 14, 2013), http://www.examiner.com/article/twitter-lynch-mob-targets-zimmerman-jury-with-death-threats.

note that they faced similar insults and questions.[63] The lack of faith the American public routinely expresses in the criminal justice system prompts Carrington to characterize Justice O'Connor's concurrence in *Herrera*,[64] in which she remarked that "[o]ur society has a high degree of confidence in its criminal trials," as "quaint."[65]

Perhaps ironically, as DNA and other scientific evidence has become more common in the criminal trial process, distrust of commentators and the public in the jury system has not ebbed, and in fact may have grown. Scholars debate the existence of a hypothetical "CSI effect" that may lead jurors—based on expectations shaped by watching crime shows on television—to expect and rely on forensic science over and above other equally (or more) reliable types of evidence.[66] Prosecutors argue that the impact of crime shows featuring forensic evidence will lead jurors more frequently to acquit defendants, believing that prosecutors who cannot offer scientific evidence are unable to fully prove their case.[67] Others argue that there is a "reverse CSI effect," wherein jurors are more likely to convict defendants who do not offer exculpatory scientific evidence, such as the DNA of the "real" perpetrator, or are likely to reify DNA over all other types of evidence.[68] Raymond notes that, "jurors will expect that, if DNA evidence exists, a defendant will use that evidence to prove his or her innocence."[69] This is especially true, as the average juror likely does not clearly appreciate what it means that the defendant does not bear this burden of proof.[70]

While the CSI and reverse CSI effects may not be as prevalent as initially assumed, scientific research increasingly has borne out that jurors are not free from bias. "[S]ocial cognition research demonstrates that fact-finders sometimes assign probative force to, or misremember evidence based on, arbitrary factors such as race."[71] Even without considering the over-layer of potential unconscious racial, gendered, or ethnic prejudices, recent research has found that when it comes to scientific evidence, jurors are most likely to believe what they need to believe to feel most safe and protected, even in the face of scientific evidence to the contrary.[72]

These concerns are compounded by research that demonstrates that numerous convictions are being obtained via "tainted or fraudulent science."[73] For example, "bite mark evidence," a trend that took hold in the 1980s and early 1990s, has been shown to produce more than 60 percent false identifications.[74] Scientists and legal scholars today are also debating the existence and extent of "shaken baby syndrome."[75] Fifteen hundred cases per year are diagnosed; however, changes in science have cast doubt on the diagnosis, leading to the filing of more than 800 criminal appeals.[76] Tuerkheimer notes that there is a "distinct possibility that our adversarial system of criminal justice may be corrupting science. It may do so by placing pressure on scientists to articulate opinions more extreme—and certainly with more confidence—than those they actually hold."[77]

These comments highlight that, although DNA evidence is "good science" with proven reliability, the use of such evidence is not unproblematic. I discuss some additional "side effects" of reliance on and promotion of DNA evidence in the subpart below.

---

63 Dorrell, *supra* note 62.

64 506 U.S. 390 at 420.

65 Carrington, *supra* note 43, at 12.

66 Victor Streib, *Intentional Wrongful Conviction of Children*, 85 CHICAGO-KENT L. REV.163, 169 (2010).

67 Mark A. Godsey & Marie Alou, *She Blinded Me with Science: Wrongful Convictions and the "Reverse CSI-Effect"*, 17 TEX. WESLEYAN L. REV. 481 (2011).

68 *Id.* at 483.

69 Raymond, *supra* note 1, at 456.

70 *Id.*

71 Smith, *supra* note 33, at 140.

72 Anthony Bastardi, Eric L. Uhlmann & Lee Ross, *Wishful Thinking: Belief, Desire and the Motivated Evaluation of Scientific Evidence*, 22 PSYCHOL. SCI. 731–2.

73 Streib, *supra*, note 66.

74 Fernanda Santos, *Evidence From Bite Marks, It Turns Out, Is Not So Elementary*, N.Y. TIMES, Jan. 28, 2007, http://www.nytimes.com/2007/01/28/weekinreview/28santos.html?_r=0.

75 Tuerkheimer, *supra* note 44, at 11.

76 *Id.* at 10.

77 *Id.* at 56.

*The Magic Bullet? DNA as a Solution to Failures of the American Criminal Justice System*

The harms of executing innocent persons cannot be underestimated. On a personal level, "those who are innocent and sentenced to death suffer the additional devastation of being blamed for a terrible crime; their names, families, and entire lives are forever tainted by such ignominy, quite apart from the death of their bodies."[78] Perhaps as importantly, the executions of such persons "deeply undermine the legitimacy of the entire criminal justice system."[79]

The advent of DNA evidence has been referred to as a "revolution," a "scientific miracle cure" for the horrible problem of executing the innocent.[80] However, while the utility of DNA in the search for "truth' is unquestionable, recent appellate cases raise important questions about the outer boundaries of such evidence. Currently all but three states routinely collect DNA from convicted felons,[81] and 17 states permit law enforcement to collect DNA from suspects post-arrest but prior to any conviction.[82]

In *Maryland v. King*[83] the United States Supreme Court recently upheld the constitutionality of a state statute providing for the warrantless collection by law enforcement of DNA from persons arrested for serious crimes. Alonzo Jay King's DNA was taken from him during an arrest on an assault charge in 2009.[84] Pursuant to Maryland's DNA collection law,[85] King's DNA was run through the State of Maryland's CODIS database, which produced a "hit" linking him to a rape committed in 2003. Disregarding the defense's arguments that, in its capacity to reveal intimate genetic details, DNA differs dramatically from other police identification procedures, the Court reasoned that, although DNA collection is a "search," the legitimate interest of the state in having "a safe and accurate way to process and identify the persons and possessions they must take into custody" outweighs what the Court characterized as a minimal intrusion into arrestees' privacy.[86] The majority categorized the intrusion in DNA collection as historically analogous to fingerprinting, simply "a natural part of 'the administrative steps incident to arrest.'"[87]

In California, the Ninth Circuit Court of Appeals is currently considering the constitutionality of that state's pre-arrest DNA collection law, which is much broader than Maryland's in that it permits law enforcement to collect DNA not only from those arrested for violent offenses but also from those who have committed any felony, including a broad litany of non-violent offenses.[88] The case before the Ninth Circuit en banc, *Haskell v. Brown*,[89] is a class action spearheaded by a woman whose DNA was collected by police as she was arrested at an anti-war protest. Though Haskell was ultimately charged only with a misdemeanor, police retained her DNA in a CODIS database with no provision that the information be expunged if the charges were dropped.[90]

A strong dissent by Justice Scalia in *King*, a five to four decision, highlights that, although DNA may in part be utilized to identify suspects, the line drawn by the *King* majority between administrative efficacy

78 Carol S. Steiker & Jordan M. Steiker, *The Seduction of Innocence: The Attraction and Limitations of the Focus on Innocence in Capital Punishment Law and Advocacy*, 95 J. Crim. L. & Criminology 587, 588 (2005).

79 *Id.*

80 Cole, *supra* note 40, at 99.

81 *Where States Stand on DNA Collection*, ProPublica (May 5, 2009, 7:40 AM), http://www.propublica.org/article/where-states-stand-on-dna-collection-505.

82 *Id.*

83 569 U.S. ___ (2013).

84 King v. State, 425 Md. 550, 42 A.3d 549, 553 (2012).

85 Maryland's DNA Collection Act authorizes state and local law enforcement authorities to collect DNA samples from individuals who are arrested for a crime of violence, an attempted crime of violence, a burglary, or an attempted burglary. Md. Code (2003, 2011 Repl.Vol.), Pub. Safety Art., § 2-504(3).

86 569 U.S. at 10.

87 *Id.* at 10, *citing* County of Riverside v. McLaughlin, 500 U.S. 44, 58 (1991).

88 CA Penal Code, § 296(A)(2)(C) was enacted after voters passed Proposition 69 in 2004.

89 Case No. 10-15152 (9th Cir. 2012). In September 2012, the Ninth Circuit heard arguments *en banc* in the case, but suspended the verdict pending the outcome of Maryland v. King. The Ninth Circuit has not yet spoken as to whether distinctions between the California and Maryland DNA collection statutes are sufficiently legally significant to keep Haskell's case alive.

90 Howard Mintz, *Federal Appeals Court to Hear Challenge to California DNA Collection Law*, Mercury News (Sept. 16, 2012, 3:55 PM), http:www.mercurynews.com/crime-courts/ci_21557952/federal-appeals-court-hear-challenge-california-dna-collection.

and investigative motives is a thin one. The promise and danger of DNA collection go well beyond mere identification. The "DNA collection cases" in fact juxtapose vital community values: on one side, the potential utility of DNA collection procedures in uncovering true perpetrators and non-invasive nature of collection; and on the other, access to our entire genetic code into the unforeseeable future. The potential consequences of permitting law enforcement broad access to this type of information cannot be underestimated. Familial DNA testing, which has been utilized in Britain for several years, is now more widely used in law enforcement in America, enabling officers to cross-reference DNA from suspects against siblings, cousins, and, parents in order to discover the perpetrator.[91] Currently legalized in four states, advocates argue that the process both renders law enforcement more efficient and, more importantly, contributes greatly to public safety by empowering the police to ferret out perpetrators of crimes they never thought possible.[92] The American news magazine *Time*, for example, chronicles the story of the arrest of Lonnie Franklin, who committed rapes and murders of more than 10 women in Los Angeles in the 1980s.[93] Police were able to identify Franklin via a search for familial DNA links using DNA collected from his son after a firearms charge in 2008.

On the other hand, as compellingly argued by advocates for Alonzo King, both pre-arrest and familial DNA testing have significant Fourth Amendment implications. Maryland's and California's statutes, for example, permit individuals to be subjected to sweeping searches without any judicial determination of probable cause. Genetic material obtained from these individuals then is added to the CODIS database, where, even years later, it may turn up as a "hit" linking them to a crime. There is no question that DNA collection is an efficient, non-invasive way to retrieve accurate information about criminal suspects. As the Maryland appeals court noted in striking down that state's DNA collection statute, however:

> The information derived from a fingerprint is related only to physical characteristics and can be used to identify a person, but no more. A DNA sample … contains within it unarguably much more than a person's identity … . [W]e cannot turn a blind eye to the vast genetic treasure map that remains in the DNA sample retained by the State … . A person's entire genetic makeup and history is forcibly seized and maintained in a government file, subject only to the law's direction that it not be improperly used and the prospect of a misdemeanor conviction if a custodian *willfully* discloses it in an unauthorized manner. No sanction is provided for if the information is non-willfully disclosed in an unauthorized manner, though the harm is essentially the same.[94]

There are also vital Fourteenth Amendment concerns that inhere in collection of pre-conviction DNA. United States Department of Justice statistics show that 48 percent of people in jail have a relative who has also been incarcerated.[95] Latinos, African Americans, Native Americans, and men continue to be seriously overrepresented in the American prison system and in arrests, meaning that such individuals are also substantially overrepresented in the CODIS system. The Association of Black Psychologists characterizes DNA collection by law enforcement as a "slippery slope":

> If you're looking at research from people who have been incarcerated, whether at the juvenile or at the adult level, and you take into consideration that the majority of those incarcerated are African-Americans … [a]nd men … .you're going to have some serious problems.[96]

While advancements in technology often are proposed as race and gender neutral, Cole argues that an "emphasis on innocence may distract from issues of inequality that affect the guilty as well as the innocent, such as the excessive punitiveness of the criminal justice system in general, the immorality and political

91 Terry McCarthy, *The Case of the Grim Sleeper*, Time Magazine, Dec. 5, 2011, http://www.time.com/time/magazine/article/0,9171,2100112,00.html.

92 *Id.*

93 *Id.*

94 King v. State, 425 Md. 550, 42 A.3d 549, 596 (2012).

95 McCarthy, *supra* note 91.

96 Rehm, *supra* note 51.

undesirability of the death penalty regardless of guilt or innocence, the race and class disparities that permeate the criminal justice system, the abuses of the prison-industrial complex and the war on drugs."[97]

Friedland describes the "turbulent and troublesome consequences" that may result from a "genetically based criminal law system":

> Genetic determinism could lead to the conviction or acquittal of people based on their physiological status rather than on their actions. Genetic information could be used to classify individuals based on the type of genetic risks they pose, particularly their level of dangerousness. In addition, a new type of discrimination may result from the creation of genetic "minorities" as people are grouped by their genetic propensities. On a broader scale, the emphasis on genetics may serve to diminish traditional functions of the criminal law, especially the provision of a moral baseline of behavior for the community.[98]

Another justice-based concern less widely discussed to date is the fact that, even if a perpetrator committed a crime years prior, there may have been mitigating circumstances, such as mental deficiency, presence of provocation, or lack of proof of causation that will be extremely difficult for a defendant to prove years after the crime. While the prosecution enters trial with the "slam dunk" of DNA after a CODIS "hit," it may be nearly impossible for a defendant to raise—or even to recall—mitigating circumstances years later. Witnesses may have died or disappeared, and the suspect's own recollection of events may be muddled. There is a real danger that the "innocent until proven guilty" standard no longer will be a tenet of the criminal justice system.

Some commentators suggest that the best solution to the issue of potentially prejudicial use of DNA evidence is the Orwellian fix—collecting DNA from every citizen. Our reaction to this suggestion as citizens is to a large extent predicated on our assessment of the balance—the search for truth versus the protection of individual liberties. As Cole notes, while universal databases have a "superficial egalitarian appeal," this is balanced by the "extension of state power and curtailment of civil liberties."[99] Our willingness to part with key information about our genetic code also depends on our view of the trial process. Do we trust in the courts and in jurors' decision-making, or should the responsibility for attributing guilt be shifted even further toward the investigator—the police and the prosecuting attorneys' office? With the rate of plea bargains already up around 95 percent,[100] perhaps there is strong evidence already as to our collective values and the way society is headed. As I discuss in the following part, the shift to reliance on DNA evidence during the pre-arrest, arrest, and trial processes has significantly impacted defendants seeking post-conviction relief.

## Part III: DNA in the Post-Conviction Context

While law enforcement moves more and more toward a system reliant on science to bring perpetrators to justice, innocence projects often advocate similar changes in the post-conviction landscape. The rise in use and collection of DNA evidence has launched significant debate in the abolitionist community with regard to the use of scientific evidence in post-conviction proceedings. Krieger observes that highlighting innocence became the preferred tactic among anti-death penalty advocates due to the "underlying psychological horror to the thought that someone who was innocent was executed."[101] "The credibility gained by innocence

---

97 Cole, *supra* note 40, at 99.

98 Steven I. Friedland, *The Criminal Law Implications of the Human Genome Project: Reimagining a Genetically Oriented Criminal Justice System*, 86 Kentucky L. J. 303, 309 (1997).

99 Cole, *supra* note 40, at 102.

100 According to the 2010 statistics from the US Sentencing Commission, 97 percent of federal defendants engaged in a plea bargain rather than go to trial. *See 2010 Sourcebook of Federal Sentencing Statistics*, Figure C, U.S. Sentencing Commission, http://www.ussc.gov/Data_and_Statistics/Annual_Reports_and_Sourcebooks/2010/FigureC.pdf (last visited Oct. 1, 2012).

101 Steven A. Krieger, *Why Our Justice System Convicts Innocent People and the Challenges Faced by Innocence Projects Trying to Exonerate Them*, 14 New Crim. L. Rev. 333, 361 (2011).

projects from their strict actual innocence stance has had a substantial effect on their ability to leverage policy making," since "DNA exonerations … are generally beyond attack by conservative critics."[102]

On the other hand, activists for reform in the criminal justice system question the consequences of privileging factual innocence over other types of innocence.[103] "The very success of the innocence argument has served to marginalize all other anti-death penalty arguments (cost, morality, suspicion of state power, redemption, and so on)."[104] Promoting factual innocence also may put anti-capital punishment advocates "in the uncomfortable position of implicitly accepting the death penalty in the unlikely event it could be made 'errorfree'."[105] For these reasons, Emily Hughes advocates "reclaim[ing] an understanding of innocence unmodified by qualifiers such as 'actual' and 'legal'."[106]

The potential impact of privileging factual innocence over other types of claims is highlighted in the comments of Lawrence C. Marshall, Legal Director for Northwestern University Law School Center on Wrongful Convictions. Marshall notes, while the "rights revolution" of the Warren Court was "controversial" and based on "value judgments, "[t]he innocence revolution is quite different, as it addresses a value that everyone shares: accurate determinations of guilt and innocence."[107] While it is true that a number of the constitutional protections recognized during the Warren era have been altered or lessened in recent years, the characterization of affording constitutional rights as a "value judgment" is problematic, particularly when juxtaposed against the "truth" revealed by DNA evidence.

There is no question that this pervasive rhetoric has altered the criminal justice landscape. In addition to falling crime rates and rising costs of incarceration, arguments regarding potential execution of the innocent have aided advocates for abolition in abolishing or enacting moratoria on the death penalty in several states.[108] The SAFE California Act, for example, which was narrowly defeated by voters in the state during a November 2012 referendum,[109] advocates commuting current death sentences to life without parole, using the primary justification that the money saved by taxpayers can be used to fund law enforcement efforts, including "us[ing] modern forensic science including DNA testing."[110] The *Los Angeles Times* newspaper, which endorsed the Act, observed, dramatically, that "eliminating the death penalty would end the risk that the hands of all Californians will be stained with the blood of an innocent."[111] The bill itself painted a remarkably unsympathetic picture of criminal defendants, with the first section beginning, "Murderers and rapists need to be stopped, brought to justice, and punished."[112] Other media outlets endorsing the measure noted,

---

102 Marvin Zalman, *Qualitatively Estimating the Incidence of Wrongful Convictions*, 48 Crim. L. Bulletin 221, 255 (2012).

103 *See, e.g.*, Steiker & Steiker, *supra* note 78; Cole, *supra* note 40; Raymond, *supra* note 1.

104 Cole, *supra* note 40, at 100.

105 *Id.*

106 Hughes, *supra* note 19, at 1124.

107 Lawrence Marshall, *The Innocence Revolution and the Death Penalty*, 1 Ohio State J. Crim. L. 573 (2003).

108 Notably, in 2000, Governor George Ryan ceased the government's execution of inmates based on his "grave concerns about [the state's] shameful record of convicting innocent people and putting them on death row." *See Governor Ryan Declares Moratorium on Executions, Will Appoint Commission to Review Capital Punishment System* (Jan. 31, 2000), *available at* http://www3.illinois.gov/PressReleases/showpressrelease.cfm?subjectid=3&recnum=359. The Governors of Connecticut, Oregon, and Maryland each have signed in measures to significantly limit application of capital punishment in those states. *See Death Penalty Fast Facts*, CNN Library (July 19, 2013), *available at* http://www.cnn.com/2013/07/19/us/death-penalty-fast-facts/index.html.

109 The proposition was *defeated* with 53 percent of voters against and 47 percent in favor. See Franklin Zimring, *Endgame for Death Penalty in California: Prop. 34's Narrow Loss a Big Step Toward Abolition of Execution*, San Francisco Chron., Dec. 8, 2012, http://www.sfgate.com/opinion/article/Endgame-for-death-penalty-in-California-4101011.php.

110 *See* Proposition 34, The "Savings, Accountability, and Full Enforcement for California Act" [hereinafter SAFE Act].

111 *Yes on the SAFE California Act*, L.A. Times, May 21, 2012, http://articles.latimes.com/2012/may/21/opinion/la-ed-death-penalty-california-20120521.

112 *Id.*

"Supporting Proposition 34 doesn't mean being sympathetic to the state's most heinous murderers"[113] and that the bill "should not be construed as any form of sympathy for these criminals nor mercy towards them."[114]

The million-dollar question is whether affirmative evidence of innocence really should be the most—or potentially only—significant factor in exonerating a defendant.[115] For one thing, although this may change over time, DNA evidence is not always available. The likelihood of finding DNA evidence depends on the type of crime committed and the scientific sophistication of individual police forces and crime laboratories. Although the crime of rape, for example, may carry a much stiffer sentence than the crime of robbery, the former is much more likely to produce DNA evidence.[116] Currently, DNA evidence is only available in about 20 percent of cases.[117] Troy Davis' argument for wrongful conviction, for example, rested on eyewitness testimony, with no physical evidence available either to tie him to the crime or to exonerate him.[118] Where jurors increasingly expect scientific evidence, the lack of such evidence may disadvantage defendants at trial.

On a normative basis, as highlighted by the comments by innocence advocates above, in privileging DNA evidence, there is the possibility that the Innocence Movement is placing the "possibility of executing innocents [as] of greater ... concern than other kinds of error" in the criminal trial process.[119] As Zalman observes, "the personnel and processes for detecting, apprehending, and prosecuting felons are far below the standards of reliability that should be demanded by a modern technological society and below levels of fairness expected in a country that takes due process and the rule of law seriously."[120] "[T]he narrative that has emerged about innocence is a dangerous one" because "the focus on DNA leads to mistaken perspectives that system is working."[121] Abbe Smith cites an offhand comment by Innocence Project founder Barry Scheck, that "he had not represented a guilty person in twenty years."[122] However, "[f]ar from being surprising, so-called 'wrongful convictions' are not 'wrongful' at all, except in the moral sense; under our system, convictions of innocent people can and should be anticipated" in a system in which the state is not required to prove a defendant's guilt to 100 percent certainty.[123]

The temptation is strong for innocence projects to frame defendants' stories as "isolated, individual tragedies that are ultimately uncovered and fixed by the system" rather than issues of systemic failure.[124] However, this potentially can lead both law students and the public to embrace a "hierarchy" of criminal defendants deserving of legal assistance, wherein defendants' rights are impacted more strongly by the initial assessment of guilt rather than the constitutional validity of their claims.[125] As Steiker and Steiker note, "The distinctive claim of the newly emerging 'innocence movement' is that the harms associated with executing innocents are of such a different kind or degree that we should not risk these sorts of errors even as we must tolerate others."[126] In an already biased criminal justice system, this "deliberate ... shift in strategy" to

113 *No to the Death Penalty—Put California's Costly and Ineffective System to Rest by Voting Yes on Proposition 34*, L.A. Daily News (Oct. 10, 2012) (noting, "These are bad people who have done unspeakable things. But the reality is that sentencing them to die doesn't result in death, just a private cell and a personal legal team dedicated to sparing their life."), http://www.dailynews.com/opinions/ci_21743781/endorsement-no-death-penalty-put-californias-costly-and.

114 *Our View: Yes on 34 to End the Death-Penalty Game*, Merced Sun-Star (Oct. 18, 2012) (observing that "[persons] on death row have been convicted of brutal, unspeakable crimes and deserve the harshest possible punishment. The reality of the situation, however, is that none will likely face their death at the hands of the state anytime soon."), http://www.mercedsunstar.com/2012/10/18/2600766/our-view-yes-on-34-to-end-the.html.

115 Steiker & Steiker, *supra* note 78, at 596.

116 Raymond, *supra* note 1, at 452.

117 Raeder *supra* note 20, at 1.

118 Smith, *supra* note 33, at 174–5.

119 Steiker & Steiker, *supra* note 78, at 596.

120 Zalman, *supra* note 102, at 277.

121 Abbe Smith, *In Praise of the Guilty Project: A Criminal Defense Lawyer's Growing Anxiety About Innocence Projects*, 13 U. Pa. J.L. & Soc. Change 315, 317–18 (2010); Raymond, *supra* note 1, at 451.

122 Smith, *supra* note 33, at 320.

123 Raymond, *supra* note 1, at 451.

124 Smith, *supra* note 33, at 324; Raymond, *supra* note 1, at 451.

125 Hughes, *supra* note 19, at 1089.

126 Steiker & Steiker, *supra* note 78, at 596.

focus on freeing the innocent necessarily refocuses public attention away from the prejudices and biases that pervade the process.[127]

On a constitutional basis, the overwhelming promotion of DNA as the "gold standard" may create what Abbe Smith calls a "CSI Effect of a different kind."[128] That is, the greater the concentration on factual innocence, the increased likelihood to overlook the claims of the "the not-quite-so-innocent but equally unfairly treated."[129] Errors in the system, such as arbitrary treatment of offenders, failure to disclose exculpatory evidence, or disproportionate punishment under the Eighth Amendment may in fact be more pervasive than execution of the factually innocent.[130] However, that the execution of an innocent person is so distinct and horrible causes society to recognize the harm of executing the innocent as "worse" than other violations.[131]

The impact of this rhetoric may be far-reaching, particularly for those claiming what the American public refers to as "technicalities."[132] For example, there may be defendants with viable Eighth Amendment claims who are guilty of something but not as great a crime as that charged. For example, a defendant may be convicted of felony murder but, on a legal basis, be guilty only of robbery.[133] There may be defendants who bring issues of error at trial, such as ineffective assistance of counsel or jury composition issues. And there may be those defendants who did the crime but were unconstitutionally deprived of their right to present evidence of mitigating circumstances. DNA evidence is not probative in these regards. "[T]he defendant with the factual innocence story throws every other defendant under the bus."[134]

The consequences of the promotion of factual innocence also mark a potentially striking shift in fact-finding from the trial process to the investigatory process. For example, the SAFE California Act employs a narrative favored by many innocence projects, presenting a "tough on crime" stance that focuses primarily on a 'search for truth" and "bringing rapists and murderers to justice."[135] The Act literally provides that the cost savings from eliminating the death penalty will be passed on to law enforcement, enabling the growth of DNA retrieval and testing.[136] However, there is currently no obligation on law enforcement to conduct either the most extensive or most reliable testing.[137] In fact, decisions such as[138] *Connick v. Thompson* and *Arizona v. Youngblood*[139] may disincentivize prosecutors from doing so, as they are insulated from liability in all but the most egregious cases of constitutional violations. At least half of defendants who were ultimately exonerated via DNA evidence had to engage in extensive litigation even to gain access to genetic testing.[140]

In the alternative, as Carrington compellingly argues, as innocence projects have grown in legislative and societal influence, it is not as though they have wholly abandoned the foundation of constitutional rights.[141] The Arizona Justice Project, for example, was instrumental in advocating for the petitioner in *Martinez v. Ryan*,[142] successfully expanding the ability of post-conviction defendants to assert ineffective assistance of counsel claims resulting from collateral state post-conviction proceedings. Other innocence projects have made substantial inroads not only toward expanding incarcerated individuals' access to post-conviction DNA testing but also toward reforming aspects of the trial process, supporting legislation to ameliorate reliance on flawed eyewitness testimony and other systemic problems.[143] Just as actual innocence provides a gateway

---

127 Krieger, *supra* note 102, at 360, 361.
128 Smith, *supra* note 33, at 324.
129 *Id.*
130 Steiker & Steiker, *supra* note 78, at 597.
131 *Id.*
132 *See generally* Smith, *supra* note 33; Carrington, *supra* note 43.
133 Smith, *supra* note 33, at 324; Hughes, *supra* note 19, at 1088–9.
134 Smith, *supra* note 33, at 324.
135 SAFE Act, *supra* note 110.
136 *Id.*
137 Dist. Att'ys Office for the Third Jud. Dist. v. Osborne, 129 S. Ct. 2308 (2009).
138 563 *U.S.* ___ (2011).
139 488 U.S. 51 (1988).
140 Hilary S. Ritter, *It's the Prosecution's Story, But They're Not Sticking to It: Applying Harmless Error and Judicial Estoppel to Exculpatory Post-Conviction DNA Testing Cases*, 74 Fordham L. Rev. 825, 827 (2005).
141 Carrington, *supra* note 43, at 19.
142 132 S. Ct. 1309.
143 Carrington, *supra* note 43, at 19–20.

to consideration of constitutional claims in a federal habeas proceeding, the increased attention brought to factual innocence by innocence projects nationwide has the potential to open the door to discussion of constitutional rights more generally. Support for the death penalty in America is currently the lowest it has been in 39 years, a phenomenon that many commentators attribute to increasingly widespread awareness of wrongful convictions.[144]

## Part IV: Conclusion

Exoneree Darryl Burton refers to himself as the "miracle man," relating the story of his exoneration—spearheaded by counsel from Centurion Ministries—as a series of signs from God.[145] For Darryl and the over 300 other persons who have been freed so far based on DNA evidence, science has indeed proved miraculous. This is all the more true because, as Raymond notes, "Whether an innocent person is able to muster the kind of evidence that constitutes conclusive proof of innocence is more or less a matter of chance."[146]

DNA evidence, at least rhetorically, bears the promise and threat of a future in which factual truth and legal truth are synonymous and where "technicalities" and value judgments are obsolete. However, for every defendant who can prove his or her factual innocence there are doubtlessly countless others who remain wrongfully imprisoned. Some belong to the 80 percent who are actually innocent but do not have the scientific evidence to overcome the significant hurdles to obtaining post-conviction relief. Others technically may have done the crime but be entitled to relief based on a constitutional violation; they may have confronted a sleeping lawyer, a racially biased jury, or an extraordinarily disproportionate sentence. As we embrace the positive impact of the DNA revolution on otherwise forgotten persons, it is important to be mindful, also, that the constitution retains the capacity to provide recourse for others who have been overlooked. As we put our faith in scientific development, we must be mindful, also, of the power that inheres in the United States Constitution.

144 Kevin Johnson, *Shifts Detected in Support for Death Penalty*, USA Today (Apr. 25, 2012), http://usatoday30.usatoday.com/news/nation/story/2012-04-24/abolish-death-penalty-movement/54515754/1.

145 Darryl Burton, Speech during Diversity Law Day, Phoenix School of Law, Phoenix, AZ (Mar. 22, 2011).

146 Raymond, *supra* note 1, at 452.

# PART IV
# Innocence Reform

# Chapter 10
# Towards a Theory of Innocence Policy Reform

Nancy Marion and Marvin Zalman

## Introduction

In less than two decades a small innocence movement has begun to generate a sizeable range of policy reforms in the investigation-prosecution-adjudication sector of the criminal process.[1] This is remarkable in that the central innocence interest group—the law school "innocence project"—is relatively weak in the panoply of American social welfare interest groups, consisting essentially of clinical programs to train students in legal practice, which typically employ one or two clinical law professors and a current class of students.[2] There are only about 50 such programs in America.[3] They are, however, networked into a cohesive organization (the Innocence Network), at least two of the projects have effective policy and research staffs (the Innocence Project and the Center on Wrongful Conviction), and the movement enjoys generally favorable public support.[4]

This chapter describes the political dynamics and policy accomplishments of three innocence reforms that occurred in the first decade of the twenty-first century: Illinois legislation stimulated by Governor Ryan's death penalty moratorium and his Commission on Capital Punishment,[5] the Innocence Protection Act passed by Congress and signed into law by President Bush in 2004; and an innocence reform package passed by the Ohio legislature in 2010. These reforms were not randomly selected; they were chosen to illustrate a variety of reform processes and a trajectory that appears to describe the growing strengths, but also the limits, of this burgeoning movement. The descriptions are designed to improve understanding of the substance of the new policies and the political dynamics that led to them. As important, we begin to explain the nature of the Innocence Movement as a policy-relevant interest group.[6]

Richard Leo admonished the criminological community for not investigating wrongful convictions and for not generating theoretical explanations of their causes.[7] In this vein we explore the Innocence Movement and its policy reform efforts in the context of growing interest in agency and system behavior theory among criminal justice scholars and draw on public policy theory to illuminate the Innocence Movement.[8] Academics and practitioners alike are interested in how policy decisions are completed, including who is able to influence

---

1 Robert J. Norris et al., *"Than That One Innocent Suffer": Evaluating State Safeguards Against Wrongful Convictions*, 74 Alb. L. Rev. 1301 (2011).

2 Jan Stiglitz, Justin Brooks & Tara Shulman, *The Hurricane Meets the Paper Chase: Innocence Projects New Emerging Role in Clinical Legal Education*, 38 Cal. W. L. Rev. 413 (2002); Keith A. Findley, *The Pedagogy of Innocence: Reflections on the Role of Innocence Projects in Clinical Legal Education*, 13 Clinical L. Rev. 231 (2006).

3 Innocence Network, http://www.innocencenetwork.org/ (last visited June 11, 2012).

4 Marvin Zalman, Matthew J. Larson & Brad Smith, *Citizens' Attitudes Toward Wrongful Convictions*, 37 Crim. Just. Rev. 51 (2012).

5 Report of the Governor's Commission on Capital Punishment (State of Illinois, Apr. 15, 2002) [hereinafter Illinois Governor's Commission] http://www.olympiafor.org/Illinois%20Moratorium%20Commission's%20complete%20report%20.pdf (last visited June 11, 2012).

6 Marvin Zalman, *Criminal Justice System Reform and Wrongful Conviction: A Research Agenda*, 17 Crim. Just. Pol'y Rev. 468 (2006); *Marvin Zalman, An Integrated Justice Model of Wrongful Convictions*, 74 Alb. L. Rev. 1465 (2011) [hereinafter, Zalman, *Justice Model*].

7 Richard A. Leo, *Rethinking the Study of Miscarriages of Justice: Developing a Criminology of Wrongful Conviction*, 21 J. Contemp. Crim. Just. 201 (2005).

8 Peter B. Kraska & John J. Brent, Theorizing Criminal Justice: Eight Essential Orientations (2d ed., 2011); Criminal Justice Theory: Explaining the Nature and Behavior of Criminal Justice (David E. Duffee & Edward R. Maguire eds., 2007).

the final policy output and in what way, i.e., to understand the "how and why" of the policy making process. Understanding the reasons why policies are made and altered provides an explanation as to how and why some issues move from a "seemingly benign existence outside the policy making arena to active areas of concern"—a process that has happened with the Innocence Movement.[9]

Academic studies of the policy making process have long supplemented general descriptions of the constitutional responsibilities of branches of government. They have provided descriptions of policy making stages, including agenda setting, policy formulation, implementation, and evaluation. This literature broadly emphasizes conflicts in making policy between interests and goals, followed by a process of cooperation, which results in public policy. Earlier assumptions of clear and orderly relationships between problems and solutions have been supplanted by a recognition that the policy process is more complex and that decision makers do not necessarily follow expected patterns. Decisions are made when opportunities or requirements arise, and involve much more internal politics, which includes bargaining and conflict among coalitions, than previously considered.[10] Agencies often do not have clear or consistent ideas about what their goals are, or how they are supposed to get there, or even who should make the decision.[11] We seek to assess innocence reform in light of these considerations and several policy making theories.

Ideally, a theory of innocence policy reform would be based on empirical analysis of a random sample of reforms. The purposive selection of the three reforms described in this chapter may omit others that would suggest alternate theoretical orientations. Kruse's case-study of the Avery Task Force in Wisconsin, for example, suggested that the Wisconsin reforms exemplified democratic experimentalism, which may be coming to replace "command-and-control style" top-down regulation with decentralized, flexible, and pragmatic approaches.[12] In the absence of interviews or quantitative data, in this exploratory study we rely on published sources for information about the three innocence reforms, acknowledging that interviews and a broader base of examples could provide more nuanced accounts.

This chapter has two goals. First, by describing the political context as well as the substance of the reform efforts, we assess the strengths and limits of innocence reform at the present time. Second, we explore the Innocence Movement and innocence projects as interest groups, assessing how closely innocence projects align with theories of policy making. Although criminal justice studies is inherently a policy field, political scientists mostly eschew the study of criminal justice, and little criminal justice research, including policy research, focuses on policy implementation.[13] Much policy making theory developed by political scientists is oriented toward federal level congressional policy level, and may not precisely fit innocence policy making at state and local levels. Our endeavor is an exploratory step toward the development of a grounded theory and may be helpful as a guide for empirical study of innocence policy making.[14]

## Part I: The Innocence Movement: The Innocence Paradigm

A brief overview of the Innocence Movement and its "innocence paradigm" helps explain our innocence reform analysis. Fortunately, two detailed analyses regarding the movement appear in this edited collection[15] as well as discussions in a recent article[16] and chapter.[17] One answer to how 50 or so innocence projects, most of which are not lavishly funded, have come to have an outsized influence on policy is that the Innocence

9 Larry N. Gerston, Public Policy Making 137 (2004).

10 Hal G. Rainey, Understanding and Managing Public Organizations (1991).

11 John F. Padgett, *Managing Garbage Can Hierarchies*, 25 Admin. Sci. Q. 583 (1980).

12 Katherine R. Kruse, *Instituting Innocence Reform: Wisconsin's New Governance Experiment*, 2006 Wis. L. Rev. 645, 673 (2006).

13 Nancy E. Marion & Willard O. Oliver, The Public Policy of Crime and Criminal Justice 4–5 (2d ed., 2012).

14 Barney G. Glaser & Anselm L. Strauss, The Discovery of Grounded Theory: Strategies for Qualitative Research (1967).

15 See, Keith Findley and Jacqueline McMurtrie, Chapter 1 and Chapter 2, this volume.

16 Zalman, *Justice Model*, *supra* note 6, at 1468–1504.

17 Keith Findley & Larry Golden, *The Innocence Movement, the Innocence Network, and Policy Reform*, *in* Wrongful Conviction and Criminal Justice Reform: Making Justice (M. Zalman & J. Carrano eds., 2014).

Movement is larger than the innocence projects, enjoys support in the information world, and has favorable public support.[18] At least two projects, the Innocence Project[19] and the Center on Wrongful Conviction,[20] are well funded and employ policy staff who work to advance innocence reform. The Innocence Network helps to amplify the policy effectiveness of the projects.

The Innocence Movement was supported at the highest levels when Attorney General Janet Reno in the 1990s fulfilled the policy-process step of *representation* even before a movement was properly underway.[21] Peter Neufeld and Barry Scheck, founders of the original Innocence Project, laid out a comprehensive and understandable reform agenda and popularized the issue,[22] while death penalty abolitionist activism in Illinois gave rise to the Center on Wrongful Convictions.[23]

Several factors help explain the presence of innocence policy reform on the public and governmental agendas. The seemingly simple story of wrongful conviction and the suffering of innocents was compelling.[24] DNA profiling, while not a factor in most exonerations, shook the confidence of criminal justice officials and the public regarding the accuracy of criminal convictions by making the case for innocence with scientific certitude in hundreds of cases.[25] Continuing study of the sources of wrongful convictions confirm that routine processing errors in cases generate wrongful convictions. Research and informed speculation support the view that the problem is significant.[26]

The policy advocacy work of innocence projects is institutionally and methodologically eclectic. They advance policies at the legislative and judicial levels, participate in bar association and government-sponsored innocence commissions, work with forensic scientists and psychologists, and engage in legal scholarship to advance innocence reforms. They work with police agencies to advance the adoption of new procedures.[27] The Innocence Project's policy director, expressing this open-ended strategy, wrote that transforming the justice system's recognized imperfections into good practice touched on the legitimate concerns of each major stakeholder in the justice process.[28]

The elements of innocence reform have been described as the innocence paradigm, a socially constructed list of factors derived from narrative accounts of actual innocence. The list reduces the complexity of actual cases into a comprehensible explanation for miscarriages of justice, and has created the now-familiar innocence reform agenda. Although the paradigm truncates some understanding of the dynamics of how cases go wrong, and avoids possible sources of error or attributes of thoroughgoing reform (e.g., police culture), it is extensive. It includes mistaken eyewitness identification and suggestive identification procedures; false confessions; tunnel vision or cognitive biases of justice system practitioners; errors in forensic analysis caused by "junk science," substandard laboratories, analyst fraud, or improper testimony; weaknesses in police

18 Zalman, *Justice Model*, *supra* note 6, at 1468.

19 Innocence Project, http://www.innocenceproject.org (last visited July 5, 2013).

20 Innocence Network, http://www.innocencenetwork.org (last visited July 5, 2013).

21 James M. Doyle, True Witness: Cops, Courts, Science, and the Battle Against Misidentification (2005); Zalman, *Justice Model*, *supra* note 6, at 1482–3, 1487–90; Charles O. Jones, An Introduction to the Study of Public Policy 54–7 (1984).

22 Zalman, *Justice Model*, *supra* note 6, at 1488–98; Barry Scheck, Peter Neufeld & Jim Dwyer, Actual Innocence: Five Days to Execution, and Other Dispatches from the Wrongly Convicted (2000).

23 Rob Warden, *Illinois Death Penalty Reform: How It Happened, What It Promises*, 95 J. Crim. L. & Criminology 381 (2005).

24 Susan A. Bandes, *Framing Wrongful Convictions*, 2008 Utah L. Rev. 24 (2008); Richard Moran, *The Presence of Malice*, N.Y. Times, Op-Ed., Aug. 2, 2007.

25 Leo, *supra* note 7; Simon A. Cole, *How Much Justice Can Technology Afford? The Impact of DNA Technology on Equal Criminal Justice*, 34 Sci. & Pub. Pol'y 95(2007).

26 Brandon L. Garrett, Convicting the Innocent: Where Criminal Prosecutions Go Wrong (2011); James M. Doyle, *Learning from Error in the American Criminal Justice System*, 100 J. Crim. L. & Criminology 109 (2010); Samuel R. Gross et al., *Exonerations in the United States, 1989 Through 2003*, 95 J. Crim. L. & Criminology 523 (2005); D. Michael Risinger, *Innocents Convicted: An Empirically Justified Factual Wrongful Conviction Rate*, 97 J. Crim. L. & Criminology 761 (2007); Marvin Zalman, *Qualitatively Estimating the Incidence of Wrongful Convictions*, 48 Crim. L. Bull. 221 (2012) [hereinafter *Qualitatively Estimating*].

27 Keith A. Findley et al., Adapting to New Eyewitness Identification Procedures: Leading Experts on Challenging Traditional Processes and Integrating New Techniques (Inside the Minds) (2010).

28 Stephen Saloom, *Adversaries as Allies: Joining Together to Prevent Criminal Injustice*, 73 Alb. L. Rev. 1235 (2010).

investigation; prosecutorial misconduct, often in the guise of not divulging exculpatory information to the defense; ineffective assistance of counsel; inappropriate judicial evidentiary rulings; failures of judges and jurors to discern the truth, and more.[29]

This familiar list is a much written about subject. We make two points regarding the innocence reform paradigm on which we base our critique. First, the paradigm is so extensive that piecemeal reform cannot be expected to produce a measurable reduction of wrongful convictions. Correcting one or two of these problems still allows other factors to generate erroneous convictions. Correcting sources of wrongful convictions in a few jurisdictions within a state will allow errors to occur in other jurisdictions. The American policy process, federalism, the radical fragmentation of local government and criminal justice, and the high level of justice-system politicization make comprehensive reform nearly impossible. Second, it will be virtually impossible to evaluate the effect of innocence reform. Wrongful convictions are invisible when they occur and come to light years or decades later by fortuitous means. As a result, innocence reform proceeds on faith that the reforms enacted and adopted by agencies will reduce miscarriages of justice.

Following our description of a trajectory of innocence reforms, we address whether and how innocence projects fit into existing theoretical concepts of policy making and speculate about adjustments to such theories and models that may better explain the role of innocence projects.

## Part II: A Decade of Change: Three Reforms

The three reforms we describe seem to follow a path of expanding societal acceptance and effectiveness of innocence reform. The Illinois reforms, enacting some recommendations of the Governor's Commission, were the unexpected product of a highly unusual political event. The Innocence Protection Act of 2004, in contrast, was a more typical product of legislative political give-and-take reflecting the rise of innocence on the social and legislative agendas. The Ohio reform package passed in 2010 seems to presage a new turn, in which innocence projects become inside players in enacting favorable legislation which is more readily adopted. A closer examination of these reforms shows that the changes were the products of differing and often contentious political strategies. The fraught politics and contingencies surrounding the reform legislation do not support the confident view that actual innocence is a fixed item on state level policy agendas.

Moreover, a closer look at the resulting policies displays their limits and partial success. Some were watered down or thwarted at the implementation stage; the range of reforms was not comprehensive, leaving other error-producing procedures untouched. In short, the enacted reforms made few demands on the criminal justice or the political systems. We begin with brief overviews.

In April 2002, the Illinois Governor's Commission on Capital Punishment, in a 200-page report, detailed 85 reforms designed to prevent sentencing innocent people to death. The 14-member commission included notables from the legal, police, and business communities, including former United States Senator Paul Simon and author Scott Turow, a former federal prosecutor. The recommended reforms ranged from videotaping a homicide suspect's entire interrogation to allowing post-conviction hearings based on newly discovered evidence of actual innocence.[30]

---

29 Garrett, *supra* note 26; Norris et al., *supra* note 1; Alissa Pollitz Worden, Andrew Lucas Blaize Davies & Elizabeth K. Brown, *A Patchwork of Policies: Justice, Due Process, and Public Defense Across American States*, 74 Alb. L. Rev. 1423 (2011); Zalman, *Justice Model*, *supra* note 6, at 1500–504.

30 Illinois Governor's Commission, *supra* note 5. Many of the recommendations pertained to all types of criminal investigations and prosecutions, not only to capital cases. For example, to paraphrase, recommendations included: police should continue to investigate after a suspect has been identified (Rec. 1); police should record all relevant evidence and turn it over to the prosecutor (Rec. 2); police should assess a suspect's mental capacity before interrogation (Rec. 9); police should conduct double-blind line-ups where possible (Rec. 10); police should inform line-up witnesses that the suspect may not be in the line-up (Rec. 11); if the line-up administration is blind, police should conduct a sequential line-up (Rec. 12); police should construct fair line-ups (Rec. 13); revoke police certification for perjury (Rec. 19); make the state forensics laboratory independent (Rec. 20); establish minimum standards for DNA evidence (Rec. 22); establish judge training on wrongful conviction factors (Rec. 35); establish prosecutor and defense lawyer training regarding wrongful conviction factors (Rec. 45); define exculpatory evidence (Rec. 49); record benefits conferred by prosecutor on witness (Rec. 50); test

Two and a half years later President George W. Bush signed into law the Innocence Protection Act of 2004.[31] The reform measure requires post-conviction DNA testing in federal cases to test innocence claims, requires the government to preserve biological evidence,[32] and encourages states to pass similar laws in order to obtain federal grants "to help defray the costs of post-conviction DNA testing."[33] The Act's second and more controversial reform established state grants to improve "the quality of legal representation provided to indigent defendants in State capital cases."[34] It was passed by offering training grants to prosecutors in states that had established effective indigent capital defense programs.[35] Compensation to wrongly convicted federal prisoners was increased from $5,000 for each year spent in prison to $100,000 for each year a prisoner was "unjustly sentenced to death," and $50,000 a year for other innocent prisoners. A "sense of Congress" encouraged states to "provide reasonable compensation" to exonerated prisoners.[36]

Ohio's governor, Ted Strickland, on April 5, 2010, signed a package of reforms into law designed to prevent wrongful convictions.[37] Senate Bill 77 was touted by a state legislator as "one of the most important pieces of criminal justice legislation in this state in a century."[38] The law enacted four changes that had by 2010 become pillars of innocence reform, and many of which had been adopted or enacted by a growing number of police departments and states. The Ohio law requires preservation of DNA evidence in all serious crimes, and expanded the categories of felons, such as parolees, who are eligible for post-conviction DNA testing. It encourages police to videotape entire interrogation sessions from beginning to end; otherwise resulting confessions are not presumed to be voluntary. It also requires that live and photographic line-ups be conducted in a double-blind fashion, meaning that the officer who oversees the procedure does not know the suspect's identity in a live or photographic line-up.

## Part III: The Politics of Innocence Reform

These reforms were not the isolated products of dispassionate research into the fallibility of the justice system. Each arose from a unique constellation of political events and actors who carved these defense-friendly changes out of a tough-on-crime, pro-prosecution culture. Although different in form, each simultaneously drew on and constructed an innocence movement. Within a decade these three innocence-inspired reforms traveled a trajectory from an extraordinary process filled with unexpected decisions and high drama, to the frustrating and drawn-out give and take of legislative politics over an issue that managed to be highly popular and highly contentious at the same time, to a seemingly more cooperative form of political decision making that occurred in the wake of these earlier battles.

---

the reliability of in-custody informant's testimony (Rec. 52); admit expert testimony regarding eyewitnesses (Rec. 55); create jury instructions regarding eyewitness testimony and cross-racial identification (Rec. 56); create jury instructions regarding reliability of in-custody informants (Rec. 57); establish educational loans, salary, and pension benefits for those entering criminal justice careers (Rec. 81); broaden recommendations to improve the criminal justice system as a whole (Rec. 83); judges should report professional misconduct by defense lawyer and prosecutors (Rec. 85). Few of these recommendations were adopted.

31 Justice for All Act, Public Law 108-405, 108th Cong. Tit. 4 (2004) (enacted); Ronald Weich, *The Innocence Protection Act of 2004: A Small Step Forward and a Framework for Larger Reforms*, 29 Champion 28 (Mar., 2005) (politics behind Act described); Michael E. Kleinert, Note: *Improving the Quality of Justice: The Innocence Protection Act of 2004 Ensures Post-Conviction DNA Testing, Better Legal Representation, and Increased Compensation for the Wrongfully Imprisoned*, 44 Brandeis L. J. 491(2006).

32 18 U.S.C. §§ 3600, 3600A (2010).

33 42 U.S.C. § 14136e (2010).

34 42 U.S.C. § 14163 (2010).

35 42 U.S.C. § 14163a (2010).

36 28 U.S.C. § 2513(e) (2010).

37 S.B. 77, 128th Gen. Assemb., Reg. Sess. (Oh. 2009), enacting Ohio Rev. Code §2933.22 (C) (1) (b) (2).

38 Carey Hoffman, *Innocence Reform Bill Crafted at UC College of Law on Verge of Becoming Ohio Law*, University of Cincinnati (Mar. 16, 2010, 12:00Am), http://www.uc.edu/news/NR.aspx?id=11573.

*Illinois*

The Illinois reform effort was initiated by George Ryan's highly dramatic decision on January 31, 2000 to place a moratorium on executions; this from a pro-death penalty, moderate Republican Governor. By 1999, it was known that Illinois, which executed a dozen inmates since the United States Supreme Court reestablished capital punishment's constitutionality in 1976, had exonerated 13.[39] Anti-death penalty groups, including the forerunner of the Center on Wrongful Conviction, lobbied Ryan to declare a moratorium. When he did, he explained that:

> I cannot support a system, which, in its administration, has proven so fraught with error, ... and has come so close to the ultimate nightmare, the state's taking of innocent life ... . Until I can be sure that everyone sentenced to death in Illinois is truly guilty, until I can be sure with moral certainty that no innocent man or woman is facing a lethal injection, no one will meet that fate.[40]

Ryan's decision was a huge impetus to a growing death penalty moratorium movement in several states.[41] He followed this execution delay by naming and adequately funding the Commission on Capital Punishment. In an even more stunning 2003 decision, shortly before leaving office he pardoned four prisoners and two ex-prisoners on grounds of innocence, and commuted the sentences of all 164 death row inmates to life or long prison terms. He announced this in public speeches before friendly audiences at local law schools. While hailed by many death penalty opponents, these pardons and commutations generated bitter opposition from prosecutors and raised the specter that they were motivated by an attempt to burnish the image of a politician facing an impending indictment for corruption.[42]

The behind-the-scenes lobbying that primed Governor Ryan's moratorium was described in detail by Rob Warden, a key player.[43] The actors in the policy initiative included a small but dedicated Coalition Against the Death Penalty (including the ACLU, Amnesty International, and religious groups); a liberal justice on the Illinois Supreme Court; Warden himself, who as a legal journalist migrated from being a "death penalty agnostic" to a firm opponent as a result of investigating the seamier side of wrongful capital cases; journalism professor David Protess, whose students uncovered wrongful convictions; Northwestern University law professor Larry Marshall, who won exonerations for a number of death row inmates and convened a national conference on wrongful convictions in 1998; and several philanthropic organizations that funded a death penalty reform conference in 1999 at Jenner & Block, a large Chicago law firm. The press played an important part by publicizing exoneration stories and running in-depth series about factors leading to wrongful convictions. The 1999 conference led to a coordinated effort by several organizations, including the Center on Wrongful Conviction,[44] which was created following the 1998 conference, to lobby for a death penalty

39 Gregg v. Georgia, 428 U.S. 153 (1976); Marshall J. Hartman & Stephen L. Richards, *The Illinois Death Penalty: What Went Wrong?* 34 J. Marshall L. Rev. 409 (2001).

40 Dirk Johnson, *Illinois, Citing Faulty Verdicts, Bars Executions*, N.Y. Times, Feb. 1, 2000, at A1.

41 Jeffrey L. Kirchmeier, *Another Place Beyond Here: The Death Penalty Moratorium Movement in the United States*, 73 U. Col. L. Rev. 1, 43 (2002); *see* James S. Liebman, Jeffrey Fagan & Valerie West, A Broken System: Error Rates in Capital Cases 1973–1995 (2000), *available at* http://www2.law.columbia.edu/instructionalservices/liebman/liebman_final.pdf (last visited July 5, 2013).

42 Steve Mills & Christi Parsons, *"The System Has Failed"; Ryan Condemns Injustice, Pardons 6; Paves the Way for Sweeping Clemency*, Chi. Trib., Jan. 11, 2003, at 19; Maurice Possley & Steve Mills, *Clemency for All; Ryan Commutes 164 Death Sentences to Life in Prison without Parole*, Chi. Trib., Jan. 12, 2003, at 1; David A. Wallace, *Dead Men Walking: An Abuse of Executive Clemency Power in Illinois*, 29 U. Dayton L. Rev. 379 (2004); Austin Sarat & Nasser Hussain, *On Lawful Lawlessness: George Ryan, Executive Clemency, and the Rhetoric of Sparing Life*, 56 Stan. L. Rev. 1307 (2004) (reviewing Governor Ryan's 22-page, hour-long explanation for his commutations in the context of the "legally sanctioned lawlessness" in a constitutional democracy and the rule of law, arguing that it is a species in the genus of the "jurisprudence of emergency"). Editorial, *Ryan's Redemption*, Chi. Sun Times, Jan. 31, 2013, p. 14 (Gov. Ryan, after release from prison, praised for his moratorium; will likely engage in death penalty issues).

43 Warden, *supra*, note 23, at 387–404.

44 Northwestern University; Center on Wrongful Conviction, http://www.law.northwestern.edu/wrongfulconvictions/ (last visited Aug. 13, 2013).

moratorium. Warden described in detail how the temper of the times and events influenced the fortunes of the moratorium movement and how Governor Ryan came to support it; in short how an interest-coalition stimulated innocence reform.[45]

*Federal Innocence Protection Act*

The Innocence Protection Act was passed by Congress as part of the Justice for All Act in 2004 and was signed into law by President George W. Bush. It was the product of protracted and less visible legislative infighting typical of most legislation, especially proposals tinged with controversy or ideological baggage. Shortly after Governor Ryan's 2000 death penalty moratorium, Patrick Leahy, Democrat of Vermont and minority leader of the Senate Judiciary Committee, introduced the Innocence Protection Act. It was motivated in part by recommendations of the National Commission on the Future of DNA Evidence, which was convened by Janet Reno, President Clinton's Attorney General.[46] At the time, the more liberal Senator Russ Feingold (D-WI) began pressing for a federal moratorium on executions.[47] A number of additional events in 2000 tilted the climate of opinion against a full-throttled application of the death penalty. A growing number of exonerees, then up to 85, were listed by the Death Penalty Information Center;[48] the popular film *The Hurricane* appeared, starring Denzel Washington, about the exonerated prizefighter Rubin Carter; Governor George W. Bush of Texas issued a rare stay of execution to allow DNA testing; Columbia University released a study finding "that appeals courts overturn two of every three death-penalty convictions, usually because defense lawyers were incompetent"; and a poll showed that support for the death penalty had declined.[49] The bill drew opposition from prosecutors who criticized its provisions as overly broad and guaranteeing "almost unlimited appeals as long as DNA testing is invoked." The most visible opponent was Joshua Marquis, an Astoria, Oregon prosecutor and member of the National District Attorneys Association board.[50] Leahy had not gained broad support in the Senate or from the Clinton Administration for his proposal by mid-2000.[51]

Hearings before the Republican-controlled Senate Judiciary Committee in mid-2000 criticized the lack of minimum attorney standards in death cases and the denial of DNA testing in Texas, the leading execution state. Governor Ryan "attended an early press conference on the Innocence Protection Act and was the star witness at the first House Judiciary Committee hearing on the bill."[52] On the other side of the issue, Oklahoma's Attorney General argued that the reform legislation aimed at improving indigent representation in capital cases could "open endless extensions of the appellate process." Seeking to moderate the initial proposal, committee chair Orrin Hatch (R-Utah) sponsored a narrower proposal.[53] Despite bipartisan support, overall support of the Innocence Protection Act was tepid and it gained little traction. In the crush of end-of-session

45 Warden, *supra* note 23, at 404–9.

46 Patrick J. Leahy, *Commentary; Execution in Error Prices Retribution Too High*, L.A. Times (Home Edition), Mar. 14, 2000; Henry Weinstein, *New DNA Evidence May Absolve Inmate in 1988 Rape Case*, L.A. Times (Home Edition), Feb. 9, 2000 ("House Judiciary Committee chairman, Henry Hyde, praised the bill as a 'very reasonable treatment of a very difficult and delicate issue' and promised a prompt hearing."); *see* National Commission on the Future of DNA Evidence, (Nov. 13, 2007), http://www.nij.gov/topics/forensics/evidence/dna/commission/Pages/recommendation.aspx (last visited Dec. 8, 2013); Editorial, *Bills to Stop Executing the Innocent*, N.Y. Times, Apr. 4, 2000, at A22. (parallel bill sponsored in House of Representatives by Ray LaHood (R-Ill.) and William Delahunt (D-Mass.)).

47 Mary McGrory, *Shock Waves*, Washington Post, Feb. 13, 2000, at B1.

48 Death Penalty Information Center, http://www.deathpenaltyinfo.org/innocence-and-death-penalty (last updated Feb. 11, 2013).

49 Mary McGrory, *supra* note 47; Leahy, *supra* note 46; Editorial, *Science and the Hangman*, St. Louis Post-Dispatch, June 4, 2000, at B2; Richard Willing, *Hatch Plans Bill to Expand DNA Testing on Death Row*, USA Today, June 13, 2000, at 6A; Henry Weinstein, *Support for Executions Declines*, L.A. Times, (Home Edition), Sept. 15, 2000, at A26.

50 Brooke A. Masters, *DNA Testing in Old Cases Is Disputed; Lack of National Policy Raises Fairness Issue*, Wash. Post, Sept. 10, 2000, at A1.

51 Willing, *supra* note 49.

52 Weich, *supra* note 31, at 29.

53 Jim Landers, *Texas Criticized During Death-Penalty Hearing: Senators Consider Attorney Standards, DNA Testing*, Dallas Morning News, June 14, 2000, at A1.

appropriation bills, the bill never got out of committee in 2000, but its supporters vowed to reintroduce it in the next session.[54]

The Innocence Protection Act of 2001 was reintroduced in the Senate with bipartisan support. By March, a third of the House of Representatives were co-sponsors of the House version of the bill.[55] When the Democrats gained narrow control of the Senate midyear, Patrick Leahy became chair of the Judiciary Committee, and his spokesman "expressed amazement … at the momentum the bill has generated."[56] Senator Hatch proposed that the less controversial DNA testing provision be severed and passed separately from more controversial provisions for improving capital defense and establishing a national commission to develop adequate-representation standards. The bill's prospects were strengthened by Justice Sandra Day O'Connor's "remarkable statement" in a speech to women lawyers in Minnesota that "the system may well be allowing some innocent defendants to be executed." This "deliberate signal" that she was "willing to grapple with unfairness and error in the application of the death penalty" in future cases was taken by Senator Leahy as a "frank assessment of these problems [that] will add to the Innocence Protection Act's momentum."[57] Nevertheless, the Judiciary Committee's embroilment in civil liberties issues spilling out of the "war on terror" and persistent prosecutorial opposition again stalled the bill, despite the fact that the number of co-sponsors continued to grow.

The year 2002 proved to be a repeat of 2001. The bill was reintroduced and had apparent momentum as the number of death sentence exonerees reached 100; editorial support continued.[58] Despite strong bipartisan support in the House, the Republican leaders did not bring it to the floor. Prosecutors objected that the bill would "severely limit or halt executions."[59] The National District Attorneys Association raised states' rights objections, claiming that federal standards would undermine local efforts to create rules tailored to local conditions and that mandated DNA testing for post-conviction.[60]

Passage of the Innocence Protection Act in 2003 was given a public relations boost by Governor Ryan's decision to commute all death sentences in Illinois. Nevertheless, prosecutorial opposition remained firm: "Joshua Marquis, co-chairman of the National District Attorneys Association's Capital Litigation Committee, countered that Ryan 'was spitting on the graves of more than 100 murder victims.'"[61] By 2003 both sides of the controversy saw that state juries were imposing far fewer death sentences and that the number of executions fell each year. There was pressure on House Speaker Dennis Hastert (R-Ill.) and Majority leader Tom DeLay (R-Tex.) to bring the House version to the floor, as the Act was "that rare—indeed, nearly extinct—piece of

54 Emily Bazar, *Death-Row Appeals for DNA Testing Stir Debate*, San Diego Union-Tribune, July 31, 2000, at ZS1; Editorial, *2003: The Year in Death*, Wash. Post, Dec. 28, 2003, at B6; *Media Stakeout with Senate Minority Leader Tom Daschle (D-SD)*, Fed. News Service, Sept. 12, 2000; Masters, *supra* note 50; Thomas B. Pfankuch, *DNA Tests Aren't Open to Everyone; Florida Legal System Prohibits Old Cases*, Florida Times-Union, July 31, 2000, at B1; David Stout, *Lawmakers See Hope for Help on Death Cases*, N.Y. Times, Sept. 15, 2000, at A26.

55 Editorial, *Death Penalty Reform*, N.Y. Times, Mar. 12, 2001, at A14.

56 Kevin Freking, *Proposed Innocence Protection Act Gains Momentum in Congress*, Arkansas Democrat-Gazette, June 12, 2001, at A4; Eric Lichtblau, *Death Penalty Reforms Gather New Momentum*, L.A. Times, June 25, 2001, at A1.

57 Editorial, *Justice O'Connor on Executions*, N.Y. Times, July 5, 2001, at A16; Charles Lane, *O'Connor Expresses Death Penalty Doubt; Justice Says Innocent May Be Killed*, Wash. Post, July 4, 2001, at A01; *see* Maria Glod, *Those Who Felt Injustice Call for a Fairer System; Ex-Convicts Testify Before Senate Panel to Support Standards for Lawyers in Capital Cases*, Wash. Post, June 28, 2001, at B2.

58 Editorial, *Pass This Bill*, Wash. Post, July 15, 2002, at A16; Editorial, *Giving Inmates Access to DNA Tests Only Just; Justice Demands that DNA Tests to Confirm Guilt or Establish Innocence Be Provided on Death Row*, San Antonio Express-News, Aug. 19, 2002, at B4; Juliet Eilperin, *Death Row Legislation Gains Support on Hill; Bipartisan Bill Would Ensure Inmates' Access to DNA Evidence, Qualified Lawyers*, Wash. Post, July 22, 2002, at A02; Deirdre Shesgreen, *Bill Would Broaden Access to DNA Testing*, St. Louis Post-Dispatch, June 30, 2002, at B1; Stout, *supra* note 54; Freking, *supra* note 56.

59 Wayne Washington, *217 Back a House DNA Bill in Capital Case, Us to Help Pay for Test*, Boston Globe, Apr. 19, 2002, at A3; Editorial, *The Death Penalty Re-Examined*, N.Y. Times, Feb. 23, 2002, at A14. Prosecutor Joshua Marquis and Sen. Patrick Leahy traded arguments in the press: *see* Joshua Marquis, Commentary, *Myths Aside, Death Row Isn't Filled With Innocents*, L.A. Times, Feb. 26, 2002, at B13; Sen. Patrick Leahy, *Death Penalty Reforms Proposed*, L.A. Times, Mar. 9, 2002, at B21.

60 Shesgreen, *supra* note 58.

61 Henry Weinstein, *Move Will Intensify Debate on Executions*, L.A. Times, Jan. 12, 2003, at A1.

legislation that draws deep support among Republicans and Democrats."[62] The politics of the moment were not entirely clear as a majority of Americans supported capital punishment, but not at the cost of executing innocents. Democratic politicians were still wary of being tarred as soft on crime if they were seen to oppose the death penalty.[63]

A powerful piece of political theater came to the fore when a DNA match was found for the killer of Dawn Hamilton in Maryland. Kirk Bloodsworth, the first DNA death row exoneree, was finally freed from any shadow of doubt of guilt for killing nine-year-old Dawn. As a white, educated, and articulate "poster boy" for the Innocence Protection Act, the ruddy-faced, gravelly-voiced ex-Marine and Eastern Shore waterman with no criminal past, who had become an active voice for reform, had a piece of legislation named for him: the Kirk Bloodsworth Post-Conviction DNA Testing Grant Program. Bloodsworth's experience transformed him into "a really, truly powerful, overwhelmingly persuasive man" with a "remarkable talent," according to former newsman and director of the Center on Wrongful Conviction, Rob Warden. It was no wonder, then, that "politicians crammed the small stage in the US Capitol studio, thanking each other for bipartisan cooperation and taking turns talking about the American people, democracy, and an Eastern Shore waterman named Kirk Bloodsworth."[64] Political theater and the warm glow of an "easy" moralistic issue led to passage of a House bill in November 2003. But the Senate had not yet acted.[65]

The Act was finally signed by President Bush days before the 2004 presidential election, after years of "institutional opposition from federal and state prosecutors as well as skepticism from senior Republican members of the Senate and House Judiciary Committees who, only a few years before, had championed the 1996 limits on *habeas corpus*" designed to speed up executions.[66] The original bill had been watered down in many ways. An entitlement to DNA testing based on the Due Process Clause was dropped, as was the requirement that states had to abide by federal competent-counsel standards in capital cases. Provisions linking the bill to stronger habeas corpus rights for prisoners were dropped. A "state's failure to live up to the bill's requirements would not alter the scope of federal review of its death sentences."[67] As noted before, the right to adequate counsel was replaced by training grant programs for defense and *prosecution* death penalty litigators. After these compromises were worked out by House and Senate leaders, "Majority Leader Tom DeLay insisted on a special rule to protect the 2001 state law under which Texas had begun to reform its own counsel appointment system. And even after the bill overwhelmingly passed the House with President Bush's proposal to expand use of the federal DNA database, the Department of Justice sent a scathing letter of opposition that emboldened Senate opponents led by Jon Kyl [R] of Arizona."[68] After a further concession, and a legislative move in the House that attached the bill "to highly popular victims' rights legislation sponsored by Kyl, … President Bush signed the bill into law … . Were it not for the election, Bush might have vetoed the bill because the Justice Department remained opposed 'to the bitter end.'"[69] These hard-won reforms involved four years of hard bargaining and concessions to law enforcement and prosecutorial interests.[70]

### *Ohio*

The path of reform leading to Ohio's legislative package was not as long or as contentious as that of the Innocence Protection Act. What is most remarkable is the central role played by the Ohio Innocence Project (OIP). The OIP began the effort in 2008 as "a joint project between the Ohio Innocence Project and the *Columbus Dispatch*,

62 Marie Cocco, *Hastert Can Help Cut Death Penalty Errors*, Newsday, Jan. 16, 2003, at A35.

63 David Firestone, *Absolutely, Positively For Capital Punishment*, N.Y. Times, Jan. 19, 2003, Week in Review, at 5.

64 Stephanie Hanes, *New Peace, New Purpose; Crusade: A Cambridge Man, Convicted of Murder and Cleared Nine Years Later by DNA Evidence, Has His Name on Federal Legislation to Extend Such Justice to Others*, Baltimore Sun, Oct. 24, 2003, at A1.

65 Editorial, *2003: The Year in Death*, *supra*, note 54.

66 Weich, *supra* note 31, at 29.

67 *Id.*

68 *Id.*

69 *Id.*

70 *Id.*; Kleinert, *supra* note 31, at 495–7.

which found serious problems in addressing and preventing wrongful convictions."[71] Relying on research by law students and consultants from the original Innocence Project's "national headquarters," the OIP crafted a bill that was introduced in the Ohio legislature in 2008 and 2009 and was enacted in the spring of 2010. The OIP worked closely with members of the Ohio Senate and House and the defense bar and orchestrated support with outside experts and media events.[72] As an indication of the networking that lay behind the legislative success, the OIP website quoted OIP director Mark Godsey as saying that those "who worked diligently to get the bill to this stage are too many to name" but listed 26 by name, including seven legislators and a former state Attorney General.[73] Even more telling was the legislative inclusion of the OIP as a consultant in a "preservation of biological evidence task force" that included representatives of justice system agencies.[74] By the end of the first decade of the twenty-first century, innocence projects had, in some places, become institutional players in innocence-oriented reform measures.

That these reforms went, within a decade, from a highly unusual policy event, to contested but relatively successful federal legislation, to a surefooted advance of an innocence project's goals demonstrates the growing strength of the Innocence Movement. At the core of these reforms lay compelling stories of suffering by innocent people who were wronged by a supposedly near-perfect system designed to do justice. Exoneree Kirk Bloodsworth was a magnet for publicity-addicted Congresspersons wanting to be seen on the right side of an emotional issue. When Governor Strickland signed the Ohio interrogation legislation, which was softened up by a highly visible newspaper campaign, several exonerees were at his side.[75]

Although prosecutors resisted some reform efforts as unnecessary obstructions to proper convictions, most of the commissioners and legislators who examined the issues instead saw necessary changes that would promote a more even-handed justice system. They could rescue innocent prisoners at relatively small costs. By 2010 some police and prosecutors had come to support the reforms. "The phrase you kept hearing from law enforcement from out-of-state was: 'It was the best thing that's ever been shoved down our throats.'"[76]

## Part IV: The Limits of Innocence Policy Reforms

A closer look at these reform efforts, however, shows the limits of these innocence reforms. Although real gains were achieved, not all recommendations were enacted; some legislation was not properly implemented or funded; and, most significantly, these early reforms addressed a small part of the potential changes needed to ensure a safer justice system.

### *Illinois*

The 85 changes proposed by the Illinois Governor's Commission regarding capital prosecutions in 2002 were not enacted wholesale.[77] However careful and realistic the proposals, they would not become policy without passing through the various constraints that face all policy recommendations: inertial, budgetary, legislative,

71 Alana Salzberg, *Press Release: Ohio Passes Major Package of Reforms on Wrongful Convictions; Governor Is Expected to Sign Bill,* Making Ohio a National Model, Innocence Project, (Mar. 16, 2010), http://www.innocenceproject.org/Content/Ohio_Passes_Major_Package_of_Reforms_on_Wrongful_Convictions_Governor_Is_Expected_to_Sign_Bill_Making_Ohio_a_National_Model.php#; *Columbus Dispatch Series: Test of Convictions*, Columbus Dispatch, http://www.dispatch.com/content/topic/special-reports/test-of-convictions-2.html, (last visited Feb. 25, 2012).

72 The OIP collaborated with the YWCA of Greater Cincinnati and the Cincinnati Museum Center to host a program featuring Jennifer Thompson-Cannino and Ronald Cotton, authors of a recent book describing their experiences as a victim who mistakenly picked the wrong man out of a line-up and the exoneree who endured the miscarriage of justice. Jennifer Thompson-Cannino, Ronald Cotton & Erin Torneo, Picking Cotton: Our Memoir of Injustice and Redemption (2009).

73 Hoffman, *supra* note 38.

74 S.B. No. 77, 128th Gen. Assemb., Reg. Sess. (Oh. 2009) amending Ohio Rev. Code §109.561.

75 Jim Siegel, *Ohio's New DNA Law Called Model; Five Men Freed from Prison by Testing See Strickland Sign Bill*, Columbus Dispatch, Apr. 6, 2010.

76 Janice Morse, *Ohio's New Criminal Court Rules Kick In*, Cincinnati Inquirer, June 30, 2010.

77 Thomas P. Sullivan, *Efforts to Improve the Illinois Capital Punishment System: Worth the Cost?* 41 U. Rich. L. Rev. 935 (2007).

organizational, and ideological. Two years after publication, Commission co-chair Thomas Sullivan reported that "many of [its] key recommendations still await legislative action, and very few have been implemented by the Illinois Supreme Court, trial courts, or law enforcement agencies."[78] Those not enacted or implemented by 2004 included reducing the number of aggravating factors that makes a convicted capital defendant eligible for the death penalty; creating a review panel to assess whether death sentences were discriminatory; replacing the state forensic laboratory's police command with civilian control; crafting jury instructions as to the limitations of eyewitness identification; and creating a state Supreme Court rule and database for death penalty proportionality review.[79] The greatest failure was disinterest on the part of the Illinois legislature or Supreme Court to extend reform proposals to non-capital cases, which constitute more than 98 percent of all felony prosecutions.[80]

Some Commission recommendations *were* adopted. Because mistaken eyewitness identification compounded by faulty line-up procedures is the factor most often associated with wrongful convictions, the Illinois legislature moved swiftly to adopt low-cost Commission-advocated reforms: "Witnesses must be told that the suspect may not be in the [line-up] array, that they are not obligated to make an identification, and that they should not assume the administrator knows which person is the suspect. In addition, line-ups and photo-spreads must be photographed or recorded when practicable."[81] The legislature drew the line at mandating more costly and controversial recommendations of double-blind and sequential live and photographic line-ups. Instead, it authorized a pilot program to test them, which led to a curious example of police and prosecutorial obstruction to reform.[82]

Another significant reform, applied to all felony investigations and not just to capital cases, was a discovery rule requiring police to turn over to the prosecution "all investigative material," including materials and information, "that would tend to negate the guilt of the accused."[83] Prosecutors, under constitutional discovery rules, must disclose material exculpatory information to the defense; this remains a contested area, and as of 2004 the state Supreme Court had not promulgated rules to that effect.[84] Other salutary rules were adopted only in regard to capital murder investigations and prosecutions. These included videotaping suspects' entire interrogations and disclosing information that could impeach informants or other witnesses.[85] The Illinois legislature expanded an already liberal law for pre-trial and post-trial DNA testing requests.[86] Some reforms applied to death sentencing rather than to innocence issues, including judicial training and expansion of mitigating factors in capital sentencing to include "emotional or physical abuse or reduced mental capacity." Another significant provision, however, was aimed directly at preventing the execution of an innocent prisoner: prohibiting death sentences "if the only evidence of guilt is uncorroborated testimony of a jailhouse snitch, a single eyewitness, or an accomplice."[87]

A 2007 update by Sullivan was mildly favorable, even though only a few more Commission recommendations were enacted. As a prominent member of the Illinois bar, Sullivan's local reporting offered a reliable assessment on the effect of reforms. He thought that police opinion came to support videotaping

78 Thomas P. Sullivan, *Preventing Wrongful Convictions—A Current Report from Illinois*, 52 Drake L. Rev. 605, 607 (2004).

79 The reforms relating only to the death penalty were rendered moot by that state's recent legislative abolition of capital punishment, a process that allegedly began with the 1998 conference at Northwestern University featuring death row exonerees, *see* Mark Guarino, *Illinois Abolishes Death Penalty, Will Other Midwest States Follow?* Christian Science Monitor, Mar. 11, 2011. As that process began with the political influence of Gov. Ryan, it can be argued that the Governor's Commission was a huge success from the death-penalty abolition perspective, *see* Warden, *supra* note 23.

80 Sullivan, *supra* note 78.

81 *Id.*, at 608 (footnotes omitted); 725 Ill. Comp. Stat. 5/107 A-5(a), (b) (1963).

82 Sullivan, *supra* note 78, at 608–9; Gary L. Wells, *Field Experiments on Eyewitness Identification: Towards a Better Understanding of Pitfalls and Prospects*, 32 L. Hum. Behav. 6 (2008); 725 Ill. Comp. Stat. 5/107A-10 (1963).

83 Sullivan, *supra* note 78, at 610; 725 Ill. Comp. Stat. 5/114-13 (1963); *see* Stanley Z. Fisher, *"Just the Facts, Ma'am": Lying and the Omission of Exculpatory Evidence in Police Reports*, 28 New Eng. L. Rev. 1, 1–4 (1993).

84 Sullivan, *supra* note 78, at 610.

85 *Id.*, at 607, 612–13; 725 Ill. Comp. Stat. 5/103-2.1 (1963); 725 Ill. Comp. Stat. 5/115-21 (1963); 725 Ill. Comp. Stat. 5/115-22 (1963).

86 Sullivan, *supra* note 78, at 613; 725 Ill. Comp. Stat. 5/116-3 (1963).

87 Sullivan, *supra* note 78, at 612–14; 725 Ill. Comp. Stat. 5/9-1(c)(6)(7), (h-5) (1963).

interrogations, as it usually benefits law enforcement, and that videotapes did lead prosecutors to decline prosecution in a few cases. Although the state provided funds for the program, police lobbied for money for other associated costs such as transcribing. Recommended training in the dangers of tunnel vision was "added to the annual refresher courses given to both new police recruits and experienced officers." Reforms to ensure proportionality review of death sentences were not enacted or adopted by the Illinois Supreme Court,[88] but the state's prosecutorial establishment adopted voluntary guidelines to guide discretion. No compliance problems were reported regarding the legislative reforms requiring the police to report exculpatory evidence in all cases and requiring prosecutors to inform the defense about benefits to informers in death penalty cases. Less happily, Sullivan reported no success in persuading a Supreme Court committee to adopt jury pattern instructions based on Commission recommendations regarding eyewitness testimony. Also, backlogs at forensic laboratories were reported, as well as problems in hiring qualified personnel.[89]

*Federal Innocence Protection Act*

The aftermath of the Innocence Protection Act similarly showed a mixed picture of effectiveness, especially in its signature reform—post-conviction access to DNA testing. By 2007 the Justice Department had not spent a penny set aside for DNA testing of potentially innocent prisoners, "while it has used $214 million to collect DNA from convicted criminals and improve crime labs … . Rules imposed by Congress have made it difficult for states to qualify for post-conviction DNA grants … ."[90] In testimony before the House of Representatives Judiciary Committee, Peter Neufeld, co-founder of the original Innocence Project, referred to the actions of the Justice Department "through Executive budgeting and Office of Justice Programs (OJP) implementation" as an "affront to justice."[91] Neufeld went on to explain that the Kirk Bloodsworth Act, Section 412 of the Innocence Protection Act (part of the Justice for All Act), which provided support for states to undertake post-conviction DNA testing, was deliberately sabotaged by the Bush Administration. Section 413 of the Act provided incentives to the states to provide post-conviction DNA testing and to preserve biological evidence. Three other sections supported training, research, and the identification of missing persons. Instead of implementing these sections, "the President created mirror programs … under the 'President's DNA Initiative.'" This initiative was funded without some of the Congressional safeguards. The OJP then created prohibitively stringent guidelines for state applications under the Bloodsworth grant program, for which Congress appropriated $8 million. Three states, Virginia, Connecticut, and Arizona, applied for Bloodsworth funding in 2006, and all three were rejected without any detailed explanation.[92] After this deliberate stonewalling, funds began to flow and a spirit of compliance with the Act emerged under the Obama Administration. A Justice Department official testified in 2009 that the National Institute of Justice "has awarded a total of more than $17.6 million to14 states through [the Kirk Bloodsworth] program."[93]

---

88 People v. Mertz, 842 N.E.2d 618 (Ill. 2005).

89 Sullivan, *supra* note 78.

90 Richard Willing, *Innocence Testing on Back Burner; $8m Targeted for DNA Appeals Gathering Dust*, USA Today, Oct. 11, 2007, at 1A. This information was reported by the National Institute of Justice, which administered the funds.

91 *Reauthorization and Improvements of DNA Initiatives of the Justice for All Act 2004; hearing before S. Comm. on Subcommittee on Crime, Terrorism, and Homeland Security, Comm. on the Judiciary*, 110th Cong. 42-106, (2008) (testimony of Peter Neufeld on behalf of the Innocence Project).

92 Neufeld, *id.*; Willing, *supra* note 90.

93 *Reauthorization of the Innocence Protection Act, Hearing Before the S. Comm. on Crime, Terrorism and Homeland Security, Comm. on the Judiciary*, 111th Cong. 7-20 (2009) (testimony of Lynn Overman, Senior Advisor to the Office of Justice Programs). *Strengthening Our Criminal Justice System: Extending the Innocence Protection Act, hearing before the Senate Judiciary Comm.* 111th Cong. 33 (2009) (testimony of Keith Findley, Professor of Law at University of Wisconsin): "In early 2009, the National Institute of Justice convened a 'Post-Conviction DNA Case Management Symposium' that assembled stakeholders from all perspectives in the criminal justice system from virtually every state to examine the issue. That symposium fostered cooperation among diverse actors in the criminal justice system on issues related to post-conviction DNA preservation and testing. Further, in particular and of special import to the Innocence Network, the spirit of the Bloodsworth Program—to provide funds to enable states to process post-conviction claims of innocence that could be proven by DNA testing—was ultimately respected under the Office of Justice Program's more recent grant funding. As noted, in FY 2008, five states applied for and received Bloodsworth Program funds. In FY 2009, another nine will receive

Another effect of the Innocence Protection Act that appeared to have significant success was in stimulating the states to pass post-conviction DNA testing laws. Such legislation passed in virtually every state by 2009, which seems to have influenced the United States Supreme Court in not establishing a due process right to post-conviction DNA testing.[94] However, on closer inspection, many of the state laws were weakened by a large number of limitations that in practice suppressed the number of inmates with deserving claims from getting DNA testing. Keith Findley, co-director of the Wisconsin Innocence Project and then president of the Innocence Network, testified before Congress and listed many flaws: failing to guarantee the preservation of evidence; failing to provide counsel to process cumbersome and complex petitions; refusing to allow post-conviction testing if it were refused at trial or if the defendant pleaded guilty; limiting DNA testing only to murder or other very serious cases; not allowing appeals from denied petitions; and not authorizing judges to order that DNA tests be compared to national DNA database profiles.[95] The cumulative effect has been to weaken the intent of Congress in providing carrots for the states to enact post-conviction DNA testing laws. Similarly, the states have been slow to follow the "sense of Congress" in adopting laws to provide compensation for wrongly convicted prisoners. Fewer than 20 had such laws prior to the passage of the Innocence Protection Act; as of 2010, 27 states and the District of Columbia passed compensation laws, a figure that had not increased by 2012. While a few are adequate, many skimp on the state's obligation to do justice.[96]

### *Ohio*

If the Illinois reforms caused by Governor Ryan's unexpected moratorium and commutations and the Innocence Protection Act's provisions have had positive but limited results on the ground, is the prospect brighter for the Ohio reform package enacted in 2010? Without taking anything away from the political skill and bridge-building that led to its passage, the Ohio law's four major reforms—preserving DNA evidence, expanding the list of those eligible for DNA testing, encouraging but not mandating the videotaping of entire interrogation sessions, and conducting live and photo line-ups in a double-blind fashion (but only photo line-ups sequentially)—had been touted for more than a decade as important to preventing wrongful convictions. Ohio was far from the first state to enact them, and these procedures had generally won police and prosecutor approval in other jurisdictions that adopted them. They were hedged in with qualifiers and exceptions. Ohio's legislators and governor, and its police and prosecution leaders, did not have to expend much political capital or exercise political courage in passing Senate Bill 77.[97] A larger view of the innocence reform movement is that by 2010 Ohio was joining a number of states reviewing a number of reforms that had already been adopted. In terms of the diffusion-of-innovations research paradigm, Ohio's adoptions of several already popular reforms places it on an S-shaped innovation curve that could contribute to adoption in other states, leading to what in popular parlance is known as a "tipping point," after which most states join the bandwagon.[98]

Looking at the Ohio 2010 reform package in its own terms presents a picture of unbridled success. But this narrow focus obscures the larger number of issues involved in a complete catalogue of innocence reforms. A much larger array of issues, for example, were tackled by the Illinois Governor's Commission,

---

funding. Many Innocence Network members are either direct recipients of or are partners with state agencies that have received Bloodsworth funding."

94 Dist. Attorney's Office for the Third Judicial Dist. v. Osborne, 557 U.S. 52 (2009). By the time of *Osborne* 46 states had "enacted statutes dealing specifically with access to DNA evidence" (Osborne, slip op. 9, 2009). As of February, 13, 2012, 48 states, excepting Massachusetts and Oklahoma, had enacted such laws, Innocence Project, http://www.innocenceproject.org/ (last visited July 5, 2013).

95 Findley, *supra* note 93.

96 Innocence Project, *supra* note 19.

97 The Ohio bill is quite detailed and it enacted a number of beneficial subsidiary reforms, such as providing police training to preserve and catalogue biological evidence, S.B. 77, 128th Gen. Assemb., Reg. Sess. (Oh. 2009), enacting Ohio Rev. Code §2933.22 (C) (1) (b) (2).

98 Everett M. Rogers, Diffusion of Innovations (5th ed., 2003); Jack L. Walker, *The Diffusion of Innovations Among the American States*, 63 Amer. Pol. Sci. Rev. 880 (1966).

but it focused mainly on infrequently occurring capital crimes.[99] Beyond the broad array of issues and processes that constitute the innocence reform agenda, each issue is quite complex and interacts with other reforms and with the justice system in manifold ways. Early implementation of the Innocence Protection Act demonstrated the resistance to, and frustration of, innocence reforms by entrenched ideological forces and institutional players. In short, however promising the reforms enacted in Ohio, Illinois, and by Congress, they are only first steps in ensuring that reforms are enacted elsewhere and that they take hold in practice to actually create justice system practices that are more fair and reliable.

## Part V: Policy Making Theory and the Innocence Movement

Justice-system policy reform was seen as a goal, perhaps the primary goal, of innocence projects from the conception of the movement in the 1990s in the writings and actions of Neufeld and Scheck establishing the Innocence Project, in Attorney General Janet Reno's unbidden promotion of the issue, and in the action that established the Center on Wrongful Conviction.[100] Having reviewed three innocence reform efforts in the first decade of "the age of innocence,"[101] we seek to assess the role of innocence projects and the Innocence Movement in terms of public policy theory.

To over-generalize, the study of interest groups focuses more on the role of groups in getting items on the public agenda, whilst the study of policy models looks more closely at the roles of groups in formulating policies once issues are on the public and governmental agendas. Each reform effort described above was the product of an innocence movement that made enough of an impact on the consciousness of policy makers to confirm that innocence was on the policy agenda. Although more work needs to be done on the rise and expansion of the innocence agenda, we focus here more on the degree to which innocence projects and the movement fits established theories about the roles played by non-government actors in the formulation and legitimation stages of public policy.[102]

Some of the theories developed to explain policy making include the policy elite and iron triangle theories, which are centralized, top-down, structural theories. In contrast, more open-ended structural approaches such as issue networks and advocacy coalitions reflected the rise of participatory democratic politics since the 1960s.[103] We also explore temporal policy making theories, including issue attention cycles and punctuated equilibrium. Finally, we will examine the "garbage can" model or metaphor, as it has been adapted by political scientists. After a thumbnail sketch of each theory we assess their fit to innocence policy making.

### *Policy Elites*

The policy elite theory of policy making suggests that policy making process participation is limited; only a relatively small group of leaders actively participate in policy making. In this view, the power to influence policy is held by a few elite members of Congress. Further, the underlying core values of the insulated elite differ from those of the general public or the "masses," which has only minimal influence over elites who seek to protect their own interests.[104] The idea is most closely associated with C. Wright Mills and Ralph Miliband.[105] They did not view the policy making process as the result of group conflict and/or group involvement, but

99 The narrow range of innocence reforms were noticeable to innocence project members, *see, e.g.*, Robert Carl Schehr, *The Criminal Cases Review Commission as a State Strategic Selection Mechanism*, 42 Amer. Crim. L. Rev. 1289 (2005) (Innocence Protection Act included no mechanism to review miscarriages of justice).

100 Center on Wrongful Conviction, *supra* note 44; *see* Zalman, *Justice Model*, *supra* note 6, at 1487–98; Warden, *supra* note 23.

101 Zalman, *Justice Model*, *supra* note 6, at 1499.

102 Jones, *supra* note 21, at 76–139.

103 David Alan Sklansky, Democracy and the Police: Critical Perspectives of Crime and Law (2008).

104 Dipak K. Gupta, Analyzing Public Policy; Concepts, Tools & Techniques (2d ed., 2001).

105 C. Wright Mills, The Power Elite (1956); Ralph Miliband, *Imperfect Competition*, *in* Public Policy: The Essential Readings 58–66 (Stella Z. Theodoulou & Matthew A. Cahn eds., 1995).

instead as based on the preferences of the power elite who make policy to reflect their minority interests.[106] The policy elite theory had more grip in the consensus era of democratic pluralism from the end of World War II to the 1960s.[107] The rise and expansion of citizen interest groups characterized the sea change in democratic practice and theory toward participatory democracy and deliberative democracy, which "led to large-scale structural changes in the public policy making process."[108]

### *Iron Triangles*

The iron triangle theory assumes that policy decisions are made by a sub-government that seeks to influence policies supporting their particular interest. The three principal actors are congressional committees, interest groups, and bureaucracies.[109] Policies result from the interaction, bargaining, and negotiation among these three groups.[110] Each unit needs the other two in order to achieve its goals, and over time they develop stable and symbiotic relationships.[111] The rise of powerful federal administrative agencies in the New Deal that regularly addressed distributive and regulatory issues that affected tangible business interests in fact generated iron triangles: congressional committees affected policy content through shaping legislation; bureaucracies possessing specialized information were responsible for implementing Congress's policies; and interest groups, possessing knowledge of issues and problems, sought to develop close ties with congressional subcommittees as a way to influence legislation.

The relationship between the actors in an iron triangle is closed to outsiders. As such, the actions of those in iron triangles are uncontrollable by the President or by those legislators who do not serve on the committees involved.[112] The negotiations between the actors are practically invisible, and the policy decisions that result from these relationships are often conducted behind the scenes and with little publicity.[113] Moreover, as these individuals work together, personal ties and friendships develop that only serve to strengthen the relationships and help build an even more powerful iron triangle.[114]

### *Issue Networks*

The issue network theory, positing that a variety of political actors attempt to influence the final output, is more descriptive of much policy making in an era of mass citizen movements and participatory politics.[115] Issue networks involve large numbers of interested parties, each of which has expertise in the policy area. The actors can include members of Congress and their staff, public officials, agency representatives, lobbyists, media, academics, members of the general public, activists, technical or policy experts, and those with intellectual, professional, or emotional interests.[116] The actors are "fluid," meaning they come in and out of

---

106 Stella Z. Theodoulou, *The Nature of Public Policy* in Public Policy: The Essential Readings 1–9 (Stella Z. Theodoulou & Matthew A. Cahn eds., 1995).

107 Sklansky, *supra* note103, at 13–32.

108 Jeffrey M. Berry, *Citizen Groups and the Changing Nature of Interest Group Politics in America*, 528 Annals Am. Acad. Pol. & Soc. Sci. 30 (1993); Sklansky, *supra* note 103, at 59–73.

109 Daniel McCool, *Subgovernments as Determinants of Political Viability*, 105 Polit. Sci. Q. 269 (1990).

110 E. Sam Overman & Don F. Simanton, *Iron Triangles and Issue Networks of Information Policy*, 46 Pub. Admin. Rev. 584 (1986).

111 James Thurber, *Dynamics of Policy Subsystems in American Politics* in Interest Group Politics 323 (Allen Cigler & Burdett Loomis, eds., 3d ed., 1991).

112 Jon W. Kingdon, Agendas, Alternatives, and Public Policies (2d ed., 1995); A. Grant Jordan, *Iron Triangles, Wooly Corporatism and Elastic Nets: Images of the Policy Process*, 1 J. Pub. Pol'y 95 (1981).

113 Randall B. Ripley & Grace A. Franklin, Congress, the Bureaucracy, and Public Policy (3d ed., 1984).

114 Stella Z. Theodoulou & Chris Kofinis, The Art of the Game (2004).

115 George J. Gordon, Administration in America (4th ed., 1992); Berry, *supra* note 108.

116 Carl E. Van Horn, Donald C. Baumer & William T. Gormley, Jr., Politics and Public Policy (3d ed., 2001); Hugh Heclo, *Issue Networks and the Executive Establishment*, reprinted in Public Administration: Concepts and Cases 408–17 (Richard J. Stillman II, ed., 4th ed., 1988).

the process depending on the issues, or may even join in or drop out as the issue develops.[117] This means that the participants vary over time, making it difficult to identify those involved. Nonetheless, the experts come together for debate and are likely to possess considerable influence over new policy that results.[118] Once the issue is resolved, the network dissolves.[119]

*Advocacy Coalitions*

Within a policy subsystem, there are people who share particular beliefs about a particular subject and can be grouped into coalitions.[120] These groups of individuals, called advocacy coalitions, share basic values, perceptions, and assumptions of problems as well as the causes and solutions to those problems. They come from many backgrounds, including elected officials, agency officials, interest group leaders, and academics.[121] They cooperate with each other to further their policy goals.[122]

The advocacy coalition framework has four basic premises. First, the time frame for policy change requires a decade or more. Second, policy change is the result of a policy subsystem that allows actors from different institutions to interact and attempt to influence policy decisions in a particular policy area. Third, the subsystems include a dimension of intergovernmental cooperation. Fourth, public policies reflect a particular set of values.[123]

*Issue Attention Cycles*

The first temporal theory of policy change we consider is the issue attention cycle. The cycle begins when a problem becomes the subject of public concern, which generates a response from government officials. This is then followed by estimates about the potential costs or other consequences of policy action, after which there is declining public interest. At this point, the media and the public grabs onto a new issue, repeating the cycle.[124] In Downs's view, public policy making results from periods where specific issues momentarily capture the public's attention, resulting in demands for government action followed by a waning of the issue.[125] This model of policy making helps us understand why certain issues dominate the attention of policy makers for a short time and then fall from attention just as quickly.[126]

The issue attention cycle has five stages. First is the pre-problem stage during which an undesirable social condition exists but because it does not receive any public attention, is not the focus of any policy action. The second stage is "alarmed discovery and euphoric enthusiasm." Here, an event or new information creates public awareness of the problem. If the event is shocking or extreme enough, the attention of the nation could be focused on the problem, and demands for government action are made. The third stage is the realization of the extent of the costs and possible consequences of the proposed changes, and the demand for action diminishes. This leads to the fourth stage, where there is a gradual decline in the intensity of the public's interest in that problem. As more and more people understand how difficult it may be to solve the problem,

---

117 Hugh Heclo, *Issue Networks and the Executive Establishment*, *in* The New American Political System 87–124 (Anthony King, ed., 1978). Van Horn et al., *supra*; Robert A. Heineman et al., The World of the Policy Analyst (3d ed., 2002).

118 Heclo, *supra* note 116.

119 Overman & Simanton, *supra* note 110.

120 Paul A. Sabatier & Hank Jenkins-Smith, *The Advocacy Coalition Framework: An Assessment*, in Theories of the Policy Process 117–66 (Paul A. Sabatier, ed., 1999).

121 Larry B. Hill, *Who Governs the American Administrative State? A Bureaucratic-Centered Image of Governance*, 1 J. Pub. Admin. Res. & Theory 261 (1991).

122 James E. Anderson, Public Policymaking (5th ed., 2003); Paul A. Sabatier, *Knowledge, Policy Oriented Learning, and Policy Change: An Advocacy Coalition Framework*, in 1 Knowledge: Creation, Diffusion, Utilization 649 (1987).

123 Hank C. Jenkins-Smith & Paul A. *Sabatier, Evaluating the Advocacy Coalition Framework*, 14 J. Pub. Pol'y 175 (1994).

124 B. Guy Peters, American Public Policy (4th ed., 1996).

125 Anthony Downs, Up and Down with Ecology—the "Issue Attention Cycle", 28 Pub. Interest 38 (1972).

126 Theodoulou & Kofinis, *supra* note 114.

they will become discouraged or even bored. In the fifth stage, or the "post-problem" stage, the issue receives less attention by the public, the media, and the policy makers.[127]

*Punctuated Equilibrium*

Another temporal theory of decision making, developed by Baumgartner and Jones, argues that during certain time periods there are more policy decisions made than during other times.[128] The punctuated equilibrium theory describes how policy making has periods of stability, or equilibrium, in which there is little change. However, these periods are sometimes interrupted when a particular issue becomes the focus of attention and is redefined in some significant way. These periods can result from new information, an event, or changes in the political or social environment.[129] The opportunity for policy change exists only for a short time,[130] but during that time, new solutions are created and rapid change may result.[131] This theory can help explain how problems are identified, how issues develop, and how the agenda is set. It also helps to explain why dramatic changes occur.[132]

*The Garbage Can Model*

The garbage can model or metaphor of decision making, developed by Cohen, March, and Olsen has two main parts.[133] First, because agencies operate under conditions of continuing ambiguity, they sometimes behave in ways that contradict current assumptions about organizational choice. And second, because of that ambiguity, they often act unpredictably. Under this theory, policy making is chaotic. They posit that an organization is a loose collection of ideas rather than a coherent structure. Problems are defined and solutions developed by those involved, who may change from one meeting to the next as different people choose to attend or not attend. Participation in decision making is ambiguous, uncertain, and changes rapidly as people leave the organization or are newly hired. Those involved are sometimes inattentive or non-participatory because other issues preoccupy them. Different units and personnel tend to have only loose communication with the others, and it is not clear who has the power to make choices. Thus, relevant problems and potential solutions appear and disappear as other conditions change.[134]

Cohen et al. state that policy choices are made when various problems and solutions are dumped into a "garbage can" by those who participate in the process. Therefore, policy choices are a product of a mix of "garbage" in a "can" (which include problems, solutions, participants, and the participants' resources) and how it is processed. Like a garbage can, decision making has a vast array of material thrown into it in a disorderly fashion. A final decision is made only when all of the elements coincide at the right time, sometimes more by coincidence than from rational actions.[135] Kingdon applied this model to government, asserting that the seemingly disorganized model of decision making in certain kinds of organizations "looks a lot like the federal government."[136] In some cases, important problems can be ignored completely because there seems to be no viable solution.[137]

---

127 *Id.*

128 Frank R. Baumgartner & Bryan D. Jones, Agendas and Instability in American Politics (2d ed., 2009); *see* Peters, *supra* note 124.

129 Christine Parsons & Brian Fidler, *A New Theory of Educational Change: Punctuated Equilibrium: The Case of the Internationalization of Higher Education Institutions*, 53 Bri. J. Educ. Stud. 447 (2005).

130 Kingdon, *supra* note 112.

131 Michael R. Mills, *Stories of Politics and Policy: Florida's Higher Education Governance Reorganization*, 78 J. Higher Educ. 162 (2007).

132 Theodoulou & Kofinis, *supra* note 114.

133 Michael D. Cohen, James G. March & Johan P. Olsen, *A Garbage Can Model of Organizational Choice*, 17 Admin. Sci. Q. 1 (1972); J.G. March & J.P. Olsen, Ambiguity and Choice in Organizations (1976); Johan P. Olsen, *Garbage Cans, New Institutionalism, and the Study of Politics*, 95 Am. Pol. Sci. R. 191 (2001).

134 Rainey, *supra* note 10.

135 Cohen, March & Olsen, *supra* note 133; Rainey, *supra* note 10.

136 Kingdon, *supra* note 112.

137 *Id.*

**Part VI: Assessment of Policy Making Theories and the Innocence Movement**

How well does the Innocence Movement, and more specifically innocence projects and the Innocence Network, fit existing policy making theories and models? An answer should be based on knowing the structure, composition, size, goals, and activities of the projects, including the levels of government to which the movement addresses its concerns. The general sketch of the Innocence Movement described above, the limited data from the three reform efforts, along with general background knowledge suggests that innocence projects and the movement reflect some aspects of established theories but do not entirely fit within any.

What is the general nature of the movement's policy goals? The Innocence Movement has elements of a social movement in its concern for a social justice issue rather than a bread-and-butter distributive policy. Since the 1960s a significantly increased number of citizens' groups have "broadened representation" in politics, leading to a "break down in sub-governments and [leading] to the rise of issue networks."[138] Nevertheless, the Innocence Movement is not a broad-based or mass citizens' movement. Although its goals may be shared by the broad public, the movement itself is quite small, with a core of about 50 innocence projects, of which only two appear to be reasonably well funded and staffed with policy and research professionals. The typical innocence project's main activity is to evaluate and investigate cases of prisoners claiming actual innocence and to litigate for those believed to be worthy of exoneration. The two best-supported innocence projects and the only two which accept cases from the entire nation, the Innocence Project and the Center on Wrongful Conviction, strongly emphasize innocence reform along the lines of the innocence paradigm, described above. The prime goal of the movement as a whole may indeed be criminal justice system reform (even if some of its members do not agree), because if the incidence of wrongful convictions each year numbers in the thousands, there will never be a sufficient number of extraordinary post-conviction exoneration cases to stem the tide.[139]

How salient is the issue of innocence reform to the public? Despite one public opinion survey indicating general familiarity with and a favorable attitude toward innocence reform,[140] general awareness of major economic issues and the kinds of social issues that erupt during American political campaigns—or even compared to major criminal justice policies like the size of prison populations, violent crime, domestic violence, and the like—suggests that wrongful conviction is a small issue to most of the public. It is so remote from the tangible or likely direct concerns of most Americans as to not ever generate a mass citizen movement. In contrast, the kinds of issues that have been the subject of the issue network and advocacy coalition theories affect the lives of millions or even all Americans. The environmental movement, for example, generated hundreds of organizations.[141] Thus, the core Innocence Movement organization is not likely to spread far beyond law school innocence clinics. It is worth mentioning, though, that the problem faced by thousands of innocent prisoners, however real, are not likely to give rise to any alternate means of redress other than the Innocence Movement. Innocent prisoners are so cloaked with the mantle of guilt and so powerlessness as to be unable themselves to effectively organize to redress the criminal justice system problems that lead to wrongful convictions in the first place. This underlying realization surely motivates innocence project lawyers to continue their efforts.

To which level of government does the Innocence Movement address its attention? The policy elite and iron triangle theories have been developed mostly with national-level policy made by Congress, federal agencies, and lobbyists concerned with tangible, distributive policies, although sub-government approaches have been evaluated at the level of the state legislature.[142] Innocence projects, however, seek to influence policy at any level. Two of our three examples in this chapter focus on state law making and one at the level of Congress. It does not appear that the Innocence Movement will become a regular player with a lobby in Washington—it simply does not have the kind of distributive ("big-money") interest or the widespread symbolic interest to

138 Berry, *supra* note 108.

139 Zalman, *Qualitatively Estimating*, *supra* note 26.

140 Zalman, Larson & Smith, *supra* note 4.

141 Baumgartner & Jones, *supra* note 128, at 184–9.

142 Kingdon, *supra* note 112; Theodore J. Lowi, *American Business, Public Policy, Case-Studies, and Political Theory*, 16 World Politics 677 (1965); Keith Hamm, *The Role of "Subgovernments" in U.S. State Policy Making: an Exploratory Analysis*, 11 Legis. Stud. Q. 321(1986).

support and sustain that kind of attention. Moreover, the Innocence Movement is promiscuous and innovative in pursuing any and all means of promoting the innocence paradigm. The Innocence Network, for example, has filed an amicus curiae brief before the United States Supreme Court,[143] and an innocence movement leader has partnered with local law enforcement and prosecutors to produce practical training materials.[144] Our background knowledge of the Innocence Movement suggests that such examples can be multiplied.

One difficulty of determining the fit of the Innocence Movement in existing policy theories has to do with the movement's organizational composition. Like the hard-to-classify platypus (*Ornithorhynchus anatinus*), which forced naturalists to reconsider biological classifications, the Innocence Movement has unusual features. It is not a mass movement, although it courts mass support with undeniably emotional appeals to the pathos of wrongful conviction. The key players are law professors, by definition a respected intellectual elite having entrée to the halls of legislative, judicial, and government-agency power, and the skills to operate effectively once they have the attention of policy makers. They have assiduously mobilized the means of modern communications to amplify their cause. By garnering support from a few state high court chief justices (e.g., I. Beverly Lake, NC; Jonathan Lippman, NY), and co-opting a few big-city chief prosecutors who have adopted conviction integrity units (Craig Watkins, Dallas Co., Texas; Cyrus Vance, New York Co. NY; Anita Alvarez, Cook Co., Ill.) the movement amplifies its message.[145] With a growing number of changes at the levels of state legislation, state court rulings, and agency action regarding videotaping confessions, conducting double-blind line-ups and the like in a growing number of jurisdictions, the large, powerful, and semi-inertial criminal justice system is beginning to bend to the arc of innocence reform. Indeed, for innocence reform to ever succeed, as one astute observer has noted, its message and agenda must be "embraced by the law enforcement community, prosecutors, and concerned politicians" requiring that the Innocence Movement adopt a policy of "cooperation with criminal justice stakeholders and lawmakers."[146]

With this background, we more closely examine the ways in which innocence projects fit the structural theories. Two earlier studies described criminal justice politics and system structures in Illinois and Chicago that provide an interesting backdrop to the Illinois innocence reforms.[147] An examination of Illinois criminal legislative activity in 1967 demonstrated that there was no major criminal justice lobby, but that a number of principal groups regularly interacted and provided a criminal law power elite: a small, mostly pro-prosecution, process-oriented, close-knit group of white men representing five organizations that were regular players in crime legislation.[148] Most were lawyers who graduated from a local law school. Writing just as the nation was embroiled in the turmoil of the late 1960s, Heinz markedly noted the exclusion of blacks, women, and defense-oriented lawyers from the criminal law deliberations.[149] This is evidence that the power elite theory accurately described policy making in the era of democratic pluralism.

Two decades later communications in the network of functioning justice agencies and personnel in Chicago had no central players—it was a network with "a sizable hole in the middle," implying that players had highly specialized roles with "little concern about the operation of the system as a whole."[150] The lack of central control actors may have reflected a point in Chicago politics when power was diffuse rather than

143 Brief for The National Innocence Network as Amici Curiae Supporting Petitioner, Melendez-Diaz v. Massachusetts, 129 S. Ct. 2527 (2009) No. 07-591.

144 Findley et al., *supra* note 27.

145 Christine C. Mumma, *The North Carolina Actual Innocence Commission: Uncommon Perspectives Joined by a Common Cause*, 52 Drake L. Rev. 647 (2004); Cyrus R. Vance, Jr., *A Conviction Integrity Initiative*, 73 Alb. L. Rev.1213 (2010); Jason Meisner, *Wrongful Convictions Spur State's Attorney Anita Alvarez to Form Review Unit for Controversial Prosecutions*, Chi. Trib., Feb. 3, 2012, at 4C; John Eligon, *State's Top Judge Seeks to Curb Wrongful Convictions*, N.Y. Times, Feb. 15, 2012, at A21.

146 James R. Acker, *The Innocence Commission: Preventing Wrongful Convictions and Restoring the Criminal Justice System, by Jon Gould*, 30 Just. Sys. J. 114, 117 (2009) (book review).

147 John P. Heinz, Robert W. Gettleman & Morris A. Seeskin, *Legislative Politics and the Criminal Law*, 64 Nw. U. L. Rev. 277 (1969); John P. Heinz & Peter M. Manikas, *Networks Among Elites in a Local Criminal Justice System*, 26 L. & Soc. Rev. 831 (1992).

148 Heinz, Gettleman & Seeskin, *supra*, at 334–43.

149 *Id.*

150 Heinz & Manikas, *supra* note 147, at 853.

centralized.[151] What we detect in the Illinois innocence reforms in the early 2000s is a more porous process. An advocacy coalition of like-minded people came together in Illinois in the late 1990s to press for action against the death penalty. These death penalty abolitionists, as well as the innocence project in Ohio, were the opposite of an establishment. The fact of a dozen Illinois capital exonerations gave this coalition a window of opportunity to make an appeal to Governor Ryan. The appeal worked, perhaps in part because of idiosyncratic and fortuitous circumstances. To this point, elements of the advocacy coalition theory and issue attention cycle theory can be discerned. It may be that the 14-member Governor's Commission reflected a policy elite, but it was an elite that included three defense lawyers (one private attorney, the Cook County Public Defender, and the Illinois State Appellate Defender) and one public member who immigrated to the United States with his widowed mother and eight siblings, and ultimately founded "one of the fastest-growing Hispanic owned companies" in the country.[152] And whilst the Illinois abolitionists of the 1990s were outside any establishment, the Center on Wrongful Conviction has become a regular presence in promoting innocence reform in Illinois and nationally.

Thus, policy elite and iron triangle theories have little place in innocence reform, especially in the classic forms of power residing in small groups closed to the public or in the congressional committee/interest group/ bureaucracy triangle. Nevertheless, all interest groups seek influence, and a sure path to influence is to become an inside player. Evidence of this regarding innocence reform is the move by the Ohio Innocence Project to be included by legislation in an ongoing task force regarding the preservation of biological evidence. Thus, beyond helping to write the legislation, the OIP secured an inside position to ensure compliance with the law.

As for the Innocence Protection Act, many people were involved—including innocence advocates, a former prosecutor, a wrongly convicted man, the ACLU, Senator Orrin Hatch, Supreme Court Justice Sandra Day O'Connor signaling concern—and the sponsorship of over 200 Representatives as well as House Speaker Dennis Hastert and Majority Leader Tom DeLay.[153] This was a far cry from the day of autocratic House and Senate committee chairmen. Also, while legislatures often pass criminal and criminal justice legislation, there is nothing like a single criminal justice regulatory agency sitting in the capital that deals with a steady stream of justice issues. Also, criminal justice bureaucracies are functional law enforcement or correctional agencies; while some may have a large lobbying presence in state legislatures, they probably defer to member organizations like police chiefs', prosecutors', and police or correctional officers' unions to be in touch with legislators. In the three reforms described herein, since there were not small groups of elites responsible for the changes, elite structural theories seem not to apply to the innocence reform movement.

Evidence from the three innocence reforms showed the existence of innocence issue networks and advocacy coalitions, but with some differences from the existing models. Innocence projects must continually form alliances with interested groups to advance one of the several items on the innocence agenda: death penalty reform in Illinois, access to DNA testing at the federal level, and DNA and eyewitness identification in Ohio. In Illinois the Governor's Commission encompassed a broad spectrum of the legal community, police, and business communities.[154] The campaign for the Innocence Protection Act attracted diverse legislators, including Patrick Leahy (D-VT), Senate Judiciary Chairman Orrin Hatch (R-UT), Sen. Arlen Specter (R-PA), House Judiciary chairman F. James Sensenbrenner (R-WI), and Rep. William Delahunt (D-MA). These groups and coalitions were generated by the dynamics of legislative politics and the politics of government commissions. Only in the case of the Ohio reforms was an innocence project seen to be an actor not only at the agenda setting and the policy formulation stages but in implementation as well.

A key attribute of issue networks is that they are temporary. Although we cannot prognosticate the future, the large number of innocence issues posed by the innocence paradigm (which sets the innocence public policy agenda), combined with the size and fragmentation of the American criminal justice system, means that there will be no quick solution to the wrongful conviction problem. Also, the Innocence Movement appears to be stable. Thus, we suggest that the innocence projects and the Innocence Network will not be temporary, but

151 *Id.*

152 Illinois Governor's Commission, *supra* note 5.

153 Margery Malkin Koosed, *The Proposed Innocence Protection Act Won't—Unless It Also Curbs Mistaken Eyewitness Identification*, 63 Ohio State L. J. 263 (2002).

154 Illinois Governor's Commission, *supra* note 5.

will continue to advocate for innocence reform for decades. Its actions will likely involve ongoing temporary campaigns in a number of jurisdictions like those seen in Ohio to generate reforms in a partially opportunistic way. Issue network theory may have to be reconfigured to help explain innocence reform activity. Thus, while particular issue networks will dissolve when a particular reform is adopted, the Innocence Network can be expected to continue to seek reform opportunities.

It is conceivable that something like an innocence advocacy coalition is being formed that helps to explain policy changes regarding the Innocence Movement. The innocence legislation discussed herein involved many interested individuals who sought to protect innocent individuals and to improve the quality of legal representation in a tough-on-crime environment. The involvement of non-members of innocence projects may have been based on their personal values and revulsion at the existence of wrongful convictions, which is a resource that can be exploited by the Innocence Movement. They received nothing in return for their actions, but instead recognized the need for change that would promote a more just system. For example, the proposed federal changes were needed, according to those involved, because the risk of executing an innocent person "shocks the conscience and offends social standards of fairness and decency."[155] As the "age of innocence" enters its second decade, then, and as the movement to protect innocent defendants continues and appears to be growing in strength if not experiencing the explosive growth of the 2000s, it may be seen to reflect many elements of advocacy coalition theory.

The problem with applying temporal policy theories to the Innocence Movement is that the movement did not exist in 1990. By 2000 a good deal of eyewitness identification research provided the foundation for line-up reform, but only a handful of innocence projects had been created. The publication of *Actual Innocence* in 2000 helped put the idea of wrongful conviction on the map, and the imagery of DNA exonerations was so powerful that innocence reforms gripped the imagination of many law professors who initiated more innocence projects. It soon led Sen. Patrick Leahy to propose the Innocence Protection Act. The decade of the 2000s saw the growth of the Innocence Movement, as seen in the three reforms described in this chapter. Whilst we think that advocacy coalition theory holds promise as an explanatory framework for innocence policy reform, it is too early to tell whether the trajectory of the Innocence Movement fits the issue attention cycle theory. In some ways it does not fit: there was no single shocking event that put the issue on the forefront of the public's agenda; nor, when compared to other issues, does it have a huge media presence. Again, when compared to many other public issues the Innocence Movement has not been the focus of intense public pressure on government officials to act or create change. Oddly enough, some innocence reform has happened "behind the scenes," so to speak, without much public outcry or media focus. Overall, the idea of an issue attention cycle does not clarify the policy process with regard to the innocence reform legislation.

Nor does the theory of punctuated equilibrium provide an explanation for the changes in laws we describe.[156] As innocence reform is a new policy issue, one decade of action is hardly enough time to assess whether it will be an issue over a span of decades, with periods of stability followed by periods when innocence becomes the focus of attention and is redefined in some significant way. It seems to us that in the past few years the Innocence Movement is continuing to be active to advance the innocence paradigm where it can, without any lulls in its activity. It continues to be on the agenda even after new policies are made. This contradicts the sudden changes that would be expected under the theory of punctuated equilibrium. There was no single event or change in the political environment that resulted in attention to innocence reform, and the change was not made quickly.

We have reserved the garbage can model for final consideration.[157] An important part of this model for the Innocence Movement is that a problem may be excluded from the public agenda because of the lack of a possible solution. If an agency or government official states publicly that it plans to solve a problem and then is unable to do so, they may be labeled as a failure and risk losing the public's confidence. That means officials may put issues on the agenda only if they already have a viable solution.[158] This may help explain why innocence reform has, despite real gains, not achieved a tipping point in any of its reform items and is not

155 Koosed, *supra* note 153.

156 *See supra* notes 128-32.

157 *See supra* notes 133-7.

158 Peters, *supra* note 124.

on the policy or action agendas in most states or in most police and prosecution agencies. Perhaps legislators and agency heads, even if they recognize the wrongful conviction problem, do not have confidence in the solutions put forward by the Innocence Movement. This problem is compounded when many legislators are elected to two-year terms and do not have time to do the research and legislative work needed to raise the problem to the action stage. The problem is made worse in states with term-limited legislatures. The hard legislative battles and compromises leading to the Innocence Protection Act provide evidence consistent with this "garbage can" finding.

This model, however, helps explain the quality of the innocence reform process that has occurred, including the many groups that were involved and the changing membership as reform efforts spread over many jurisdictions. The leadership of the innocence projects and the Innocence Network has not changed much, but it has only been in existence for a decade. The movement seems to be both loosely coupled (50+ projects; a changing array of policy initiatives) and tightly coupled (the main actors among the innocence projects seem to have been stable and cohesive). Paradoxically then, the Innocence Movement allows for a changing cast of many people (legislators, courts, agency personnel) to have an opportunity to influence policies, although at the same time the prime movers of reform, innocence project lawyers, have apparently not changed substantially in composition in the first decade of the Innocence Movement's policy presence. The politics surrounding the Illinois reforms were highly unusual and would be difficult to replicate. The passage of the Innocence Protection Act suggests that most innocence reform legislation will be met by opposition supported mostly by prosecutors. And the Ohio reforms suggest that even relatively easy reforms require a great deal of skillful legislative work. This suggests that the kinds of analysis conducted by political scientists inspired by the garbage can model may be useful in assessing innocence policy reform.[159]

## Part VII: Conclusion

This chapter is a preliminary exploration of the policy work of the Innocence Movement in light of existing policy making theories. As the data relied on primarily are available printed material, this chapter can only be suggestive of what may be found if the Innocence Movement were studied by interview methods that have been productive in explaining public policy.[160]

We have suggested that elements may be borrowed from existing theories to explain innocence reform, in part because the Innocence Movement has unusual structural features compared to more typical social-issue movements. As Berry writes, "No one argues that there are only issue networks or only sub-governments active in policy making. Rather, the argument is over what is most typical and most descriptive of the policy process. Which should serve as our framework for analyzing how laws and regulations are made?"[161] It is difficult to say that one theory helps us to understand policy change in every policy arena. It could be that different theories operate better in different situations. Such a research project may not appeal to political scientists who seek grand theories. On the other hand, criminal justice scholars and social scientists for whom middle-level theorizing may generate satisfying explanations of diverse behaviors and results could seek to generate a theory of innocence reform grounded in data peculiar to that policy arena but informed by alternate theories of policy making.[162]

159 Kingdon, *supra* note 112.
160 Heinz, Gettleman & Seeskin, *supra* note 147; Heinz & Manikas, *supra* note 147; Kingdon, *supra* note 112.
161 Jeffrey M. Berry, The Interest Group Society (2d ed.) (1989).
162 Glaser & Strauss, *supra* note 14.

# Chapter 11
# Innocence Commissions in America: Ten Years After

Sarah Lucy Cooper[1]

## Introduction

The year 2002 was a landmark year in the Innocence Movement in America. Twenty-five men were exonerated that year, making it one of the most active years for post-conviction DNA exonerations to the date of this chapter.[2] In April 2002, Ray Milton Krone was the one-hundredth person to be exonerated by post-conviction DNA evidence in America, after spending over a decade in prison, including four years on death row, for a murder he did not commit.[3] Krone quickly became the poster-boy for the failings of the American criminal justice system and the media became hungry to expose them.[4]

Later, in October, 2002, Barry Scheck and Peter Neufeld, the godfathers of the Innocence Project, wrote an article —*Toward the Formation of "Innocence Commissions" in America*—questioning why the American criminal justice system "has no institutional mechanism to evaluate its equivalent of a catastrophic plane crash, the conviction of an innocent person."[5] Scheck and Neufeld argued for the creation of state and federal innocence commissions to address the institutional problems that contribute to wrongful convictions[6] by

---

1 I would like to thank Professor Christine Mumma, Professor Jon Gould, Professor Daniel Blinka, and Mr. Drew Edmondson for taking the time to share with me their fascinating experiences of leading and/or working with American innocence commissions. The conversations we had proved pivotal to the design and content of this chapter. I would also like to thank Professors Gould and Blinka, Professor Lissa Griffin, and the scholars at the University of Liverpool's 2013 International Postgraduate Conference for providing feedback on an earlier draft. Finally, I must give special thanks to my colleague, Lauren Haddock, who helped me organize the resources needed to develop this chapter, and my Graduate Research Assistants, Daniel Gough LLB, LLM, and Amna Nazir, whose intellectual and editorial instincts are enviably sharp.

2 *Case Profiles*, Innocence Project, http://www.innocenceproject.org/know/Browse-Profiles.php (last visited Mar. 3, 2013).

3 *Ray Krone Profile*, Innocence Project, http://www.innocenceproject.org/Content/Ray_Krone.php (last visited Mar. 3, 2013).

4 Bill Kurtis, *Clarence Darrow Keynote Address, Symposium Protecting a National Moral Consensus: Challenges in the Application of* Atkins v. Virginia, *Seventeenth Annual DePaul Law Review Symposium*, 57 DePaul L. Rev. 643, 646 (2008).

5 *See* Barry C. Scheck & Peter J. Neufeld, *Toward to the Formation of Innocence Commissions in America*, 86 Judicature, 98, 98 (2002) ("In the United States there are strict and immediate investigative measures taken when an airplane falls from the sky, a plane's fuel tank explodes on a runway, or a train derails. Serious inquiries are swiftly made by the National Transportation Safety Board (NTSB), an agency with subpoena power, great expertise, and real independence to answer the important and obvious questions: What went wrong? Was it system error or an individual's mistake? Was there any official misconduct? And, most important of all, what can be done to correct the problem and prevent it from happening again? … The American criminal justice system, in sharp contrast, has no institutional mechanism to evaluate its equivalent of a catastrophic plane crash, the conviction of an innocent person.").

6 There is a substantial debate surrounding the definition of "wrongful convictions" and "innocence." See Keith A. Findley, *Defining Innocence*, 74 Alb. L. Rev. 1157, 1158, 1159, 1160 (2011) ("The debate about the definition of 'innocence' largely treats the question as identical for both policy and case litigation purposes, subsuming both under a general category of 'wrongful conviction.' Typically, the definition runs something like, 'the innocence movement focuses on wrongful convictions in the factual sense, where the wrong person is convicted for a crime, or is convicted for a crime that did not occur.' While such a definition is appropriate and accepted, it is deceptively oversimplified. It masks the reality that deciding who counts as 'the wrong person' can be difficult and unclear, and that there are multiple standards for determining innocence that are context dependent. Some scholars break 'innocence' into several separately defined categories. Margaret Raymond, for example, identifies what she calls 'burden of proof innocence,' 'legal innocence,' and 'factual innocence.' Cathleen Burnett also distinguishes three types of innocence, which she calls 'actual innocence,' 'factual innocence,' and 'legal innocence.' In a slightly different way, William Laufer recognizes three categories of innocence—again, legal

investigating, monitoring, and reforming errors in the criminal justice system.[7] Around the same time, a ground-breaking meeting took place in North Carolina. Concerned by a number of high-profile exonerations in the state, the then Chief Justice of the North Carolina Supreme Court, I. Beverly Lake, Jr., invited a diverse group of representatives from across North Carolina's criminal justice system to a meeting to discuss wrongful convictions.[8] The meeting ended with a "commitment on the part of participants to establish a commission to study the problems they had discussed in depth."[9] Eventually, that commitment resulted in America's first innocence commission—the North Carolina Actual Innocence Commission.[10]

This chapter explores the development of innocence commissions in America since 2002.[11] Part I will consider the different definitions and functions of innocence commissions that have evolved since 2002. Part II will tell the stories of a selection of innocence commissions that have emerged since 2002 in California, Connecticut, Florida, Illinois, Oklahoma, New York, North Carolina, Pennsylvania, Texas, Wisconsin, and Virginia. Part III will evaluate the main criticisms lobbied at innocence commissions in light of those stories. Part IV will conclude by suggesting what the future looks like for innocence commissions in America.

## Part I: Definitions and Functions of Innocence Commissions

The term "innocence commission" is used to describe a variety of organizations that are different in name, function, power, resource, composition, permanency, and conception.[12] These organizations form part of a nationwide system response to concerns caused by wrongful convictions,[13] but tend to operate practices and procedures that are tailored to the specific challenges and idiosyncrasies of the states they serve. Despite some natural overlap, three general categories[14] of innocence commissions have emerged since the start of the new millennium: error correction commissions; systemic reform commissions (including blue-ribbon commissions); and integrity programs.

### *Error Correction Commissions*

Error correction commissions review and investigate existing post-conviction cases in order to unearth wrongful convictions.[15] In order to have his case reviewed, a defendant must typically relinquish a bundle of his rights[16] and meet a certain threshold; for example, have fresh scientific evidence that demonstrates a

innocence, actual innocence, and factual innocence—which he distinguishes by varying requisite degrees of proof. I argue that these distinctions are largely meaningless in our system of justice and that there is really only one functional category of 'innocence,' although how innocence is determined can vary depending on context.").

7 *Id.* at 99.

8 See Christine C. Mumma, *The North Carolina Actual Innocence Commission: Uncommon Perspective Joined by a Common Cause*, 52 Drake L. Rev. 647 (2004).

9 *Id.* at 649.

10 *Id.* at 648.

11 Note that although post-2002 innocence commissions are the focus of this chapter, the chapter does consider Governor Ryan's Commission on Capital Punishment in Illinois, which was created in the year 2000. This is because it is generally viewed as an important example of the power of innocence in the context of this chapter.

12 Kent Roach, *The Role of Innocence Commissions: Error Discovery, Systemic Reform or Both?*, 85 Chi.-Kent L. Rev. 89 (2010) ("The phrase 'innocence commission' has been used to describe a wide variety of very different institutions.").

13 *See Innocence Commissions*, Innocence Project, http://www.innocenceproject.org/fix/Innocence-Commissions.php (last visited Dec. 27, 2012); *see also* Brandon Garrett, *Aggregation in Criminal Law*, 95 Cal. L. Rev. 383, 435 (2007).

14 Justice projects and innocence projects might legitimately be considered another category, but not for the purposes of this chapter. For more information about justice projects and innocence *see* Jacqueline McMurtrie, Chapter 2, this volume.

15 Roach, *supra* note 12, at 91–2. An error correction commission may also investigate cases of manifest injustice, i.e., convictions that have resulted from a flawed legal process, but that is not the focus of this chapter.

16 For example, this is the case for inmates applying to the North Carolina Innocence Inquiry Commission. *See*, N.C. Gen. Stat. §15A-1467(b) (2010) ("No formal inquiry into a claim of innocence shall be made by the Commission unless the Director or the Director's designee first obtains a signed agreement from the convicted person in which the convicted person waives his or her procedural safeguards and privileges, agrees to cooperate with the Commission, and agrees to provide full disclosure regarding all inquiry requirements of the Commission.").

credible innocence claim.[17] In the event that a credible claim is established, for instance an exculpatory DNA test is obtained, such an organization can either provide relief to the defendant by way of its own authority (although this practice is not utilized in America)[18] or refer the case to a judicial or quasi-judicial panel that can, should the burden of proof required be met, provide the defendant with relief. Ideally, these bodies are (to the largest extent possible) independent of the state, so as to reduce the potential for actual or perceived conflicts in interest.[19]

*Systemic Reform Commissions*

Systemic reform commissions are perhaps best described as "research, recommendation, and reform" commissions. These commissions are typically mandated to research system failures by engaging in a meticulous analysis of wrongful conviction cases in a specific jurisdiction where the defendant has already been afforded relief,[20] or by investigating a particular issue such as false confessions or eyewitness misidentifications. Using the findings of its research as a compass, the commission typically makes recommendations aimed at eliminating and/or reducing the likelihood of those failings reoccurring, which can then be transformed into practicable reforms.[21] These commissions can take a broad-brush approach and research a plethora of issues and cases, or be appointed (often by the state) to examine a specific issue or high-profile case.[22] The latter are generally known as "blue-ribbon" commissions. No matter the findings of these commissions, however, they tend not to be able to refer cases for judicial examination.[23] The vast majority of innocence commissions in America are systemic reform commissions.[24]

*Integrity Programs*

Integrity programs are internal regulation programs operated within prosecutorial offices (or other organizations that handle the "front-end" of the criminal justice process, such as crime laboratories or law enforcement agencies) to help ensure the integrity of convictions, prosecutions, and people working in the criminal justice system.[25] The aim of these programs is to reduce the likelihood of wrongful convictions occurring or going unnoticed.[26] By engaging with internal and external stakeholders and experts in the criminal justice process, these programs *inter alia* aim to identify best practices for reviewing and investigating cases, representing different parties, dealing with scientific evidence and police protocols, and to foster accountability, facilitate education, and implement processes by which meaningful innocence claims can be dealt with promptly.[27]

17 For example, inmates applying to the North Carolina Innocence Inquiry Commission must have a "claim of factual innocence," which is defined as "a claim on behalf of a living person convicted of a felony in the General Court of Justice of the State of North Carolina, asserting the complete innocence of any criminal responsibility for the felony for which the person was convicted and for any other reduced level of criminal responsibility relating to the crime, and for which there is *some credible, verifiable evidence of innocence* that has not previously been presented at trial or considered at a hearing granted through post-conviction relief." *See* N.C. Gen. Stat. §15A-1460(1) (2010).

18 Roach, *supra* note 12, at 92 ("Although it would be possible to give an innocence commission the power to reverse or quash a conviction, it is widely accepted in Anglo-American jurisdictions that innocence commissions should only have the power to refer a case back to the judiciary.").

19 *Id.* at 91–2.

20 *Id.* at 104.

21 *Id.*

22 *Id.*

23 Samuel Wiseman, *Innocence After Death*, 60 Case W. Res. L. Rev. 687, 728 (2010).

24 *Id.* (This is also demonstrated by this chapter).

25 See generally, Barry Scheck, Professional and Conviction Integrity Programs: Why We Need Them, Why They Will Work, and Models for Creating Them, 31 Cardozo L. Rev. 2215 (2010). Mike Ware, Dallas County Conviction Integrity Unit and the Importance of Getting It Right The First Time, 56 N.Y.L Sch. L. Rev. 1033 (2012); Cyrus Vance Jr., A Conviction Integrity Initiative, 73 Alb. L. Rev. 1213 (2010).

26 *Id.*

27 *Id.*

Professional integrity programs specifically aim to amend office processes that contribute to prosecutors failing to carry out their duties adequately and remedy individual errors of incompetence and/or misconduct.[28]

Since 2002, tens of innocence commissions,[29] which John Rago describes as a "quilt work in designs,"[30] have started up in America. Grouping them by the categories above, Part II of this chapter will introduce a selection of those commissions coordinated in California, Connecticut, Florida, Illinois, Oklahoma, New York, North Carolina, Pennsylvania, Texas, Wisconsin, and Virginia.

## Part II: Innocence Commissions in America

### *A. Error Correction Commissions*

#### *i. North Carolina Innocence In quiry Commission*

The North Carolina Innocence Inquiry Commission (NCIIC) is the only error correction commission in America.[31] It materialized following a proposal by the North Carolina Actual Innocence Commission (NCAIC) and, after some stagnation, was signed off by the North Carolina legislature in 2006.[32] The NCIIC is an independent and state-funded[33] body that solely reviews claims of factual innocence which meet initial criteria.[34] It is based on its English equivalent—the Criminal Cases Review Commission.[35] The NCIIC has eight commission members[36] from various criminal justice backgrounds,[37] and has the power to investigate claims of innocence by issuing subpoenas and compelling the attendance of witnesses.[38] If, after a hearing before all eight commission members, "five conclude there is sufficient evidence of factual innocence to merit judicial review,"[39] the case is referred to a superior court judge.[40] Subsequently, the Chief Justice will appoint a three-judge panel to hold a hearing.[41] If the panel unanimously concludes that the convict is innocent by "clear and convincing evidence," it must vacate the conviction and dismiss the charges.[42] The decisions of the NCIIC and panel are final and not subject to appeal or judicial review.[43] As of November, 2012, the

28 *Id.*

29 In this chapter, unless stated otherwise, the term "innocence commission" will be used to refer to these three general categories collectively.

30 John Rago, *Fine Line Between Chaos & Creation: Lessons on Innocence Reform from the Pennsylvania Eight*, 12 Widener L. Rev. 359, 421 (2006).

31 Wiseman, *supra* note 23, at 728. *See also*, Steven M. Cytryn, *Guilty Until Proven Innocent: Providing Effective Relief to the Actually Innocent in New York*, 10 Cardozo Pub. L. Pol'y & Ethics J. 469, 499 (2012).

32 Jerome M. Maiatico, *All Eyes on Us: A Comparative Critique of the North Carolina Innocence Inquiry Commission*, 56 Duke L.J. 1345, 1358 (2007).

33 Roach, *supra* note 12, at 103.

34 North Carolina Innocence Inquiry Commission Rules and Procedures, Article 2, *available at* http://www.innocencecommission-nc.gov/rules.html (last visited Mar. 4, 2013).

35 David Wolitz, *Innocence Commissions and the Future of Post-Conviction Review*, 52 Ariz. L. Rev. 1027, 1032 (2010).

36 *Id.* at 1049 ("In addition, the Commission is empowered to hire—and has hired—an executive director and other staff to carry out day-to-day administrative, investigatory, recordkeeping, and other tasks.").

37 *Id.* ("Specifically, the Act created a commission of eight members to be composed of one superior court judge, one prosecutor, one criminal defense attorney, one 'victim advocate,' one sheriff, one member of the general public, and two people to be appointed at the discretion of the Chief Justice."). N.C. Gen. Stat. §15A-1461 (2010).

38 N.C. Gen. Stat §15A-1467 to -1468 (2010).

39 N.C. Gen. Stat. §15A-1468(c) (2010). If the inmate's conviction is based on a guilty plea, all eight commission members must agree. *Id.*

40 *Id.*

41 The three-judge panel must not include the original trial judge.

42 N.C. Gen. Stat. § 15A-1469(h) (2010).

43 Wolitz, *supra* note 35, at 1071.

NCIIC had received over 1,200 applications, had seven cases in formal inquiry, sent five cases to a three-judge panel, and achieved four exonerations.[44]

*B. Systemic Reform Commissions*

*i. North Carolina Actual Innocence Commission*

In late 2002, stakeholders from across North Carolina's criminal justice system were sent an invitation to a roundtable discussion with then Chief Justice I. Beverly Lake Jr. The purpose of the meeting was to review "innocence issues"[45] relevant to North Carolina which had been highlighted by multiple exonerations. The meeting resulted in an agreement that the causes of wrongful convictions needed to be understood by "all members of the enforcement and justice system and that corrective options should be identified and actions implemented where possible."[46] Resultantly, the NCAIC, the first study commission of its kind in America, was established and members began an open dialogue at topic-focused meetings, set across lunch hours and in venues organized to maximize face-to-face contact between unusual collaborators.[47] The NCAIC zoned in on the issue of eyewitness misidentification and its eventual, adopted reform proposals are viewed as a "gold standard" for law enforcement across America.[48]

*ii. California Commission on the Fair Administration of Justice*

Appointed by the government, the California Commission on the Fair Administration of Justice (CCFAJ) was created by the California Senate in 2004. Its mandate was to (1) study failures of the California criminal justice process that had resulted in wrongful convictions; (2) examine ways of safeguarding against such failures; and (3) make recommendations designed to further ensure that the California criminal justice system is applied and administered in a "just, fair, and accurate" manner.[49] The commission's 25 members included lawyers, academics, religious leaders, police, and victim advocates.[50] The CCFAJ issued a final report in 2008, which contained various (but not all unanimous) recommendations related to *inter alia* police practices, snitch testimony, scientific evidence, professional responsibility, and capital punishment.[51] The recommendations were described as the product of "hard-fought comprise and a delicate balancing of interests";[52] but despite approval in the legislature, bills relating to the recommendations were mostly vetoed by then California Governor Schwarzenegger.[53]

*iii. Connecticut Advisory Commission on Wrongful Convictions*

The Connecticut Advisory Commission on Wrongful Convictions was created through legislative action in 2003, to promote measures to prevent wrongful convictions by encouraging dialogue, identifying best

---

44 *See Case Statistics*, NC Innocence Commission, http://www.innocencecommission-nc.gov/stats.html (last visited Mar. 4, 2013).

45 Mumma, *supra* note 8, at 649.

46 *Id.* quoting: "*See NCAIC Mission Statement, Objectives, and Procedures*, Innocence Project, http:// www.innocenceproject.org/docs/NC_Innocence_Commission_Mission.html (last visited Apr. 14, 2004) (setting forth the Commission's mission statement, objectives, and procedures)."

47 Mumma, *supra* note 8, at 651–2.

48 *See*, NCAIC Recommendations for Eye Witness Identification, http://www.innocenceproject.org/docs/NC_eyewitness.pdf (last visited Mar. 4, 2013).

49 *See* CCFAJ Charge, http://www.ccfaj.org/charge.html (last visited Mar. 4, 2013).

50 *See* CCFAJ Membership, http://www.ccfaj.org/membership.html (last visited Mar. 4, 2013).

51 *See* CCFAJ Final Report, http://www.ccfaj.org/documents/CCFAJFinalReport.pdf (last visited Mar. 4, 2013).

52 *Id.* (letter from the chair).

53 *Gov. Vetoes 3 Bills on Crime Case Procedures*, L.A. Times, Oct. 16, 2007, at B4. That said, the governor did sign off on a wrongful conviction compensation statute that is now in law. *See* http://www.leginfo.ca.gov/pub/09-10/bill/asm/ab_0301-0350/ab_316_bill_20091011_history.html.

practices, and satisfying public desire that "something meaningful be done."[54] Members of the commission,[55] most of whom can rotate, include usual stakeholders in the criminal justice system and "other members,"[56] and it was hoped members would also reflect the "racial, ethnic, geographical, municipal, and socioeconomic diversity of the State."[57] The commission is funded by criminal justice agencies, although academic institutions may pursue grants to assist its work.[58] The commission was mandated to meet every quarter, make decisions by simple majority votes, and issue reports after completing relevant study.[59] It issued its major report concerning *inter alia* compensation for wrongfully convicted persons in February, 2009.[60] However, despite there being no identifiable sunset period for the commission's work, it now appears to lie dormant.[61]

*iv. Florida Innocence Commission*

The Florida Innocence Commission (FIC) was established by an administrative order of the Chief Justice of the Florida Supreme Court in July, 2010,[62] after 68 petitioners requested that Florida establish an Actual Innocence Commission.[63] Funded by the state legislature and Bar Association to the eventual sum of $376,862.10,[64] the primary aim of the FIC was to make recommendations that would reduce the likelihood of wrongful convictions.[65] The FIC's 25 members, including judges and legislators,[66] met approximately every eight weeks to facilitate this aim, and completed their final report in June, 2012.[67] The report made a number of recommendations,[68] which were foreshadowed by a strong message from the commission's chairman, Chief Judge Belvin Perry Jr., that "some of these recommendations will cost money and some may even argue the price of justice is too high. But the consequence of inaction is injustice, and injustice is not what this Country was founded upon."[69] The report made it clear that the creation of an error correction commission was a matter for the three branches of government, however.[70]

---

54 *See Mission Statement*, Advisory Comm'n on Wrongful Convictions, http://www.jud.ct.gov/committees/wrongfulconviction/#MISSION (last visited Mar. 4, 2013).

55 *See Composition Requirements*, Advisory Comm'n On Wrongful Convictions, http://www.jud.ct.gov/committees/wrongfulconviction/#COMPOSITION (last visited Mar. 4, 2013).

56 *Id.* The "other members" are to be appointed by the Chief Court Administrator.

57 *Id.*

58 *See Funding*, Advisory Comm'n On Wrongful Convictions, http://www.jud.ct.gov/committees/wrongfulconviction/#FUNDING (last visited Mar. 4, 2013).

59 *See Rules*, Advisory Comm'n On Wrongful Convictions, http://www.jud.ct.gov/committees/wrongfulconviction/#RULES (last visited Mar. 4, 2013).

60 *Report on the Advisory Commission on Wrongful Convictions*, Advisory Comm'n on Wrongful Convictions, http://www.jud.ct.gov/committees/wrongfulconviction/WrongfulConvictionComm_Report.pdf (last visited May 30, 2013).

61 According to its main web page, the Connecticut Advisory Commission on Wrongful Convictions meeting history has not been updated since March, 2008. It appears its last action was to issue a report in February, 2009. *See* http://www.jud.ct.gov/committees/wrongfulconviction/WrongfulConvictionComm_Report.pdf.

62 *See* Administrative Order AOSC10-39 on July 2, 2010.

63 Florida Innocence Commission, Final Report to the Supreme Court of Florida, 5 (2012) ("On December 11, 2009, a Petition for a Rule Establishing an Actual Innocence Commission was filed with the Supreme Court of Florida by Talbot D'Alemberte, Esquire, on behalf of sixty-eight petitioners. On July 2, 2010, Chief Justice Charles T. Canady established, by Administrative Order AOSC10-39, the Florida Innocence Commission.").

64 *Id.* at 10.

65 *Id.* at 6.

66 *See Commission Membership List*, Florida Inn. Comm'n, http://www.flcourts.org/gen_public/innocence.shtml (last visited Mar. 3, 2013).

67 *Final Report*, Florida Inn. Comm'n, Final Report to the Supreme Court of Florida, June 25, 2012, *available at* http://www.flcourts.org/gen_public/innocence.shtml.

68 *Id.* at 166–70. The report included recommendations concerning snitches, scientific evidence, the preservation of evidence, professional responsibility, and funding for the criminal justice system.

69 *Id.* at 13.

70 *Id.* at 7 ("Whether Florida chooses to create a new commission modeled after the North Carolina Innocence Inquiry Commission, or form another commission to study criminal justice issues, is left to the sound discretion of the judicial, executive, and legislative branches of government.").

*v. Governor Ryan's Commission on Capital Punishment*

Throughout the 1990s, 13 people were exonerated from Illinois' death row.[71] This led Illinois' then governor, George Ryan, to issue a moratorium on executions and establish a blue-ribbon commission (that had relative free reign) to "assess the capital justice system in Illinois and determine what needed to be fixed" in 2000.[72] The commission's members included the usual stakeholders plus some atypical ones, such as a novelist and president of a janitorial firm.[73] The commission reviewed all Illinois death penalty cases since 1978 (paying close attention to the 13 exonerations) and engaged in expert testimony and public hearings.[74] The commission issued its final report in 2002 and made 85 specific recommendations for reform.[75] Although death penalty-specific, Lawrence Marshall argues that this commission is a "strong testament to the power of the innocence issue to have a bold impact ...."[76] In March, 2011, Illinois became the sixteenth state to abolish the death penalty.[77]

*vi. Oklahoma Justice Commission*

The Oklahoma Justice Commission (OJC) was established by the Oklahoma Bar Association in 2010 to take appropriate measures to enhance the "reliability and accuracy of convictions."[78] Led by conservative veteran prosecutor Drew Edmondson,[79] the OJC looked to build upon wrongful conviction research already undertaken across America, by creating a dialogue between stakeholders in the criminal justice system.[80] The OJC, which has now adjourned, "inspired"[81] the Oklahoma Innocence Collaboration Bill, which sought to mandate collaboration between the Oklahoma State Bureau of Investigation (OSBI) and relevant institutions when there was a possibility that scientific evidence might prove an inmate was factually innocent.[82] The bill died in conference in May, 2012.[83]

---

71 Lawrence C. Marshall, *The Innocence Revolution And The Death Penalty*, 1 Ohio St. J. Crim. L. 573, 578 (2004).

72 *Id.*

73 Keith Findley, *Learning From Our Mistakes: A Criminal Justice Commission To Study Wrongful Convictions*, 38 Cal. W. L. Rev. 333, 349 (2009).

74 *Id.*

75 George H. Ryan, Report of the Governor's Commission on Capital Punishment (Apr. 15, 2002), at i–ii. Keith Findley summarizes the proposals as follows: "to require videotaping of interrogations in capital cases; to review police procedures for obtaining eyewitness identifications; to reduce the number of circumstances under which the death penalty may be imposed; to increase the funding and training for lawyers and judges involved in capital cases; to intensify the scrutiny of the testimony of in-custody informants; and to implement new procedures for review of capital sentences." Findley, *supra* note 73 at 349.

76 Marshall, *supra* note 71, at 579.

77 S.B. 3539, 96th Gen. Assemb., Reg. Sess. (Ill. 2011).

78 Oklahoma Bar Association Resolution, *establishing* The Oklahoma Justice Commission: A Commission Dedicated to Enhancing the Reliability & Accuracy of Convictions, *available at* http://www.okbar.org/members/justice-commission/ (last visited Mar. 4, 2013).

79 *Edmondson to Chair Justice Commission*, Oklahoma Bar Association (Jan. 28, 2011), http://www.okbar.org/news/front/2011/01/28-edmondson-head-justice-commission.htm; *see also* M. Scott Carter, *Edmondson Heads Commission to Improve Oklahoma's Judicial System*, The Journal Record (Oklahoma City, OK), June 29, 2011.

80 The Oklahoma Bar Association resolution that established the OJC required that the OJC include representation from district attorneys, defense attorneys, trial and appellate court judges, police, sheriffs, legal scholars, legislators, the office of the Attorney General, Oklahoma State Bureau of Investigation, victim advocates, public defenders, Council on Law Enforcement Education and Training expert or liaison from the innocence community, a forensic science consultant or expert, and a member of the general public.

81 Telephone interview with Drew Edmondson, attorney, GableGotwals (Aug. 2, 2012).

82 Michael McNutt, *Oklahoma State Bill Authorizing Innocence Investigations Advances*, News OK (Feb. 14, 2013) http://newsok.com/oklahoma-house-bill-authorizing-innocence-investigations-advances/article/3648698 (The OSBI would work with higher education institutions or agencies to investigate, consult, and screen scientific evidence that may conclusively prove a person convicted and incarcerated for a felony offense is innocent.)

83 *See Bill Information for HB 2652*, Oklahoma .State Legislature, http://www.oklegislature.gov/BillInfo.aspx?Bill=HB2652&Session=1200 (last visited Mar. 4, 2013).

*vii. The Avery Task Force and Wisconsin Criminal Justice Study Commission*

In 2003, Steven Avery was exonerated by DNA evidence after spending over 17 years in prison for a rape he did not commit.[84] Embarrassed and concerned, Representative Gundrum appointed a legislative committee—the Avery Task Force (ATF)—to examine the causes of wrongful convictions. The ATF brought together a cross-section of professionals whose eventual recommendations resulted in a "breath-taking" course of reform in Wisconsin.[85] However, in 2005, Avery was charged (and later convicted) of murdering a freelance photographer, and the ATF was effectively "wiped" from record.[86] Soon after, the Wisconsin State Attorney General, State Bar of Wisconsin, Marquette Law School, and University of Wisconsin Law School collaborated to form the Wisconsin Criminal Justice Study Commission, which continues to build upon the work of the ATF.[87]

*viii. New York State Justice Task Force on Wrongful Convictions and New York State Justice Task Force*

The 22-member State Justice Task Force on Wrongful Convictions began work in June, 2008. The group studied wrongful conviction cases in New York, examined other states' experiences, devised specialist sub-committees, and conducted public hearings in order to identify what factors were attributable to wrongful convictions.[88] It cast a wide net, examining the criminal justice "process all along the line, from the innocent person's arrest to interrogation of witnesses, the evidence collected, and everything that happens up to the moment of indictment."[89] Its final report was issued in April, 2009.[90] One month later, Chief Judge of the New York Supreme Court, Jonathan Lippman, created the New York State Justice Task Force with a mission to "eradicate the systemic and individual harms caused by wrongful convictions" and recommend reforms to "safeguard against ... such convictions in the future."[91] He called wrongful convictions an "ugly stain on the reputation of the courts."[92] The New York State Justice Task Force soon ruffled the feathers of the legislature by recommending the expansion of New York's DNA database.[93] The Task Force has also made recommendations concerning post-conviction access to DNA testing, frameworks for improving the reliability of eyewitness identifications, and the electronic recording of interrogations.[94]

*ix. Pennsylvania Advisory Committee on Wrongful Convictions (PACWC)*

In 2006, a Pennsylvanian Senate Resolution requested that an advisory committee be created to study the causes of wrongful convictions and develop a consensus on recommendations intended to reduce the possibility of future wrongful convictions.[95] The subsequent, approximately 50-member committee focused on eight issues,[96] undertook a robust study, and produced proposals that were, according to the Innocence

84 *See Steven Avery Profile*, INNOCENCE PROJECT, http://www.innocenceproject.org/Content/Steven_Avery.php (last visited Mar. 4, 2013).

85 Katherine R. Kruse, *Instituting Innocence Reform: Wisconsin's New Governance Experiment*, 2006 WIS. L. REV. 645, 646 (2006).

86 *See Steven Avery Profile*, *supra* note 84.

87 John T. Rago, *A Fine Line Between Chaos & Creation: Lessons on Innocence Reform from the Pennsylvania Eight*, 12 WIDENER L. REV. 359, 423 (2006).

88 James R. Acker, *Protecting the Innocent in New York: Moving Beyond Changing Only Their Names*, 73 ALB. L. REV. 1245, 1247 (2010).

89 Scott Ehlers & Liza Kaplansky, *State Legislative Affairs Update*, 32 JUL CHAMP. 53, 54 (2008).

90 Acker, *supra* note 88, at 1247.

91 *See* Carol DeMare, *Panel: Expand Use of DNA*, THE TIMES-UNION (Albany, NY), Feb. 19, 2011 (Final Edition).

92 *Id.*

93 *Id.* ("For some time, expansion of the state DNA databank has been a political hot button among state lawmakers and those in the criminal justice field. Many legislators have resisted expanding the databank.").

94 *Task Force Recommendations*, N.Y. STATE JUSTICE TASK FORCE, http://www.nyjusticetaskforce.com/recommendations.html (last visited May 25, 2013).

95 S. Res. 381, 2006 Gen. Assemb., Reg. Sess. (Pa. 2006).

96 REPORT ON THE ADVISORY COMM. ON WRONGFUL CONVICTIONS, *available at* http://www.deathpenaltyinfo.org/documents/PAwrongfulconvictions.pdf (The report identified eyewitness identification, confessions, indigent defense services, informant testimony, prosecutorial practice, post-conviction relief, redress and science as the key operative issues.).

Project, "thoroughly researched, cost effective and important to justice."[97] That said, numerous reports have surfaced about there being a "deep division" within the Pennsylvanian committee.[98]

*x. Innocence Commission for Virginia (ICVA)*

The ICVA was formed by a "small band of lawyers, academicians and activists" in 2006.[99] It was a "non-profit, non-governmental, non-partisan project dedicated to improving the administration of justice in Virginia,"[100] which relied on the *pro bono* efforts of law firms and law schools to undertake a detailed examination of 11 specially selected wrongful conviction cases in Virginia.[101] Following the examination of each case, legal research, and surveys of justice agencies, the commission convened a steering committee and then an advisory committee to consider its findings.[102] The ICVA produced its seminal report—*A Vision for Justice*—in 2005,[103] recommending "a conservative agenda for reform."[104]

*xi. Timothy Cole Advisory Panel on Wrongful Convictions (TCAP)*

Timothy Cole was the first man to be posthumously exonerated by DNA evidence testing in Texas.[105] In September, 2009, a panel was created, in Cole's name, by the Texas legislature to advise the State Task Force on Indigent Defense about the causes of wrongful convictions.[106] After 10 months of hearings and meetings, the panel produced 11 recommendations that related to numerous facets of the criminal justice system,[107] and called for the novel creation of a Texas Innocence Commission that would not stand alone, but would formalize the work of Texas-based innocence projects.[108] Subsequently, Senator Rodney Ellis used

---

97 *See PACWC Report*, Innocence Project, http://www.innocenceproject.org/Content/Pennsylvania_Advisory_Committee_on_Wrongful_Convictions_Report_Establishes_Need_for_Reform.php (last visited Mar. 5, 2013) ("This commission has undertaken one of the most robust examinations of wrongful conviction to date. The proposals put forward are thoroughly researched, cost effective and important to justice. The Commission was sensitive to the various realities and concerns in Pennsylvania when forming their recommendations and in some areas chose a more moderate approach than the research suggested. States across the country are enacting similar reforms, and readers of this report will see that the Commission's work and recommendations are the right fit for Pennsylvania's criminal justice system," said Rebecca Brown, Senior Policy Advocate for State Affairs at the Innocence Project.).

98 *See, e.g.*, Sara Ganim, *Panel Suggests DNA Testing, Recorded Interrogations to Reduce Wrongful Convictions in Pennsylvania*, Penn Live (Sep. 20, 2011), http://www.pennlive.com/midstate/index.ssf/2011/09/panel_suggests_dna_testing_rec.html; *see also* Pennsylvania Innocence Project, White Paper on Conviction Integrity Proposals in Pennsylvania, *available at* http://www.innocenceprojectpa.org/newsandevents/docs/whitepaperonconvictionintegrity.pdf (stating "14 members of the Advisory Committee submitted to the Senate Judiciary Committee a separate Independent Report, questioning the process by which the Advisory Committee conducted its business and whether the recommendations were truly based upon a 'consensus' process or one 'largely decided upon in advance, and … designed solely to benefit criminal defendants[']").

99 Jon B. Gould, The Innocence Commission: Preventing Wrongful Convictions and Restoring the Criminal Justice System 5 (2008). This "band" involved contributions from the Innocence Project of the National Capital Region, the Administration of Justice Program at George Mason University, and the Constitution Project, part of Georgetown University's Public Policy Institute.

100 Rago, *supra* note 87, 422 n.339.

101 *See* Innocence Comm'n for Virginia, *A Vision for Justice: Report and Recommendations Regarding Wrongful Convictions in the Commonwealth of Virginia* (Mar. 2005), *available at* http://www.exonerate.org/ICVA/full_r.pdf.

102 *Id.*

103 *Id.*

104 Gould, *supra* note 99, at 239.

105 *See Timothy Cole Profile*, Innocence Project, http://www.innocenceproject.org/Content/Timothy_Cole.php (last visited Mar. 4, 2013).

106 *See* Timothy Cole Advisory Panel on Wrongful Convictions, http://www.txcourts.gov/tidc/tcap.asp (last visited Mar. 5, 2013).

107 *Report to the Texas Task Force on Indigent Defense*, Timothy Cole Advisory Panel on Wrongful Convictions, ii, *available at* http://www.txcourts.gov/tidc/pdf/FINALTCAPreport.pdf (last visited Mar. 4, 2013).

108 *Id.*, recommendation 10: ("Formalize the current work of the innocence projects that receive state funding to provide further detail in the projects' annual reports and distribute those reports to the Governor, Lieutenant Governor, Speaker of the House, and Chairs of the Senate Jurisprudence, House Corrections, House Criminal Jurisprudence and Senate Criminal Justice Committees. Report input should be solicited from other innocence projects, interested bar associations, judicial entities, law enforcement agencies, prosecutor associations, and advocacy organizations.").

the TCAP's work to propose an "Innocence Protection Package"—four bills aimed at reducing wrongful convictions—to the Texas legislature.[109] Ellis' previous attempts at establishing a systemic reform innocence commission in Texas had been labeled a "needless addition to state bureaucracy" by Texas Governor Rick Perry.[110] To date, only one of the Innocence Protection Package bills, aimed at improving access to DNA testing, has come into effect.[111]

*C. Integrity Programs*

*i. Texas Criminal Justice Integrity Unit*

The 12-member Texas Criminal Justice Integrity Unit (TCJIU) was created by the Texas Court of Appeals in June, 2008, and was described as a "call to action"[112] following an increasing tally of exonerations in Texas.[113] The TCJIU shares some commonalities with systemic reform commissions, in that its purpose is to review the Texas criminal justice system in order to make recommendations that would increase its accuracy and fairness.[114] However, what distinguishes the TCJIU (in the author's view) is its focus on making "pro-active changes at the front-end of the system"[115] by means of collaborating with pivotal organizations, and thereby effectively internally regulating and enhancing their practices.[116] For example, the TCJIU has worked with the Texas Commission on Law Enforcement Officer Standards to integrate eyewitness evidence training into core curriculums so that law enforcement officers can spot weak identifications early.[117] It has also facilitated specialist defender units such as the Texas Mental Health Task Force,[118] and proposed a traveling DNA laboratory that would 'spot check' the quality of crime laboratory processes.[119]

*ii. Conviction Integrity Program (CIP), New York*

The District Attorney's Office of Manhattan created the CIP in March, 2010 to ensure cases brought by the office were stronger for victims and fairer to defendants.[120] It has three main components: (1) a Conviction Integrity Committee, which comprises 10 District Attorney Office staff who review practices and policies within the office and ensure meaningful claims of innocence are dealt with in an orderly way that is quick and

---

109 *See* Press Release, Sen. Rodney Ellis, *Ellis Introduces "Innocence Protection Package" for 2011 Legislative Session, available at* http://www.ellis.senate.state.tx.us/pr10/p110810a.htm ("Senator Rodney Ellis introduced an ambitious package of criminal justice reform bills to prevent wrongful convictions. The Houston Senator's 'Innocence Protection Package' incorporates many of the recommendations from the Tim Cole Advisory Panel on Wrongful Conviction … . The Innocence Protection Package includes legislation to: increase the accuracy and reliability of eyewitness identification procedures (SB 121); require electronic recording of custodial interrogations for serious felonies (SB 123); improve the state's post-conviction DNA testing statute (SB 122); and update the Fair Defense Act to improve criminal defense representation for indigent defendants (SB 170).").

110 Scott Ehlers & Liza Kaplansky, *State Legislative Affairs Update*, 32 Jul Champ. 53, 54 (2008).

111 *Bill SB122 Progress*, Texas Legislature Online, http://www.capitol.state.tx.us/BillLookup/BillStages.aspx?LegSess=82R&Bill=SB122 (SB122 Improving the state's post-conviction DNA testing statute). The legislative process was not completed for the other bills.

112 *Texas' Top Criminal Court Creates Unit to Study Justice System*, Star-Telegram (Fort Worth), June 4, 2008.

113 *Id.*

114 Judge Barbara Hervey & D. Kaylyn Betts, *Beyond the Bench: The Texas Court of Criminal Appeals' Work to Improve the Criminal Justice System Outside the Box*, 73 Tex. B.J. 560 (2010).

115 *Id.*

116 *Id.* "For example, some of the issues initially addressed include: Improving the quality of defense counsel available for indigent defendants, implementing procedures to improve eyewitness identification, making recommendations to eliminate improper interrogations and to protect against false confessions, reforming the standards for collection, preservation, and storage of evidence, improving crime lab reliability, and improving attorney practices and accountability." Thus, the TCJIU set out to work with "front-end" organizations such as law enforcement, forensic specialists, and District Attorney and Public Defender offices.

117 *Id.*

118 *Id.* at 561.

119 *Id.* at 560.

120 *See Preventing Wrongful Convictions*, New York District Attorney's Office, http://manhattanda.org/preventing-wrongful-convictions (last visited Mar. 6, 2013).

methodical; (2) a Conviction Integrity Chief, who coordinates the Committee and leads the re-investigation of any meaningful innocence claims; and (3) a Conviction Integrity Advisory Panel of criminal justice experts who advise the District Attorney's Office.[121] As such, like an error correction commission, the CIP will review actual innocence claims, but as part of ensuring the integrity of its internal practices, not as an independent body with the sole purpose of identifying wrongful convictions.

The innocence commissions detailed in Part II demonstrate the three general categories of innocence commissions that have evolved in America since the early stages of the new millennium, and demonstrate why the term "innocence commission" is used to describe a variety of organizations. Although these commissions have engaged in some positive "heavy lifting" between 2000 and 2012, it is evident that several criticisms can be (and have been) aimed at their work. Part III will evaluate some of these criticisms.

## Part III: A Critical Evaluation of the Criticisms Aimed at Innocence Commissions in America

American innocence commissions are subject to a myriad of criticisms that, in the author's view, can be funneled into six general categories: (1) tensions with the criminal justice system; (2) legitimacy; (3) framing; (4) group dynamics; (5) resources; and (6) erroneous vindications. These criticisms will be evaluated in turn.

### *1. Tensions with the Criminal Justice System*

There are tensions between innocence commissions and traditional facets of the American criminal justice system.[122] This criticism is largely aimed at error correction commissions because they provide unconventional processes for defendants to gain post-conviction relief. These tensions generally fall into two spheres.

First, there is a "deep-seated"[123] aversion to innocence-based post-conviction relief because the inquisitorial nature of error correction commissions' work is viewed as "un-American"[124] and undermines "tough-on-crime" political policies.[125] This is reflected by the fact there is only one error correction commission—the North Carolina Innocence Inquiry Commission—operating in America,[126] and by the typically complex nature of American post-conviction frameworks.[127] In fact, Christine Mumma, Director of the Center on Actual Innocence in North Carolina, has said that the complex nature of post-conviction relief procedures is what galvanized the need for the NCIIC.[128] As Professor Daniel Blinka, a member of the Wisconsin Criminal Justice Study Commission, puts it, "innocence commissions are not an inbuilt feature of the criminal justice system … as demonstrated by the tangled web of post-conviction relief."[129] Despite this, however, the NCIIC has managed to successfully root itself into the North Carolina criminal justice system. To date, it has achieved four exonerations through its unconventional post-conviction processes,[130] and set in motion an audit that uncovered pervasive, disturbing flaws in the processes and practices of the North Carolina State Bureau of Investigation.[131]

---

121 Vance, *supra* note 25.

122 *See generally* Wolitz, *supra* note 35; Erik Lillquist, *Improving Accuracy in Criminal Cases*, 41 U. RICH. L. REV. 897 (2007).

123 Wolitz, *supra* note 35, at 1041.

124 Scheck & Neufeld, *supra* note 5, at 101.

125 GOULD, *supra* note 99, at 5 (2008). (Jon Gould, Director of the Innocence Commission for Virginia, commented that the Virginia commission's final report pushed a "conservative" reform agenda in part because he believes that no recommendations "will be enacted simply by appealing to civil liberties or a call to the higher good. … No one ever was elected in this country by appearing 'soft on crime.' … The policy proposals have not changed; only the supporting rhetoric has.")

126 Wolitz, *supra* note 35. (Although the "error correction" work of the Conviction Integrity Unit ran by the New York District Attorney's Office should be noted).

127 Carrie Sperling, Chapter 8, this volume.

128 Telephone interview with Christine Mumma, Adj. Professor of Law, Univ. N. Carolina (July 23, 2012).

129 Telephone interview with Daniel Blinka, Professor of Law, Marquette Univ. Law School (July 20, 2012).

130 *See Case Statistic*, NCIIC, http://www.innocencecommission-nc.gov/stats.html (last visited Mar. 4, 2013).

131 Paul C. Giannelli, *The North Carolina Crime Lab Scandal*, 27 CRIM. JUST. 43 (Spring 2012).

Second, innocence commissions disrupt traditional functions and values of the criminal legal process. For example, exonerations resulting from the work of error correction commissions disrupt finality and usurp the roles of the judge and jury.[132] However, Blinka argues that "finality is one value out of many, getting it right is more important."[133] Blinka suggests there is more value in having an "institutional recognition that the system makes mistakes and will deal with them."[134] Mumma agrees, saying "getting it right and being accountable for mistakes is an American value too."[135] Scholars also argue that error correction commissions may "lower the cost" of jurors returning erroneous verdicts.[136] In other words, the existence of innocence commissions may encourage jurors to lower the evidence threshold required to convict a defendant because they are aware that there is a "safety net" to catch wrongly convicted innocents. Wolitz's hunch, however, is that "the existence of an innocence commission is unlikely to change juror or jury psychology in any measurable way. An innocence commission is unlikely to figure into the minds of jurors any more than appellate courts, or the governor's pardon power, or the remote possibility of habeas review."[137]

Scholars also argue that innocence commissions undermine the jury and judge's roles by "second-guessing a factual finding"[138] and related legal decisions respectively. By agreeing to review a case post-conviction, innocence commissions arguably diminish "the trial court's authority and thus undermine its sense of responsibility."[139] However, although it often comes in second best to the law's desire for proof, the law's ultimate quest is for truth.[140] Therefore, arguably, if an innocent man is there to be identified it would be unconscionable for traditional notions of legal process to hinder attempts to relieve him, at any time. For instance, there would be little, if any, opposition to arguing that the four exonerations achieved by the NCIIC and the over 300 post-conviction DNA evidence exonerations across America to date are a "good thing," despite the average time served by the latter pool, before attaining relief, being over 13 years.[141] As Blinka questions, "What's objectionable about an innocence commission looking at egregious mistakes?"[142]

*2. Legitimacy*

Legitimacy is an important characteristic of any institution, especially those that are tasked with uncovering errors.[143] As Professor James Gibson argues in relation to truth commissions:

> Without legitimacy in the eyes of ordinary people, a truth commission cannot effectively promulgate its views about the past. Legitimate institutions are credible, and credible institutions hold the potential to persuade people. To the extent that people can be persuaded to adopt a nuanced view of the struggles of the past, reconciliation itself becomes possible.[144]

---

132 Wolitz, *supra* note 35, at Part I.

133 Telephone interview with Daniel Blinka, *supra* note 129.

134 *Id.*

135 Telephone interview with Christine Mumma, *supra* note 128.

136 Lillquist, *supra* note 122, at 908.

137 Wolitz, *supra* note 35, at 1066.

138 *Id.* at 1034 (citing Lee v. Moore, 213 So. 2d 197, 198 (Ala. 1968)).

139 *Id.* at 1056.

140 Thomas Weigend, *Should We Search for the Truth, and Who Should Do It?* 36 N.C. J. Int'l L. & Com. Reg. 389, 389–90 (2011). ("Many purposes have been ascribed to the criminal process. In Continental legal thinking, the criminal process is said to be geared, alternatively or cumulatively, to enforcing the criminal law, creating the basis for a just and fair judgment, restoring social peace, or simply 'finding the truth' about a criminal incident. Anglo-American writers, by contrast, tend to emphasize the conflict-resolving potential of the criminal process. None of the potential purposes of the criminal process can be reached unless the judgment has been based on a search for the truth. To reach any of its goals, the process must reflect an honest effort to determine what 'really' happened.").

141 *See Know The Cases*, Innocence Project, http://www.innocenceproject.org/know/ (last visited Mar. 4, 2013).

142 Telephone interview with Daniel Blinka, *supra* note 129.

143 See James L. Gibson, *On Legitimacy Theory and the Effectiveness of Truth Commissions*, 72 Law & Contemp. Probs. 123 (2009).

144 *Id.* at 141.

Given truth and innocence commissions share some common ground, this view can arguably be adopted for innocence commissions.[145] Innocence commissions require legitimacy to persuasively promulgate their views about the work they carry out to review active cases and/or safeguard against wrongful convictions and secure their place as a credible facet of a system that is beholden to notions of tradition and finality.

Innocence commissions face a question of legitimacy for a number of reasons. First, innocence commissions are criticized for being "non-starters," in that they have start-up issues, have only a temporary existence, and, even if permanent, go dormant. Start-up problems (that often persist despite the passage of time) are common amongst innocence commissions, whether they be in the form of skepticism, operational difficulties, and/or resource problems, as documented by Christine Mumma and Professor Jon Gould in respective writings about the North Carolina Actual Innocence Commission and the Innocence Commission for Virginia.[146] Furthermore, experiences in Connecticut show how such efforts can peter out (unnoticed) because of such problems.[147] The Connecticut Advisory Commission on Wrongful Convictions is also an example of a commission struggling to secure its position within the state criminal justice system, as much of the commission's work overlapped with other agencies.[148] Moreover, as shown in Part I, many commissions are temporary. That said, many commissions have overcome initial obstacles and persisted to produce results, as shown by all those commissions, detailed in Part I, that delivered on their mission to produce final reports of their findings. The bigger concern lies in what is done with those findings.

Thus, the second criticism concerning the legitimacy of innocence commissions is their ability to achieve tangible reforms. This criticism has rung true for a number of the commissions detailed in Part I. For example, the California Commission on the Fair Administration of Justice had the numerous bills underpinned by its work vetoed by then Governor Schwarzenegger;[149] bills emanating from the New York State Justice Task Force's recommendations were stalled by the New York State Senate;[150] and Texas Senator Rodney Ellis failed to pass through the Texas legislature all of the recommendations emanating from the Timothy Cole Advisory Panel on Wrongful Convictions.[151] That said, there are many examples of commissions achieving tangible reforms. For instance, the result of the Avery Task Force's work can be seen in Wisconsin Assembly Bill 648 that led to improved procedures concerning the recording of interrogations, preservation and testing of biological evidence, and eyewitness identifications.[152] Moreover, the North Carolina Actual Innocence Commission's work led to the creation and continued work of the North Carolina Innocence Inquiry Commission, and changes to police protocols concerning eyewitness identification that have propelled changes America-wide.[153] Other tangible reforms can be seen in the initiatives organized and funded by the Texas Criminal Justice Integrity Unit to better educate stakeholders about forensic science and indigent defense, and bills passed to help less populated Texas counties store biological evidence more conveniently to ensure the integrity of the evidence is preserved.[154] All of these results have helped engender a view that these commissions are working toward improving public confidence in the criminal justice system. This is reflected by the media support given to the various commissions' work.[155]

---

145 A truth commission is a commission tasked with discovering and revealing past wrongdoing by a government (or, depending on the circumstances, non-state actors also), in the hope of resolving conflict left over from the past.

146 Mumma, *supra* note 8; Gould, *supra* note 99, at 56–60.

147 *See supra* note 61 (noting the apparent lack of action of the Connecticut Advisory Comm. on Wrongful Convictions).

148 *See* Dave Collins, *Conn. Wrongful Convictions Panel Sits Idle for 2 Years*, Associated Press, *available at* http://www.boston.com/news/local/connecticut/articles/2010/11/26/conn_wrongful_convictions_panel_idle_for_2_years/.

149 *Gov. Vetoes 3 Bills on Crime Case Procedures*, L.A. Times, Oct. 16, 2007, at B4.

150 Stephen Saloom, Editorial, *Wrongful Convictions Affect All New Yorkers*, Buffalo News (New York), Mar. 4, 2012 Sunday, at G4.

151 *See* Ellis, Press Release, *supra* note 109.

152 *See* Wis. Legis. Reference Bureau, Legisl. Brief 06-18, Criminal Justice Reforms, 2005 Wisconsin Act 60 (2006).

153 *Case Studies*, Innocence Project, http://www.innocenceproject.org/Content/Criminal_Justice_Reform_Commissions_Case_Studies.php#nc (last visited Mar. 4, 2013).

154 Hervey & Betts, *supra* note 114.

155 *See, e.g.*, Saloom, *supra* note 150; Editorial, *Legislature Must Act on Cole Panel Plan*, San Antonio Express News, Aug. 30, 2010, at 12A; Editorial, *Texas Can Do Better on Wrongful Convictions*, San Antonio Express News, Oct. 3, 2010, at 8B; Editorial, *More Progress Needed; Improved Procedures By Investigators Will Help Prevent Wrongful Convictions*, Buffalo News (New York) at A6.

These achievements, however, bring up the issue of "easy" and "hard sells." It is arguable that some of the reforms achieved by innocence commissions, to date, are merely "easy sells" and thus have limited impact. For instance, reforms such as those that preserve biological evidence,[156] help lawyers better understand forensic science,[157] and minimize the potential for law enforcement to make mistakes when carrying out eyewitness identifications[158] all have a laudable primary aim—to prevent and/or minimize wrongful convictions—that makes them attractive, "easy sells" to gather support for implementation. After all, most people would agree that the criminal justice system should not convict the innocent.[159] That said, each of these reforms could also be considered "hard sells" because they result in additional expense in a crippled economy, thwart police efficiency by requiring extra processes and paperwork, and burden the state with extra responsibilities.[160] Nevertheless, it is still arguable that innocence commissions avoid the really "hard sells." For example, the Florida Innocence Commission avoided taking a view on whether Florida should create an error correction commission,[161] and the North Carolina Actual Innocence Commission decided not to discuss the legitimacy of the death penalty.[162]

The third criticism aimed at the legitimacy of innocence commissions is their lack of powers, which is often related to concerns about their inability to achieve tangible reforms. Scheck and Neufeld argue that innocence commissions should have the power to (1) investigate any wrongful conviction and to recommend any public policy reforms they deem necessary; (2) order reasonable and necessary investigative services; and (3) "subpoena documents, compel testimony, and bring civil actions against any person or entity that obstructs its investigations."[163] Scheck and Neufeld label these powers "indispensable,"[164] which is supported by Professor Jon Gould's experiences as chair of the Innocence Commission for Virginia:

> Without the availability of subpoenas or other powers to demand answers, investigators have been unable at times to go beneath those facts already published in the press or available in court documents. We have tried to work around these limitations by extensive interviews and intensive document review, but our findings would be even more detailed with state powers to compel evidence. For example, as the ICVA was completing its report, the State Crime Commission decided to conduct its own survey of identification procedures used by Virginia law enforcement agencies. We understand that their findings are likely to be similar to those published by the ICVA, but, not surprisingly, the State Crime Commission enjoyed a higher response rate to its surveys.[165]

156 *See supra* Part II. C. i.

157 *Id.*

158 *See supra* Part II. A. i.

159 See generally, Abbe Smith, *In Praise of the Guilty Project: A Criminal Defense Lawyer's Growing Anxiety about Innocence Projects*, 13 U. Pa. J. L. & Soc. Change 315 (2010).

160 *See, e.g.*, Avraham M. Levi & R.C.L. Lindsay, *Lineup and Photo Spread Procedures*, 7 Psychol. Pub. Pol'y & L. 776, for a good overview of the advantages and disadvantages of the reforms recommended by the 1999 Technical Working Group for Eyewitness Evidence to police eyewitness identification practices. Although the changes discussed in this article did not relate to the work of an innocence commission, they reflect many of the recommendations of the innocence commissions that have focused on this area post-2002.

161 Florida Innocence Commission, Final Report to the Supreme Court of Florida, June 25, 2012, at 7. ("Whether Florida chooses to create a new commission modeled after the North Carolina Innocence Inquiry Commission, or form another commission to study criminal justice issues, is left to the sound discretion of the judicial, executive, and legislative branches of government.").

162 Mumma, *supra* note 8, at 654–5.

163 Scheck & Neufeld, *supra* note 5.

164 *Id.*

165 Gould, *supra* note 99, at 70.

That said, Gould makes the point that the ICVA's private status gave the organization the power to "do/say what we wanted without having to answer to public officials."[166] He also points out that the ICVA's ability to "marshal resources from top law firms lent a different, important form of legal legitimacy to our work."[167]

To date, however, there is no American innocence commission that fully embodies Scheck and Neufeld's ideal innocence commission.[168]

Fourth, innocence commissions can be accused of being unaccountable, biased (towards innocence), and non-independent.[169] The fact that most commissions have to file interim and/or final reports about their expenditure, progress, and/or findings to the state or other organizations challenges the idea that they are not accountable.[170] Furthermore, the diverse composition of the majority of innocence commissions challenges the notion that innocence commissions are biased as a consequence of the affiliations of their members, albeit that state representatives have, on occasion, felt outcast.[171] Horan suggests "If sufficiently motivated persons who are truly independent of political and judicial influence were not appointed, an Innocence Commission might function merely as an invidious rubber-stamp of wrongful convictions or a further branch of the police and prosecutors' offices."[172] However, it is clear that the appointment of leaders with a particular political persuasion is a way of actually injecting legitimacy into an innocence commission in some states. For instance, former Chief Justice Lake, who galvanized efforts in North Carolina, had a reputation for being a strong conservative jurist. The same can be said of Drew Edmondson, a veteran prosecutor and death penalty supporter, who was appointed chair of the Oklahoma Justice Commission, and Judge Barbara Hervey, who created the Texas Criminal Justice Integrity Unit. In many ways, independence is a double-edged sword for innocence commissions. True independence would relieve this criticism, but leave innocence commissions, especially those in jurisdictions that have a strong conservative backbone on criminal justice issues, struggling to undertake the commission's mandate and achieve tangible reforms. This is because both tasks would likely require, in the eyes of the public and political entities in those jurisdictions, legitimate leadership—i.e., conservative leadership. Furthermore, with regards to implementing tangible reforms, it is likely that to achieve results that are underpinned by legislation and/or have state endorsement, there is a need for political representatives to be a part of the commission's composition to engender a political will for change. This naturally dilutes the commission's independence. Still, the validity of this view is supported by efforts in Wisconsin and New York. By involving legislatures in its work, the Avery Task Force in Wisconsin achieved

---

166 Email from Jon Gould, Professor, Dep't of Justice, Law & Soc'y, School of Public Affairs to Sarah Cooper, Senior Lecturer in Law, Fellow, Arizona Justice Project (Apr. 18, 2013) (on file with author).

167 *Id.*

168 *See generally*, Robert Norris et al., *"Than That One Innocent Suffer": Evaluating State Safeguards Against Wrongful Convictions*, 74 Alb. L. Rev. 1301 (2011) (although note that the North Carolina Innocence Inquiry Commission has various powers to investigate meaningful innocence claims, and many systemic reform commissions have a wide latitude to carry out their work).

169 David Horan, *The Innocence Commission: An Independent Review Board for Wrongful Convictions*, 20 N. Ill. U. L. Rev. 91, 174–81 (2000).

170 *See, e.g.*, Florida Innocence Commission, Mission Statement, Objectives, and Operating Procedure, IV (5), *available at* http://www.flcourts.org/gen_public/innocence.shtml; Oklahoma Bar Association Resolution, *establishing* The Oklahoma Justice Commission: A Commission Dedicated to Enhancing the Reliability & Accuracy of Convictions, Section 3, *available* at http://www.okbar.org/members/justice-commission/; N.C. Gen. Stat. § 15A-1475 (2006) (specifying the NCIIC is to issue an annual report to the NC General Assembly).

171 *See, e.g.*, *supra* Part II. B. ix. and accompanying note 97 (discussing the divisions within the PACWC between those in favour of stronger reforms and law enforcement and prosecutors who issued a separate report as a result of concerns about the impartiality of the commission).

172 Horan, *supra* note 169, at 175.

tangible results,[173] whereas the New York State Justice Task Force, which failed to work with legislators, struggled, failed to galvanize political support, and had its recommendations stalled in the state Senate.[174]

*3. Framing*

Framing the role, work, and product of innocence commissions is crucial to their legitimacy. Even the name of an innocence commission is important, as demonstrated by the experience of the Avery Task Force in Wisconsin. This is because there is a view that the rhetoric of innocence is arrogant, accusatory, and detrimental to other areas of the criminal justice system.[175]

As shown in Part I, American innocence commissions come under a variety of names—innocence commissions, task forces, integrity units, and criminal justice commissions. Professor Abbe Smith argues that "There is a level of self-righteousness that gets under my skin when people talk about Innocence Projects. I confess that even the name of the organization rankles."[176] This view can be transferred to innocence commissions, given the commonalities between the two types of organizations.

The work of innocence commissions is inherently finger-pointing. This is because it involves identifying and investigating mistakes (be it with the defendant imprisoned or retrospectively), which typically leads to the identification of a person or organization that is responsible, to some extent, for those mistakes. For example, the work of the NCIIC identified deep flaws in the North Carolina State Bureau of Investigation, and in particular with the work of one examiner.[177] The media perpetuate the drama of uncovering these issues too.[178] Blinka agrees that innocence can be "inflammatory" and perhaps it would be better to focus on emphasizing that each commission is a "getting it right" commission.[179] Mumma agrees that the naming of a commission is important because it conveys a message, but says that the advantage of the word "innocence" is that few can disagree with it.[180] In other words, it accords with the notion that most people would agree that innocent people should not be convicted of crimes they did not commit.[181] It is hard to oppose an organization

173 Rago, *supra* note 30, at 425 ("the integrated Wisconsin model appears to have been especially effective ... The Avery Task Force, formed in 2002 by Wisconsin legislator Rep. Mark Gundrum after the exoneration of Steven Avery, has now finished its work. In its wake is the Wisconsin Criminal Justice Study Commission that consists of four entities[:] the Wisconsin State Attorney General, the State Bar of Wisconsin, the Marquette Law School, and the University of Wisconsin Law School. Almost from its outset, Wisconsin's reform movement has included academics, the Wisconsin Supreme Court, the State Attorney General, and the legislature. The political legitimacy and viability of this integrated approach has been clear in the product of its legislative and judicial responses. The Wisconsin Supreme Court has decided multiple cases with consequences for wrongful convictions, while the State Attorney General has implemented cutting-edge guidelines for eyewitness identification. The Attorney General also is in the process of implementing guidelines for the electronic recording of interrogations capping off several years of highly productive work on innocence reforms.").

174 Saloom, *supra* note 150.

175 Smith, *supra* note 159.

176 *Id.* at 321.

177 Giannelli, *supra* note 131.

178 For example, the role of investigative journalism in exposing wrongful convictions has increased exponentially in the past two decades; the Innocence Network now presents an annual award for investigative journalism; *see Awards*, Innocence Network, http://www.innocencenetwork.org/conference/awards. Similarly, Northwestern University Law School works alongside Medill School of Journalism in the Wrongful Convictions Clinic; *see* Laura Aucoin, *Righting Wrongful Convictions*, Northwestern Magazine (Spring 1999), *available at* http://www.northwestern.edu/magazine/northwestern/spring99/convictions.htm.

179 Telephone interview with Daniel Blinka, *supra* note 129.

180 Telephone interview with Christine Mumma, *supra* note 128.

181 Smith, *supra* note 159, at 322. ("In the criminal justice system, neither side wins when an innocent person is convicted. The victim is denied justice because the real culprit remains unpunished. Police and prosecutorial resources are squandered. Public confidence in the system is undermined if and when the mistake is revealed. And, of course, the innocent person who is convicted suffers most of all. Innocence movement lawyers and their compatriots see this and trumpet it. They are saving the wrongfully convicted and the entire system. Perhaps this crusading view has led to the construction of a related identity for those working within the innocence movement. Innocence advocates might come to see themselves as not merely righting a specific wrong—vindicating a wrongfully convicted person—but caring for everyone, redressing all systemic wrongs, and doing something that approaches real justice. Unlike changeable, whimsical ordinary justice—the kind of justice that is in the eyes of the beholder—no one would disagree with this justice.").

that works to relieve and/or carry out work to prevent innocent people from being convicted. Furthermore, "innocence" draws attention. As Abbe Smith says, "There is nothing more compelling than a story about an innocent person wrongly convicted and ultimately vindicated."[182] Thus, "innocence" is undeniably a platform for bringing to the forefront issues that have historically been neglected. Moreover, it has educated the masses on the causes of wrongful convictions and galvanised the media to encourage change.[183]

As shown in Part III (2), in order for innocence commissions, especially systemic reforms commissions, to be legitimate they must be able to produce and encourage tangible outputs, whether that is in the form of unanimous recommendations, police protocols, legislation, and/or the creation of new organizations. To do this, innocence commissions must frame their outputs thoughtfully—they must present a case that is attractive to all stakeholders. For example, they cannot appear to be too soft on crime, biased, or impracticable. If an innocence commission frames an issue inappropriately, they risk a backlash. An example of this can be shown in New York, where verbal blows were traded by various stakeholders after the New York State Justice Task Force recommended the expansion of the New York DNA Database to include DNA samples from everyone convicted of a misdemeanor.[184] Drew Edmondson, chair of the Oklahoma Justice Commission, confirms that a certain kind of framing is required in practice. In his view, a "good"—i.e., well framed—set of outputs would be (a) based on unanimous recommendations from the commission; (b) have the support of law enforcement; (c) ensure the prosecution of guilty parties; and (d) be inexpensive.[185]

The rhetoric of innocence, spurned by innocence commissions, may cause wider implications too. For example, it may hoodwink law students into thinking they will only ever represent innocent clients, which undermines important tenets of criminal defense,[186] or cause the stories of "the not-quite-so-innocent but equally unfairly treated" to be undervalued.[187] As Abbe Smith puts it, "the defendant with the factual innocence story throws every other defendant under the bus."[188] In other words, the rhetoric of innocence arguably rations justice. In response to the former point, Professor Tucker Carrington, Director of the Mississippi Innocence Project and Innocence Clinic, "could not disagree more"[189] because, *inter alia*, innocence work serves a significant pedagogical purpose.[190] Tucker argues that, in relation to the cases students work on:

---

182 *Id.* at 315.

183 *See generally* Richard A. Leo, *Rethinking the Study of Miscarriages of Justice: Developing a Criminology of Wrongful Conviction*, 21 J. Contemp. Crim. Just. 201, 202 (2005) ("In the past decade, there have been more newspaper stories, magazine articles, and television documentaries on the plight of the wrongfully convicted than ever before").

184 John Eligon, *The Politics of the States DNA Database (Who's In It, Who Can See It)*, City Room Blog, N.Y. Times (June 24, 2011, 7:39 PM), http://cityroom.blogs.nytimes.com/2011/06/24/the-politics-of-the-states-dna-database-whos-in-it-who-can-see-it/ ("A bill that would let the state take DNA samples from anyone convicted of any crime—including misdemeanors—has stalled in Albany, where the State Senate and the Assembly have butted heads over what the bill should include."). Note, however, this bill (with some amendments) was signed into New York State law in March, 2012. *See* Maggie Clark, *New York Expands DNA Databank*, Stateline (Mar. 29, 2012), http://www.pewstates.org/projects/stateline/headlines/new-york-expands-dna-databank-85899378965 (New York will now take and catalog DNA samples from more offenders than any other state. Supporters say the expansion will make it easier for police to solve crimes and for defendants to prove innocence, but opponents say it's an invasion of privacy.).

185 Telephone interview with Drew Edmondson, *supra* note 81.

186 Smith, *supra* note 159, at 326 ("I worry that students in Innocence Projects representing only factually innocent people will think they can have a career in which, like Abraham Lincoln or Perry Mason, they represent only innocent people. Worse, I worry that they will come to think that it is somehow beneath them—as law students and lawyers—to represent people who actually did something wrong or bad. One of the most important lessons students learn in a criminal defense clinic is that they are not so different from their clients, no matter who the client is or what he or she may have done. Students come away recognizing that we all make mistakes, do stupid things, lose our tempers, give in to temptation or greed, and fall in with the wrong crowd. This is a transformative revelation for some.").

187 *Id.* at 324.

188 *Id.*

189 W. Tucker Carrington, *"A House Divided": A Response to Professor Abbe Smith's In Praise of the Guilty Project: A Criminal Defense Lawyer's Growing Anxiety about Innocence Projects*, 15 U. Pa. J. L. & Soc. Change 1, 22 (2012).

190 *Id.* ("I also take issue with her claim from a much more practical pedagogical standpoint. Identifying, investigating and litigating claims of innocence contain all of the base ingredients for the type of experience Professor Smith claims as the purview of 'guilty projects.'").

> To read the appellate opinions on these cases is to read a record that is replete with a version of guilt. From a purely factual perspective, the trial record is generally no better. What interests us is a rape kit that may never have been submitted for testing … or a recanting witness who had been a co-defendant who had gotten a deal. Those facts standing alone do not mean by any stretch that the person is innocent—only that there exist hallmarks of possible innocence in a case that may or may not turn out to be—after significant work—a viable case. Until that point, though, students are working on a "guilty" person's case.[191]

With regards to the latter concern—"the deleterious effects on criminal defendants generally"[192]—Tucker concedes there is much support for it.[193] However, as shown in Part I, the mission of nearly all innocence commissions, and in particular systemic reform commissions, is to identify appropriate measures to reduce and/or eliminate wrongful convictions, and this has commonly resulted in systemic reforms that do not apply narrowly to innocent defendants. By and large these reforms—such as improved measures relating to eyewitness identification, forensic science, false confessions, indigent defense services, snitch testimony, post-conviction relief, and prosecutorial practices—are attempts to provide safeguards at both the front and back end of the criminal justice process, for *all* defendants.

*4. Group Dynamics*

As demonstrated in Part I, innocence commissions typically bring together representatives from across (and occasionally beyond) the criminal justice system. This approach aims to encourage collaboration and create reforms that take into account each representative's interests. However, as Scheck and Neufeld point out, "it is not a simple matter to get these comparatively autonomous actors to engage in co-ordinated or uniform change."[194] This view is reflected by the experiences of a number of innocence commissions and, in particular, by divisions between representatives of the state and other commission members.

For instance, there were deep divisions within the Pennsylvania and Florida innocence commissions. In Pennsylvania, there were differences of opinion on *inter alia* access to DNA testing and eyewitness identification procedures,[195] which eventually led to 14 members of the Pennsylvania Advisory Committee on Wrongful Convictions—from law enforcement, district attorney, and victim advocate backgrounds—to publicly claim that the committee's final proposals were "flawed and biased and excluded their contributions."[196] This led to two dueling reports being presented to the Pennsylvania Senate Judiciary Committee in 2011.[197] In Florida, there was blunt resistance from law enforcement to the proposed statutory implementation of double-blind line-ups, which needed to be administered by a law enforcement officer who does not know which photo is the suspect.[198] It was publicly argued by law enforcement that such a set-up was impossible to carry out in-house because certain agencies were so small.[199]

191 *Id.*

192 *Id.* at 16.

193 *Id.*

194 Scheck & Neufeld, *supra* note 5.

195 *See* Ganim, *supra* note 98.

196 *Id.*

197 Sara Ganim, *Committee Presents Dueling Reports on Wrongful Convictions in Pennsylvania*, Penn Live (Sep. 20, 2011) http://www.pennlive.com/midstate/index.ssf/2011/09/mixed_reactions_to_four-year_s.html; Report on the Advisory Comm. on Wrongful Convictions, *supra* note 96; Independent Report of Law Enforcement and Victim Representative Members of the Advisory Comm. on Wrongful Convictions, *available at* http://www.phila.gov/districtattorney/pdfs/Law_Enforcement_Report.pdf (last visited Mar. 3, 2013).

198 A double-blind line-up is where the officer administrating the line-up does not know which persons are fillers and which person is the suspected culprit. The purpose of this procedure is to avoid the office intentionally and/or inadvertently influencing an eyewitness identification witness.

199 Rene Stutzman, *State Senator to Cops: Clean Up the Way You Do Police Line-Ups*, Orlando Sentinel, Feb. 28, 2011, http://articles.orlandosentinel.com/2011-02-28/news/os-innocence-eye-witness-bill-20110228_1_lineups-witness-photos.

The experiences of Pennsylvania and Florida are perhaps unsurprising. As Mumma describes, in relation to the famous meeting called by then Chief Justice Lake in North Carolina in 2002, "everyone came with their traditional role hats on … they didn't trust who was sitting on the other side of the table."[200] This skepticism, however, was a key ingredient to the eventual success of efforts in North Carolina. The initial distrust between the invitees meant that no one wanted to be "left outside of tent,"[201] which lead to a long-term, collaborative, and open dialogue. Similarly, the Oklahoma Justice Commission created relationships and "lots of respect"[202] between its diverse members, as the commission provided a venue for members to cordially deliver firm opinions and listen to different perspectives.[203] In fact, the experiences of all the commissions discussed in this chapter show, to differing degrees, usually autonomous actors coming together to encourage change, as all commissions have had some sort of productive output.

*5. Resource Implications*

Innocence commissions require significant amounts of money, people, and other operational resources over considerable amounts of time. As such, it is questionable whether the benefits of having innocence commissions outweigh the cost of them.

It is difficult to identify a constituency of people that want to spend money on "trouble-makers."[204] Thus, the argument that innocence commissions squander state funding (and numerous do rely on state funding) on inmates with frivolous claims, when money could be channeled to law enforcement or other state agencies and used to serve (law abiding) civilians, is unsurprising. There are a number of points that challenge this argument, however. First, of all the commissions detailed in Part I, only the NCIIC and the New York Conviction Integrity Program consider "live" claims, and both employ a high threshold before accepting a case and spending resources on reinvestigating.[205] In other words, expenditure on frivolous claims is avoided. Second, on the whole, state funding to such endeavors appears minimal. Moreover, a proportion of commissions, for example the Innocence Commission for Virginia, have made use of private funding and *pro bono* contributions. Third, scholars argue that the process of identifying and/or studying wrongful convictions is "not a place to save money."[206] As Gould puts it, "the issue should be caring not cost."[207] Fourth, reports show that the cost of imprisoning an innocent man is just as high as for exonerating him. For example, the cost to the state of Virginia for wrongfully imprisoning 13 men was over $2 million, and that is without considering the "human cost"—i.e., the negative effects on the innocent person, their family, the victims, and the public's loss of confidence in the criminal justice system.[208] These latter costs are considered to be "beyond measure."[209] Arguably, therefore, the savings made by minimizing wrongful convictions outweigh the costs associated with processing exonerations, researching common causes of wrongful convictions, and implementing appropriate safeguards.

*6. Erroneous Vindications*

The work of innocence commissions may lead to the release and/ or celebration of a guilty party or a person who goes on to commit another crime. This was the case for the Avery Task Force in Wisconsin; when Steven

200 Telephone interview with Christine Mumma, *supra* note 128.

201 *Id.*

202 Telephone interview with Drew Edmondson, *supra* note 81.

203 *Id.*

204 Telephone interview with Daniel Blinka, *supra* note 129.

205 In order to qualify for review the Conviction Integrity Program in New York requires inmates to have been convicted in New York County and have a claim of "actual innocence." The NCIIC requires inmates to have a factual innocence claim where "credible" and "verifiable" evidence of factual innocence exists.

206 Telephone Interview with Daniel Blinka, *supra* note 129.

207 Telephone Interview with Professor Jon Gould, American University, College of Law (July 19, 2012).

208 *A Vision for Justice*, ICVA Report, at xvi, *available at* http://www.exonerate.org/ICVA/full_r.pdf (last visited Mar. 5, 2013).

209 *Id.*

Avery, the Task Force's namesake, was correctly exonerated for a rape he had been convicted of, but then went on to murder a woman after his release.[210] Demonstrating how crucial this concern about innocence commissions is, in order to maintain the credibility of the work undertaken in Wisconsin, Avery's name was quickly "dropped" and it is now very difficult to find literature bearing the "Avery Task Force" label. That said, with regards to error correction commissions achieving an erroneous exoneration, Lillquist thinks the potential problem is "fairly trivial,"[211] citing the example of the high burden of proof—"clear and convincing evidence"—required (unanimously) by a three-judge panel before exonerating a defendant whose case has journeyed through the North Carolina Innocence Inquiry Commission's relief processes.[212] In fact, Mumma reports that the NCIIC was designed with this concern in mind, and that is why measures such as a high burden of proof, waiver of the inmate's rights, and multiple levels of review were implemented.[213] This, Mumma suggests, makes the potential for a wrongful exonerations "impossibly low."[214] Professor Lissa Griffin also agrees. Griffin comments that because the phrase "wrongful conviction" tends to mean factually innocent in the United States, it is "unlikely in the extreme" that anyone who is actually guilty will be exonerated.[215]

Part III has demonstrated that a myriad of criticisms can be aimed at American innocence commissions, with and without challenging arguments. Part IV will conclude by suggesting what the future looks like for innocence commissions in America.

## Part IV: Conclusion

With record numbers of DNA exonerations, a rally call for measures to prevent wrongful convictions from Barry Scheck and Peter Neufeld, and the start of an unprecedented drive to resolve "innocence issues" by the Chief Justice of the Supreme Court of North Carolina, 2002 was a pivotal year in the Innocence Movement. Since then, tens of innocence commissions have been established across America and three general categories of commissions have emerged: error correction commissions; systemic reform commissions; and integrity programs. America showcases examples of each of these categories; however, systemic reform commissions are by far the most common.

On the basis of the arguments and examples presented in this chapter, the following conclusions can be made:

1. In America, the term "innocence commission" can be used to describe a variety of organizations that differ in name, function, power, resource, composition, permanency, and conception.
2. American innocence commissions are subject to a myriad of criticisms, including the tensions they have with other facets of the criminal justice system and the struggles they face in terms of fostering legitimacy, persuasively framing their work, navigating the group dynamics of their diverse membership, handling resources, and avoiding erroneous vindications.
3. Each of these criticisms can be both supported and challenged by scholarly arguments and the experiences of multiple innocence commissions.
4. Measuring the success of an innocence commission is difficult, primarily because of their varying constitutions, although it is clear some have been more productive that others.
5. There is much overlap between the work of many innocence commissions, especially systemic reform commissions, and many have used their predecessors' product as a platform for their own initiatives.

---

210 *See Steven Avery Profile*, *supra* note 84.

211 Lillquist, *supra* note 122, at 908.

212 *Id.*

213 Telephone Interview with Christine Mumma, *supra* note 128.

214 *Id.*

215 Email from Lissa Griffin, Professor, Pace Law School, to Sarah Cooper, Senior Lecturer in Law, Fellow, Arizona Justice Project (Apr. 26, 2013) (on file with author).

6. Innocence commissions have provided an unprecedented forum for the various stakeholders in the criminal justice system to collaborate for an uniform purpose, engage in a constructive dialogue, and yet promote their professionally affiliated viewpoints.
7. Innocence commissions show a desire to prevent wrongful convictions and thus better the criminal justice system for victims, the public, and defendants.

In light of these conclusions, a key theme for the future of innocence commissions in America is going to be whether or not their work leads to meaningful change. As it stands, systemic reforms commissions and integrity programs have laid foundations for the development of a plethora of initiatives in many key areas across the criminal justice system. Similarly, America's only error correction commission—the NCIIC—has become a commendable example of an unconventional yet successful post-conviction process. Yet more needs to be done. For instance, systemic reform commissions and integrity programs need to be legitimized further by having their recommendations rolled out state-wide to foster consistency, and validated by the state in terms of appropriate resource allocation, sponsorship, and legislative action in order to prevent their work becoming static, outdated, and/or dispensable. Similarly, as Mumma explains, the NCIIC should be more efficient and process more credible innocence claims at a quicker rate.[216] Moreover, the exclusivity of the NCIIC is problematic, as the opportunities it presents to both inmates and the state system are confined to one state.

In the author's view, the future perhaps lies in a three-pronged approach that would further define (and likely rename) the roles of the three types of innocence commissions that have evolved in America. This approach would involve an integrity program, systemic reform commission, and error correction commission all operating in each state. The integrity program would focus on the internal regulation of lawyer offices and other related "front-end" organizations, whereas the error correction commission would operate as safety-net, weeding out wrongful convictions and targeting "back-end" issues to ensure a smoother post-conviction process. The systemic reform commission would then act as an umbrella commission that continuously facilitates dialogue between stakeholders, identifies new focus areas, undertakes research projects, updates reform ideas, and collaborates with relevant bodies to implement reforms and obtain resources. This approach would aim to avoid overlaps in work, foster a structured and layered approach to reducing the potential for wrongful convictions, and install innocence commissions as a legitimate and valuable cog in the mechanics of the criminal justice system.

---

216 Telephone interview with Christine Mumma, *supra* note 128.

# Index

For Product Safety Concerns and Information please contact our EU representative GPSR@taylorandfrancis.com Taylor & Francis Verlag GmbH, Kaufingerstraße 24, 80331 München, Germany

**Batch number: 10726294**

Printed by Printforce, the Netherlands